Events: The Force of Inte

Events: The Force of International Law presents an analysis of international law, centred upon those historical and recent events in which international law has exerted, or acquired, its force. From Spanish colonisation and the Peace of Westphalia, through the release of Nelson Mandela and the Rwandan genocide, and to recent international trade negotiations and the 'torture memos', each chapter in this book focuses on a specific international legal event. Short and accessible to the non-specialist reader, these chapters consider what forces are put into play when international law is invoked, as it is so frequently today, by lawyers, laypeople or leaders. At the same time, they also reflect on what is entailed in naming these 'events' of international law and how international law grapples with their disruptive potential. Engaging economic, military, cultural, political, philosophical and technical fields, *Events: The Force of International Law* will be of interest to international lawyers and scholars of international relations, legal history, diplomatic history, war and/or peace studies and legal theory. It is also intended to be read and appreciated by anyone familiar with appeals to international law from the general media, and curious about the limits and possibilities occasioned, or the forces mobilised, by that appeal.

Fleur Johns is a Senior Lecturer in the Faculty of Law, University of Sydney and Co-Director of the Sydney Centre for International Law.

Richard Joyce is a Lecturer in the School of Law, University of Reading. He works in the fields of legal theory, international law and intellectual property.

Sundhya Pahuja is an Associate Professor in the Law School, University of Melbourne and Director of the Law and Development Research Programme at the Institute for International Law and the Humanities.

Events The Force of International Law

Edited by
Fleur Johns, Richard Joyce
and Sundhya Pahuja

Routledge
Taylor & Francis Group

a GlassHouse book

First published 2011
by Routledge
2 Park Square, Milton Park, Abingdon, Oxfordshire OX14 4RN
Simultaneously published in the USA and Canada
by Routledge
711 Third Avenue, New York, NY 10017
A GlassHouse book

Routledge is an imprint of the Taylor & Francis Group, an informa business

First issued in paperback 2011

© 2011 editorial matter and selection Fleur Johns, Richard Joyce and Sundhya Pahuja, individual chapters the contributors

Typeset in Garamond by
Taylor & Francis Books

British Library Cataloguing in Publication Data
A catalogue record for this book is available from the British Library

Library of Congress Cataloguing in Publication Data
Events : the force of international law / edited by Fleur Johns, Richard Joyce and Sundhya Pahuja.
    p. cm.

1. International law. I. Johns, Fleur. II. Joyce, Richard John, 1978–
III. Pahuja, Sundhya.
KZ1250.E93 2011
341–dc22   2010008190

ISBN13: 978-0-415-55452-7 (hbk)
ISBN13: 978-0-203-84446-5 (ebk)
ISBN13: 978-0-415-66846-0 (pbk)

For Peter Fitzpatrick

Contents

Acknowledgements   x
List of abbreviations   xii
Notes on the editors   xiv
Notes on contributors   xv
Foreword by Martti Koskenniemi   xviii

Introduction   1
FLEUR JOHNS, RICHARD JOYCE AND SUNDHYA PAHUJA

1 The international law in force: anachronistic
   ethics and divine violence   18
   JENNIFER BEARD

2 Absolute contingency and the prescriptive force of
   international law, Chiapas–Valladolid, ca. 1550   29
   OSCAR GUARDIOLA-RIVERA

3 Latin roots: the force of international law as event   43
   PETER FITZPATRICK

4 Westphalia: event, memory, myth   55
   RICHARD JOYCE

5 The force of a doctrine: art. 38 of the PCIJ
   Statute and the sources of international law   69
   THOMAS SKOUTERIS

6 Paris 1793 and 1871: *levée en masse* as event   81
   GERRY SIMPSON

7   Decolonization and the eventness of international law   91
    SUNDHYA PAHUJA

8   Post-war to new world order and post-socialist
    transition: 1989 as pseudo-event   106
    SCOTT NEWTON

9   The liberation of Nelson Mandela: anatomy of a
    'happy event' in international law   117
    FRÉDÉRIC MÉGRET

10 Political trials as events   130
    EMILIOS CHRISTODOULIDIS

11 The Tokyo Women's Tribunal and the turn
    to fiction   145
    KAREN KNOP

12 Many hundred thousand bodies later: an analysis
    of the 'legacy' of the international criminal
    tribunal for Rwanda   165
    DENISE FERREIRA DA SILVA

13 From the state to the Union: international law
    and the appropriation of the new Europe   177
    PATRICIA TUITT

14 The emergence of the World Trade Organization:
    another triumph of corporate capitalism?   191
    FIONA MACMILLAN

15 The World Trade Organization and development:
    victory of 'rational choice'?   207
    DONATELLA ALESSANDRINI

16 Protesting the WTO in Seattle: transnational citizen
    action, international law and the event   221
    RUTH M. BUCHANAN

17 Globalism, memory and 9/11: a critical Third World
    perspective   234
    OBIORA CHINEDU OKAFOR

18 Provoking international law: war and regime
   change in Iraq   246
   JOHN STRAWSON

19 The torture memos   260
   FLEUR JOHNS

   Index   279

Acknowledgements

This book emerged, by a rather circuitous route, from a series of workshops dedicated to critical approaches to international law that were held in 2003, 2004 and 2006 at Birkbeck College, University of London. In the first two instances, these were co-sponsored by the now-disbanded Foundation for New Research in International Law, based in The Hague, and drew upon the seemingly illimitable energy of Thomas Skouteris for which we are ever grateful. The third of these workshops was made possible by the support of the United Kingdom's Arts and Humanities Research Council and the Leverhulme Trust. All three workshops benefited from the support of the Birkbeck College School of Law and its staff, above all Professors Peter Fitzpatrick, Fiona Macmillan and Costas Douzinas. We are indebted to them and to all who participated in those workshops for the opportunities that they afforded for vibrant and fruitful exchange.

From those beginnings, and via related routes, we are fortunate to have assembled an extraordinarily talented group of authors to contribute to this book. We are immensely grateful to those authors for their willingness to take up questions posed in the original brief for this book in such fascinating ways, and to see the whole through to publication with patience and good humour.

In bringing this book to fruition, we have depended on the assistance of many. Susan Cirillo, Laura Griffin and Sadhana Abayasekara worked tirelessly to wrestle the manuscript into shape and to assist in the development of particular sections. John Warburton brought a fresh eye and a keen intellect to the final editing phase. From the book's conception, Colin Perrin has been a wonderful source of encouragement and advice. He, Holly Davis and all at Routledge have exhibited supernal patience throughout its preparation. We are thankful to all of them. The making of this book was also supported in various ways by the faculties of which we are fortunate, respectively, to be part: the Faculty of Law at the University of Sydney; the School of Law at the University of Reading; and the Melbourne Law School.

We are deeply grateful to Gerhard Richter for permission to reproduce his 1984 painting *Holländische Seeschlacht* (Dutch Sea Battle) on the cover of this book.

Finally, this book would never be in print were it not for the support of our families, several members of whom arrived in the midst of its production. To Jeremy, Peter, Premala: thank you for coming along for the ride and for the countless contributions that you made to this project's realisation at all the crucial moments. To our delightful abecedary of offspring – Ananya, Arlo, Benjamin, Claude – thank you for teaching us more than anyone about the potential for newness in the world.

List of abbreviations

AES	actually existing socialism
ANC	African National Congress
CERD	1969 Convention on the Elimination of All Forms of Racial Discrimination
Charter	1945 Charter of the United Nations
CIA	Central Intelligence Agency
CLS	Critical legal studies
COSATU	Congress of South African Trade Unions
DAIG	Inspector General of the US Department of the Army
DAN	direct action network
ECJ	European Court of Justice
EU	European Union
FDI	foreign direct investment
FLN	Front de Libération Nationale (National Liberation Front, Algeria)
GA Res	United Nations General Assembly Resolution
GATS	General Agreement on Trade in Services
GATT	General Agreement on Tariffs and Trade
ICC	International Criminal Court
ICJ	International Court of Justice
ICRC	International Committee of the Red Cross
ICTR	International Criminal Tribunal for Rwanda
IFIs	international financial institutions
IL/IR	International law and international relations
IMTFE	International Military Tribunal for the Far East
INGOs	International non-governmental organizations
ISAK	Isolera Sydafrika-Kommittén (Isolate South Africa Committee)
LN	League of Nations
NAFTA	North American Free Trade Agreement
NAIL	new approaches to international law
NATO	North Atlantic Treaty Organization

NGOs	non-governmental organizations
NIEO	new international economic order
OAU	Organization of African Unity
OED	*Oxford English Dictionary*
OPEC	Organization of the Petroleum Exporting Countries
OSCE	Organization for Security and Co-operation in Europe
PCIJ	Permanent Court of International Justice
PMC	Permanent Mandates Commission
POWs	prisoners of war
Torture Convention	1984 Convention against Torture and Other Cruel, Inhuman or Degrading Treatment or Punishment
TRIPs Agreement	Agreement on Trade-Related Aspects of Intellectual Property Rights
TWAIL	Third World approaches to international law
TWT	Women's International War Crimes Tribunal for the Trial of Japan's Military Sexual Slavery
UDHR	Universal Declaration of Human Rights
UK	United Kingdom
UN	United Nations
UNCTAD	United Nations Conference on Trade and Development
UNGA	United Nations General Assembly
UNSC	United Nations Security Council
US	United States of America
USSR	Union of Soviet Socialist Republics
VCLT	1969 Vienna Convention on the Law of Treaties
VOC	Verenigde Oost-Indische Compagnie (United East India Company)
WTO	World Trade Organization

Notes on the editors

Fleur Johns (BA, LLB (Hons) (Melb.); LLM, SJD (Harvard)) is a Senior Lecturer in the Faculty of Law, University of Sydney and Co-Director of the Sydney Centre for International Law. Fleur's publications include the edited book *International Legal Personality* (Ashgate, 2010). Fleur is Articles Editor for the *Leiden Journal of International Law* as well as serving on a number of other editorial boards.

Richard Joyce (BA, LLB (Hons) (Melb.); PhD (Lond.)) is a Lecturer in the School of Law, University of Reading. He works in the fields of legal theory, international law and intellectual property.

Sundhya Pahuja (BA, LLB (Hons) (Melb.); LLM (UBC); PhD (Lond.)) is an Associate Professor in the Law School, University of Melbourne and Director of the Law and Development Research Programme at the Institute for International Law and the Humanities. Sundhya is the author of *Decolonising International Law* (forthcoming, CUP). She serves on the editorial boards of *Law, Justice and Global Development*, the *Australian Feminist Law Journal* and the *Melbourne Journal of International Law*.

Notes on contributors

Donatella Alessandrini is a lecturer at Kent Law School, University of Kent, UK. She obtained her PhD at the School of Law, Birkbeck, University of London where her doctoral project focused on the development approaches of the international trading regime. Her research interests are in the areas of trade theories and practices, development studies, neo-liberalism and political economy.

Jennifer Beard is currently on a leave of absence from the University of Melbourne Law School, having accepted an appointment to the Australian Migration and Refugee Review Tribunals. Jennifer researches in the fields of law and development, public international law and legal theory. Her research interests include the concepts of sovereignty, borders, power, development, underdevelopment and post-colonialism.

Ruth M. Buchanan is currently an Associate Professor at Osgoode Hall Law School in Toronto. Her research interests span the fields of law and development, political theory and film studies. She has written on the role of Westerns in framing understandings of law, constitutionalism and pluralism in relation to the WTO, and the unintended consequences of NAFTA's labour side agreement.

Emilios Christodoulidis is Professor of Legal theory at the Law School of the University of Glasgow. His interests lie mainly in the area of the philosophy and sociology of law and in constitutional theory. He has written on the relationship between law and politics, on the tensions between constitutionalism and radical democracy, on transitional justice and political trials and on critical legal theory.

Peter Fitzpatrick is currently Anniversary Professor of Law at the School of Law, Birkbeck, University of London. He has taught at universities in Europe, North America and Papua New Guinea and published books on legal philosophy, law and social theory, law and racism, and imperialism, the latest one being with Ben Golder, *Foucault's Law* (Routledge, 2009).

Oscar Guardiola-Rivera is Senior Lecturer at the School of Birkbeck Law, University of London, and member of the Birkbeck Institute for the Humanities' Steering Board. He is author of *Being Against the World: Rebellion and Constitution* (Routledge, 2008) and *What If Latin America Ruled the World?: How the South Will Take the North into the 22nd Century* (Bloomsbury, 2010).

Karen Knop is Professor at the Faculty of Law, University of Toronto and Editor of the *University of Toronto Law Journal*. Her book *Diversity and Self-Determination in International Law* (Cambridge University Press, 2002) was awarded a Certificate of Merit by the American Society of International Law. She is the editor of *Gender and Human Rights*.

Fiona Macmillan is a Professor at the School of Law, Birkbeck, University of London. Previously, she has held academic positions at the University of New South Wales, the University of Leicester, Murdoch University in Western Australia and the Institute of Advanced Legal Studies, University of London. Her research interests include intellectual property, cultural property and international economic law.

Frédéric Mégret is an Assistant Professor of Law at the University of McGill, as well as the Canada Research Chair on the Law of Human Rights and Legal Pluralism and the Director of the McGill Clinic for the Sierra Leone Special Court.

Scott Newton is Lecturer in the Laws of Central Asia in the School of Law at the School of Oriental and African Studies (SOAS), University of London. His research/publications concern the relation of law to the political economy of post-colonial development and post-socialist transition, as well as critical international law, human rights, and law and contemporary conflict. He has served as legal technical adviser in Central Asia, Russia, the Caucasus, Central Europe and South Asia.

Obiora Chinedu Okafor is a Professor at the Osgoode Hall Law School of York University, Toronto, Canada. He holds a PhD from the University of British Columbia, Vancouver, Canada; and is the author or co-editor of six books and over fifty other scholarly writings.

Denise Ferreira da Silva is Associate Professor of Ethnic Studies at the University of California, San Diego. She serves as the Director of Latin American Studies Program at the same university. She writes in the fields of political theory, legal theory, racial and cultural studies, and human rights. She is the author of *Toward a Global Idea of Race* (University of Minnesota Press, 2007).

Gerry Simpson holds a Chair of Law at the University of Melbourne Law School, where he is Director of the Asia-Pacific Centre for Military Law and the Global Justice Studio, and is a Visiting Professor of Public International Law at the London School of Economics. His latest book is *Law, War and Crime: War Crimes Trials and the Reinvention of International Law* (Polity, 2007), and he is currently writing about the law and literature of war. Gerry has two small children, Hannah and Rosa.

Thomas Skouteris is Assistant Professor at the American University in Cairo while on leave from Leiden University. He also serves as Secretary General of the European Society of International Law and General Editor of the *Leiden Journal of International Law*. He works in the fields of public international law and legal history.

John Strawson is Reader in Law at the University of East London and works in the areas of international law and Middle East studies with a special interest in post-colonialism. His publications include: *Partitioning Palestine: Legal Fundamentalism in the Palestinian–Israeli Conflict* (Pluto Press, 2010).

Patricia Tuitt is Professor of Law and Executive Dean of the School of Law, Birkbeck, University of London. She has published widely in the field of international refugee law, including the book *Race, Law, Resistance* (Glasshouse Press, 2004). Her current research focuses on forced migration, critical race theory, law and narrative forms, human rights, and post-colonialism.

Foreword

One memory I retain vividly from work in the Foreign Ministry is that for the political decision-makers, every situation was always new, unprecedented and very often (and not least for that very reason) a crisis. It then became the legal adviser's task to calm down that decision-maker by explaining that situations of a similar type had arisen last year, five years ago, 30 years ago and that far from being singular or unprecedented, the situation (the 'event' in the language of this book) was in fact part of a recurrent pattern and could therefore be treated in the same way as 'we' had done with those previous cases. As the editors of this book observe, this type of reduction is a quintessentially legal activity. International lawyers do this constantly, not only to soothe the nerves of anxious decision-makers, but also to argue before courts and tribunals and to persuade the readers of law reviews and books of the moral or political power of whatever it is they wish to argue for. We routinely make points about precedent and custom, and dress our claims in terms of general principles and institutional practices. Indeed, the very act of qualifying something in legal terms – an action, a form of behaviour, an instrument – is to reduce it from its singularity by subsuming it under a rule. And there is no more lawyerly activity than rule-application.

Law is also a polemical activity. The reduction of an event into a pattern or a rule ('qualification') is meaningful to the extent it works as a prelude to action or decision. The advice in the Foreign Ministry, for example, contained the implicit (and sometimes quite explicit) suggestion: we *should* deal with this case like we did with *those*. To move from singularity to rule is surely a key part of the expertise of a legal counsel pleading for a client – a state explaining its action as 'self-defence' or a war crimes prosecutor claiming that the acts of the accused amounted to 'genocide'. And yet, it seems clear that the ability to make the reverse reduction must be equally important; one must often argue for the opposite case as well. To distinguish the precedent, to argue that the case ought to be appreciated in view of its singularity (and not only by reference to qualities that make it resemble something else) is to deny that it should be reduced to a pattern and thus be treated like those *other* cases. Typical techniques performing this include arguing from the exception instead of the rule, from equity or for example from 'circumstances precluding wrongfulness' under Chapter V of the International Law Commission's 2001 Draft Articles on State Responsibility. With such points we highlight the event's 'eventness', the way it cannot properly and without injustice be treated by reducing it into a pattern.

The many cases discussed in this book show the stakes in either making the event stand out proudly on its own or having it slowly disappear as part of the background so that we can no longer distinguish anything remarkable in it. Neither reduction is 'innocent', of course. Each involves choice and interpretation that is inspired by the need to take a decision, to move from reflection to action. Should we think of this case in view of its singular properties, or by drawing attention to the way it resembles other cases? Should we apply the rule or the exception? Ought we to do like we did last year, or should we perhaps reconsider the position? Is Kosovo a *sui generis* situation or is it not?

The important lesson is this: a situation or a case is never an 'event' or 'part of a pattern' in itself but always appears as one or the other as a result of language and argument. Moreover, the legal argument is never disinterested. Although aesthetic judgement is crucially involved in both reductions, they are never just about aesthetics. The legal judgment seeks to intervene in the world so as to produce an effect on the distribution of material or spiritual resources. To see somewhere a singular 'event' is to claim that the routine of patterned choices ought not to be applied *now*. It appeals to the imagination and a sense of (informal) justice in the decision-maker that appreciates things in their individuality and events by their 'eventness' and suggests a decision on that basis. To view the thing as part of a pattern, by contrast, is to deny the decisive significance, here and now, of whatever it was that first struck us in the special character of the moment, and thus to call for a decision that is familiar and reassuring.

There are cultural and political assumptions involved in each reduction (event to pattern; pattern to event). The propensity of lawyers to reduce things to rules is at least in part responsible for the tendency to think of law as an intrinsically conservative profession. The reduction appears to deny – and *does* deny – the colourful multiplicity of the world. It makes everything appear grey and bureaucratic. To overlook the singularity of the event is to fall back on a routine that may support conservative biases – *plus ça change* ... Against this, pointing to the striking uniqueness of the event may appear as a liberating, profoundly anti-conservative move; it appeals to our sensitivity about what is out of the ordinary: thinking outside the box. The intuitive appeal of this surely results from the way it invites us to break the routine and freshen things up, to awaken from apathetic slumber and make us once again *feel* that life has unique things to offer.

But these cultural and political associations are never this stable. Each may be made to serve purposes not initially associated with it. Although much

recent political and legal philosophy, as the editors observe, has tended
to stress the 'event' as a radical alternative against the monotonies of
routine, the purposes of that philosophy may sometimes be better served by
imaginative reduction in the opposite sense. Emphasising the speciality of
'terrorism' for example, may be a deeply conservative move against which it
might seem useful to reduce it into another law-enforcement 'problem'. Even
as 'eventness' and pattern, just like the exception and the rule, are effects of
aesthetic imagination, they inform action we take in the world. A skilful
lawyer moves in a field of aesthetic alternatives with awareness about the
consequences of particular choices and readiness to choose the strategy that
is most likely to bring about the right decision or the desired type of
action. This involves sensitivity to the fact that in particular (legal, political)
institutions, one type of reduction often predominates so that accomplishing
that may be the right strategy to follow. Yet, it is always also possible to
bring out the contrary effect. We stare at a wall, and what first appeared as a
boring pattern of evenly painted surface slowly begins to yield some form
that will finally end up striking us with its singularly expressive power – or
we admire the imaginative uniqueness of an artwork until we learn that it
reproduces the aesthetic canons of this or that 'school' and we learn to read
it as a typical representative of its 'period'. The rule becomes the exception,
the exception the rule, the foreground and the background change place in a
subtle use of legal imagination. Neither reduction has a privileged moral or
political status in law. Both involve cultural gestures and political associations that are important to recognize and then to appreciate in what they can
be made to do. It is hard to think of a more powerful series of reflections and
illustrations on this theme than the essays collected in this book.

Martti Koskenniemi
Helsinki
March 2010

Introduction

Fleur Johns, Richard Joyce and Sundhya Pahuja

Wars, forced migrations, environmental catastrophes, pandemic outbreaks, trade breakdowns, mass grave exhumations, technological breakthroughs: the international legal imaginary is littered with ruptive instances. For international lawyers, Louis Henkin's famous observation – that 'almost all nations observe almost all principles of international law and almost all of their obligations almost all of the time' – continues to be the source of great reassurance (Henkin 1979: 47). From the venous hum of postal services, flight routes and financial transactions, international lawyers discern a disciplinary heartbeat and conviction that an operative body of law remains in place. Yet international lawyers listen, above all, for the screech accompanying an event, when that hum seems to recede and reparation of one kind or another is urged. Of such acute moments is a sense of disciplinary life strung together; of the episodic international law makes an everyday.

The snapshots from that disciplinary life that are assembled in this book are among its most familiar. From the mythic dimensions of the Peace of Westphalia of 1648 to recent revelations of torture perpetrated or sponsored by the US and its allies: the chronology is commonplace. Even its lurches across centuries, unlikely conjunctions and inevitable omissions will be unsurprising to any student of international law. Yet, in their very conventionality, these episodes have much still to relate, or so the contributors to this book will demonstrate.

But before introducing (or reintroducing) international law in all its momentousness in the chapters that follow, we need briefly to explain what this book is about. Impelling the collection is a wish to refresh international legal thinking around events. For if international law is organized around events, then rethinking the event is crucial for a critical international law. What, then, might be entailed in the exercise of 'eventing' international law; of finding in international law an opening, or having it come to pass anew (OED 1989)?

Eventing international law

The normative expectations that political analysts infer from events are the substance of much of contemporary international law ... Yet, at least on first consideration, it is startlingly inconsistent with our accepted notions of law to suggest that one ought to orient oneself in the international legal system by reference to these incidents rather than primarily by reference to statutes, treaties, venerable custom, and judicial and arbitral opinions.

(Reisman 1988: 7)

Since at least the nineteenth century, international lawyers have prospected among events for certain possibilities for international law. Late twentieth-century efforts in this regard are exemplified in the work of Michael Reisman, an influential figure associated with the so-called New Haven School of policy-oriented thought in international law. For Reisman, a focus on the event (or, as he preferred, the 'incident' of conflict between two or more actors within the international system (Reisman 1988: 15)) could yield four properties of which international law has sometimes been perceived as chronically short.

Such a focus offered, first, prospects for international law's continual renewal: each incident was cast as capable of generating that which seemed 'startlingly inconsistent' with that which had come before. Second, it offered substance or content: events were perceived as the raw material out of which international law could be made and remade over time. Moreover, insofar as the events in question could not fully be accommodated by other legal rubrics, a focus on the event offered means by which international law could continue to lay claim to a distinctive field of operation. It could also mark itself as distinctive from other forms of law on the basis of the *extent* of its sensitivity to what happens: witness the grounding of international law in custom, in practice, and the way in which balances and imbalances of power structure its institutions.

For Reisman, a focus on incidents or events offered, third, relevance or a point of intimate connection with power. For him that power resided mostly with 'political analysts' and the 'effective elites' of which they were part (Reisman 1988: 7). What was important for international lawyers, in Reisman's account, was 'not so much what happened [in a particular event] as what effective elites think happened and how they react' (Reisman 1988: 21). In the shared enterprise of 'think[ing] [what] happened', international lawyers could commune with those whose decisions they most sought to inform.

Fourth and finally, a focus on the event, or rather a series of events, offered international law a code or sequence by which to orient itself and generate a sense of disciplinary movement. That orientation has been, above all, towards progress and improvement. By stringing events together into evolutionary narratives, international lawyers have generated a collective disciplinary past, emboldening themselves to navigate its favoured routes into the future. Yet here we see too the beginnings of a tension between events as 'raw material', to which international law must respond, and events as discursive phenomena whose interpretation (and consequent incorporation) is what counts.

For international lawyers of today, Reisman's instincts about the promise latent in the event remain compelling. International legal texts – scholarly and practical – continue to be organized around events as a matter of routine (Charlesworth 2002). Applications to the International Court of Justice, for instance, typically begin with a 'chronology of relevant events' (e.g., International Court of Justice 2009: 2). The 2003 edition of a popular international law textbook observes, in its preface, that '[c]ertain key events must be noted, for they have combined to shift the orientation of international relations'. The paragraph continues with a brief discussion of 'human rights violations committed in the Kosovo Province of Yugoslavia in 1998–99 [that] precipitated an air attack by NATO', 'the attack on the US on 11 September 2001', 'military operations' in Afghanistan and 'the campaign against Iraq' (Shaw 2003: xxiii). Both the 2003 edition and a 2008 edition of the same book highlight the significance of the 'decisive events' of colonial empires' 'disintegration' and 'the birth of scores of new states in the so-called Third World' as pivotal to 'the evolution of international affairs since the Second World War' (Shaw 2003: 38; Shaw 2008: 38). Such occurrences appear as events in these texts at least partly because of the grandness of their scale – a scale in part evidenced by their ability to provoke a response from the law that purports to apply to the whole world. Perhaps, too, this scale is enacted in and by the international legal record itself, in the moment that the local is elevated to the worldwide through these events' apparent contribution *to* international law.

Just as international law might elevate some occurrences to events on a grand scale, so too does it operate as a mode of reduction and containment with respect to events. With reference to new states' appearance and questions of state succession, for example, Shaw's text remarks that '[i]nternational law has to incorporate such events into its general framework with the minimum of disruption and instability' (Shaw 2003: 861; Shaw 2008: 956). Here, then, we see the event performing similar functions as in Reisman's work, albeit with a rather different scholarly handling: events orient international law and shift its centre of gravity or focus 'decisive[ly]' from time to time. Nonetheless, the event holds dangers of 'disruption and instability' levelled at international law's 'general framework' that must be overcome.

International law thus provides a field in which the disruptive potential of events meets directly with an imperative to account for, respond to, contain, incorporate and overcome them. In this process, past events which appear to disrupt the established framework become part of – and indeed to a large extent constitutive of – international legal order. As such events become part of international law's evolutionary narratives, they often cease, it seems, to be unstable or surprising. However, international law does not seek only to reduce past events to its characteristic narrative forms; it seeks to draw in the future as well. It does this by marking itself as the standard against which actors in future international events will come to be judged, by asserting itself as capable of shaping the behaviour of those actors, and announcing in advance the progress it seeks to achieve. In the reduction of the past and the future to a narrative of unfolding progress, it often seems that nothing could happen to international law which it has not either anticipated or claimed the ability to capture: nothing surprising, nothing confronting, nothing, perhaps, capable of constituting an 'event' in 'the strong sense' (Derrida 2002: 234).

Caught between irruption and containment, events, then, seem to confront international law in a contradictory way. It is at this point of contradiction that the contributions to this book are situated. They are situated generally, it may be said, with a view to emphasizing the possibilities which remain, or the continuing operation of instability and potential in events, even after their ostensible containment by international law.

Nonetheless, as preceding paragraphs have emphasized, the turn to events in and for international law is anything but new; indeed, for most international lawyers it is a matter of reflex. What is distinctive about this book, by way of a contribution to international law literature, is its reflection upon this very reflex in the course of its re-enactment. While in one way performing one of international law's most familiar routines – namely, the discipline's recurrent reference to a chronology of events – contributors to this book have sought to raise questions other than those conventionally provoked by the events in question. Those questions include the following. What does international law make of the events by which it orients itself? How has 'eventness' been registered in and by the discipline? How, in particular, have international lawyers envisaged that which is previously unforeseen or unimagined being brought about? What might be some effects of enlivening registers of 'eventness' within this familiar disciplinary record other than those oriented towards progress as such? Might some of international law's most familiar modes of understanding yet be made strange and if so, to what end (if ends are what should concern us)? In addressing these questions and others, the aim of this book is not to inscribe a more definitive or authentic account of international law's 'key events' as much as to demonstrate and explore continuing possibilities for these events to exert ruptive force.

In these inquiries, the contributors to this book are, as they acknowledge, far from alone. Rupture, dislocation and 'the shock of the new' have been matters of intense study across a range of disciplines for centuries (Hughes 1980). In various modes, these have been characteristic preoccupations of the modern era. Many of these inquiries have, moreover, circulated around different iterations of the event. Indeed, as a preoccupation of particular modes of philosophical and political inquiry, the Event has attained the status of a proper noun.

Evental moments and evental sites in contemporary thought

In philosophy of a left or critical bent, the Event has been a recurring figure of 'groundlessness' or the impossibility of absolute foundations (Marchart 2007). What Marchart calls 'post-foundational' thought challenges the familiar shift brought on by the advent of modernity to the scientistic, and the corollary belief in the possibility of positive 'foundations' (Steinmetz 2005). Post-foundational thought rejects the accepted view that the institutions of society (including law and politics), and society itself, are founded on principles, categories and identities which are undeniable, immune to revision and located outside themselves or outside society (Herzog 1985: 20). In terms of the Event, then, what the rather disparate approaches we can gather under this banner arguably share is 'a radicalized notion of the event as something one encounters and which cannot be subsumed under the logic of foundation: rather *event* denotes the dislocating and disruptive moment in which foundations crumble' (Marchart 2007: 2).

For some, '[t]he surprise – the event – does not belong to the order of representation' (Nancy 2000: 173). This suggests a category of something like genuine Events which 'exceed [...] everyday patterns of thinking and acting, opening up a space beyond [themselves]' (Passavant and Dean 2004: 315). For others, the turn to the Event marks a more interpretative orientation, suggesting the need to take some analytical and strategic distance from 'what might (quaintly?) be called world historical events' and to reconsider ostensibly banal ones with the aim of 'decentering the event, working around it, treating it as contingency or symptom' (Brown 1997). Such interpretative approaches might be taken as a refusal of the time of events, adopting a certain 'resistance to [their] immediate terms and intensity' so as to be better able to reflect, to conceptualize and above all, to contextualize (Fitzpatrick 2003).

Other approaches in the interpretative vein draw on discourse analysis and theories about the performativity of language in order to encourage us to see that events and their representation, or form of expression, are inextricably bound together. Understanding that 'event attributions do not simply describe or report pre-existing events, they help to actualize particular events in the social field [...]' illuminates how a description within a particular social context determines something as a particular kind of event (Patton 1997). This also explains why the description of an event will often be the site of active contestation by political actors.

The commonality of the approaches to which we have referred – such as it is – is to open events, or the event, to the political. 'The political' here does not mean institutionalized politics, nor wider social practices that we might call politics. Instead it indicates precisely that which escapes political domestication. To relate it back to grounds, or the idea of foundation, the political is that which is precluded by the actual grounding of society and institutions. The ontic practices of conventional politics to attempt to ground society are, according to these accounts, always unsuccessful. This is because the grounds themselves can never be complete, or to oversimplify, themselves be grounded. This is not necessarily a bad thing. Nonetheless, in order to account for society's absent ground, a term was needed for 'the founding difference that [prevents the social] from closing and becoming identical with itself' (Marchart 2007: 5). This term, within a long and rich vein of critical social thought, is 'the political'. 'The political' thus gestures toward the fact that something is always lost when society is instituted.

In the work of some post-foundational scholars, the event, like the political, is in the foregoing sense a figure of groundlessness or contingency. Other figures of groundlessness include freedom, truth or the real. These figures 'stand' on society's non-ground. The moment of the political – a moment some render as event – is the instant when society's absent ground becomes palpable (Marchart 2007: 8).

To gather post-foundational scholarship in this way is, of course, to elide much in the work of the scholars in question, divergences especially. Many renderings of the event in contemporary philosophy are neither fungible with, nor gathered comfortably alongside, other understandings of the term. The work of Alain Badiou, for instance, has invested the event with a precise meaning formulated axiomatically on the basis of extensional set theory (or a rendering of the latter in Badiou's own name). Within that field, the event is the name that Badiou gives to that which is 'always an abnormal multiple'; the supernumerary (Badiou 2007: 179). So derived, the event, per Badiou, is a haphazardly occurring mark of the localized possibility of 'laicized grace'; 'neither an ontological attribute nor a historical result but something that occasionally comes to pass, from time to time' (Hallward 2003: 115; xxxii). Furthermore, the event is not instantaneously emergent as such. Rather, the properties of an evental site are such as to force a decision whether to intervene to generate the singular 'discipline' of realizing some unrepresentable 'newness in being' on which we might wager the name event (Badiou 2007: 207–9). In this sense, the event is, for Badiou, foundational; evental sites are 'absolutely primary terms' within a situation (Badiou 2007: 175).

For all its density and difficulty, Badiou's work on the event nonetheless installs a marker for emancipatory politics in the plural. Badiou's writing seeks to recoup and 'subtract[] the sheer "what happens" from the general determinations of "what is"' (Badiou 2004: 100). Politics, in Badiou's account, begins with thought, rather than opinion, group, class or social configuration (Badiou 2005: 5). His is, then, a 'radical inaugural gesture' of thought that seeks to 'set out on an entirely different path' to that which political philosophy has previously inscribed (Badiou 2004: 104; Badiou 2005: 23). That is a path opposed to 'every vision of consensual politics' and to 'the humanist vision of the bond, or the being-together' (Badiou 2005: 23, 66). Instead, each evental site in Badiou's account is the locus for 'the inception of a politics' of absolute singularity through which a subject – or subjective universality – expressive of an egalitarian logic may be induced (Badiou 2005: 23; 143; 148–49).

For Jacques Derrida, on the other hand, the event expresses not so much a point or site from which one could found or even depart toward a new politics, but rather an opportunity to glimpse the relationship between the impossible and the possible, the unconditional and the conditional. For Derrida, the event depends on the 'dangerous modality of the "perhaps"': there 'is no future and no relation to the coming of the event without an experience of the "perhaps"'. (Derrida 2002: 234, 235). This modality is one of exposure to that which cannot be determined in advance, anticipated or conditioned, or made subject to rules – even the rules by which it could be understood. An event 'in the strong sense' would suppose an *irruption* that punctures the horizon, *interrupting* any performative organization, any convention, or any context that can be dominated by a conventionality. Which is to say that this event takes place only where it does not allow itself to be domesticated' (Derrida 2002: 234). If events are the 'raw material' out of which international law is made, this line of thought would emphasize their rawness.

Derrida would concede that an event is produced by the performative which claims only to speak of it (Derrida 2002: 234). Yet also, and inversely, the very act of speaking of and for the event, of interpreting it, of giving it a meaning and a context (for example, placing it within a narrative conditioned by international law's modes of conventionality) neutralizes its character as 'event' in Derrida's terms. For Derrida, '[i]f what arrives belongs to the horizon of the possible, or even of a possible performative, it does not arrive, it does not happen, in the full sense of the word' (Derrida 2002: 234). Indeed:

> The event belongs to a *perhaps* that is in keeping not with the possible, but with the impossible. And its force is therefore irreducible to the force or the power of a performative, even if it gives to the performative itself, to what is called the *force* of the performative, its chance and effectiveness.
>
> (Derrida 2002: 235)

In these terms, events provide a dangerous kind of raw material for international law. Events give international law what it needs to in order to announce and impose itself on the world, things to comprehend, explain, abhor, judge, regulate *et cetera*. And yet events cannot be totally and finally reduced to international law's own ends: the 'force of the event is always stronger than the force of a performative ... in the face of what ... happens ... all performative force is overrun, exceeded, exposed' (Derrida 2002: 235). No conditioning, contextualizing and reduction can totally neutralize the disruptive potential of events. They remain open to new modes of appropriation, new interpretations. Something like this possibility underlies many of the contributions to this book. Nonetheless, per Derrida, difficulty lies in keeping the singular, unconditional force of the event in operation, in spite of ever-present sovereign modes of capture and reduction (Derrida 2002: 235).

The chapters

Fittingly, Jennifer Beard opens the chapters by examining the relationship between the two key events by which modern international law is often thought to have been founded: the Peace of Westphalia of 1648 and the discovery of the New World. Beard's concern is with the violent event of 'discovery' as constitutive of the two worlds instantiated in contradistinction in the Peace of Westphalia: 'the Old World of Europe and a New World that was to be subjected to colonisation'. The claim of peace and universal law embedded in Westphalia is, Beard argues, anachronistic; it is a form of legalized or mythical violence in Walter Benjamin's terms. From this event of history- and law-making violence, Beard invites us to gaze 'beyond historical time' to spaces 'where the multitude threatens the place of the state subject'.

From Beard's chapter, we move back in historical time to the mid-sixteenth century and the Valladolid Debates between Juan Ginés de Sepúlveda, Bartolomé de Las Casas and Francisco de Vitoria concerning the status, entitlements and self-governing capacities of Amerindians. We stay, nonetheless, with Benjamin's notion of mythic violence. In Oscar Guardiola-Rivera's account, it is the pragmatic common sense of international law and international relations that enacts the mythical in its unending 'index of the totality of cases'. From Vitoria and Sepúlveda contemporary international lawyers have drawn an idea of law's constancy through time and space, Guardiola-Rivera maintains. In this concern with constancy, international lawyers have disavowed the event, that is, the unprecedented or improbable. Against this tendency, Guardiola-Rivera retrieves the 'memory' of Felipe Guaman Poma de Ayala's writings, particularly his presentation of 'the challenge of extinction' and thus the 'non-totalisable nature of reality'. From this, Guardiola-Rivera extracts possibilities for 'a conception of the event freed from its limits in experience' and an ethical disposition of openness towards the nonexistent.

Peter Fitzpatrick's chapter also takes the work of Francisco de Vitoria as a point of departure. In its straddling the divide between the medieval and the modern, Fitzpatrick finds in Vitoria's work the preservation of a contradiction within international law that standard modern accounts would suppress. In the standard account, Fitzpatrick contends, international law gains its force 'solely from the sovereign and secular nations out of which it dependently emanates'. Yet, as Fitzpatrick shows, these entities are dependent on international law to provide the terms on which they are constituted. Taking this contradiction (between the singular nation state and the community of the international) as itself constitutive of the force of international law, Fitzpatrick demonstrates its salience both in Vitoria's writings and by way of reflection on the event as such.

Richard Joyce's chapter returns us to the Peace of Westphalia and the common claim made for its being the founding event of modern sovereignty; a foundation which in turn is taken to ground international law. Joyce examines recent claims to the contrary – claims that the content of the Westphalian treaties did not inaugurate or consolidate an unequivocal principle of sovereign statehood, and that its status as the founding event of international law is the work of myth rather than history. Between these positions, Joyce argues that the continued significance of Westphalia for modern sovereignty lies precisely in the disjuncture between the historical record and that for which it is remembered. One measure of this significance lies in the way in which the complexity of political forms in the Westphalian treaties might help to put in perspective current 'crises' in modern sovereignty. Another is the way in which Westphalia highlights both the importance of myth to our understanding of modern sovereignty and law and the way in which that importance is often denied.

Thomas Skouteris (re)visits the adoption of article 38 of the statute of the Permanent Court of International Justice (PCIJ), a classic event in most treatises of international law. This article, adopted with the court's statute in 1920, lists normative forms to which the court may have regard in deciding what the law is to be applied to any decision. Notwithstanding its seemingly modest aim, the article became the unintended point of origin for what later became the modern doctrine of the sources of international law. Skouteris uses this 'seminal' doctrinal moment in the development of international law as a case study for analyzing notions of progress in international law, in terms of both form and function. In Skouteris' argument, the adoption of article 38 operates retrospectively within sources doctrine, and implicitly within international law as a whole, as a founding moment for a new determinacy within international law. But, he argues, this determinacy is putative; it can be asserted only through the negation of what went before. Certain techniques such as standardization and formalization are involved in that negation, but are themselves dependent on a modernization story. Skouteris' chapter shows that while those techniques seem to help us to discern the difference between law and non-law ever more clearly, they ultimately rely on gestures or incantations, of pragmatism and rationality in particular, to conjure up a point of arrival for the modernizing movement forward. The event of article 38, and the formation of a determinate doctrine of sources, thus turn out to be matters of fantasy, or at least a myth of origin, but one which is ideologically operative through its (re)iteration.

Gerry Simpson's chapter continues the theme of the instability of the distinctions on which legal categories are founded with a consideration of the *levée en masse*, or event of mass uprising, beginning with that which occurred in France in 1793. This event, which Simpson suggests, 'may or may not have occurred, and which might only exist as a possibility', has yet shaped our experience of war and resistance through its occupation of the unstable space of differentiation between the two. Simpson traces two competing conceptions of the *levée en masse* to show the way the poles which the conceptions respectively occupy operate on one level as a kind of 'ground' for the laws of war. On another level, those poles themselves come full circle, bleeding into one another in fact, and implicitly stabilizing one another in principle. The *levée* is thus a paradoxical moment in which an event which threatens to exceed law can do so only by its demand for recognition *by* law. Without its liminal status being marked by law itself, the event simply becomes illegal. Yet once marked by law, arguably that liminal status dissolves in favour of incorporation into the regulation of violence and the event of *levée en masse* is neutralized.

The evental character of law's instability is further explored in Sundhya Pahuja's chapter as she draws out the character of a post-colonial event in international law. Specifically, Pahuja offers an account of the way in which a heterogeneous series of political demands for independence after the end of the Second World War are narrated into the smooth event of 'decolonization' within international law. As in many other chapters in the book, this narrative emollient is provided in Pahuja's account in large measure by a story about progress, or a movement forward, embodied here by the concept of development. Like Simpson and others in this volume, Pahuja is interested in the way that certain demands (which may in themselves take the form of events) threaten to disrupt the categories of international law, which categories address that ruptive potential via a process of incorporation. In doctrinal terms, the extension of legal principle to include a particular political claim embodied in an event marks the success of that political claim. In other ways, that inclusion is precisely a depoliticization of the more radical dimensions of the claim. Like the mass uprising and its (re)categorization as a *levée en masse*, claims for decolonization are neutralized as they are recognized as acts of self-determination by nation states within the legal frame. The specifically post-colonial character of the event of decolonization in Pahuja's account arises from the way the universal promise of international law itself both facilitates the demands for decolonization through a certain illimitability of that promise and facilitates those demands' incorporation within law's body.

Scott Newton's chapter also focuses on the way in which the disruptive potential in events might be reduced by their containment within a narrative determined by dominant voices. Newton's concern is with the collapse of state socialism in Eastern and Central Europe in 1989 and the subsequent collapse of the Soviet Union two years later. As Newton shows, these collapses seemed to provide the opportunity for the realization of an international system promised in 1945, but held back by the Cold War. Nineteen eighty-nine thus 'rapidly assumed the dimensions of an epochal Event', Newton recounts. He argues, however, that this 'Event' is better characterized as a '"psuedo-Event," staged or managed (or co-opted) by an existing configuration of power or authority, rather than spontaneously generating any new such configuration on the basis of new revolutionary subjectivities'. This is exemplified, for Newton, by the way in which the language and practice of 'transition' (of the former socialist states' economies into market economies) deprived societies in these states of the critical standpoints necessary to maintain fidelity to the event (in Alain Badiou's sense) of the collapses themselves.

In narrating the story of Nelson Mandela's release from prison, Frédéric Mégret's chapter highlights the way in which 'external' events are incorporated into international law, again as part of a narrative of progress. This time the story is one of a progressive journey to freedom which certain traditions of contemporary international law see themselves as bringing about. Mégret's chapter resonates tellingly with Pahuja's observations about the uncontainability of the promise of justice within international law, illustrating ways in which that promise can be mobilized against pragmatic, bureaucratic and 'apologetic' tendencies within international law (Koskenniemi 2006). Mandela's release, for Mégret, is neither a triumphant narrative of a victory over oppression nor a condemnation of international law's impuissance in the face of a gross injustice. Instead, Mégret offers a subtle account of the way this peculiar, even unique, event called international law to account for itself, breathing life into its promise of justice and resuscitating near-moribund institutions. The disruption caused by this event is thus slightly different to most others in the book. Mégret focuses on the way the emancipatory character of international law's affirmation of human rights can be operative through the narration of a radical event as one 'belonging' to international law, and in this continuing operation, generative of institutional renewal. This stands in contrast to other chapters' accounts of the incorporation and deradicalization of events challenging the order of international law.

In Emilios Christodoulidis' chapter, on the other hand, we encounter the event in quite a distinct sense: that derived from the work of Alain Badiou. We encounter it also in a sense more familiar for international lawyers: the event in question is that of an explicitly politicized trial and the trials discussed are matters of historical record and international legal concern: the French trials of Algerian militants and the Milošević trial. Drawing from Badiou, the political trial is considered first as situation, then as eventual site within that situation. Through its Badiouvian framing as evental site, Christodoulidis seeks in the trial 'the possibility of challenging existing distributions of subject positions and entitlements' or 'break[ing] out of ... situational confinement'. Within a trial situation, he asks, how are immanent possibilities for resistance to the orders of capital created?

Karen Knop's chapter also concerns the trial and possibilities for its re-enactment in a register of resistance. Knop recounts a trial performed as a retrospective remaking of historical events, or an 'act of going back in time and taking another path': the 2001 Women's International War Crimes Tribunal for the Trial of Japan's Military Sexual Slavery. This 'as if' act was structured, Knop observes, to blend fact and fiction. As such it comprises, in Knop's innovative reading, a distinctive form of critique. For all its limits, Knop suggests, this critique helped to create 'a feminist past *manqué* for international law' with some of the force of precedent.

Denise Ferreira da Silva's chapter concerns another 'landmark' trial in international law: the first decision of the International Criminal Tribunal for Rwanda (ICTR), in 1998, *The Prosecutor v Jean-Paul Akayesu*. For da Silva, however, this event enacts less a disruption than a consolidation: specifically, a consolidation of 'the place of humanity in ... international law through the particular deployment of cultural difference that sustains the [ICTR] Chamber's decision'. Like other contributors, Da Silva regards the event as constitutive of subjectivity. Hence she asks: 'What sort of juridical subjects does this deployment produce?' Surmising that the subject of crime against humanity may present 'the latest refashioning of the global subaltern subject', she seeks ways to 'comprehend its conditions of emergence and effects' by reading through and beyond 'early' critical approaches pre-occupied with 'racial othering'.

Tackling further landmarks of institution building, Patricia Tuitt's essay takes on the usual account of the European Union's establishment as having been achieved by the force of 'positive legal norms alone'. For Tuitt, by contrast, the creation of the European Union relied, just like the creation of the 'New World', on land appropriation. In both cases, this process necessitated the presentation of the space which would be appropriated as 'free' despite being both 'populated and governed'. Tuitt argues that the assertion of the four freedoms in the Rome Treaty (the free movement of goods, services, workers and capital) effected this transformation of the territory of Europe into a space which could simultaneously ground and have imposed on it a new sovereign order. For Tuitt, it is by accepting 'that the European Union relies for its existence on modes of sovereign assertion that pre-dated (and made possible) the state system' that we might come to understand the 'uneven distribution of rights among the people of Europe'.

Emergence and structural effects are, in a different yet related sense, the foci of Fiona Macmillan's chapter on the establishment of the World Trade Organization (WTO) in 1995. In Macmillan's account, the WTO's creation, and the rise of 'corporate capitalism' within which she situates it, are traceable to the establishment of the English East India Company and its Dutch counterpart at the beginning of the seventeenth century. As such, the international regulatory strategies borne out in the WTO's creation are linked to corporations' complex interdependence with states, interstate competition for mobile capital and the growth in corporations' capacity to wield influence on their own behalf within processes of supranational institution building and structural change. Rather than being an interruption, the rise of the WTO is cast as a response to an interruption in 'the process of corporate-led globalisation'; that interruption being the introduction of non-tariff measures in the wake of 'exogenous shocks' of the 1970s and 1980s. This response, Macmillan suggests, echoes repeated turns from war to international (economic) law-making as a means of managing conflict. Past failures in these efforts, Macmillan suggests, should give us pause before re-enacting them amid 'the current period of economic turbulence'.

Underlining the multiplicity of this event and its openness to many readings, Donatella Alessandrini's chapter also examines the WTO's establishment. For Alessandrini, however, the questions raised by this institution's emergence surround 'the development dimension' of international trade. Specifically, Alessandrini engages critically the notion that the WTO's creation signalled a victory for rational choice approaches to the pursuit of development goals, over the 'ideological' claims by which earlier periods of development thinking were said to be marked. Like other contributors, Alessandrini identifies continuity where some would announce rupture. The late-twentieth-century neo-liberal 'revolution' in development thinking is less revolution than reformulation, in Alessandrini's account: political assumptions underpinning earlier development theories were overthrown, only to usher in 'a new and powerful construction of developing countries' "backwardness"'. At the same time, Alessandrini takes issue with prevailing interpretations of that shift in development thinking, rejecting the notion that it resulted from stakeholders' rational pursuit of the most efficient trade policy. This change in thought has not been a flowering of reason, Alessandrini maintains; rather, it is an outcome of multiple material, structural and regulatory factors, some of the most important of which have been too easily dismissed. Challenging the WTO's development agenda is, then, less a matter of reasoning towards greater efficiency than of '[r]ecognising how the "development mission" of the international trading regime has operated since inception'. Openings reside elsewhere than among trade-offs framed in rational choice terms.

Ruth Buchanan's chapter identifies openings as well. Buchanan explores street-level mobilizations against international institutions as 'direct interventions into ongoing legal debates over the legitimacy and accountability of that institution'. Actions taken in 1999 in Seattle against the WTO serve as her exemplary case study. Using Arendt's notion of the event, read alongside that discernible in writings of activist participants in the 1999 demonstrations, Buchanan seeks to extend critical thinking about citizen action, the constitutive force of resistance and the role of social movements within international law. In their unpredictable, performative dimension, Buchanan argues, these actions may counter-actualize politics and reveal 'something new in the world', understood in the sense of Arendt's writing on political events.

Continuing in the vein of resistance, Obiora Chinedu Okafor is interested in what we might think of as resistant international law theory, and in particular, Third World Approaches to International Law or 'TWAIL'. In his chapter, Okafor seeks to use a TWAIL approach to explore the reconfigurations of the international sphere in the aftermath of 11 September 2001, and to ask what ways of understanding the world have become prominent since events of that date. Like others in this volume, Okafor is interested in the continuities of practices of domination and subordination in the world in both material and epistemological terms. These continuities are concealed in new techniques, but may be unearthed through an insistence on history, and on remembering the past in the face of what seems ever new. In line with this insistence, Okafor reminds us of the colonial roots of intervention, and the putative universality of its justifying norms. He also reminds us of the familiarity for the Third World of practices such as torture. These acts, marked as exceptional and necessary to respond to the unprecedented events of *now*, can be seen as almost routine in the context of interventions into the Third World, justified, then as now, by the threat of barbarism and the need to protect the 'international community'. Scrutinized through this lens, what Okafor calls 'security relativism' is therefore shown to be something international lawyers must resist, lest we join the long list of 'friendly torturers', justifying their barbarity in the name of security.

Concerned also with violence precipitated by 11 September and continuities enacted thereby, John Strawson's chapter takes as its point of departure the common assumption that the invasion of Iraq in 2003 was illegal under international law. In Strawson's account, the invasion does not provide a clear example of a breach of international law, but rather highlights the limited nature of the prohibition on the use of force by states. In particular, Strawson emphasizes the scope left to states themselves to determine whether circumstances exist justifying the use of force in their self-defence. None of this is surprising, Strawson argues, once the role played by colonization in shaping the norms and structure of international law (and, in particular, the prerogatives of sovereign statehood and attendant ambiguities on the use of force) is recognized. The example of the Indian invasion of Goa in 1961 is offered as another 'event' in which the relationship between international law and the self-justified use of force by a sovereign state is at stake. In that instance, however, 'war was seen as a means to enforce law'. Drawing a link between Goa and Iraq, Strawson argues that colonialism bequeathed an international law on the use of force which has not been challenged head on, but instead remains open for 'competitive appropriation' by states who seek to determine its meaning in their own interests.

Closing the book, Fleur Johns' chapter, on the release of the so-called torture memos between 2004 and 2009, is concerned with something new coming into the world as international law understands it, however marked with convention and continuity. The newness in question is the law-making capacity of a figure to which Johns gives both the name 'detainee-combatant' and the name 'event', the latter framed in terms drawn from Alain Badiou. In the piecemeal record of detainee-jailer interactions taken from various reports, Johns discerns efforts, on the part of detainees, to activate the errancy of the category 'unlawful combatant' and contest the law-making endeavours in which all parties seemingly recognized themselves to be engaged. For Johns, the torture memos' release amounted to a public announcement of this novatory law making, revealing law directly enabling and enabled by violence. In Johns' account, the persistence of this errancy explains the intensity and vigour of international lawyers' efforts to redeem themselves and remake their disciplinary situation in the memos' wake.

Conclusions and beginnings

Fittingly, then, the book concludes with an announcement of newness and a record of both its persistence and its domestication in international law. From the book's chapters, no shared conception of the event emerges. Even so, contributors to the book are working from a more or less common canon of 'post-foundational' writing surrounding the event (Marchart 2007) and an equally incendiary tradition of international law's renewal through historical critique. It has become customary to look to the former for diagnosis and direction in contemporary international legal scholarship. This book suggests that 'mainstream' international lawyers' libraries could perhaps be as rich, in this regard, as those of their more 'interdisciplinary' colleagues, given the attentive readings exemplified in its chapters.

By subverting or sideswiping the usual interpretations given to the events under consideration, or by bringing to light things about them which may have been neglected, the contributors to this book put in question both the specific events they have addressed (their meaning and significance for international law, that is) and also the possibility of a singular narrative for international law as a whole. As this book's contributors show, events can be seen to have a generative force in relation to international law. However, the relation is at least circular, for international law also makes of certain occurrences 'events' with ramifications extending well beyond international law's disciplinary field. In light of these generative relations, and their divergent impacts, recognizing and exploiting the multiplicity of possible readings of international law's 'seminal' events prompts a rethinking of what international law and international lawyers might yet do. It does not, however, point towards a clear answer to that question. If both international law and the event itself are characteristically caught between irruption and containment – between the threat and promise of the new on the one hand, and the incorporation of what happens into a pre-existing, dominant narrative on the other – then perhaps a useful critical stance will be one which is not held hostage to the imperative to fashion for each an integrative disciplinary response or resolution. Indeed, we might just as well conclude that what we learn from international law's relation to the event is precisely a reminder that the chance and challenge to determine what international law does, and what it is for, remain open.

References

Badiou, A. (2004) *Badiou: Theoretical Writings*, trans. R. Brassier and A. Toscano, London, New York: Continuum.

——(2005) *Metapolitics*, trans. J. Barker, London, New York: Verso.

——(2007) *Being and Event*, trans. O. Feltham, London, New York: Continuum.

Brown, W. (1997) 'The time of the political', 1:1 *Theory and Event* http://muse.jhu.edu/journals/theory_and_event/v001/1.1brown.html.

Charlesworth, H. (2002) 'International law: a discipline of crisis', 65 *Modern Law Review* 377.

Derrida, J. (2002), 'The university without condition' in J. Derrida, *Without Alibi*, trans. P. Kamuf, Stanford: Stanford University Press, 2002.

Fitzpatrick, P. (2003) 'The irresponsibility of the intellectual', opening address given at *Professing to Educate and Educating to Profess,* McGill University Law School, Montreal, Canada (July 2003). Copy on file with the authors.

Hallward, P. (2003) *Badiou: A Subject to Truth*, Minneapolis: University of Minnesota Press.

Henkin, L. (1979; 1st edn 1968) *How Nations Behave*, New York: Columbia University Press.

Herzog, D. (1985) *Without Foundations: Justification in Political Theory*, Ithaca: Cornell University Press.

Hughes, R. (1980; 2nd edn 1991) *The Shock of the New*, New York: Knopf.

International Court of Justice (2009) *Application Instituting Proceedings by the Kingdom of Belgium Against the Republic of Senegal* (16 February 2009). Available online at: <www.icj-cij.org/docket/files/144/15054.pdf#view=FitH&pagemode=none&search=%22events%22> (accessed 10 December 2009).

Koskenniemi, M. (2006, 2nd edn) *From Apology to Utopia: The Structure of International Legal Argument*, Cambridge: Cambridge University Press.

Marchart, O. (2007) *Post-Foundational Political Thought: Political difference in Nancy, Lefort, Badiou and Laclau*, Edinburgh: Edinburgh University Press.

Nancy, J. L. (2000) *Being Singular Plural*, Stanford: Stanford University Press.

The Oxford English Dictionary (OED) (1989, 2nd edn), *The Oxford English Dictionary*, Oxford: Oxford University Press. OED Online. Available: <http://dictionary.oed.com/> (accessed 15 December 2009).

Passavant, P. A. and Dean, J. (2004) *Empire's New Clothes*, New York and London: Routledge.

Patton, P. (1997) 'The world seen from within: Deleuze and the philosophy of events … ' 1:1 *Theory and Event*. Available online at: http://muse.jhu.edu/journals/theory_and_event/v001/1.1patton.html (accessed 18 January 2010).

Reisman, W. M. (1988) *International Incidents: The Law that Counts in World Politics*. Princeton, NJ: Princeton University Press.

Shaw, M. N. (2003, 5th edn) *International Law*, Cambridge: Cambridge University Press.

——(2008, 6th edn) *International Law*, Cambridge: Cambridge University Press.

Steinmetz, G. (ed.) (2005) *The Politics of Method in the Human Sciences: Positivism and its Epistemological Others*, Durham, NC: Duke University Press.

Chapter 1

The international law in force

Anachronistic ethics and divine violence

Jennifer Beard

Introduction

Most textbooks on international law state the founding event of modern international law to be the Peace of Westphalia of 1648 that followed the Thirty Years War. This is the event in which a European society of sovereign states is said to have been established and, so, the law of nations. The peace was set out in two treaties between the Roman Empire and various European powers at Osnabrück on 15 May 1648 and at Münster on 24 October. The treaties recognized the existence of nascent, territorial states comprising their own legal and religious jurisdictions. Prior to the peace, these territories had been subject to the jurisdiction of the Holy Roman Empire, which had been ruled by the Catholic Church over a number of centuries. European peoples were not the only peoples over whom the Catholic Church had claimed jurisdiction by virtue of its divine duty to save all souls. However, the Peace of Westphalia remained silent about the territorial rights of the peoples of the 'New World' and their territories. In that respect, the peace was founded on older claims of legitimate rule that had sanctioned the objectification of a New World. That same objectification enabled European legal theorists to incorporate the violence of colonization into new theories supporting the law of nations that arose out of the Peace of Westphalia. This division between the Old World of Europe and the New World, understood as an effect of pre-modern violence, remains a part of international relations today. In consequence, I suggest that the Peace of Westpahlia should be considered as much a culminating event of violence as a foundational event of modern, international law.

A critique of the foundations of international law

I have found it useful to explore the founding events behind the force of international law by engaging with Walter Benjamin's 'Critique of violence', particularly through a reading of that text by Judith Butler (Benjamin 1986; Butler 2006). This section of the chapter explains why

Benjamin's critique is relevant to the relationship of violence and international law. The following section will engage with the violent events surrounding the discovery of the New World. The aim will be to show how the sanctioning of imperial violence produced a mythical and conceptual separation between Europe and the New World, which was incorporated into the legal system established by the Peace of Westphalia. The point is to question the kind of justice that exists in an international law that is so intimately related to violence.

Benjamin's 'Critique of violence'

In his 'Critique of violence', Benjamin examines how violence is legitimized through its relation to law and justice (Benjamin 1986). Benjamin first distinguishes between natural law and positive law. He says, 'Natural Law attempts, by the justness of ends, to "justify" the means', positive law to 'guarantee' 'the justness of ends through the justification by legal sanction of the means' (Benjamin 1986: 278). Benjamin argues that positivism is the better basis upon which to begin his analysis of the legal justification of violence because of its theoretical distinction between 'historically acknowledged, so-called sanctioned violence, and unsanctioned violence' (Benjamin 1986: 279).

The treaties establishing the Peace of Westphalia are interesting in that respect. These treaties are a good example of how legal agreements were used to legitimize the emergence of a new society of legal subjects (states) and a system of laws to regulate those subjects. Benjamin argues that a positivist 'legal system tries to erect, in all areas where individual ends could be usefully pursued by violence, legal ends that can only be realized by legal power' (Benjamin 1986: 280). The Peace of Westphalia marks the beginning of a new 'balance' of power in Europe that is secured by the legal constitution of a particular way of dividing and occupying territory and populations. The aim of the peace was to check the violence of territorial acquisition and conflicts over legitimate rule by establishing a system where violence (and power) would not appear to function regardless of, or outside of, the law (Benjamin 1986: 280–81). Benjamin argues that these kinds of legalized violence can be divided into law-making (*rechtsetzend*) violence and law-preserving (*rechterhaltend*) violence. Benjamin distinguishes both of these forms of violence from what he calls divine violence.

Law-making violence occurs when violence is used to bring about a new legal order. Here law is used to sanction the use of violence by 'recognising the new conditions as a new "law", quite regardless of whether they need *de facto* any guarantee of their continuation' (Benjamin 1986: 283). There is an inherent 'law-making character' to all such violence. In terms of international law, for example, we might say that the Peace of Westphalia sanctioned the reality of a nascent system of state-based relations that emerged as a result of a long period of violence. This was an event of law-making violence.

Once 'made', the law must be preserved. Theories of positive law rely on violence to preserve the law in the name of the common good. Benjamin might have argued that international law is preserved by the constant reassertion of the founding act of the Westphalian Peace. The primary essence of the peace is the maintenance of a system of sovereign, territorial states. Today, international law may not support the concept of absolute state sovereignty, but it certainly maintains the formal principles of territorial integrity and sovereign equality as basic norms. This kind of violence might be understood as the law in force. There are many technologies of power and state practices that constrain or compel legal subjects to ensure the law's preservation. These forces are complex and broad-ranging. As Orford has argued, a crisis of legal authority pervades the discipline of international law (Orford 2004). International law is constantly 'called upon to renew itself and reassert its relevance' (Orford 2004: 441). Those who seek to rely on and give force to international law are constantly seeking 'a new sovereign ground for the law, whether that be in the form of international organizations or of powerful national sovereigns who stand outside the law and guarantee its operation' (Orford 2004: 441). Regardless of this crisis of authority, I would argue that the foundational structure of international law is always maintained. That structure is the state system. The 'peace' offered by the Westphalian system is the 'inalienable right' of all peoples to 'the exercise of their sovereignty and the integrity of their national territory' (GA Res 1514 1960). The legal subject of the state is essential to the existence of international law and contemporary relations of power. International legal norms reflect the effects of these power relations by ensuring that state boundaries and populations remain relatively static while issues of governance such as rights-based approaches to human development or the choice of economic policies are regulated in ways that do not affect the existence of the state subject as such.

Benjamin suggests that both 'law-making' and 'law-preserving' violence can be understood in terms of a kind of 'mythical violence'. In this sense, the law is there to justify power. In myth, 'the law' is the power of gods explained. In constitutional law, law is explained as the power of the state to instate and maintain the 'peace' within and around its frontiers (Benjamin 1986: 295). Benjamin gives as an example the idea that 'in the beginning all right was of the kings or the nobles – in short of the mighty ... ' (Benjamin 1986: 298). The power behind international law is also aimed at securing existing power structures that rely on the system of sovereign states established by the Peace of Westphalia. For Benjamin, power lies behind all forms of violence envisioned by the legal theories of natural law and positivism. He concludes that legal theories of justice are merely a form of reasoning inherent in the justification of means and ends arising from what is ultimately violence imposed by fate (Benjamin 1986: 294). In consequence, Benjamin argues that any violence justified by legal sanction is not necessarily morally just.

Benjamin concludes that the only form of violence to fall outside of the law is 'divine violence'. He says that if 'mythical violence [i.e. legalized violence] is law-making, divine violence is law-destroying' (Benjamin 1986: 297). The human response to divine violence, according to Butler, is an anarchistic one that happens 'without recourse to principle' (Butler 2006: 214). There is no reinstatement of a new law that might arise from divine forms of violence. According to Butler, 'no law is made from this place, and the destruction is not part of a new elaboration of positive law' (Butler 2006: 214). Divine violence is said to work against the positive law 'that binds a subject to a specific legal system and stops that subject from developing a critical, if not a revolutionary point of view on that legal system' (Butler 2006: 203). According to Butler, such violence is not 'justified through a set of ends but constitutes a "pure means"' (Butler 2006: 211).

Laws that are enacted in the name of a particular religion are not forms of divine violence. For example, the violence of colonization is not divine violence, although for centuries the Catholic Church justified its imperial practices as a means to save souls. The violence of colonization is better understood as a form of mythical violence. The violence can be understood as mythical in the sense that the fate of colonized peoples was interpreted through the sovereign and legal authority of the Catholic Church as one that was somehow justified because of the particular conditions or status of the peoples themselves. That mythical belief in the legitimation of imperial violence was incorporated into the system of sovereign relations established by the Peace of Westphalia. Hence, the Peace of Westphalia can also be understood as a mythical event, primarily concerned with legitimizing the constitutional powers of individual European territories. But in marking out a system of inter-sovereign relations, the peace maintained the right of states to colonize foreign territory and populations. This right had already been established during the period of discovery in the fifteenth century pursuant to the belief held by the Catholic Church of its duty to save all souls. The next section of this chapter explores the conceptual effects of such a mythological interpretation of events.

The event of discovery

As stated in the introduction, international law is founded on the Peace of Westphalia, which was the culmination of a religious war. One of the effects of bringing the war to an end by declaring a new legal order was to bring the violence of the self-declared universal jurisdiction of the Roman Catholic Church within the terms of the Westphalian Peace. The distinction between Christian and non-Christian worlds legitimized by the Catholic Church remained a legitimate reality in the establishment of the Peace of Westphalia and the constitution of two worlds: the Old World of Europe and a New World that was to be subjected to colonization. In this section I explore how this distinction between the Old World and the New World was constituted through violence and justified through law in the event of discovery.

When Columbus set off with the sanction of the Catholic Pope and the Spanish monarchs to find a western route to the Indies, there was no sense of the earth's territories divided into spaces of equal, sovereign power. Instead, 'new' territory was subject to possession through treaty, occupation or conquest. From his diaries, we know that there was never any doubt that Columbus' intention was to possess the territories he discovered in the name of the king and queen of Spain, by force if necessary or by peaceful conversion. As Columbus encountered each territory, he claimed it. In this way, pursuant to papal bull, Spanish law became the law to be enforced. At the time, the Catholic Church was an extremely powerful force in Europe, which was by then largely Christian. All Christian monarchs were expected to defer to the divine authority of the pope. One of the many powers vested in the pope was the authority to grant dominion over territory. Papal bulls issued by Pope Nicolas V in 1452 and 1455 to King Alfonso V of Portugal had confirmed to the crown of Portugal dominion over all lands discovered or conquered by Portuguese explorers. These bulls were revoked in bulls issued in 1493. Pope Alexander VI issued these latter bulls to King Ferdinand and Queen Isabella of Spain. They stated that one Christian nation did not have the right to establish dominion over lands previously dominated by another Christian nation. The bull also assigned to Castile the exclusive right to acquire territory and to trade in the lands lying west of the meridian situated 100 leagues west of the Azores and Cape Verde Islands. These bulls mark the beginning of the imperial competition between Westphalian states to acquire foreign colonies. Here we see how the mythology of divine authority vested in the papal bulls was relied on to justify imperial violence and to preserve the empire. The fateful event of discovery was instituted by force of law and in turn was justified and enforced through law. In this way, the 'triumph of fate is the establishment of law itself' (Butler 2006: 208). The Christian empire rising from the west of Europe would lay down the word through the colonization of these territories by monarchs deferring to the Roman Catholic empire. The legal rights proclaimed by Catholic popes have since been reasserted over time in different events.[1]

Underlying that instantiation of law is the myth of a world newly discovered. If the Old World of Christian Europe was to justify its conquest and destruction of the New World then it had to believe that it held the promise of salvation – that the conquest of the New by the Old signified the fall of one world into the promise of another. The colonization of the New World was justified figuratively by the Old World in its promise that the two worlds belonged to a single history. Columbus understood his discovery of the Americas as part of an eventual unification of the world's peoples under one Christian religion. He wrote that the unification of humanity, following the conversion of the Chinese and the Muslims, would precipitate the Last Judgement and a return to that ultimate reunification with God (Beard 2007). Law and violence are thus bound together to create a form of global justice based on a particular Christian ethos.

The Christian ethos that had been formed and reformed in Europe could only ever have been imposed on the territories of the New World by a papal claim to commonality through violent means. Any such ethos that instrumentalizes 'violence to maintain the appearance of its collectivity' raises serious questions of morality that have not been properly addressed even today (Butler 2005: 4). That is not to say that the ethos of a particular society is morally right simply because it is not universal. Particularities are also prone to ethical and moral debates. The focus here, however, is on the ethos and technologies of international law's universalism. The universality of international law today can be characterized not by its incapacity to accept certain norms, commonly described as 'non-western', but rather by the failure of international law to recognize these differences as law. This may be an inevitability of an international law. Just as law can be understood as sanctioned violence, difference could be understood as an unsanctioned reality. Law can thus be used to delegitimize difference. For if the law were to recognize difference, that recognition would entail a delegitimation of the violence effected in the claim to commonality. Colonial peoples can only be recognized in and through the rendering of commonality: first as Christian souls; and ultimately as populations destined to self-determination through the Westphalian state system.

Moreover, by binding all of humanity to the same promise, which was subject to a particular Christian system of natural justice, the New World was also obliged to recognize the debts it incurred to the Old World in that extension of justice. In contrast, the Old World was mythically located in a previously unredeemed time possessed by God alone. The New World became a place where the Old World already was but also what it had cast out; it was that part of itself that was denied. In mythical terms, the division of worlds told a story about subjects transformed by divine intervention. In the case of the transformation of the New World, the violence of fate dealt out to the societies of American peoples cast them into the body of a Christian (political) subject held responsible for that violence. The discovery was not experienced first as an infraction against the laws of discovery, occupation or conquest. Rather, the encounter with the New World, based as it was on violent conversion and possession, became the 'precipitating condition of an anger' (Butler 2006: 208). Neither that angry response nor indeed the injury that caused it is circumscribed in advance by law (Butler 2006: 208). This anger, to keep with Butler's analogy, worked performatively 'to mark and transform' the New World as a fallen subject. The New World became a political subject as much as a legal object that was 'accountable, punishable, and punished' through law but not of law (Butler 2006: 208). Since post-colonial times, the society of underdeveloped states has assumed that responsibility even though its peoples have achieved the status of legal subjectivity through statehood (Butler 2006: 208; Beard 2007).

The violence of Christian imperialism during the Roman Empire continued into the Westphalian Peace. In time, the bifurcated structure of two worlds was interpreted variously as the division between the civilized and the barbaric; and ultimately as the developed and the underdeveloped. Also over time, the idea of an international society of independent states governed by a law of nations spread from Europe across the world. In that process of decolonization, any society that wanted to participate in the (re)constitution of the law that would govern these new entities was required to take the form of a sovereign state. States depended on international law's universal capture to maintain the system of sovereign equality that began to be applied in Europe and was expanded to apply to all of the world's territories during the post-colonial era. Land taken, societies formed: these are events of fate. But the law is what brings recognition to these territories and turns a population into an accountable, legal subject. Hence the importance of the mythical belief in a universal law to the Westphalian states system (Beard and Noll 2009).

As Butler has argued, 'the problem is not with universality as such but with an operation of universality that fails to be responsive to cultural particularity and fails to undergo a reformulation of itself in response to the social and cultural conditions it includes within its scope of applicability' (Butler 2005: 6). International law remains a preservation of state power structures because it upholds the state system as a given. For many international lawyers, the fact that the state does not hold legitimacy for millions of people living in the world is not a valid reason to rethink the justice of international law. Rather, it is a reason to enforce and preserve the law more and more violently. This is particularly so where law's illegitimacy poses a threat to law's monopoly of violence. In the Westphalian system sovereign power and international law are mutually constitutive. An objective of both forms of power is to use law, and where necessary this includes the use of violence, to ensure that the state structure is maintained and legitimized despite the existence of competing socio-political structures. But as Adorno argues, 'an ethical norm that fails to offer a way to live or that turns out, within existing social conditions, to be impossible to appropriate has to become subject to critical revision' (Butler 2005: 6). Butler argues in turn that:

> [i]t is one thing to say that a subject must be able to appropriate norms, but another to say that there must be norms that prepare a place within

the ontological field for a subject. In the first instance, norms are there, at an exterior distance, and the task is to find a way of appropriating them, taking them on, establishing a living relation to them. The epistemological frame is presupposed in this encounter, one in which a subject encounters moral norms and must find his way with them. But did Adorno consider that norms also decide in advance who will and who will not become a subject? Did he consider the operation of norms in the very constitution of the subject, in the stylization of its ontology and in the establishing of a legitimate site within the realm of social ontology?

(Butler 2005: 5)

If we apply these thoughts to international law, we can say that post-colonial struggles are concerned primarily with the appropriation of existing norms. These norms establish and preserve the Westphalian system of state relations. But as Butler suggests, assuming the state as norm fails to challenge the fact that these norms determine who will and who will not have a voice on the international stage. They also determine who does and who does not belong to a particular territory; or who becomes part of a minority as opposed to a majority. These norms regulate the flow of people, goods, services and capital in particular ways conducive to certain forms of power and exploitative of others. This is not to say that international law and its universal presumptions are responsible for all of the suffering of people in the world. As Benjamin argues, suffering and death are conditions of being human. An ethical dilemma arises, however, when people are bound to the law in structural terms because they are sinful, of a fallen race or an underdeveloped world. As Butler suggests:

[c]oercive law seeks to transform all suffering into fault, all misfortune into guilt. By extending accountability beyond its appropriate domain, however, positive law vanquishes life and its necessary transience, both its suffering and its happiness. It turns subjects into wailing stones. If the positive law establishes a subject accountable for what she suffers, then the positive law produces a subject steeped in guilt, one who is compelled to take responsibility for misfortunes that are not of her own doing, or one who thinks that, by virtue of her will alone, she could put an end to suffering altogether.

(Butler 2006: 216)

Power is behind the establishment of the Westphalian system of sovereign states. Power is also behind the preservation of that system. Today, power is still very much structured along the same lines of division evident during the eras of empire. Post-colonial states may have achieved formal independence but their subjectivity is still conditioned on their compliance to particular views of what a state must be and how it is to be governed. Indeed, all states are subjected to these requirements of legal recognition. Any population that attempts to challenge the Westphalian system, including contemporary ways of understanding state governance, must do so violently. Such a revolt would be dealt with violently and probably, as I have tried to argue, lawfully.

If we are to understand these effects of power, we must concern ourselves with the history of international law and its anachronistic structure of universalism. We must look critically at the material effects that structure continues to have on the lives of people and their environment. In the event of the discovery of the Americas by Columbus, Christianity's claim to universality was a degenerate anachronism. The diverse ethical conditions of peoples of a world not even entirely known by Europe were not commonly shared. The so-called fathers of international law, such as Grotius and Vitoria, drew on Christian universalism to establish the claims of a universal law. In doing so, they were always already writing of the idealization or indeed the globalization of a common universal ethos made impossible by difference. Even today, religious, cultural, economic, military and political forces (to name a few) prevent international law from achieving a 'common sense' of universalism (Umozurike 1979; Fitzpatrick 2001; Pahuja 2005; Beard 2007). It is no wonder that the forces used to maintain a universal state system have become so immense.

The universalism of international law is as mythical an allusion as the Christian presumption of universal dominion over all of humankind. Certainly, it is universally applied to all of its subjects, but that raises the questions: Who are its subjects? Who is able to speak in this domain? It is one thing to speak of the constitution of the human subject by law. But what are the ethical implications of the constitution of a subject that is legal but not human (Arvidsson, 2009)? How do we locate an ethical position in the multiple souls of conscience of a lifeless but forceful subject like a state or a world? In the Westphalian 'epistemological frame' it is difficult, if not impossible, to consider how the political subject might engage in a negotiation of moral norms (Butler 2005: 9).

International law is applied so that states may take on a living relation to each other as legal subjects. My point is that it does so through a mythical claim to a common ethos that was always already an anachronistic ethos. According to Butler, Adorno warns us of any collective ethos that maintains a unity that 'attempts to suppress the difficulty and discontinuity existing within any contemporary ethos' (Butler 2005: 4). Butler explains that when the unity of an ethos is no longer shared, 'it can impose its claim to commonality only through violent means' (Butler 2005: 4). Butler argues, '[i]n this sense, the collective ethos instrumentalizes violence to maintain the appearance of its collectivity. Moreover, this ethos becomes violence only once it has become an anachronism' (Butler 2005: 4–5). International law and violence are bound together.

Benjamin has argued that the only form of violence that is not bound to law is that of divine violence. This is not a form of violence open to human rationality or will. International laws operate as a form of sanctioned violence to maintain the Westphalian system of sovereign states with an established order of rights and responsibilities. States in turn are transformed into 'forms of legal and moral accountability that make sure individuals remain forcibly obligated to act according to the law, indeed, to gain their civic definition by virtue of their relation to the law' (Butler 2006: 204). This is not to say that millions of people are not living virtually oblivious to state power or in protest against state power, rebelling against state power or migrating as if state boundaries did not exist. From the perspective of these individuals and peoples, there is no common ethos that they can work with and encounter as constitutive parts.

Conclusion

In responding to the responsibility for one's own fate, the legal subject, who is also a moral subject, a human subject, struggles with a solitary ethical demand (see Arvidsson 2009). In struggling against the myth of a universal ethos of international law, the moral subject must choose whether to obey or struggle against the coercions of the law (Butler 2006: 218). If we look to international law for justice we may find only violence. The question is what kind of violence will we find? If we are looking for divine violence, we may not find it in explicit claims of post-colonial struggle; at least not where those struggles are concerned with the reconstitution of the Westphalian state system. Perhaps we need to look to those millions of people crossing state borders 'illegally'. We may find divine violence there in the force of human survival that renders open the body of a state. Perhaps we will find it in the villages of territories not yet touched by the violence of sovereign power struggling to gain recognition as a post-colonial state. It is probable that these instances of pure violence, acts of difference or rebellion will end as soon as the law arrives to coerce its subjects back into the state and its power. But until law's arrival, there are spaces on this earth where the multitude threatens the place of the state subject. Here, beyond historical time, you may find a substitute for the anachronistic nature of international law's universal force. But it may not be the particular alternative you are looking for.

Note

1 In terms of the Americas, see the Treaty of Tordesillas signed by Spain and Portugal on 7 June 1494; as well as the US cases *Johnson v M'Intosh* (1823); *Cherokee Nation v Georgia* (1831); *Worcester v Georgia* (1832).

References

Anghie, A. (2005) *Imperialism, Sovereignty and the Making of International Law*, Cambridge: Cambridge University Press.

Arvidsson, M. (2009) 'Rendering oneself ethical: law, force, body and subjectivity in the office of the administrator in contemporary international law', Ph.D. thesis in progress, on file with author.

Beard, J. (2007) *The Political Economy of Desire: International Law, Development and the Nation State*, New York: Routledge-Cavendish.

Beard, J. and Noll, G. (2009) 'Parrhesia and credibility: the sovereign of refugee status determination', *Social and Legal Studies*, 18(4): 455–77.

Benjamin, W. (1986) 'Critique of violence', in P. Demetz (ed.), *Reflections: Essays, Aphorisms, Autobiographical Writings*, New York: Schocken Books.

Butler, J. (2005) *Giving an Account of Oneself*, New York: Fordham University Press.

——(2006) 'Critique, coercion, and sacred life in Benjamin's "Critique of violence"', in H. de Vries and L.E. Sullivan (eds), *Political Theologies: Public Religions in a Post-Secular World*, New York: Fordham University Press.

Fitzpatrick, P. (2001) *Modernism and the Grounds of Law*, Cambridge: Cambridge University Press.

GA Res 1514 (1960) General Assembly Resolution 1514 (XV) 14 December 1960.

Orford, A. (2004) 'The destiny of international law', *Leiden Journal of International Law*, 17: 441–76.

Pahuja, S. (2005) 'The postcoloniality of international law', *Harvard Journal of International Law*, 46: 459–69.

Umozurike, U.O. (1979) *International Law and Colonialism in Africa*, Enuga, Nigeria: Nwamife Publishers.

Chapter 2

Absolute contingency and the prescriptive force of international law, Chiapas–Valladolid, ca. 1550

Oscar Guardiola-Rivera

Law and event

As it is commonly understood, the discipline of international law and international relations (IL/IR) deals with the order of foundations, power and generations. This means to say that its jobs are often associated with the marking out of territory, with war (not simply as the end of peace but also as the life-spending power at the source of culture) and with the stability and persistence of given communities. Such is the *doxa*, the common opinion in the discipline.

The aim of the present chapter is to question the predominant opinion just outlined. In what follows I will be putting forward a thesis about that dominant position and call for a switch of standpoint. Common opinion in IL/IR assumes the centrality of group survival and the necessity of the realization of the inherent potential of the group in a 'perfect community' or a state-form that must persist at all costs. The possibility of bracketing war in international law emerged as a corollary of this assumption. 'Total war', which was related to credal disputes and the problem of just cause, gradually became a matter of 'state war'. The crucial element in this transformation was the emergence of the state as a spatially defined unit recognizable as a public person by other similar units.

It will be argued that the assumption and its corollary are a persistent feature in international law since at least the 1550s debates at Burgos and Valladolid. The units referred to above were first described by Francisco de Vitoria in the context of such debates. He named them 'perfect communities' for the first time. He defined the 'perfection' or realized potential of these communities and others during the course of such debates, in contrast with the 'lesser perfection' of the communities found in the Americas. Only 'perfect' communities would recognize one another as public persons of the same character and similar rights, and thus, the conduct of war could be formalized only between them. European soil would become the *theatrum belli* in which politically and militarily organized 'perfect communities' could test one another under the watchful eye of other sovereigns.

These debates took place at a crucial moment in the history of mankind. After the European 'discovery' of the Americas, the ruler of the Holy Roman Empire and king of Spain, Charles V, convened a meeting of experts or *junta* to establish the legal title of the occupation and appropriation of the Americas by European powers. At stake was a realm of relative reason, distinguishing between 'legal partners in war' and an outer space exempted from such co-relative recognition. In spite of profound changes in the discipline and its practice, particularly the evacuation of metaphysical concerns in favour of a more pragmatic approach, the division between 'perfect' and 'perfectible' communities would withstand the test of time. The justice of war, as one European internationalist put it, 'no longer [would be] based on conformity with the content of theological, moral or juridical norms, but rather on the institutional and structural equality of political forms' (Schmitt 1950: 143).

This chapter will focus on the Valladolid debates of 1550 in order to isolate that distinction. That will be our 'case study', helping us to focus on the inaugural event of international law. In keeping with such a 'switch of standpoint', the starting point of our argument is twofold: on the one hand, three elements of public discourse (foundations, power and generations) will be explored together, so that we can posit a connection between them in relation to the theme of 'foundational sacrifice'. The latter term refers, in secular contexts, to the calculus of costs and benefits posited as necessary for group survival. In turn, group survival is seen in the context of the predominant *doxa* as necessarily desirable and violence appears paradoxical: violent conflict, often seen as a foreign element threatening group survival, is necessarily undesirable and must be contained by means of ... violence. On the other hand, the assumption that group survival is necessarily desirable means that any concern with the long term and the long distance (the beyond of the city's marked frontiers) is limited by the experiential notion that the future must resemble the present and the past. And if we cannot ultimately justify this knowledge from experience, then we must simply pose it under another form that makes it amenable to treatment.

I contend that this is precisely what distinguishes IL/IR as an 'expert' discourse: the question no longer consists in proving the resemblance of the future and the present or the past, so that the *doxa* according to which group survival is necessarily desirable and conflict necessarily undesirable becomes warranted beyond doubt. Rather, the dominant position in international law merely tries to describe the existing practice or set of practices (mainly reasoning and argumentation, whose job is associated with group survival and conflict management) so as to extract its implicit rules.

Put otherwise, the history of the professionalization of IL/IR runs parallel to the progressive abandonment of the search for a metaphysical foundation of the assumption concerning group survival and its replacement with a question that evacuates all ontological problems, applying itself instead to the description of the effective practices of the community of experts, mainly state politicians and international lawyers.

What remains profoundly problematic in this movement from metaphysics to pragmatic expertise is the realization of a deep-seated tendency to disavow the event. In its more or less metaphysical (professional) orientation, the discipline of international law applies itself to guarantee the survival of the group as a 'perfect community' (more on this later). Implicit in this assumption is a definition of the legal and the political as concerned with constancy and preservation in the face of the future and the stranger.

In the more refined and less metaphysical orientations, the suggestion is that one cannot deduce in univocal fashion all future or distant occurrences permitted by the law, and their succession. But it is posited that at the very least, one can in principle index these occurrences in their totality, even if their apparent infinity prohibits their definitive foreclosure. Notice, however, that in both cases (the metaphysical and the allegedly post-metaphysical or 'expert') this entails the disavowal of 'violent', unpredictable, incalculable or non-totalizable interruption: the event.

The latter refers to the force of historically unprecedented transformation, the improbable contingency, or the hopeful interruption of the world as it appears to us in the present, disavowed in the name of expertise and experience. Likewise, this world-weary experience and expertise posits that everything will have to continue more or less as it is now (for it is 'complete', self-sufficient, it works now and so it must also work at all times), or at the very least, that any potential occurrence could be described in all or most of its outlines as an anticipated possibility and, if necessarily undesirable, prevented. It is as a result of this position that preservation, prevention and containment have become the common sense of IL/IR.

My proposal in this chapter is to contest the evacuation of all ontological problems from IL/IR in the name of experience and expertise, precisely because this evacuation allows no room for the possibility of a true event. Crucially, the question of the event in law can be formulated in terms of the claim that the long term (the future) and the long distance (the stranger) might not resemble the past or the familiar (the given) in any way. If in the *doxa* in IL/IR what matters is foundational sovereignty, power and generations, then the proposal here is to go beyond that common sense and open up research in IL/IR to an exploration of the significance of the future and the stranger as they impact upon and decisively transform (or call for the transformation of) the given.

The objective of the chapter is also twofold: on the one hand, to point out that the common-sense experience and expertise of IL/IR knows nothing about the event, for 'an event that could be described and predicted in all of its outlines would not be an event' (Cornell 2008: 145). On the other hand, this chapter seeks to rescue the disavowed redemptive and disruptive dimension from within the history of IL/IR. In the latter sense, the chapter can be seen as an exercise of internal constructive critique: the retrieval of a past memory for the purposes of an imaginatively different future. Put otherwise, the objective is to 'fan the spark of hope' even as we look and force ourselves to see the suffering inscribed in the images of the present situation (from El Alto in Bolivia to Abu Ghraib in Iraq), as Walter Benjamin might have put it (Benjamin 1968: 255). The chapter will conclude that the common-sense experience and expertise of IL/IR is, to put it once again in Benjamin's terms, mythical.

Legacy and significance of the Valladolid debates

In historical terms, the problem of the event in international law is but a retrieval and refinement of the question that pitted the translator of Aristotle and Spanish crown jurist Juan Ginés de Sepúlveda against the dissident Bishop of Chiapas, Bartolomé de Las Casas during the debates at Burgos and Valladolid, but also occupied 'the opaque and uncertain founder of what was a more resolute international law', Francisco de Vitoria, in the sixteenth century (Fitzpatrick 2009: 324). The question emerged at the inaugural point of IL/IR, during and after the debates concerning the self-governing capacities of Amerindians, which took place between the 1530s and 1600s.

For Sepúlveda (1494–1573), faced with the challenge of strangers one's loyalty must be with the 'we', and thus, the principle of order and constancy of the community that derives from natural law is better served by the containment and re-channelling of violence against 'them', the latter being dispossessed of reason and therefore less than human. He argued thus in *Apologia pro libro de iustis belli* (Sepúlveda 1941), itself a summary of the best-known *Democrates secundus* (Sepúlveda 1951). In contrast, both Las Casas (1474–1566) and Vitoria (1486–1546) dismantled the Aristotle-inspired theories about the natural slavery of the Amerindians and their lack of dominion, thereby asserting that they were possessed of reason and discounting sovereign use of force against 'them' as justified. Noticeably, they all drew on ancient sources, on Aquinas, and the *ius gentium* (the law of nations). And although Las Casas and Vitoria found reason in the strangers, this did not prevent them from providing a justification for their colonial subordination, derived from the *ius gentium*.

However, later in life, by the time Las Casas collaborated in the 1560 memorandum addressed to King Phillip II of Spain (co-authored with his colleague in Perú, Domingo de Santo Tomás) (Las Casas 1958) and the so-called *Twelve Doubts*, Las Casas' initial position had changed into a more radical rejection of the claims concerning sovereign intervention and colonial subjection. Not only did he thoroughly condemn 'any foreign sovereign's intervention' as 'a violation of natural law' (Las Casas 1958: 489) and demanded the restitution of indigenous territories; he pointedly argued that this remedial action was required because of the foreseen decrease in the

Andean population. Crucially, this anticipatory statement depended on the recognition of the immense complexity of the effects caused on actual and future populations by such political technologies of government and regulation as the *encomienda* (system of colonial trusteeship) and the *corregimiento* (administrative unit or subdivision), which were characteristic of the imperial enterprise. That is to say, on the non-totalizable nature of the reality of these consequences. And where the Dominicans in South America spoke of a mere decrease in the Andean population, earlier local critics like the Peruvian Guamán Poma de Ayala anticipated their extinction (Adorno 1978: 128).

It is crucial to understand the contrast: as we will see later, Vitoria and Sepúlveda relied upon the notion of perfect and imperfect possibilities or potentialities in order to grasp the manifestation of law in nature through time and space, and derived from it an idea of constancy embodied in the 'perfect community' as the true source of international law. The latter would thus be based on a principle of reciprocity, for a perfect community, a 'surpassing and singular nation can effect the impossibility of a complete, quasi-imperial control of the domain of its relations to others' (Fitzpatrick 2009: 326). This is expressed in terms of a duty (to civilize), which is the counterpart of another's right (to be civilized, or to develop), which in turn is seen as the like of one's own right. It is assumed that this likeness extends through time as well as space. Therefore, it could be said on this basis that constancy in the long term and long distance is the norm and that if the succession of cases cannot be deduced univocally at least one can in principle index these cases in their totality. One could then argue that every postulation of a law operates in this way, as an index of the totality of cases. And by the same token, that unprecedented interruption or extinction is unlikely or improbable.

Contrariwise, Las Casas, and much more decisively Ayala, introduced in their arguments a principle of the non-reciprocity of duties to the future. Following Las Casas, Ayala speaks of the extinct and the non-existent who make no demands and therefore cannot suffer violation of their rights (Ayala 1968). More radically, what is at stake in the argument is the realization that in principle they (the Andean Amerindian population) have no right to exist at all before they in fact exist. And yet, the ethic and politics that these earlier critics sought concerned precisely these non-existent beings; thus, the principle of responsibility implicit in that ethic and politics had to be independent of any idea of right and therefore also of reciprocity. Put otherwise, the question 'what have they [the future Amerindians, the strangers] ever done for me?' or 'Do they respect my rights?' cannot be validly posited. Thus, the framework of 'justice' and/or 'just war' (which is the one used by Sepúlveda and Vitoria), based upon notions of likeness and constancy (i.e. justice and war among perfect states) and ultimately, on the perfection or imperfection of potentialities to the exclusion of the true event, fails for the purposes of the argument. Rather, it becomes central to find instances of elementary nonreciprocal responsibility and duty.

Nature, some might say, provides one such instance in the case of children and the sex relationship bound up with such a demanding original sphere of action (Jonas 1984: 39). However, although fundamental, this archetype may prove insufficient for the purposes of our (Ayala's) argument. It has been noticed that the duty to care for children can be based upon the responsibility of the existing cause for its effect (Jonas 1984: 39). Therefore, like the language of justice or rights, this duty is also present oriented. And given the force of the childlike metaphor in earlier and later justifications of colonial subordination (backwardness, economic underdevelopment, cultural insufficiency, and so on) and in understandings of nation, sovereignty and war (as fatherhood), one can speculate that someone at the receiving end of such justifications, like Ayala, would prefer not to develop the argument for the non-reciprocity of duties to the future and the nonexistent upon such basis. Imaginatively, Ayala refused to frame his argumentation within the standpoint of 'just war' and patriarchal protection; instead, he appealed to the story of an original 'donation' of the Tawantisuyu (the Americas) to the European sovereign by the ambassador of the Inca Huascar in a fictitious meeting at Tumbes in 1532 (Ayala 1968: 375–6).

Pointedly, a donation generates for the European king first, a duty towards a future humankind even if no descendants of his are among them, and second, a duty to ensure their quality of life. This duty can be derived neither from the fact of fatherhood (the duty of the begetter towards the life already begotten) nor from the pragmatically sufficient reasoning that we can assume continued existence as such and directly turn to the more concrete subject of duties towards its future quality. Such duties have, of course, the advantage of being derivable from more familiar principles of morality (solidarity, sympathy, equitableness, compassion) and their observance helps also secure the mere existence that is presupposed; in fact, this is the predominant approach in contemporary practice, immediately recognizable under such names as humanitarianism, rights-based approaches, philanthropy and aid. This predominant approach operates through a fiction of contemporaneity or sympathetic relationality between the present and the future or the distant stranger, and our prospective respect of their right, anticipated as existing, on the other side. However, it would be insufficient for our (Ayala's) argument: first, because setting aside for a moment its patronizing nature, this duty toward the quality of 'their' life remains subject to the condition that there be future or distant life, and this condition – and the duty it entails – answers to no right whatsoever. Second, this approach is insufficient because what is at stake is not so much 'their' existing *right* to happiness or whatever, but rather, that they be capable of complying with their *duty* to be fully human (Jonas 1984: 42).

Put simply, what Ayala recognizes is that a gift is taxing. After the dona-tion, Europeans are not simply obliged to behave as good fathers or more civilized 'equals', or be sympathetic to the foreigners whose land and wealth they profited from. Beyond that, they have to watch over the duty of others (non-Europeans, Amerindians in this case) to be truly human, and thus over their capacity for this duty and even the capacity 'to even attribute it to themselves at all', which is, to borrow Jonas's more contemporary language, what 'we' (Europeans in this case) could possibly rob them of 'with the alchemy of our "utopian" technology' (Jonas 1984: 42). This entails the recognition of virtual, rather than potential, equality and capacity, but also of the virtual freedom that accompanies being possessed of the capacity to be truly human.

'Virtuality' stands here for the force of a becoming that transforms the given set of possibilities, in this case the prescription to ensure a future for Amerindians in the face of extinction. It explains why Ayala, radicalizing the demands made by his Dominican fellow travellers, pressed for the immediate restitution of lands to the Amerindians, rather than some calcu-lated compensation vis-à-vis future potential damages. Ultimately, Ayala's 'donation argument' confronted nascent IL/IR with the challenge of extinc-tion, and thus with the incalculable and non-totalizable nature of reality. Like extinction, a true gift is precisely what is non-totalizable: it is unpre-cedented, incalculable and it cannot be paid back. It gives place to an infinite and non-reciprocal demand: to ensure that there be future life, and with it future subjects of right.

Similarly, this duty answers to no right or rights whatsoever and thus finds no basis on any assumption of likeness or constancy in nature in the long term and the long distance; rather, this duty is the source of such rights. In our terms, Ayala confronted nascent IL/IR – based upon the assumption of constancy in nature and the completability of the community – with the true event, found it wanting, and proposed instead a new foundation on the non-reciprocal duty to posterity. Speaking in ontological terms, the latter entails the contingency of laws and observable constants and the incomplet-ability or non-totalizable nature of reality. This translates into a challenge to most postulations of legality, whether deterministic or aleatory, that identify reality with a universe of possible cases indexable (and amenable to survey) in principle, such as the reigning *doxa* in IL/IR.

Let us explain further. To project his resolution on the newly discovered world, Vitoria adapted two types of *ius gentium* found in Roman law. One was the law common to all civilized peoples, according to which wars of intervention were just because they 'would save many innocents, who [some Amerindians] immolate each year, from great injustices', as Ginés de Sepúlveda put it, citing Vitoria (Hanke 1974: 89; Sepúlveda 1941: 155). The other was the *ius inter gentes*, 'the law governing relations between peoples and latterly international law' (Fitzpatrick 2009: 324–5). In this way Vitoria posited that while extending to all people, *ius gentium* is fully realized only by some. The latter are self-sufficient or 'perfect communities' (Vitoria 1991: 310), with complete capacity for self-government and duty to intervene (to care), within which different sources of power (monarchical and popular) operate through the mediation of divine law and its derivative, natural law. Vitoria argued that 'access or attachment to that divine law was not necessary for either the integrity or efficacy of natural law, or indeed for the ability to know it' (Fitzpatrick 2009: 326; citing Vitoria 1991: 164) for it can be known by man's reason being applied to nature. A determinable natural law can thus exist without revelation, even if the godhead did not exist, for it must be 'externally manifest' (Vitoria 1991: 155) and thus it could be rendered as an earthly *ius gentium* (Fitzpatrick 2009: 326).

Vitoria's argument about natural law enabled, among other things, the subjection of religious power to the political, and thus the positing of the singular nation (Vitoria's 'perfect community') by later writers such as Grotius, Leibniz and Vattel as the true source of the *ius gentium*. Crucially, Vitoria's account of natural law rests upon the idea that there is constancy in nature. Nothing, not even God himself, could 'destroy or change in general the natural propensities of things' (Vitoria 1960: 1099). This ontological axiom of order and constancy underwrites the argument of experience according to which we shall know the unfamiliar through the familiar, and thus to disavow the event.

Importantly, such an 'epistemology' played and arguably continues to play a definitive role in the rise and rise of empire and coloniality, even after the theologians departed the scene (Singh Mehta 1999: 190). In his study on nineteenth-century British political thought, Uday Singh Mehta wonders how liberals committed to the idea of national self-determination 'see in an ancient civilization like India none of the teguments of a nation or of a people?' (Singh Mehta 1999: 191). The answer is that when liberal theorists and practitioners gaze at an unfamiliar world, that of the stranger and the future, they see those forms as provisional, as mere unrealized possibilities. In our terms, they see their equality and freedom as potential, subject to chance, rather than virtual, subject to an interrupting event. Put otherwise, in justifying 'light' empire, liberal theorists disavowed liberation and revolution. Furthermore, in the face of such pure potentialities, they saw it as right, indeed as obligatory, to seek to complete that which was incomplete, static, backward, and to hitch it to a more meaningful teleology. That teleology, soon enough couched in quasi-biological and mathematical language, as Frantz Fanon rightly observed, goes by the name of 'civilisation', progress or, more recently, 'development', economic or human (Gordon, 2007: 5–12). Its study is no longer a matter for onto-theology, but rather for that other theology and natural jurisprudence that, oblivious to its own origins, calls itself economics and counts itself among the social sciences.

The principal means of doing so were and continue to be political and legal. As Singh Mehta notices, it is in part 'from the perspective of a liberal political vision that the judgment of provisionality itself stemmed'

(Singh Meta 1999: 190). However, as we now know, that judgement was made possible by the obverse judgement of 'completeness' that emerged in Vitoria's argument concerning the realization of *ius gentium* in the context of the Valladolid debates concerning the self-governing capacities of Amerindians. Both judgements, that 'we' are complete while 'they' are provisional, provide the conceptual and normative core of the mercantilist and liberal justifications of coloniality and empire. In fact, as Singh Mehta observes (1999: 192–94), the sedimentation of that core made unnecessary the continued use and debate of arguments concerning the right of conquest or the imminence of external threat.

This is the story of the secularization and the professionalization of IL/IR. The latter was presupposed and subsumed by the former. In this way, too, the ontological question at the heart of debates regarding the right of conquest gradually disappeared. Ontology gave way to a normative description (socio-legal, econo-legal) of the most effective political and legal means to intervene in 'their' lives or shape the future in accordance with 'our' forecasts: a description permitted by the judgement of colonial nations' completeness and the provisionality of the colonized. In turn, this 'expert' practice depended on the idea that every postulation of legality identified the world with a universe of possible cases indexable in principle, pre-existing their ultimate discovery, and thereby 'constituting the potentialities of that universe' (Meillassoux 2007: 70).

According to professionalized IL/IR, any possible hazard (governing change) is construed as a 'risk', not a challenge, presupposing the essential fixity of such change, since 'chance' or 'risk' or 'probability' can only mean the possibility of the advent without reason of one of the cases permitted by the initial (indexed, totalized) initial universe. What remains excluded is precisely what Ayala's 'donation argument' calls for: the freedom of rebellion against that world, that universe, to bring forth cases that do not belong to the set thus defined (for instance, the fully capable, truly human Indian or Amerindian). Contemporary thinkers call this belief in the aleatory (cost–benefit, risk-like) legality of the world a 'metaphysics of chance', 'necessity' or 'occurring time' (Meillassoux 2007: 70–71; Guardiola-Rivera 2009; Dupuy 2004). This is so insofar as chance 'supposes the postulation of a law which would prescribe the fixed set of events within which time finds itself free to oscillate without any determined order' and incorporates the belief in the factual necessity of determinate probabilistic laws that can only be accounted for via the assumption of time/space as a fixed background necessity (Meillassoux 2007: 70. See also Unger and Smolin 2005). Following these thinkers, it can be argued that the metaphysical legacy of the Valladolid debates survived the departure of the theologians, and it is present even in the more refined, expert accounts of IL/IR.

Decisively, the judgement that emerged out of those debates, the pair complete–provisional, corresponds to a view of the world and reality as totalizable, an 'all' that can be surveyed. This 'all' possesses constant laws that can be extracted, plural bifurcations that are manifest in nature and amenable to being arranged in a hierarchy or according to their merits or more-or-less realized capacities, processes that can thus be sorted out into realized and not-yet realized possibilities and thereby rendered subject to chance and probability. This is precisely the language of experiential knowledge, of calculability, of cost–benefit analysis, of risk-scenario planning, of 'realism' and pragmatism. From our historical and conceptual perspective, the picture and the experience of this 'all' can be seen as a late repetition of the language, metaphysics and epistemology of the *machina mundi* (worldly machine) that dominated thought, cosmography and geopolitics already in the sixteenth century (Wey Gómez 2008: 59, 229). More importantly, what this picture and experiential language exclude is the 'non-all', the notion that reality is non-totalizable and thus that the improbable can occur. Once again, in our terms, it disavows the event: the really unfamiliar and the objectively uncertain.

Conclusion: IL/IR is mythical

The conclusion of this chapter is that the common-sense experience and expertise of IL/IR is mythical. This can be understood in two senses: first, in the sense that its practical postulation of legality (as a universe of possible cases indexable in principle) ultimately depends on the incorporation of a belief in the necessity of constants. That is, its legality depends upon observable aleatory or determinate probabilistic laws, background-dependent action and fixed background legality. For all its allegations concerning 'realism', 'pragmatism' and 'post-metaphysics', even the most refined or expert orientations of IL/IR turn out to be metaphysical. Its post-metaphysical self-perception is therefore a myth. To unlock the secrets of the 'common language' that nowadays unites humanitarians, the military and the politicians (Kennedy 2004: 327–28), one has to think metaphysics: think Leibniz, think Vitoria. Alas, these are the opaque, uncertain, half-forgotten founders of the discipline.

Second, this chapter contends that IL/IR is mythical in a sense that can be seen, at least partially, in the notion repeated over and over again throughout the 1990s and hammered with renewed force after 9/11, according to which the dream of a redeemed humanity (one that realizes the truth of its freedom in democratic control over the means of guaranteeing a future for humankind) had itself died (Jonas 1984: 38–46; Cornell 2008: 137). As Drucilla Cornell points out, there is an obvious irony here in what it means to condemn a dream, a visionary image of the future, to death. 'After all', she writes, 'isn't a dream exactly what cannot be killed off because it does not have actual existence?' (Cornell 2008: 137–38). A dream is, after all, a detotalization of the possible; a 'donation', as Ayala might have put it.

Cornell observes that the rhetoric of the 'death of a dream' in the name of realism and pragmatism has an implicit agenda to marginalize those who still identify themselves as socialists, decolonizers and idealists. No less important, her remark about the ontological status of dream-images matters most for the purposes of examining the claims to knowledge made by IL/IR as an 'expert' discourse and practice. Particularly after 9/11, and in the wake of the 'war on terror' in the global North and South, dreamers, idealists, humanitarian activists and all who dare to make dissident speech-acts in human rights and IL/IR are condemned by experts in the profession as hopelessly out of contact with reality.

According to the experts in the profession, such people are 'do-gooder' relics of the past, irresponsible romantics who insist on judging power from without and 'pathetically try to preserve their ethical vision' (Kennedy 2004: 327–28). They are, according to the prevailing IL/IR view, radicals who believe in abstract generalizations, do not accept responsibility for the long-term consequences of their actions and are happy to criticize governments from the margins. Unlike governments and policy makers, they do not carry out cost–benefit analyses of their activities. Furthermore, their commitment to broad principles of improving humanity to be carried out through constitutional reform, legal measures and institution building blinds them to the inadequacy of the tools and the adverse effects of their activities. In sum, because they see themselves as outsiders, avert their eyes from power generally and their own power specifically, and are, in general, out of touch with reality, these dissidents are actual obstacles in the becoming global of the common language that nowadays unites humanitarian experts with the military and the politicians (Kennedy 2004: 327–29; for critique, see Douzinas 2008: 7; 223–25).

The proper question to ask these experts is: what do you mean when you speak of reality in this manner? What they mean by 'reality' is the picture of the present and future world put together by a certain form of mathematics and calculability associated with cost–benefit analysis, risk forecast and probabilistic reasoning. Setting aside for the moment the problems of passing an ideological agenda as 'social science' and the quasi-sacrificial representation of dissidents as 'obstacles' in the path of the discipline's progress, one must wonder about the status of the image of the world put together by 'expert' discourse vis-à-vis the dream-image put forward by dissidents and rebels, the inheritors of Las Casas and Ayala. To use once again terms that are familiar already to the reader of these pages, it turns out that the former is, ontologically speaking, an image of the totalized possible, while the latter is an image of the improbable.

Crucially, the possible is not real since it will always be the case that what is postulated as possible may or may not happen, and therefore can never be verified or falsified outside of the heads of those who exchange the belief in the potential occurrence of whatever is announced (often a catastrophic occurrence that warrants a licence for catastrophic intervention). Notice that the obverse of the belief in the possible is not the impossible, but rather the correlative belief in a recurring claim that this is a reality, and that if 'this' works now it shall do so at all times. The belief in the possible is thereby characterized not by faith, but rather by fate; fate in the sense of an eternal recurrence. It is thus a myth, in Benjamin's parlance (Benjamin 1978: 308). To put it in more familiar terms, experts in the field of IL/IR, now married to the empiricist–pragmatist outlook, forsake any discussion of the necessity of laws (as opposed to so-called logical necessity); it is simply assumed that either the future must resemble the past, or else that to question such a necessity would lead us to (epistemological) failure and disorder in practice. Conversely, this assumption serves to reinforce the opinion that the aim of law (as a discipline) is to maintain order and avert or permanently defer disorder (i.e. that group survival is necessarily desirable and conflict always undesirable).

On the contrary, we shall say, after Ayala and others, that what does not have actual existence is virtual but nevertheless real. Even in the most brutal reality we see an opening 'that can illuminate another way of being in the world that allows us at least to have a glimpse of what a redeemed world might look like and, perhaps more importantly, what is our responsibility for those who have lived and died for it', but also, it should be added, for those who do not exist yet (Cornell 2008: 138; see also Jonas 1984: 39 and Benjamin 1978: 308). In this respect, the 'expert' images of the present and future world effectively wipe out the chances for any meaningful moral agency. Notice that for the common position the reality of the world is, particularly after 9/11, that 'we' are pitted against 'them' and therefore all we can do to guarantee group survival is to go after them because this is the way the world must be. For all its purported concern with the long term, this view is informed by a present-oriented ethic of the existent based on the principle of reciprocity. Contrariwise, the dissident image that we have retrieved from within the history of IL/IR calls for an ethic of the non-existent based on the principle that our duty is to use the past and the present to ensure a future for all. And since the non-existent make no present demands and therefore cannot suffer a violation of rights (conceived as negative liberties against those others present here and now), it may seem problematic to speak of our responsibility towards the non-existent.

Yet this is precisely the ethic that we need when confronted by the threat of unending war, permanent unemployment and economic catastrophe for 'disposable' peoples as a result of the failure of globalist finance capitalism and planetary climate change. We face, like Ayala in the sixteenth century, the challenge of extinction. This is to say that what is required in IL/IR today is an ethic of the non-existent and the improbable independent of any principle of reciprocity; and therefore, one for which the 'expert' notion of human rights and cost–benefit calculation seems totally insufficient.

It cannot be based on the experiential knowledge of what is possible, which actually paralyzes our capacities for action while condemning us to a vicious circularity trapped inside a time warp ('we' have to catch 'them' before 'they' attack 'us', but then, on what basis can 'we' justify our containment of 'them'?).

Thus, another kind of experience is called for: one prompted not by the knowledge of what is possible, but rather by the idea that because we cannot know what is improbable, we are left with our own responsibility, in whatever context we are, to transcend that context. We cannot fathom what is improbable, virtual or non-existent in the sense that every experience points beyond itself to its limit, both defining what counts as experience and yet marking it as directed towards a different order of experience. This statement counts both for Kennedy's 'common language' of glorified cost–benefit analysis and for the big narratives of socialism and liberation.

Instead of presupposing a law, itself immutable, regulating the future changes of current constants or practices 'that work', we need to reopen the question of the interruption of what now 'works', insofar as its workings threaten the very reality of a future for all. This can be expressed as an insistence on the absolute contingency of all laws. The emphasis on absolute contingency must be understood as an invitation to enquire about the necessity or the absence of necessity of experienced norms and constants. Thus, it should not be taken to mean that experienced norms must change in the future, but rather that it is contingent that they should be recurrent. This suggests a contingency so radical that it would incorporate all conceivable, anticipated and calculable futures of the present laws, including a future in which they do not change at all (Meillassoux 2007: 59).

In turn, such a suggestion opens up the possibility of positing a conception of the event freed from its limits in experience. If in the expert discourse of IL/IR the event is disavowed in the image of a 'scientific' survey of all anticipated futures and a correspondent policy of prevention and containment, in the dissident discourse there is space for the true event, which is governed by no necessity whatsoever. This can be expressed as the prescriptive force of law. Such a situated dynamic seems a better basis for true ethical and political action, carried out *in situ* through a refusal of fate, and thus predicated on those whose present and future situation is often presented as a matter of fate, those who live or will have to live with the poverty left by empire and in the shadow of racism; the non-existent. But it also points to the ethical interest of those who count themselves among the privileged or the oppressors: those who live with all of the privileges of coloniality and empire, and the spoils of racism. The latter also have an ethical interest in finding 'in themselves a source of responsibility that is not self-punishing but unfolds from an aspiration to be worthy of happiness' (Cornell 2008: 146).

References

Adorno, R. (1978) 'Felipe Guaman Poma de Ayala: an Andean view of the Peruvian viceroyalty, 1565–1615', *Journal de la Société des Américanistes*, 6: 121–43.

Ayala, G. P. de (1968) *Nueva Corónica y Buen Gobierno*, Paris: L'Institut D'Ethnologie.

Benjamin, W. (1968) 'Theses on the philosophy of history', in H. Arendt (ed.), *Illuminations*, New York: Shocken Books.

——(1978) 'Fate and character', in P. Demetz (ed.), *Reflections: Essays, Aphorisms, Autobiographical Writings*, New York: Schocken Books.

Cornell, D. (2008) *Moral Images of Freedom*, Lanham and Plymouth: Rowman & Littlefield Publishers.

Douzinas, C. (2008) *Human Rights and Empire*, London: Routledge.

Dupuy, J.-P. (2004) Complexity and uncertainty: a contribution to the work in progress of the 'Foresighting the New Technology Wave' high-level expert group, Brussels: European Commission.

Fitzpatrick, P. (2009) 'Legal theology: law, modernity and the sacred', *Seattle University Law Review*, 32: 321.

Gordon, L. R. (2007) 'Through the hellish zone of non-being', *Human Architecture: Journal of the Sociology of Self-Knowledge*, V, special double issue, summer 2007, 5–12.

Guardiola-Rivera, O. (2009) *Being Against the World*, London: Routledge & Birkbeck Law Press.

Hanke, L. (1974) *All Mankind is One: A Study of the Disputation Between Bartolomé de Las Casas and Juan Ginés de Sepúlveda in 1550 on the Intellectual and Religious Capacity of the American Indian*, Illinois: Northern Illinois University Press.

Jonas, H. (1984) *The Imperative of Responsibility*, Chicago: University of Chicago Press.

Kennedy, D. (2004) *The Dark Side of Virtue*, Princeton: Princeton University Press.

Las Casas, B. de (1958) *Obras Escogidas de Fr. Bartolomé de Las Casas*, ed. J. Pérez de Tudela Bueso, Madrid: Ediciones Atlas.

Meillassoux, Q. (2007) 'Potentiality & virtuality', *Collapse*, 2: 55–82.

Sepúlveda, J. G. De (1941 [1550]) *Tratado sobre las Justas Causas de la Guerra contra los Indios* (ed.) Marcelino Menendez y Pelayo and Manuel Garcia-Pelayo, Mexico DF: Fondo de Cultura Económica.

——(1951 [1545]) *Democrates Secundus*, Madrid: Editorial Angel Losada.

Schmitt, C. (1950) *The Nomos of the Earth in the International Law of the* Ius Publicum Europaeum, trans. G. L. Ulmen, New York: Telos Press.

Singh Mehta, U. (1999) *Liberalism and Empire: A Study in Nineteenth-Century British Liberal Thought*, Chicago, IL: University of Chicago Press.

Unger, R. and Smolin L. (2005) 'Changing laws', audio recording online. Available at: <www.perimeterinstitute.ca/activities/scientific/cws/evolving_laws/agenda.php> (accessed 22 April 2009).

Vitoria, Francisco de (1960) *Obras de Francisco de Vitoria: Reflecciones Teológicas*. Ed. by T. Urdánoz. Biblioteca de Autores Cristianos: Editorial Católica.

——(1991) *Political Writings* in A. Pagden and J. Lawrence (eds), trans. J. Lawrence, Cambridge: Cambridge University Press.

Wey Gómez, N. (2008) *Tropics of Empire*, Massachusetts: MIT Press.

Chapter 3

Latin roots

The force of international law as event

Peter Fitzpatrick[*]

> The greatest events and thoughts – but the greatest thoughts are the greatest events –
> are the last to be comprehended: generations that are their contemporaries do not
> *experience* these sorts of events, – they live right past them.
>
> (Nietzsche 2002: 171 [285])

Introduction

An inexcusably brief adventure into the seeming infinity of philosophical
engagement with 'the event' serves to focus the argument of this chapter, an
argument that the imperative quality of the event as and in modernity provides the force of international law. The chapter also has its own generative
event, an event that makes possible the modern notion of event generally,
and that event is one of the more improbable deaths of God – 'improbable'
because it was effected by a scholastic theologian of the sixteenth century,
Francisco de Vitoria. With Vitoria, that epochal event fuses with his being
at the origin of international law. Manuals of the trade would consign
Vitoria's contribution to international law to the preliminary and the
peripheral, and this in favour of a later contender, most often the ubiquitous
Grotius. Even Vitoria's relegation of the deity has been trumped by the
succès de scandale of Grotius in proclaiming that the discovering of natural
law 'would take place though we should even grant, what without the
greatest Wickedness cannot be granted, that there is no God ... ' (Grotius
2005: 89; cf. Stumpf 2004: 163–64, n. 52). The point of the comparison
with Grotius, however, will be that Vitoria accommodates an essential
quality of international law, a quality aligned with the force of the event,
and a quality suppressed in the reception of Grotius in standard-issue
accounts of the subject.

The allure of Vitoria for present purposes is that he straddles the sharp
divide between a medieval world supposedly under 'the tyranny of Heaven'
(cf. Milton 1949: 236) and a secularized modernity. The same could be said
of Grotius, but Grotius has been received and reduced in a way that provides

a template for a modern international law the force of which derives solely from the sovereign and secular nations out of which it dependently emanates. That derivation meant, in Vattel's stark formulation from the eighteenth century, that the society of nations was to have no overarching commonality, and this to such a complete extent that none of its members 'yield ... rights to the general body', each sovereign state being 'independent of all the others' (Vattel 1916: 9; cf. Cavallar 2002: 306–17). The definitive or primary type of politico-legal formation is thence the sovereign principality or state, ultimately the nation state. Vitoria has proved resistant to relegation in any such terms. What such resistance reveals is a contradiction in that standard scheme, a contradiction that does not dissolve the scheme but, rather, goes to constitute it. And it is in his accommodating the divide between the medieval and the modern that Vitoria preserves this constituent contradiction, and in so doing centres the force of international law not just on the assertion of a sovereign statehood but also on the quality, the communal quality, of the international. Further, it could and will be said that *the* force of international law ultimately inheres in the fusion of these two forceful sources – the force of the singular nation state or of other subjects of international law, and the force of the community of the international. And, so the argument runs, it is in and as the event that we can, as it were, find this intrinsically contradictory yet combinative force of international law.

This is the way in which that modest agenda will now be followed. First, I will instance and abruptly theorize the constituent contradiction just mentioned, the contradiction that is international law and its force. Next, that force is transposed to the quality of the event, and pointedly to what can thence be seen as the event of international law. Then we come to the engagement with Vitoria. This focuses on how his thought initiates and makes both possible and imperative such an 'eventful' idea of international law. Admittedly, and to an extent, this is an anachronistic exercise. The terms and language of international law as such emerged after Vitoria's time, yet this very anachronism serves to reveal what was involved yet denied when the constituent forces of international law were combined and one of those forces, that emanating from the international, effectively denied.

The logic of (inter)national law

To begin at a beginning, how do these sovereign states, quite 'independent of all the others' (Vattel 1916: 9), come to be 'in the first place'? They come to be through being recognized in and by international law. Which immediately plunges us into circularity and a seeming inconsequence with the nation state creating an international law which creates it. To borrow the beginnings of an escape from such circularity, the study of international law offers us 'two principal theories as to the nature, function and effect of recognition': one is the *constitutive* theory' in which 'recognition alone' creates the nation state; and the other, and the more widely accepted, is 'the *declaratory* or *evidentiary* theory' in which the nation state 'exists as such prior to and independently of recognition', recognition then being 'merely a formal acknowledgement of an established situation or fact' (Shearer 1994: 120 – his emphasis). The disparity between the theories is instantly sharpened on finding that the lineaments of the 'situation or fact' are themselves provided by international law in such as article 1 of the Montevideo Convention of 1933 where it is said that 'a person of international law' should have '(a) a permanent population; (b) a defined territory; (c) a Government; and (d) a capacity to enter into relations with other States'.

Now, common assurance to the contrary, facts do not speak for themselves. They come to be through various performative modes endowing them with operative existence. This could be an observational mode, for instance – a recognition of the existence of the facts through the way in which they are observed. And doubtless law, any system of living law, depends upon some such observation. It depends upon recognizing what, as it were, comes to it factually. But this ability, as Derrida has it, is of the law itself: the incipient relation to 'nonlaw' is 'in law' (Derrida 2002: 269). What is involved here becomes not just the 'declaratory' observation of some factual evidence. What is involved is also a 'constitutive' legal decision responding to a legal claim, with both decision and claim being based on legal criteria relating to whether an entity is to be endowed with the requisite legal personality to participate in an international legal system. And even if this entity could aptly match the 'factual' indicia of recognizable existence, the law can still deny it legal personality because, for example, of some illegality involved in its self-affirmation as a nation state, including some 'offending [of] fundamental norms of the international legal order' (Shearer 1994: 87).

All of which leaves us with a confirmed circularity, but that will in a sense be the leitmotif of this chapter. In terms of the theories of recognition, we have with one the 'fact' of a self-subsistent singularity of the nation state, a singularity which calls for recognition. This includes recognition as an entity of the kind on which the existence of international law depends. With the other, what becomes prime is the 'constitutive' dependence of the nation state on international law. Given such a seeming impasse, it would be as well to move on to the next stage of the argument. In doing so, I will cede full force and effect, as it were, to the classic assertion that international law is the creation of nation states that remain self-subsistent. The argument will proceed by taking that assertion through a straightforward logic from which the rest of the chapter is meant to follow. Disagreement will at least spare you the burden of reading further.

That logic, what could be called a sociologic, would portend the dependence of singular entities existing in common on a determinate commonality, a dependence necessary for their very singularity. The detail goes as follows:

1) If without more, singular entities were still to exist in common, then the only available commonality would be one where they were the same as each other and singularity would be lost.
2) If the commonality were not determinate and apart, there would be nothing to stop it merging into the singular entities, and there would then be a replay of 1).
3) Yet the determinate commonality cannot be so much apart from the singular entities that it ceases to relate responsively to them in a way sufficient to be their commonality.
4) Alternatively, if the relation to the singular entities were so pervasive as to become a totalized comprehension, then the singularity of each entity would again be lost.
5) A totalized comprehension need not be total in its terms. The claim to hold the commonality in some enduringly determinate 'part' would require a totalized comprehension. This would be needed both to hold the part in an ungiving stasis and also to determine its relation and possible relation to everything else. In that configuration also, the singularity of each entity would be lost.

In all, for singular entities existing in common, the commonality has to be assuredly determinate but not ultimately determinate. It has to be illimitably responsive but not ultimately responsive. This opposition yet relation is generative of the commonality, of community – of, we could now go on to say, the event of community.

The philosophical engagement with 'the event' is enormously diverse and proliferating, but here only one of its strands will be touched on. This strand, emanating of late mainly from France, would see the event as constituently combining the dimensions of the determinate and the responsive just located in and as community, and in that very combining the event is a generative force (e.g. Derrida 2005: Part I, ch. 8, Part II, ch. 2; Deleuze 2004: 164, 172).[1] If the event were fixedly determinate and unresponsive, it would come to lack relation to a world changing around it and thence disappear into irrelevance. Yet if it were so responsive that its determinacy dissipated, it would thence disappear into deliquescence. Without this combinatory force of these two dimensions, the event could not (continue to) exist or be coming to exist. A convenient instance here is the event of law – the event that is any instantiation of law as well as the 'eventness' of law itself (Derrida 2002: 256–7; Moore 2007: 43). These dimensions of law, its determinacy and its responsiveness, will be augmented when we come to Vitoria, but first a prelude that may help take us to him.

With the story so far, the event is constituted in a necessary irresolution. Given the terms of that constitution, it becomes impossible to quell the irresolution through some enduringly posited, some positive determination. Perhaps, however, the tangible ethos of the event can be discerned negatively – discerned in a negative reflection of what it would be if the event were supposedly to be 'wholly comprehended and appropriated' (Borradori 2003: 148). In engaging with a specific event as event, Derrida would ask what could be 'the system of interpretation, the axiomatic, logic, rhetoric, concepts, and evaluations that are supposed to allow one to *comprehend* and to explain precisely something like "September 11"' (Derrida 2003: 93 – his emphasis). Such a comprehension takes one operative form as 'the *discourse* that comes to be, in a pervasive and overwhelming, hegemonic fashion, accredited in the world's public space' (Derrida 2003: 93 – his emphasis). Such a discourse lays claim to 'the worldwide movement of the world, life on earth and elsewhere, without remainder'; and it is ramified in 'international law, a world market, a universal language … ' (Derrida 2003: 98–9). While the denial of the 'eventness' of this event calls for a totalizing position, a position surpassing of 'the world' rather than a coming from within it, the existence of any such position is not confined to the imperial. Theocratic pretension would do just as well (see Derrida 2005: 33). Both imperialism and theocracy now set the scene for Vitoria, at last.

Vitoria and the event of the event

At this point, the most convenient of the contradictions that were or became Francisco de Vitoria – and we will come to others – is that between his being a committed scholastic theologian and his being hailed as a pioneering humanist and rationalist, and even, as it is claimed, a modern intellectual who, among others, initiated modern political philosophy and the study of society (D'Ors 1946: 124–5, 132; Pagden and Lawrance 1991: xiii–xiv; Collins 1998: 525). First, the theologian and, for present purposes, more particularly the exponent of natural law: 'For Vitoria, as for Aquinas, the law of nature was the efficient cause which underpinned man's relationship with the world about him and governed every practice within human society' (Pagden and Lawrance 1991: xv). Although drawing on the Divine Doctor's scheme of things, Vitoria mapped natural law onto the attributes of the monotheistic deity rather more pointedly than did Aquinas. The ineffable god of revelation exercised divine will; the god of reason, a god of determinate order and perfect constancy, was the assured source of natural law or the law of nature: 'the rules of law are in God *as in a thing which is to rule*' (Vitoria 1991: 155–57 and 163 for the quotation – his emphasis).[2] This was a god caught by 'his' own laws, by 'nature', the same as the god later forbidden by Malebranche to 'disturb the simplicity of his ways' (see Riley 1986: 40). This all-sufficing natural law was projected back onto the divine will, binding the deity and the divine will to natural law. And so Vitoria would 'think that God could not have made the fire, which is hot by nature, cold, or that it were not warm by nature; nor the snow black; the soil, light; nor could God destroy or change in general the natural propensities of things' (Vitoria 1960: 1099).[3] Neither access nor attachment to the divine will and revelation were necessary for the integrity and efficacy of natural law, or indeed for the ability to know it (Vitoria 1991: 164). It can be known comprehensively by human reason being brought to bear on nature, and all people, even if they are not Christians, have that faculty (Vitoria 1991: 155, 164). Bluntly, God was not necessary. A determinable, all-sufficing natural law can exist without divine revelation, and it can exist even if the godhead did not. All of which would accord with Vitoria as a supposed humanist, a modern political theorist, and such. This disposal of the deity left a natural law derived and formulated through and as reason – the defining quality Vitoria attributed to all law. Law was not produced by will and revelation, but by reason. Reason, however, was then as thoroughly adaptable as it has remained.

For what became international law, one of the more extravagant accomplishments of this amenable reason was the endowing of natural law with content derived from Roman law. In a resort to what would be the Institutes of Gaius, Vitoria found that 'the law of nations (*ius gentium*) ... either is or derives from natural law, as defined by the jurist: "What natural reason has established among all nations is called the 'law of nations'"' (Vitoria 1991: 278). Vitoria extended this *ius gentium*, this law common to all nations, to include another category of Roman law, the *ius inter gentes*, the law governing relations between different peoples, different nations (Stein 1999: 94–95). This fusion of the two varieties of law could have come to match the constituent dimensions of international law outlined earlier by way of the sociologic. And as those dimensions were also aligned with the event, Vitoria's disposal of the deity could be seen as making the event, including the event of international law, both possible and necessary. The departure of the deity is the event of the event. With it goes any transcendental resolution of the antinomies of the event, and they could thence take on their own combinatory force – a force also described earlier. Likewise, the event of international law could take on its own force – a force cohering solely in the commonality of its singular subjects. Matters, rather obviously, have not entirely turned out that way. The protean Vitoria perversely provides the reasons why this is or became so, and they will now be sketched in. Indulging still in anachronism, they can be encapsulated in one nineteenth-century word, nationalism, and encapsulated in the modern meaning assumed by another word also in the nineteenth century, imperialism. Both can be set in further Vitorian contradictions.

Taking imperialism first, Vitoria is perhaps most remembered for espousing the interests of indigenous populations against a predatory Spanish colonisation of the Americas. Of late, however, this espousal tends to be seen more as a refined justification of imperial acquisition (Anghie 2005: ch. 1; Bowden 2005: 8–13; Williams 1990: 96–108). Vitoria did oppose the more resolutely genocidal of the Spanish invaders, oppose their 'butchery and pillage'

(Vitoria 1991: 331, 333). In the same vein, he also opposed the division of the world, including a papal division, into areas of Christian lawfulness and areas without law, and thence ripe for free acquisition (Vitoria 1991: 259–61). Papal generosity in allocating the lands of others, as well as naked monarchical acquisition of territory, were countered by Vitoria's drawing on the *ius gentium* and on Aquinas to affirm that 'the Indians', by virtue of being human and thence possessed of reason, had *dominium*; or in other words they had a mastery of property and a mastery of rule 'public and private' – all of which was evidenced by their living in communities and by their having families, hierarchical government, legal institutions and something like religion (Vitoria 1991: 239–50).

This same obliging *ius gentium*, however, allowed of certain modes of acquiring 'just title', modes developed by Vitoria so as to identify 'the legitimate titles by which the barbarians could have been subjected to Christian rule' (Vitoria 1991: 252). There are several of these but, it may be a relief to read, Vitoria gives predominant emphasis to the first two. The first emanated from a right to trade, to travel and to dwell in the countries of the barbarians – a right extending beyond trade narrowly conceived to include intercourse and communication generally (Vitoria 1991: 278–84). The second right founding a putative just title was the right to proselytize: 'Christians have the right to preach and announce the Gospel in the lands of the barbarians' and that even against their will, conversion being 'necessary for their own salvation' with the barbarians being 'obliged to accept the faith' if it were adequately presented to them (Vitoria 1991: 271, 284–85). The *barbari* being often found resistant to both these rights, 'it becomes lawful' for the Spaniards 'to do everything necessary to the aim of war' to ensure a compliance Vitoria found to be necessary; territorial acquisition by conquest ensued, and Spain's imperial domination could continue with only marginal adjustments (Vitoria 1991: 282–3, 285–6, 291–2).

Obviously a difference was being observed. The *ius gentium* in its universal essence was tied to Christianity. A Christian nation could not treat another Christian nation in this way, and although the *barbari* were included in this Christianized *ius gentium*, they were also excluded from it. In terms that even then were far from original, Vitoria found the barbarians to be undeserving of full inclusion because they were akin to madmen or children, cannibalistic, sexually perverted and culinarily outrageous, a making unnatural and so much so that they were considered well neigh impervious to a reforming natural reason (Vitoria 1991: e.g. 207–30, 290–1; and see also Pagden 1982: 86–91, 100–3). That difference set the recognized cohering force of an emergent international law. And it was a continuing force the perception of which is obscured by depictions of an abrupt transition from the religious to the secular, from a Christian to a 'European' international law (e.g. Schmitt 2003: 127). Even as Christianity and natural law faded at the cohering core of international law, they merged into what became that law's most sustained substitute, civilization – a substitute supported at times by racist ascription and developmental dictates (Anghie 2005). The upshot is a perpetual machine in which those constituently excluded are futilely bidden to enter. What complements this constitution in exclusion or negation positively is the claim of the definitively included to exemplify the universal, a claim that can only be quasi-transcendental, but a claim that can be made now without resolving reference to a deity transcending the world. From that same quasi-transcendental position, the included assert a prerogative hold on international law, matching its determinate dimension and its determining force to their own power. In the process, law's responsive dimension is comprehensively subordinated to this determinacy. An imperial law does go responsively into the world, but its response must be entirely oriented to its own enduring determinacy (e.g. Schmitt 2003: 69–70).

Coming now to nationalism and our final Vitorian contradiction, with one Vitoria there is the dedicated Catholic theologian and churchman, and with the other a closet Protestant and nationalist (cf. Pagden and Lawrance 1991: xiii–iv). While these latter characteristics may be wide of the mark, Vitoria did reject various papal dictates to do with the colonization of the Americas. That was, of course, a rejection of the authority of the head of the 'universal' church. And while this rejection was grounded in the *ius gentium* as natural law, it was a rejection that served the cause of a burgeoning and proto-nationalist Spanish empire, and Vitoria did explicitly support the colonizing thrust of that cause. Also, and finally, Vitoria's writings on law and on the civil power were conceived as consonant with the contemporary Spanish state, with the kingdom of Castile and Aragon. More pointedly, this was also his purport with the Aristotelian conception of 'the perfect community' – 'perfect' being 'complete in itself' (Vitoria 1991: 301). The same kingdom of Castile and Aragon was, with a few others, at the forefront of an emergent nation-building. This entailed a distancing from, and at times a rejection of, the power of the papacy and of the Holy Roman Empire.

Nonetheless, there is some accuracy in the standard view that it was not until Grotius and after that international law was considered the product of autonomous nation states, states which remained completely independent of each other. This is to simplify Grotius and to endow him with the gift of prophecy, but what usually happens in the texts of international law is that the terms of the Peace of Westphalia of 1648 are overlaid on his contribution. The Westphalian settlement of the engulfing Thirty Years War in Europe accentuated the separate and sovereign quality of the 'European' nation states and principalities in opposition to an encompassing religious authority, the religion practised within the nation being determined by its ruler. This also was a simplification (see Krasner 1993: 242–46), but it was an apt envisaging of the role the nation state came to play as a deific substitute. Mediated initially by ruling pretensions to divinely endowed authority, the European nation state came to be, in Nietzsche's terms, the 'new idol' that takes over 'the ordaining finger of God' (Nietzsche 2006: 34–35).[4] From yet another quasi-transcendent position, law takes on its predominant modern guise as the contained creature of the 'sovereign' nation state.

It would, to say the least, be difficult to comprehend all that may sustain the quasi-transcendence of nation in the modern period, but perhaps the role of imperialism has not been sufficiently addressed. As a progenitor of modern nation, Spain can continue as our guiding instance. Kamen provides the apt perspective: 'we are accustomed to the idea that Spain created its empire: but it is more useful to work with the idea that the empire created Spain' (Kamen 2003: xxv). Nor was the range of imperial creativity confined to the 'common cause' it generated within the nation; Spain was something of a managing director of an imperial enterprise closely involving many European and other peoples (Kamen 2003: xxv, 13). And imperial identities were being assumed also by other national powers. But what sheets this identity home is the imperial constitution of international law. That is something which can be handled by way of a conclusion.

Conclusion

The argument of this chapter was initially impelled by the inadequacy yet relevance of standard conceptions of international law as the dependent creation of the singular nation. There was something of a reversal of that dependence since nation was found to depend, and to depend for its very singularity, on the commonality, the community of nations, and to depend on the law of that community, international law. The perception of that dependence was derived here initially from the rules of recognition in international law, but we could have started just as well with other examples of international law existing beyond the discrete reach of nation – instances such as the customary element of international law and its general principles, so-called. Force was then given, I hope, to that perception of dependence in the outlining of a sociologic of mutual and constituent dependence between singularity and commonality. That same sociologic showed that the force of the commonality was to be found in the opposition yet integral relation between its necessary dimensions of determinacy and responsiveness. That force was then encapsulated in the notion of the event, and this notion was then transposed to law, and to international law in particular.

The rest of the chapter, with a touch of the retroactive, brought that line of argument to one of the ancestor figures of international law, Francisco de Vitoria. The aptness of Vitoria for present purposes lay in his preceding the modern reduction of ideas of international law. With Vitoria, one could still discern the generative force of the commonality or community in and as international law, or what became international law. Yet Vitoria was also found to be modern in his providing the lineaments of that rendition of international law as the deracinated creation of the nation state. This tragedy was then somewhat summarily attributed to nationalism and imperialism, and most pointedly to the imperial appropriation of international law. Thus far, the argument ended with intimations of the imperial quality of nation as sustaining its supposed and singular ability to create international law.

The constituent claims of imperium and of the sovereign nation are evidently similar. Both can wondrously fuse being determinate with an unconstrained efficacy, and do so without resort to a transcendental resolution of that impossibility. For a time there was some resolving mediation by way of ruling claims to divine authorization. Those having largely disappeared, nation becomes itself a deific substitute. What now sustains this substitution? Confining an answer to our current concerns, the substitution is sustained by the imperial arrogation of international law. With Vitoria, and for some time after, the law of nations in its generative operation was confined to Christian nations, and imperial domination could extend to peoples who were not Christian. But that identity, that being within and defined by a 'comity' of Christian nations, was not confined to those who were operatively imperial. This talismanic identity was shared by all Christian nations, and then by the substitutes for the Christian, most constantly by the criterion of the civilized.

A culminating irony now returns us to that reversal of dependency we found in international law, an irony which serves to explain the nation state's strange and solitary ability to create such law. Instead of, and as well as, international law being the dependent creation of the singular nation state, we found that the nation state depended on international law for its very being. Yet the 'civilized' nation state depends on a community of the international and its law that derives its operative unity and identity from imperialism. The singular nation thence takes on imperial qualities through its being part of and dependent on this community and its law, but that dependence cannot be recognized because the constitution of the community and of its law in the sociologic is incompatible with imperialism. As Heraclitus had it: 'The real constitution is accustomed to hide itself' (in Kirk *et al*. 1957: 192).

Notes

* Many thanks to José Bellido for invaluable translation, to Maria Carolina Olarte Olarte for eventful research and for the tracing and translating of a crucial source, and to Richard Joyce for editorial guidance and generosity.
1 Examples could be multiplied and a more nuanced account would accommodate the diversity in which they are expressed, but my hope is that this formulation 'captures' it. See also Badiou's clarion (2003: 54–55).
2 Vitoria (1991) is a superb and readily available collection and translation of the works of Vitoria particularly relevant here. In case more specific identification is wanted of the works referred to in the text these are 'On Law' (153–204), 'On Dietary Laws, or Self-Restraint' (205–30), 'On the American Indians' (231–92), 'On the Law of War' (293–327), and 'Letter to Miguel de Arcos' (331–3).
3 The English translation is provided by Maria Carolina Olarte Olarte.
4 From the First Part 'On the New Idol'. For 'the finger of God' see e.g. *Exodus* 8:19.

References

Anghie, A. (2005) *Imperialism, Sovereignty and the Making of International Law*, Cambridge: Cambridge University Press.

Badiou, A. (2003) *Infinite Thought: Truth and the Return to Philosophy*, trans. O. Feltham and J. Clemens, London: Continuum.

Borradori, G. (2003) 'Deconstructing terrorism: Derrida', in G. Borradori, *Philosophy in a Time of Terror: Dialogues with Jürgen Habermas and Jacques Derrida*, Chicago, IL: University of Chicago Press.

Bowden, B. (2005) 'The colonial origins of international law: European expansion and the classical standard of civilization', *Journal of the History of International Law* 7: 1–23.

Cavallar, G. (2002) *The Rights of Strangers: Theories of International Hospitality, the Global Community, and Political Justice Since Vitoria*, Aldershot: Ashgate Publishing.

Collins, R. (1998) *The Sociology of the Philosophies: A Global Theory of Intellectual Change*, Cambridge, MA: Belnap Press of Harvard University Press.

Deleuze, G. (2004) *The Logic of Sense*, trans. M. Leicester with C. Stivale, London: Continuum.

Derrida, J. (2002) 'Force of law: the "Mystical Foundation of Authority"', trans. Mary Quaintance, in J. Derrida, *Acts of Religion*, New York: Routledge, 2001.

——(2003) 'Autoimmunity: real and symbolic suicides', trans. P.-A. Brault and M. Naas, in G. Borradori, *Philosophy in a Time of Terror: Dialogues with Jürgen Habermas and Jacques Derrida*, Chicago, IL: University of Chicago Press.

——(2005) *Rogues: Two Essays on Reason*, trans. P.-A. Brault and M. Maas, Stanford: Stanford University Press.

D'Ors, A. (1946) 'Francisco de Vitoria, intellectual', *Revista de la Universidad de Oviedo*, VII: 155–33.

Grotius, H. (2005) *The Rights of War and Peace Book I*, trans. J. Morrice *et al.*, Indianapolis: Liberty Fund.

Kamen, H. (2003) *Empire: How Spain Became a World Power 1492–1763*, New York: HarperCollins.

Kirk, G.S., Raven, J.E. and Schofield, M. (1957, 2nd edn) *The Presocratic Philosophers: A Critical History with a Selection of Texts*, Cambridge: Cambridge University Press.

Krasner, S. (1993) 'Westphalia and all that', in J. Goldstein and R.O. Keohane (eds), *Ideas and Foreign Policy: Beliefs, Institutions and Political Change*, Ithaca: Cornell University Press.

Milton, J. (1949) 'Paradise Lost', in J. Milton, *The Portable Milton*, New York: Penguin Books.

Moore, N. (2007) 'Icons of control: Deleuze, signs, law', *International Journal for the Semiotics of Law*, 20: 33–54.

Nietzsche, F. (2002) *Beyond Good and Evil*, trans. J. Norman, Cambridge: Cambridge University Press.

——(2006) *Thus Spoke Zarathustra*, trans. A. Del Caro, Cambridge: Cambridge University Press.

Pagden, A. (1982) *The Fall of Natural Man*, Cambridge: Cambridge University Press.

Pagden, A. and Lawrance, J. (1991) 'Introduction', in F. de Vitoria, *Political Writings*, trans. J. Lawrance, Cambridge: Cambridge University Press.

Riley, P. (1986) *The General Will Before Rousseau: The Transformation of the Divine into The Civil*, Princeton: Princeton University Press.

Schmitt, C. (2003) *The Nomos of the Earth in the International Law of the Jus Publicum Europaeum*, trans. G.L. Ulmen, New York: Telos Press.

Shearer, I.A. (1994, 11th edn) *Starke's International Law*, London: Butterworths.

Stein, P. (1999) *Roman Law in European History*, Cambridge: Cambridge University Press.

Stumpf, C.A. (2004) 'A comparison between the theo-political concepts of Richard Hooker and of Hugo Grotius', in C. Stumpf and H. Zaborowski, *Church as Politeia: The Political Self-Understanding of Christianity*, Berlin: W. De Gruyter.

Vattel, E. de (1916) *The Law of Nations or the Principles of Natural Law Applied to the Conduct and to the Affairs of Nations and Sovereigns*, vol. 3, trans. C.G. Fenwick, Washington: Carnegie Institute.

Vitoria, F. de (1960) 'De homocide', in F. de Vitoria, *Obras de Franciso de Vitoria: Relecciones teológicas*, trans. from Latin to Spanish Teófilo Urdánoz, Madrid: Editorial Católica, Biblioteca de Autores Cristianos.

——(1991) *Political Writings*, trans. J. Lawrance, Cambridge: Cambridge University Press.

Williams, R.A. (1990) *The American Indian in Western Legal Thought: The Discourses of Conquest*, Oxford: Oxford University Press.

Chapter 4

Westphalia

Event, memory, myth

Richard Joyce

[T]he origin makes possible a field of knowledge whose function is to recover it, but always in a false recognition ... The origin lies in a place of inevitable loss.

(Foucault 1977: 143)

Introduction

The Peace of Westphalia of 1648 is routinely cited as the 'event' which marks the emergence of the modern sovereign state. From this point on, so the story goes, states are freed from religious and imperial rule and now provide the basis for their own authority. In doing so, they ground the existence and authority of international law. This event thus looms large in the international legal memory as its foundational moment.

However, the notion that the Peace marked a decisive break between medieval notions of political authority and the modern states system has been called into question. The debate is keenest in the field of international relations. For Stephen Krasner, the 'widely held view among international relations theorists and international lawyers which sees Westphalia as a major, perhaps a decisive, break marking the transition from the medieval to the modern world' – a world now divided into sovereign states – 'is wrong' (Krasner 1993: 235, 238). As Krasner points out, political entities with more or less exclusive control over defined territories existed well before the Peace, and medieval forms of political authority – including authority exercised by the Holy Roman Empire and the papacy – continued well after it (Krasner 1993; see also Beaulac 2004). Responding to this debunking of the conventional view, Daniel Philpott has attempted to 'rescue' the 'prestige of Westphalia' by once again establishing its place at 'the origin of modern international relations' through an 'updated defense, more subtle and qualified than the conventional wisdom' (Philpott 2001: 76–77). Philpott accommodates the existence of elements of sovereignty prior to Westphalia by characterizing it as 'the consolidation, not the creation *ex nihilo*, of the modern system', and those medieval forms of authority which persisted after Westphalia as 'anomalies' (Philpott 2001: 77).

For Philpott the classic notion of sovereignty was consolidated at Westphalia, and by the time European colonies received their independence had 'come closer to enjoying universal explicit assent than any other principle of political organisation in history' (Philpott 2001: 3, 74–96). What animates Philpott's analysis is an unequivocal view of what sovereignty 'is'. Within 'invisible lines that we call borders ... supreme political authority typically lies in a single source – a liberal constitution, a military dictatorship, a theocracy, a communist regime. This is sovereignty' (Philpott 2001: 3). With this, another of modernity's conventional views safely in place, Philpott could turn his attention to the question of how 'it' developed and, more precisely, when 'it' gained sufficient currency to be regarded as having emerged or been consolidated.

For all its subtlety, rigour and attention to historical detail, Philpott's analysis is limited in two key ways. First, by taking the object of his study as a given, Philpott reduces the analysis to a question of whether or not Westphalia can be taken as a major (or the major) event in the emergence of the sovereign state. Taking this approach renders the study of the historical record surrounding Westphalia incapable of shedding any (new) light on what modern sovereignty 'is'. It shuts down the possibility of asking whether, for example, the 'anomalies' which, for Philpott, prompt a mere 'qualification' of the conventional view of the origin of state sovereignty, might actually reveal something previously overlooked in our understanding of sovereignty itself. The second limitation is that by focusing on sovereignty as a question of 'supreme political authority', Philpott does not consider sufficiently the question of law. In modernity, the state is taken to be the source from which all legal authority and all law flows. It is the original site of modern law. Thus, if Westphalia is the origin of the modern state, then it is the origin of the origin of modern law. Even if Westphalia is only taken as a mere consolidation of state sovereignty, it would still mark the moment at which this form became widely enough accepted to make possible a claim to universality (a claim necessary to ground state sovereignty as the sole or primary governing principle of modern law and international law as a law which derives its force from the collective authority of sovereign states). As we will see in the second part of this chapter, qualities pertaining to modern law make it hard to place its origins at all, imperative though this task is made to appear.

In this chapter I will argue that the continued significance of Westphalia for modern sovereignty lies precisely in the disjuncture between the historical record and that for which it is remembered. This is for two reasons which might appear at first to contradict one another, but which I will argue sit well together. The first has to do with the value of uncovering those elements of Westphalia which would challenge the conventional view. The second has to do with understanding the significance of the suppression (or ignorance) of such elements. The first reason is that the messiness of the contested and conflicting settlement at Westphalia can shed light on the complex array of political forms currently operating in international society. We may be minded then to think less in terms of the birth, rise and fall of the sovereign state, and be more attuned to how different political communities and forms of authority relate to one another. In this sense, uncovering a more accurate historical record of Westphalia is important for putting our current condition in perspective.

The second reason lies in what we can learn about sovereignty from the way the Peace of Westphalia operates as myth. For Stéphane Beaulac, the disjuncture between the historical record of Westphalia and what it is remembered for having inaugurated reveals the word 'Westphalia' to be 'one of those powerful words which has its own existence as an active force within human consciousness' (Beaulac 2004: 182). It operates as shorthand for an 'aetiological myth' (a myth 'concerning the origins of things') which, through its large-scale adoption and iteration, has 'created a new reality, a mythical reality, about the present international state system' (Beaulac 2004: 186, 212).

Taking up and extending Beaulac's concern with Westphalia's significance as myth, I will argue that the Peace provides an example of how, in modernity, myths of origin are both necessary and suppressed. They are necessary because we need such myths to explain ourselves to ourselves. Since we are always changing, we need our understanding of our origins to be protean rather than fixed, and beliefs in myths are much better at this than strict attachment to the historical record. (In this short chapter, the distinction between myth and historical record will be presented more starkly than really it should be. It is true that a strict separation between myth and historical record is impossible (since myths often rely on history, and history is never transparent). The argument presented here, though, is that since the modern sovereign state's myth of origin carries certain fabulous traits to which no historical event could be equal, it makes sense to use them as opposing terms.) But just as a myth of origin is necessary, so too must it be suppressed. One of modernity's chief claims is that it marks the triumph of universal secular reason, a claim it makes by distinguishing itself from limited and particular superstition. As such, its origins are meant to be traceable to actual events in history (a universal history, no less). Just as modern sovereignty needs myth, so too does it need history. Westphalia's continued significance lies in its ability to satisfy both these needs.

History and memory

In conventional readings of the history of international law, the Peace of Westphalia of 1648 marks the moment at which the sovereign state emerged as the principal actor in European political life and the foundation for a new, international, law. The conventional view variously holds it to be the origin, consolidation or consecration of the sovereign state; at the very least the moment when that form became sufficiently widespread to create a 'sovereign states system' (see Philpott 2001: 83; Nussbaum 1962: 115–18; Butler and Maccoby 1928: 100–101). It also is taken to mark the point at which the idea that states ground their own legal authority became sufficiently accepted such that it could be said to express a new dominant view of political authority detached from religious authority and medieval institutional forms (Poggi 1987: 89; Gross 1948; Crawford 2006: 10). Although the precise formulations vary, the following quotations from Leo Gross's 1948 article encompass the gist of this conventional view. Gross wrote that:

> It can hardly be denied that the Peace of Westphalia marked an epoch in the evolution of international law ...
>
> (Gross 1948: 26)

In particular, it:

> marked man's abandonment of the idea of a hierarchical structure of society and his option for a new system characterized by the coexistence of a multiplicity of states, each sovereign within its own territory, equal to one another, and free from any external earthly authority. ... This new system rests on international law and the balance of power, a law operating between rather than above states and a power operating between rather than above states.
>
> (Gross 1948: 28–29)

Against the conventional view generally, and that of Gross in particular, Krasner argues that Westphalia did not mark a turning point in history (Krasner 1993: 235, 264). Beaulac's historical analysis leads to a similar conclusion (Beaulac 2004: 211). In what follows, I will draw on those aspects of the Westphalian treaties which Krasner and Beaulac identify as revealing a gap between the historical record and that for which Westphalia is remembered. This focus is not intended to suggest that everything about the treaties is inconsistent with the conventional view; counter-examples can be found (see Philpott 2001). But even Philpott admits the existence of this gap, disagreeing only as to its extent (Philpott 2001: 73). And so in this section I will focus on the divergences between the historical record and the memory of Westphalia, rather than the convergences, in order to provide the context for my arguments concerning what the existence of this gap reveals about Westphalia's continuing significance.

Both Krasner and Beaulac rely on the existence of centralized authority in France, England and in the major northern Italian cities well before 1648 as evidence that such forms were not born at Westphalia (Krasner 1993: 253–55; Beaulac 2004: 194–95). This observation helps to challenge the idea of

Westphalia as a major historical break. However, to the extent that the conventional wisdom holds Westphalia to be a moment of consecration or consolidation of the sovereign state, the existence of isolated precursors does not contradict that wisdom. More significant is the affirmation of medieval conceptions of authority within the Westphalian treaties and their persistence beyond 1648. The provisions in the Westphalian treaties concerning diplomacy, territory and religion did not reveal the unequivocal emergence of a widespread notion of modern sovereignty or the establishment of a coherent system at the heart of which lay the sovereign state. Instead, they revealed the continued influence of medieval ideas and institutional forms.

First, diplomacy. The aspect of the Westphalian treaties most often cited in support of the conventional view concern the ability of princes within the Holy Roman Empire to conduct foreign relations. The article of the Treaty of Münster which bestowed on the princes the right to conclude treaties provided that 'it shall be free perpetually to each of the States of the Empire, to make Alliances with Strangers for their Preservation and Safety' (Treaty of Münster 1648: art. 65). However, this right was heavily qualified and in no way made the princes 'sovereign' in a modern sense (Krasner 1993: 245; Beaulac 2004; 203–204; cf. Philpott 2001: 85). Article 65 also stated that no treaty could result in an alliance 'against the Emperor, and the Empire, nor against the Public Peace'. Other 'marks' of sovereignty (as Jean Bodin might have described them) remained located in the Empire, albeit with extensive rights of consultation conferred on the states. Again, the same article gives the princes and states of the Empire the:

> Right of Suffrage in all Deliberations touching the Affairs of the Empire; but above all, when the Business in hand shall be the making or interpreting of Laws, the declaring of Wars, imposing of Taxes [and] levying or quartering of Soldiers.
>
> (Treaty of Münster 1648: art. 65)

All of which assumes that the so-called sovereign princes themselves did not have ultimate authority over law, war and tax – three things most commonly associated with state sovereignty.

The territorial settlements also reveal a messy picture. These were directed at satisfying the demands of France and Sweden against the Holy Roman (Hapsburg) Empire and the German princes (Krasner 1993: 240–42; Beaulac 2004: 201–203). The French claims were satisfied by a transfer of certain territories (including the bishoprics of Metz, Toul and Verdun), which was explicitly stated to be a transfer of 'all Jurisdiction and Sovereignty' (Treaty of Münster, 1648: art. 76). However, the transfer to France of Austria's rights in certain parts of Alsace was not so neat. Austria's rights in Alsace had been subject to a superior claim by the Holy Roman Empire on which various local bishoprics and mayories depended. The transfer to France of

Austria's rights did not affect those imperial rights (and the local rights derived from them). The relevant article thus contains complicated reservations reflecting the existing medieval arrangements (Treaty of Münster, 1648: art. 92; see Beaulac 2004: 202). By virtue of those reservations, the French king, whilst in receipt of certain rights in relation to the Alsatian territories, could not 'pretend any Royal Superiority over them' (Treaty of Münster, 1648: art 92). The settlement of Sweden's claims was based even more on medieval and imperial institutional forms than those of France (Krasner 1993: 241; Beaulac 2004: 201–203). Sweden was granted rights in territories on the south shore of the Baltic. However, these rights were not absolute and the territories did not become part of a singular Swedish Crown. Instead, they were transferred in 'perpetual and immediate Fief of the Empire' (Treaty of Osnabrück 1648: art. 10). These grants of fiefdoms gave the ruler of Sweden the right to sit in the Imperial Diet as representative of the regions covered by the grants. As such, not only did the settlement keep in place the medieval form of the fief, it also cast the Swedish Crown in multiple roles – sovereign over certain territories, a subject of the Empire in others. As Krasner argues, the 'statesmen at Osnabrück and Münster had available to them a variety of institutional forms, and they saw no problem in cobbling together arrangements that now appear anomalous' (Krasner 1993: 242).

The presence of overlapping forms of authority in post-Westphalian Europe is instructive not only for reinterpreting the 'event' of Westphalia itself, but also for understanding our current condition. Adherence to the conventional view of Westphalia tends to result in the characterization of our current condition as one in which state sovereignty is in decline. In this telling, 'Westphalian' sovereignty represents a high point of state autonomy and independence from which we are now departing. Philpott, for example, argues that increasing intervention under United Nations auspices (e.g. in Iraq (in 1990–91), Somalia, Haiti, Rwanda, Bosnia, etc.) and increasing European integration present 'conspicuous challenges' to the classic notion of modern sovereignty (Philpott 2001: 3). His interest in Westphalia as a formative event in the development of modern sovereignty arose precisely because of a sense of present rupture. He set himself the task of considering: '[i]f our sovereign state system is cracking, how did it ever come to be?' (Philpott 2001: 3).

But finding a complex interrelation between political forms operating at supranational and local levels embedded in the Westphalian settlement could prompt a different understanding of our current condition and might help put in perspective the current challenges posed to sovereign statehood. The question of military intervention under UN auspices is one example which will be taken up later. Another example is the challenge posed by international organizations (like the World Trade Organization or the International Monetary Fund). These organizations are commonly seen as imposing on state sovereignty by virtue of their broad reach over a vast range of policy areas and capacity to influence national law through overtly punitive (e.g. enforcement of loan conditions, approving trade sanctions) and more subtle techniques (e.g. the provision of 'technical assistance'). However, in formal terms, these organizations adhere to notions of state sovereignty and indeed rely on them to some extent to ground their own authority (their members are states, after all). The presence and actions of these organizations thus call into question a rigid distinction between national and supranational authority; a distinction which Westphalia might show was never that neat. Other challenges are situated at the local level, such as that provided by indigenous peoples in post-colonial states, whose persistent presence calls into question the self-generating and all-encompassing authority of the sovereign state. Observing in Westphalia a complex interaction of overlapping authorities, rather than a simple story of how exclusive state authority came to be, might make us more attuned to seeing how current political forms interact instead of simply viewing these challenges to the sovereign state as indications of its demise. We might also be capable of grasping with more acuity the way in which the sovereignty of the state has always been, and continues to be, both constituted and challenged by those political forms which oppose it.

The persistence of medieval political forms is only one way in which the historical record of Westphalia departs from the memory of it as the event which marks the emergence or consolidation of the modern sovereign state. Most significantly, the complex territorial settlement reveals that Westphalia did not establish or consolidate a principle that states constitute their own authority in and of themselves. And it is that principle which best characterizes the classical view of the modern sovereign state — a political entity which, having grounded its own authority, can then join with others to ground the authority of international law. Instead, we find that at Westphalia, the demarcation of the scope of authority of the various parties involved (even if we arbitrarily limit this to the ones which most closely resemble the classical idea of modern sovereignty) was determined in the course of negotiations. Their 'sovereignty', such as it was, was not purely self-positioned, nor did it come out of nothingness, nor out of fidelity to an abstract principle of state sovereignty. Rather, the extent of their authority (which would be how, even on the conventional view, one would measure what it meant to be 'sovereign' after Westphalia) was determined in the course of the relation between competing powers. It did not somehow pre-exist that relation. This would call into question the notion that state sovereignty exists prior to, and is the constitutive condition of, international law.

The religious settlement also reveals a disjuncture between the historical record and the conventional view of Westphalia. As a settlement to the Thirty Years War, one of the main objectives of the Peace was to set in place a more stable structure to accommodate the conflict between Catholic and Protestant rulers (and, most importantly, between these rulers and those of their subjects who adhered to the opposite denomination) than had been achieved by the Peace of Augsburg in 1555. That earlier treaty established the right of a ruler to determine the religion of subjects within their territory. This, of course, was a direct and substantial challenge to the authority of the papacy (both religious and temporal). But it was not a stable solution, particularly to the extent that a change in ruler (or a conversion of a ruler) could necessitate the conversion of a whole population.

The Peace of Westphalia kept intact the principle that the ruler could determine the religion of their subjects. It could thus be regarded as an affirmation (if not the inauguration) of the principle that religion was subject to an all-encompassing sovereign political authority. However, the contribution of the Peace of Westphalia was to make this principle subject to a number of new restrictions. Most significantly, the Treaty of Osnabrück provided that a ruler who changed their religion could not compel their subjects to follow suit (Treaty of Osnabrück, art. 11; see Beaulac 2004: 200). Moreover, the treaties provided for a limited notion of freedom of religion regardless of the denomination of the ruler. Article 5 of the treaty of Osnabrück provided that anyone:

> who ... shall profess and embrace a Religion different from that of the Lord of the Territory, shall ... be patiently suffered and tolerated without any Hindrance or Impediment to attend to their Devotions in their Houses and in private, with all Liberty of Conscience, and without any Inquisition or Trouble.

In addition to this private right of worship, the same article gave such people the right to engage in public works in accordance with their beliefs and also to educate their children according to their religion either at home or in foreign schools. All of which was in turn subject to them otherwise being dutiful subjects of their ruler and not causing 'Disturbance or Commotion' (Treaty of Osnabrück 1648: art. 5).

Connected to these substantive obligations was a guarantee made by the parties to enforce them. For Gross, who as we saw above is the writer most often associated with the conventional view of Westphalia, this guarantee marked a step *away* from sovereign autonomy. Gross quotes with approval David Jayne Hill's description of the treaties as having given Europe 'what may fairly be described as an international constitution, which gave to all of its adherents the right of intervention to enforce its agreements' (Gross 1948: 24). Of course, to the extent that Westphalia is conventionally taken to mark the origin of international law (as well as the consolidation of the sovereign state), the existence of such a right still fits with this part of the conventional view. But close attention to it might put into question the characterization of the interventions to which Philpott refers (in Iraq, Somalia, Haiti, Rwanda and Bosnia) as marking a decline from 'Westphalian' state sovereignty (irrespective of whatever else might be said about their relationship to, and what they reveal about, international law: see e.g. Bowring 2008).

This religious settlement at Westphalia can be read as the imposition of a constraint on the power of the so-called sovereigns. But, to the extent that Westphalia can be said to have inaugurated or consolidated the idea of the modern sovereign state, it would be more accurate to read it as having imbedded this constraint within the very meaning of sovereign statehood. The guarantee of toleration of religious minorities within states was not simply an obligation which applied to states, but was constitutive of what it meant to be a state in the post-Westphalian system. Indeed, it was the corollary of freedom from the papacy (i.e., for a ruler to be free from imperial religious domination also meant to lack the power to impose a state religion yourself). As such, at the moment in which the idea of a complete and absolute sovereign state is meant to have emerged, one finds not only that its formal condition is determined by its relation to other entities, but that a substantive content applies to it in advance of it undertaking obligations as such.

The existence of substantive content to the meaning of sovereign statehood is a result of the process alluded to above, by which the terms of relation between states constitute what they are. And it has ever been the case. One of the earliest writers on what would only later become known as 'international law', Francisco de Vitoria, elevated European sovereignty by distinguishing (in a rather more complex fashion than many later writers, it must be said) between civilized nations and their colonial other (Vitoria 1991: 233–92). This distinction reached its most extreme form in the period of nineteenth-century colonization (when the ranks of the 'civilized' shrank quite dramatically in order to accommodate the expansion of those being colonized) and continued into the period of decolonization, with standards of 'civilization' remaining the marker of a positive content of sovereignty (see Fitzpatrick 2001: 157). A more recent manifestation of this can also be observed in the standards of human rights, democracy, the rule of law and facilitation of free markets (particularly the free movement of capital) prescribed, to take one conspicuous recent example, as the 'single sustainable model for national success' (Bush 2002: preface; Bush 2006: paras I, II, VI). At each moment, the determination of the meaning of sovereign statehood and the scope of state authority occurs in the context of a relation between states, and between states and other forms of political organization – a relation which is not purely formal and devoid of content. Things do not begin with a stable notion of (state) sovereignty.

Sovereignty and myth

We have seen above how the event marked by the words 'Peace of Westphalia' did not actually happen. In this section, I will argue further that it *could* not happen. No historical process could be equal to what Westphalia is remembered for having inaugurated. Only as myth can Westphalia be taken as the origin of modern sovereignty. But why should modern sovereignty, and an international law said to be dependent on it, require myth (and in particular, a myth of origin)? Should not modernity mark the end of a reliance in myth and the triumph of secular reason? Is not the origin of the sovereign state and of international law one of those events which can be plotted in modernity's history of unfolding progress and perfectibility?

Borrowing a general answer to this question from Peter Fitzpatrick, I would argue that modernity's denial of myth 'is the myth' (Fitzpatrick 1992: ix). As Fitzpatrick argues, 'Enlightenment's obsession with origins is perhaps the most obvious substitute for the mythically transcendent' (Fitzpatrick 1992: 48). In these terms the object (here, the modern state) could 'no longer take its being from the transcendent source provided in a myth of origin. Its essence now was simply found in its origin' (Fitzpatrick 1992: 48). In the origin of things, as Foucault reminds us, we think that we will see 'the moment of their greatest perfection, when they emerged dazzling from the hands of a creator or in the shadowless light of a first morning' (Foucault 1977: 143). Applied to the present case, this myth of modernity suggests that we should be able to find in Westphalia the essence of modern sovereignty. But in the return of what is denied, we find that only as myth can such an essence be found there.

In searching for the origin and essence of our current condition, our chief goal is to explain ourselves to ourselves. Such searches generally begin with a good sense of what we are looking for. In searching for origins we are not concerned to learn how things are; we are concerned to ground (and thereby confirm) what we already know to be true about them. In the case of the modern sovereign state, there are certain features which we take as characteristic. The most important characteristic is that the state itself is the source of law. It does not derive its authority from any external source and especially not a deity. It is independent of other political entities and of religious authority (even theocratic states do not defer to religious authorities external to the state itself). It is autonomous and self-sufficient. It is capable of entering into relations with other states but is not obliged to do so. These qualities overlap, of course, and together spark a number of variations and applications. One significant example would be the way in which the qualities of independence and autonomy are taken to ground a right against external interference in domestic affairs (a right which no matter how often qualified or infringed is nonetheless taken as a conceptual starting point).

When we look at the Peace of Westphalia with these characteristics already in mind, it is possible to find material to marshal in support of its status as the origin of the modern sovereign state. Westphalia did mark a step away from the political power of religious (papal) authority. It did mark a step away from imperial rule (even if, as shown above, this step was much smaller and more tentative than is commonly thought). It did give local princes some rights to conduct foreign relations (even if this was less extensive than the rights we would now associate with sovereign statehood). The existence of these features is crucial. Without them, it would not even be possible to claim to ground modern sovereignty in Westphalia as a historical event. And without that possibility, modernity's claim that the origin of things can be found in historical events would be too easily and obviously exposed as false and it would not be able to keep its reliance on myth suppressed. Nonetheless, something more is needed to overcome the disjuncture between the historical record and the fabulous characteristics the modern state is taken to have. What is needed is another of modernity's myths: the idea that history unfolds in a linear progression which takes the present as inevitable and reduces the past to a series of steps leading towards it.

If we take as given the question of what the sovereign state became, we only need to find its perceived characteristics in incipient form at Westphalia in order to assert that they originated there. For all its detail and subtlety, it is this move which grounds Philpott's attempt to defend the conventional view of Westphalia as the origin of modern sovereignty (Philpott 2001: 75–96). And since they need only to have been subsequently realized, substantial differences from the origin can be accommodated through a narrative of linear progression from the origin to the present time. As Fitzpatrick argues, in modernity, '[o]riginary time is connected with the present object in a process of development or civilisation in which the continuity of the object is maintained even while it changes' (Fitzpatrick 1992: 48). When we begin with the present object the path towards it can be presented as inexorable and its origin thus secured. Hence the idea of Westphalia as the origin of the modern sovereign state can survive even quite substantial attacks on its historical accuracy. In effect, since we ground the origin in our understanding of the present, the origin itself takes on an ahistorical, mythical, quality.

This ahistorical quality becomes even more apparent when one considers more closely the attributes of modern sovereignty, in particular its status as the source of law and its lack of reliance on any authority outside of itself. In modernity, the state is the unmoved mover – and its sovereignty prime and generative of all law, both domestic and international. If all legal authority flows from states, and states are not reliant on any external authority (earthly or transcendent), then states must ground their own authority. This assumes that the state is capable first of producing itself without any reliance on anything beyond it – emerging fully formed in that 'shadowless light of a first morning' to which Foucault refers (Foucault 1977: 143). It is here that we can see Philpott's claim – that Westphalia can be both an origin *and* something which was not created *ex nihilo* but rather consolidated a preexisting situation – fails to account for the conventional view of modern sovereignty as the original source of law. This pure self-grounding must have a pure origin, otherwise the state would be found to be dependent on whatever created it (and modern law thus ultimately dependent on something other than the sovereign state). Of course, there is no such thing as a pure origin. The authority claimed by and for states requires a *belief* in its self-grounding capacity and its status as the source of all law. These qualities can be asserted and practised *as if* they exist, but they are not things which can be proved to exist, much less shown to have derived from an originating event.

But the origin of modern sovereignty and law must not only be made to fit what we currently are. It must also be made to fit all that we might become. This quality pertains both to the content of the law itself and also its foundation. In terms of content, modern law sets itself out as universally applicable in its forms (of which sovereignty would be key) and more precisely in terms of its ability to apply itself to any situation both present and future (see Fitzpatrick 1992: 56–59). It must be able to respond to infinitely changing circumstances (Fitzpatrick 2007: 185). This protean quality within law requires a sovereign capable of mediating between the current situation and what might be brought to bear on it. As such, the grounds on which that sovereign bases its authority must, like the law itself, be capable of adapting to new circumstances. Its characteristics cannot be fixed. As Derrida writes:

> the structure of law ... tends towards universality ... it must extend beyond the historical, national, geographical, linguistic, and cultural limits of its phenomenal origin. Everything must begin by uprooting. The limits would then appear to be empirical contingencies.
>
> (Derrida 1987: 22)

Modern sovereignty must be able not only to find its ground in a distant past but also in its own present affirmation of what it currently is and what it might become. And as part of this iterative process, the history on which this affirmation is based must be capable of being appropriated to new ends. Turning to Derrida again, '[i]terability makes it so that the origin must [*doit*] repeat itself originarily, must alter itself to count *as origin*, that is to say, to preserve itself' (Derrida 2002: 277–78 – his emphasis).

As such, for Westphalia to retain its status as the origin of modern state sovereignty, the characteristics of statehood thought to have originated there must be sufficiently protean to be relatable to new circumstances. Only as myth can Westphalia have this protean quality. To the extent that we rely on the historical record, we can do so only by focusing on incipient rather than realized qualities and by suppressing or marginalizing those features which might be inconsistent with our present understanding of modern sovereignty.

Conclusion

The aim of this chapter has been to consider the implications of the gap between that for which the Peace of Westphalia is remembered (as the 'event' which gave birth to the modern sovereign state and the states system) and the historical record. One set of implications concerns the way in which closer attention to the complexity of the Westphalian settlement might put current challenges to sovereign statehood into perspective. It might enable us to see the construction of state sovereignty as ongoing rather than complete or (even more deterministically) in decline. Instead, we might view it as a concept formed and re-formed by the relation between rival powers which are constantly forced to reassert themselves in the face of contemporary challenges. The other set of implications touched on in this chapter concern the way in which myth has been used to close the gap. This, I have argued, provides a way into thinking about the importance of myth to our understanding of modern sovereignty and law even as that importance is denied. Westphalia 'as origin' provides an excellent example of a modern myth – enough history to make it plausible and enough myth to make it pliable. Westphalia only operates as an effective ground for modern sovereignty (and international law) to the extent that it can adapt itself to and match the illimitable qualities modern sovereignty claims for itself. Only in myth can these fabulous qualities find their ground.

References

Beaulac, S. (2004) 'The Westphalian model in defining international law: challenging the myth', *Australian Journal of Legal History* 8: 181.

Bowring, B. (2008) *The Degradation of the International Legal Order? The Rehabilitation of Law and the Possibility of Politics*, Abingdon: Routledge-Cavendish.

Bush, G.W. (2002) *The National Security Strategy of the United States of America*, Washington, DC: Office of the President of the United States.

——(2006) *The National Security Strategy of the United States of America*, Washington, DC: Office of the President of the United States.

Butler G. and Maccoby S. (1928) *The Development of International Law*, London: Longmans, Green and Co.

Crawford, J. (2006, 2nd edn) *The Creation of States in International Law*, Oxford: Clarendon Press.

Derrida, J. (1987) 'The laws of reflection: Nelson Mandela, in admiration', M. Caws and I. Loenz (trans.) in J. Derrida and M. Tlili (eds), *For Nelson Mandela*, New York: Seaver Books.

——(2002) 'Force of law: the "Mystical foundation of authority"', M. Quaintance (trans.) in G. Anidjar (ed.), *Acts of Religion*, New York: Routledge.

Fitzpatrick, P. (1992) *The Mythology of Modern Law*, London: Routledge.

——(2001) *Modernism and the Grounds of Law*, Cambridge: Cambridge University Press.

——(2007) 'What are the Gods to us now?: secular theology and the modernity of law', *Theoretical Inquiries in Law* 8: 161.

Foucault, M. (1977) 'Nietzsche, genealogy, history', in D.F. Bouchard (ed.), *Language, Counter-Memory, Practice: Selected Essays and Interviews*, Ithaca: Cornell University Press, 139–64.

Gross, L. (1948) 'The peace of Westphalia: 1648–1948', *American Journal of International Law* 42: 20.

Krasner, S. (1993) 'Westphalia and all that', in J. Goldstein and R.O. Keohane (eds), *Ideas and Foreign Policy: Beliefs, Institutions and Political Change*, Ithaca: Cornell University Press, 235–64.

Nussbaum, A. (1962) *A Concise History of the Law of Nations*, New York: Macmillan.

Parry, C. (ed.) (1969) *The Consolidated Treaty Series*; *Treaty of Münster* (1648); *Treaty of Osnabrück* (1648), vol. 1, New York: Oceana Publications.

Philpott, D. (2001) *Revolutions in Sovereignty: How Ideas Shaped Modern International Relations*, Princeton: Princeton University Press.

Poggi, G. (1987) *The Development of the Modern State: A Sociological Introduction*, London: Hutchinson.

Vitoria, F. (1991) *Political Writings*, A. Pagden and J. Lawrence (eds and trs.), Cambridge: Cambridge University Press.

Chapter 5

The force of a doctrine

Art. 38 of the PCIJ Statute and the sources of international law

Thomas Skouteris[*]

Introduction

The history of international law is strewn with accounts of progress: events (institutional, doctrinal, methodological, other) celebrated by the discipline as examples of some kind of evolution or advance. We are all familiar with the cases in point: 1899 and 1907 and the Hague Peace Conferences; 1945 and the Charter of the United Nations; 1946 and the Nuremberg and Tokyo Trials; 1948 and the Universal Declaration of Human Rights; 1949 and the Geneva Conventions; 1969 and the Vienna Convention on the Law of Treaties; and so on. The same holds true for processes spanning longer periods of international law's development, such as the abolition of slavery, decolonization, the codification of international law, the limitation of the reserved domain of states, the prohibition of the use of force, the obligation to peacefully resolve international disputes, to name a random few.

Responding to the theme of the book, this chapter addresses one of the most acclaimed early disciplinary events, namely the adoption of article 38 of the Statute of the Permanent Court of International Justice (PCIJ) in 1920 and the subsequent emergence of the doctrine of the sources of international law. The argument sidesteps the ontological question of whether our event *really* signifies progress for international law. Rather, it follows the more unusual tack of exploring what makes events such as the adoption of article 38 appear to professional consciousness to constitute progress. It is therefore an investigation about how meanings of progress may be produced in international law discourse.

The idea of progress is astonishingly pervasive in international law's language and modes of thinking. Progress in our methods and techniques, in our understanding, in solving problems, in achieving goals such as maintaining peace, bringing justice or protecting human rights seems so natural a goal that questioning its premise appears pedantic. But is it really that obvious? Although 'progress' or 'progressive' have powerful connotations, they are also notions that acquire concrete meaning only when situated in a particular story, namely an explanation of how things were before and what they ought to become. Progress, in that sense, has no essence but a narrative. The following pages make the narrative itself the centre of our investigation. This analysis is therefore not about truth or falsity but about the structures within a discourse that make something appear true or false. It is not about 'external' critique (whether a narrative 'truly' represents reality) but 'internal' critique (whether the narrative has internal contradictions and gaps).

By investigating how meanings about progress are produced by texts, one may come to understand how rhetorical strategies remove from sight the ideological dimensions of legal argument. To put it in crude terms, if progress talk proves to be a powerful ideological rhetorical strategy of (de)legitimation, one may be forced to reconsider some well-rooted assumptions about international law. These include such assumptions as international law being a formal discourse without gender, religion, culture, ideology, economic theory, and so on. Most importantly, one may be able to understand better the structure of specific debates that invoke or rely on the idea of progress as part of their rhetorical apparatus. The above considerations constitute the starting point of this enquiry.

The 'event' of article 38

In professional talk, the 'doctrine of the sources of international law' is a term of art used to signify an agreed-upon set of abstract normative forms (e.g. treaties, customary law, general principles of law) that determine two essential parameters of the system: law creation (how international law is made) and law ascertainment (how we distinguish between legally binding and non-binding norms). In plain terms, for a norm to be one of international law it needs to have a form (or to be created through a process) stipulated by the doctrine of the sources. Along these lines, a norm is binding *because* it qualifies as a source of international law. Present-day textbooks, especially in Europe, trace the moment of the creation of the modern doctrine of sources to the 1920 adoption of article 38 of the Statute of PCIJ, which reads:

> The Court shall apply:

> 1. International conventions, whether general or particular, establishing rules expressly recognised by the contesting States;
> 2. International custom, as evidence of a general practice accepted as law;
> 3. The general principles of law recognised by civilised nations;
> 4. Subject to the provisions of Article 59, judicial decisions and the teachings of the most highly qualified publicists of the various nations, as subsidiary means for the determination of rules of law.
>   This provision shall not prejudice the power of the Court to decide a case *ex aequo et bono*, if the parties agree thereto.

The story of the adoption of the Statute of the PCIJ has been told at length elsewhere (Sanchez de Bustamante 1925: 97–111; Spiermann 2002). Suffice it here to remember that, although article 38 was finally adopted by consensus, it was a highly contentious provision for the members of the Advisory Committee of Jurists who drafted the Statute (Permanent Court of International Justice, Advisory Committee of Jurists 1920: 293–338). The article was initially intended to serve as a standing order for the Court, stipulating the normative forms that the PCIJ should take into account when deciding cases. Nevertheless, soon after its adoption article 38 acquired importance and meaning beyond the one anticipated by its drafters. It rapidly became synonymous with the 'doctrine of the sources of international law'; a closed list enumerating the abstract normative categories that comprise the body of international law. The formative impact of the text of article 38 on post-1920 theory and practice is hard to overstate. During the interwar years the adoption of the article was heralded as a giant leap forward, 'the solid bed of rock on which the fabric of international law has now to be built' (Williams 1939: 38–39), a development that ended an 'embarrassing uncertainty' (Lauterpacht 1927: 67–68) about the sources of international law. Recent scholarship, especially in Europe, remains attached to the wording of article 38, albeit with a range of caveats varying from one author to the next.

Professional orthodoxy about article 38 revolved around the idea that the adoption of the article ended the uncertainty about the sources of international law. As the story goes, before 1920 there was no clear understanding of the processes that produce universally binding norms, and the normative taxonomy of international law was open to contention. Article 38 'changed all that' by providing a clear and finite list of the sources of international law. This was perceived as bringing certainty and predictability to the legal process and improving the quality of the judgements of the PCIJ. Further, article 38 acknowledged the important role of 'general principles of law', which symbolized the corrective normative standards of justice.

This conventional account was well embedded in the rhetoric of interwar mainstream thought.[1] Interwar sociological jurisprudence largely shared five argumentative tropes that paved the way for the wide acceptance of article 38. First, it used the Great War as the historical surface upon which a new beginning for international law could be projected (e.g. Hudson 1925). Second, it called for the reconstruction of international law in the ashes of the Great War into a 'new international law'. Third, it contended that 'critique' had to begin by scrutinizing the foundations and methods of pre-war international law. Such critique was mostly targeted towards the attachment of international law to (what was perceived as) theoretical dogmatism instead of pragmatic thinking, and especially to the stilted versions of the traditions of naturalism and positivism that were believed to form the prevailing approach before the war (Kennedy 1996). Fourth, it proclaimed that 'reconstruction' should take place by means of clarifying the legal methods for the development of the law and, primarily, by creating more law and more determinate law. The term frequently used to refer to this activity was 'legislation' and the method *par excellence* for its attainment was 'codification'. The idea was that the development of new rules would 'annex' within the law previously unregulated areas and prevent future setbacks. Fifth, it ascertained the existence of a new spirit, a new internationalist mentality and sensibility, with which the project of international law's reconstruction should be undertaken (Hudson 1925: 23; Álvarez 1930: 37).

Formalization and standardization

Let us look more closely at how the literature reckoned with the adoption of article 38. The following paragraphs focus on two narrative moves common to the literature of the time, which I call *standardization* and *formalization*. These moves are not only symptomatic of interwar sources discourse. They are also enabling moves: they actively create the discursive space for the doctrine to be accepted as an element of progress by telling a story about international law's past, present and future.

Standardization

Standardization may be defined in plain terms as a conscious process by which reality, in all its diversity, is organized on the basis of categories that carry the promise of universal legitimacy and applicability. Standardization in the sources of international law is precisely what article 38 came to stand for. Prior to 1920, sources did not exist as a doctrine or even as a settled domain of scientific or professional knowledge. Ideas about law making were derived directly from theories about the basis of obligation in international law, which could be positivist, naturalist or other (Koskenniemi 1989: 264). Authors appeared to have their own terminology, taxonomy and lateral views about the number and properties of the sources of international law. Thus, while most authors agreed that international custom and international treaties should be listed among the sources of international law, others included in their lists concepts such as divine law, natural law, ancient law, general history, Roman law, principles of justice and reason, the opinion of eminent jurists, the universal consent of nations, international usage, decisions of tribunals (prize courts, mixed tribunals, local courts), ordinances, commercial law and municipal law, international state papers other than treaties and diplomatic correspondence and documents, international conferences, instructions issued by states for the guidance of their own affairs and tribunals, the sea laws of various ports, international public opinion, and so on (e.g. the enumerations in Davis 1908: 26; or Maine 1894: 14). While under the 'old' international law one was not sure to which sources a tribunal was likely to appeal in determining the legal points at issue, the new model of the sources has 'changed all that' (Williams 1939: 38–39).

Article 38 has indeed 'changed all that', albeit gradually. By the mid-1930s, the great majority of textbooks adopted Article 38 as the standard starting point of any discussion of sources. Specialized literature on the sources of international law appeared for the first time and sources became a recognized field of academic study. Let us look at a telling example. The 1928 edition of Brierly's popular textbook makes no reference whatsoever to article 38 PCIJ but states that the sources of international law are custom and reason, while one is 'probably justified' to add treaties as a third source (Brierly 1928: 38–46). Eight years later, the book's next edition begins the same section by directly citing the text of article 38. No explanation is given except that this is a text of 'highest authority' and that one may 'fairly assume' that it expresses the duty of every tribunal that is called upon to apply international law (Brierly 1936: 46). The rest of the passage replicates the structure of article 38, following the order of the sources as listed there. 'Reason' is no longer listed as a source of law.

What does it mean to reduce an open-ended list of sources to the text of article 38? What is at stake in such a move? Standardization in sources discourse organizes a diversity of normative forms and processes of law creation into a 'closed' and 'universal' model. The new doctrine of sources thus becomes at once 'closed', in the sense of comprising a determinate and finite list of sources, and 'universal', in the sense of being applicable to all states and all areas of international practice. Law of the sea, diplomatic law or the law of jurisdiction are now subject to the same normative categories of sources as listed in article 38; and the physical space of the globe, from Latin America to Asia and Africa, now constitutes a new global field of norms of universal application. The question 'What are the sources of international law?' can be answered by a mere reference to the list of article 38.

This is a crucial before/after narrative move. It tells a story of disciplinary evolution by describing the possibility of a universal, one-size-fits-all doctrine replacing a chaotic and indeterminate prior state of affairs. In doing so it reduces, denies, or sets aside the diversity of law-making methods in the actual practice of states. Standardization carries the political message that finality and universality is better than fragmentation. Difference is toned down (or set aside) for the purpose of reaching a generally acceptable formulation. For standardization to be acceptable, it must invoke scientific method in discerning common denominators, at the cost of reducing reality into essence.

The amount of information about the object is reduced, with the result of foregrounding specific properties only. In sources theory, the process occurs by dissecting content from form, by regarding sources as abstractions that exist independently from the content of the rule that they embody. The new doctrine of sources refers to a set of criteria (tests, conditions, standards) that must be met by any norm, in whatever field and whatever its content. As a field of scholarly study, the topic 'sources of international law' refers to an enquiry aimed at defining or refining such criteria and their modes of application without reference to a specific area of the law's application. The doctrine of sources is, in this sense, an exercise in abstraction. The abstraction, however, is not only descriptive: it is also prescriptive. Sources doctrine is not only a tool for telling how 'legal' norms are but also how those norms must look in order to acquire binding effect. It is an endeavour to demarcate, in the best possible way, a set of ideal-type forms that, when applied to an infinite range of situations by an infinite number of professionals or institutions, would lead to reliable determinations of whether a particular norm is legal or not.

Formalization

Like standardization, *formalization* is crucial in understanding the adoption of article 38 as a moment of progress. By formalization, I refer to a process that proclaims a transcendental object (the sources doctrine), whose properties are unaffected by the analysing subject (the international lawyer, the court, and so on). In interwar literature, the formalizing move is manifested in different ways concerned precisely with creating space for an autonomous doctrine of sources to operate without reference to an external point. Politics, philosophy and legal theory, for example, all become divorced from sources discourse.

The literature of the time tries at length to separate the practical application of the doctrine from the question of the basis of obligation in international law. The 'registers' of high theory and practical application are postulated as two separate and autonomous levels or planes of contemplation. Under the veil of 'terminological clarity', authors distinguish between one's theoretical ideas about the basis of obligation in international law and generally accepted normative forms or law-creating processes (Corbett 1925: 21; Gihl 1957: 53). Authors explain the differences between terms such as 'source', 'cause', 'basis', 'evidence', 'material source', 'historical source', and so on. This separation does not require one to be agnostic about the basis of obligation. Rather, the emphasis is on finding a way to insulate practical application from the grand debates of high theory.

Formalization is a narrative move that claims the possibility for the doctrine of sources to operate autonomously and on a different register than theoretical contemplation or political contest. The 'I' of the subject applying the law is at most the catalyst for the application of the doctrine or else is removed from the picture entirely. Without formalization, practical application would be pinned on an external, non-objective point of reference and, as a consequence, disagreement could continue interminably without a possibility of closure. Determining whether a particular norm is customary would therefore depend not on the practical application of the formal criteria of 'state practice' and '*opinio iuris*' but on one's idea about the basis of obligation in international law. The doctrine and its application now acquire an objective, technical, mechanical property. Hence, when we speak of criteria or 'tests of validity' of international law, we think precisely of criteria that could be applied by an infinite number of people in an infinite number of circumstances and yield similar results. This way the process of law identification seems like a technical exercise, removed from the realm of politics or philosophy, situated in the realm of technical–professional expertise. Thus a norm of customary law is ascertained categorically when the conditions of state practice and *opinio iuris* are met. A formal model would allow this conclusion to be reached by a trained professional, regardless of whether she thinks that the specific norm should be binding, fair, just, good, and so on. Determinations no longer have to be derived from state consent (positivism) or natural justice (naturalism). But if not state consent or natural justice, then what?

The pursuit of correctness

Standardization and formalization frame a discursive space that seems insulated from indeterminacy. Together they create a style of argument that seems new, formal, stable, determinate and superior to that of the 'old' international law. The 'new' doctrine of the sources under article 38 is not directed at revealing justice or truth. Contemplation turns instead to decisions and judgements of practical thinking, or what Minkkinen calls 'correctness' (Minkkinen 1999: 3 and 9–47). If one cannot determine what is just or true, the decision could just as well be correct according to the rules of the game. For nearly a century sources writing has been devoted to determining verifiable juridical phenomena: whether norm x 'is' a norm of law according to the doctrine of sources; or whether interpretation y of norm z is 'correct'. The quest is for a technique, tool or standard that would enable correctness to be determined decisively. By regarding itself not as an enterprise of high theory but as an exercise in practical thinking, the new field is invested in inventing and sharpening abstract criteria (boundary conditions, tests of validity, definitions), the tools of the trade of making correct professional statements about the law. Article 38, initially concocted as a procedural guideline for the PCIJ, became the first generally accepted list of such professional criteria.

The pursuit of correctness in sources discourse often appears in the guise of the quest for determinacy or relevance. The quest for determinacy aims for definitions and formulations of the doctrine (and of each source) which are as clear as possible. Thus, crude or imprecise expressions have to be replaced or supplemented with finer, more precise ones – or additional (second-generation) tools must be developed. If article 38 does not sufficiently define the concept of a treaty, then an additional definition is needed (e.g. by means of a convention on the law of treaties). At other times, the problem of indeterminacy can be traced to the lack of clear hierarchy between sources. In this case scholarship must create conflict resolution doctrines in the form of hierarchical systems that privilege in a decisive way one source over another. The last century has witnessed the creation of an intricate web of additional conditions, practices and second-generation criteria to such effect. These additions distinctly mark the way each period understands sources doctrine.

In turn, the quest for relevance leads to a doctrine that is in sync with the will and the practice of states. The classic example here is the various waves of literature concerned with 'new' sources, from General Assembly resolutions and unilateral acts of states to relative normativity and studies of law-making practices in new or emerging fields, such as international economic law, international environmental law, and so on. The problem of relevance can be resolved by modernizing, recasting or adapting the doctrine in such a way that it can assimilate, to the greatest extent possible, such new practices. The idea is to flex our understanding of each source (e.g. the formation of customary law) in order to include developments in practice, but to stop firmly before an imaginary breaking point. It is a question of moving the metaphorical Rubicon to a different location, while allowing sources doctrine to maintain its on/off quality. So, for example, although General Assembly resolutions, codes of conduct and other soft-law instruments cannot be considered to be sources of international law proper, these new forms of law making could nevertheless be brought within the ambit of article 38 by means of upgrading their relevance in the determination of existing sources of law, such as international customary law. Similarly, the definition of a treaty could be flexed to include memoranda of understanding, and so on.

The paradox of the doctrine of the sources is that it claims to be both the product of social observation (standardization) and a defence against the indeterminacy of external theory (formalization). In striving to be anti-foundationalist it falls into the trap of essentializing the science of social observation. Things seem to appear in a world 'out there', passing before the eyes of the scholar who merely reports them. The problem, as Koskenniemi remarks, is that "'social facts' do not come before our eyes "an sich"" (Koskenniemi 1989: 340). To understand what takes place in the social world we need to interpret, and this involves external elements as well as a subjective understanding. Thinking about sources in terms of correctness is about what Kennedy calls a quest for a 'decisive discourse' (Kennedy 1987: 95), or a way of continually distinguishing binding from non-binding norms, while remaining open to expressions of sovereign will. Whenever confronted with interminable disagreement about whether or not a particular norm is customary international law, the discipline translates this problem as one of correctness, as a technical lapse, without accepting that no end may be brought to the debate unless a choice is made by reference to an external point of view. Deliverance is found in the creation of even more doctrinal tools, which may relocate the problem but cannot resolve it.

Take the example of a treaty. Disagreement as to whether a treaty exists or is binding would require a definition of a treaty, as provided by article 2 of the 1969 Vienna Convention on the Law of Treaties (VCLT). This article would only be helpful if it was not amenable to 'hard' and 'soft' arguments, which appear equally legitimate or which would transmute into each other. The International Court of Justice has on many occasions battled with the question with contradictory results.[2] Is a given agreement a treaty because the parties intended it to be a treaty or because it 'objectively' meets the definition of article 2, or is it considered as such in order to maintain the legal certainty of the system regardless of the intention of the parties? And who decides what was the initial intention of the parties? Is it the parties themselves, or must there be some objective evidence of their intentions? Since article 38 of the PCIJ Statute and article 2 of the VCLT do not in themselves bring determinacy, one must resort to yet another doctrine to interpret the evidence in a way that would help one apply these definitions. A doctrine of interpretation, say articles 31 and 32 of the VCLT, would, however, also be open to 'hard' and 'soft' arguments. In order to interpret a treaty provision, should one look at the intention of the drafters ('hard'), the objective meaning of the terms, or the object and purpose? The search for a 'decisive discourse' can continue indefinitely and without closure.

In closing

Responding to the theme of this book, this chapter turned to the 'event' of the adoption of article 38 PCIJ Statute to highlight two of the narrative moves in the literature of the time that helped produce meanings about progress in international law. This narrative presents the pre-1920 doctrine of sources as unable to fulfil its role as a tool for separating law from non-law. The reason given is that the doctrine was indeterminate: it was too open-ended (nobody knew the exact number and nature of the sources of international law) and too dependent on arbitrary theoretical or political opinion (underpinned by partial philosophical theories). On the other hand, the post-1920 doctrine of sources (encapsulated in article 38 of PCIJ Statute) is presented as hugely superior on account of it being determinate. The problem of open-endedness was resolved with the move to standardization; a new 'closed' and 'universal' list of sources. The problem of dependence on arbitrary political or philosophical opinion was resolved with the move to formalization (the creation of a set of secondary rules belonging to a different register than 'high theory' or politics). The transition from fragmentation to standardization, from philosophy/politics to technique, from academic formalism to pragmatism, is a totalizing narrative that produces meaning about progress in sources discourse. The narrative moves of standardization and formalization capitalize on a background story that privileges determinacy, scientific technique and pragmatism, leaving no choice as to the meaning of progressiveness in doctrinal debates. The only way for this story to perform its discursive effect is to buttress its claim to objective truth. The terms themselves (determinacy, pragmatism, technique) need also to be assumed as having stable and determinate meaning. A mystified opposition between a primitive past and an advanced present/future becomes the interpretative device for understanding doctrinal progress (correctness, determinacy, social relevance).

The projected virtue of the determinacy of the new doctrine is based on notions that are themselves neither stable nor determinate. Closure and universality are subverted each time they are applied. The only way to bring closure is to invoke yet another 'decisive' discourse, this time external to article 38. The same holds for the narrative move of formalization. Formalization aspired to disconnect the 'registers' of high theory and practical application in order to allow a technical (non-political, non-theoretical) application of the doctrine. It was, however, demonstrated that the two registers collapsed into each other each time one sought their autonomous application.

Standardization and formalization, far from having a stable content, can be better understood as a trope or style of argument that helped legitimize a project for the reconstruction of public international law. 'Talking sources' is not more determinate than 'talking theory'. But at the same time, the language of sources doctrine is able to capture anew the fantasy of the international lawyer as amounting to a discourse able to jump over the ruptures of everyday experience. Legitimacy in sources discourse is thus produced not because article 38 of the PCIJ Statute has the capacity to tell decisively whether a certain norm is one of public international law. Legitimacy is produced via the *invocation* of the vocabulary of pragmatism and article 38. In that sense, progress in sources discourse does not have an essence: it is the product of a narrative whose essence is floating, allowing a multiplicity of meanings according to the occasion. One could argue that the iteration of meanings is what enables the success of the language of sources doctrine. As explained above, literature on sources has found peace in bracketing (setting aside) all the difficult questions that would expose the indeterminacy of the doctrine. The feeling of certainty in the literature is forged by standard references to classical cases and materials. In such references the iteration of the vocabulary is either silenced or underplayed. The authors of the new doctrine are not the authors of a determinate and rational set of technical tools but the users of a set of discursive structures that legitimize legal–social outcomes.

Notes

* An expanded version of this argument appears as Chapter 3 in Thomas Skouteris, *The Notion of Progress in International Law Discourse* (T.M.C. Asser Press: The Hague, December 2009).

1 For the interwar sociological movement see Koskenniemi 2002: 266–412; Kennedy 1996: 385; Berman 1992: 353.

2 See, for example, the findings in the Aegean Sea Continental Shelf Case (*Greece v Turkey*) (Judgment of 19 December 1978), ICJ Rep. (1978), at 3; South West Africa Cases (*Ethiopia v South Africa; Liberia v South Africa*) (Judgment of 21 December 1962), ICJ Rep. (1962), at 319; Case Concerning Maritime Delimitation and Territorial Questions Between Qatar and Bahrain (*Qatar v Bahrain*) (Jurisdiction and Admissibility) (Judgment of 5 February 1995), ICJ Rep. (1995), at 6. In each of these cases, the court resorted to a different criterion to determine whether a certain instrument was an international treaty, ranging from the intentions of the parties (SWA Cases) to subsequent reliance (Aegean Sea) to a 'reasonable man' criterion (*Qatar v Bahrain*). For a discussion, see Chinkin 1997.

References

Álvarez, Á. (1930) 'The new international law', *Transactions of the Grotius Society*, 15: 35–51.

Berman, N. (1992) 'A perilous ambivalence: nationalist desire, legal autonomy, and the limits of the interwar framework', *Harvard International Law Journal*, 33: 353.

Brierly, J.L. (1928, 1st edn) *The Law of Nations – An Introduction to the International Law of Peace*, Oxford: Clarendon Press.

——(1936, 2nd edn) *The Law of Nations – An Introduction to the International Law of Peace*, Oxford: Clarendon Press.

Chinkin, C. (1997) 'A mirage in the sand? Distinguishing between binding and non-binding relations between states', *Leiden Journal of International Law*, 10: 223.

Corbett, P. (1925) 'The consent of states and the sources of the law of nations', *British Yearbook of International Law*, 6: 20–30.

Davis, G.B. (1908, 3rd edn [revised]) *The Elements of International Law, With an Account of its Origin Sources and Development*, New York and London: Harper & Brothers Publishers

Gihl, T. (1957) 'The legal character and sources of international law', *Scandinavian Studies in Law*, 1: 53–92.

Hudson, M.O. (1925) 'The prospect for international law in the twentieth century', *Cornell Law Quarterly*, 10: 419–559.

Kennedy, D. (1987) *International Legal Structures*, Baden Baden: Nomos.

——(1996) 'International law and the 19th century: the history of an illusion', *Nordic Journal of International Law*, 65: 385.

Koskenniemi, M. (1989) *From Apology to Utopia: The Structure of International Legal Argument*, Helsinki: Finnish Lawyers' Company.

——(2002) *The Gentle Civilizer of Nations: The Rise and Fall of International Law 1870–1960*, Cambridge: Cambridge University Press.

Lauterpacht, H. (1927) *Private Law Sources and Analogies of International Law (With Special Reference to International Arbitration)*, London: Longmans.

Maine, H.S. (1894, 2nd edn) *International Law (The Whewell Lectures)*, London: Murray.

Minkkinen, P. (1999) *Thinking Without Desire: A First Philosophy of Law*, Oxford: Hart Publishing.

Permanent Court of International Justice, Advisory Committee of Jurists (1920) 'Procès verbaux of the proceedings of the committee June 16th – July 24th 1920', The Hague: Van Langenhuysen Brothers.

Sanchez de Bustamante, A. (1925) *The World Court*, New York: Macmillan.

Spiermann, O. (2002) '"He who attempts too much does nothing well": the 1920 Advisory Committee of Jurists and the Statute of the Permanent Court of International Justice', *British Year Book of International Law*, 73: 187–260.

Williams, J.F. (1939) *Aspects of Modern International Law: An Essay*, London: Oxford University Press.

Chapter 6

Paris 1793 and 1871

Levée en masse as event

Gerry Simpson

> The inhabitants of a territory which has not been occupied, who, on approach of the enemy, spontaneously take up arms to resist the invading troops, without having had time to organise themselves in accordance with Article 1, shall be regarded as belligerents if they carry arms openly and it they respect the laws of war.[1]
>
> (Hague Convention IV, 1907, article 2, definition of *levée en masse*)

1793 and 1949

Violence in war is subject to feverish regulation.[2] This regulation, partly, depends on a categorization of human beings as either combatants or non-combatants (and, in a not quite overlapping categorization, soldiers or civilians). The principle of 'distinction' is founded on the stability and recognizability of these categories and this principle, in turn, is a constitutive preoccupation in the work of international humanitarian and military lawyers. All of this is threatened, though, by a sense that the distinction cannot work: because war is now total, or because resistance is multiple, spontaneous and permeable, or because law is sidelined by the imperatives of insurrection, occupation or annihilation, or because these categories are continually bleeding into one another.[3]

The event that provides an earlier origin for this crisis may be the *levée en masse*. This can be understood in two, perhaps contrasting, ways: either as a moment in French political history (23 August 1793), when a Committee of Public Safety creates modern war through a form of mass recruitment; or, instead, as the ongoing possibility of unplanned, impulsive revolt against invasion, occupation or domination. The latter idea is found in the Hague Regulations and in the lineaments of article 4 (6) of the Fourth Geneva Convention, and has at least one of its precursors (or, perhaps, analogues) in an iconic event in the history of revolutionary struggle: the Paris Commune of 1871.

In the legal imagination, conceptions of the *levée en masse* alternate between spontaneous, uncontrollable event and planned, ordered regimentation;

between uprising and recruitment; and between fluid, ad hoc resistance and stratified war making. The *levée*, it might be argued, encapsulates war's romantic and strategic aspects. More importantly, it reflects and speaks to law's openness to subversion, opposition and political self-determination on one hand, and its insinuations in hierarchy, bureaucracy and management on the other. The *levée en masse* is where war's modern hierarchical impulses (the invention of state-led, mass participation war) meet its romantic counterpart (the possibility of a politics of resistance without or outside the state).[4] The *levée en masse*, precisely, is poised between conscription and rebellion.

The *levée*, then, makes 'warlaw' (Byers) or 'lawfare' (Kennedy) possible and impossible at the same time. It is made possible in the sense that modern war and the laws of war can be understood as a response to the rise of the conscripted mass army in 1793; it is made impossible in the sense that the *levée* as rebellion (1871) threatens to eliminate the very distinctions upon which the laws of war rely for their power and coherence. These two conceptions are entrenched in two competing stories told about the *levée en masse*.

In the first, the *levée* as conscription is the ground on which is created the post-Napoleonic, militarized state and the possibility of total war. It is an ongoing project for enforcing state power and assimilating citizenship to warriorship: the opposite of an 'event' (Badiou 2007: 285–89).

State-building in Europe at the time of Westphalia and for a century and half after depended largely on the creation of small professional armies, large-scale bureaucracies and potent state ideologies.[5] In China, though, at least during the warring period of the Ming Dynasty, the *levée* was a state enterprise designed to create enormous armies of up to 2 million men and women (and, sometimes, as was the case in parts of nineteenth-century China, children too). This was a different sort of total war with citizens as participants (as well as victims). The Chinese model was not adopted (and the Westphalian model abandoned) in Europe until August 1793 when a badly outnumbered and outgunned French state under Napoleon introduced the *levée* in order to fight the Spanish, the Austrians, the Prussians, the Dutch, the British and the Spanish:

> From this moment until such times as its enemies shall have been driven from the soil of the Republic, all Frenchmen are in permanent requisition for the services of the armies.[6]
>
> (Hazen 1932: II, 666)

This innovation led in turn to more regular forms of conscription, and the *levée* became associated with two forms of state action: mass mobilization or universal conscription, and the potential deployment of large contingents of reservists. Napoleonic France, then, provides an opening for the future history of war. After all, when the 'women make tents and clothes ... the children turn linen into lint ... ' then all are at war (Anderson 1908: 184–85).[7] This provides the basis for total war and introduces the ambiguous figure of the 'warring citizen': a non-combatant who becomes indispensable to war-making.[8] And while the Great War continued this Napoleonic tradition of the conscripted army and the warring citizenry, the Second World War took it to its logical conclusion. Everyone became a combatant. The *levée en masse* reaches its apotheosis at Dresden, in Chongquin, in Coventry, in Hamburg, in Tokyo and at Nagasaki.

But following the Second World War, there is the appearance of a division between those subject to the logic of the *levée* and those who apply its logic. Its locales were now found in Pyongyang and Hanoi and, more latterly, in Gaza and Fallujah, where the technologically supreme states made war on enemy populations. The Committee on Public Safety had merely requisi-tioned 'all Frenchmen'; the *levée*, by the beginning of the twenty-first century, had threatened to requisition half of humanity.

The *levee en masse*, though, has its romantic counter-narrative to this Napoleonic trajectory.[9] This narrative supplants the role of the state and its compulsory requisitions with a more revolutionary conception of the *levée* that has its roots in the politics of mass resistance. It is, as it were, extra-curricular self-defence: self-defence against (the Paris Commune) or in the name of (the Geneva Conventions, where the revolt must be directed towards external enemies in order to qualify for protection) the state. It represents a moment of self-defence defined by the very absence of organization or the time for such organization. A contemporary model for this version of the *levée* is the Warsaw Uprising of 1944: a spontaneous, instinctive and hopeless gesture of resistance that draws on the history of earlier Polish *levée*s and is squashed by an occupying state (Germany) with the connivance of the soon-to-be 'liberating' state (the Soviet Union).

Putatively concerned largely with the clash of armies on legalized plains, international humanitarian law is a project continually wrestling with its disruptive 'other': the irregular combatant, the civilian, the soldier *hors de combat*. Put differently, the law of war is built on the logics of the *levée*: the *levée* as bureaucratic conscription and the *levée* as provisional rebellion (and potential event). Article 4 of the First Geneva Convention is typical in this regard.[10] Prisoner-of-war status is to be accorded to regular armies (conscripts and professionals) (4(1)), to militias and volunteer corps 'forming part of such armed forces' (4(1)) and to 'organised resistance movements' (4(2)). Thus article 4 largely is concerned to protect the hierarchically ordered war-fighting unit. But article 4(6) accords Geneva POW status to:

> Inhabitants of a non-occupied territory who, on the approach of the enemy, spontaneously take up arms to resist the invading forces, without having had time to form themselves into regular armed units, provided they carry arms openly and respect the laws and customs of war.

Of course, this is a restrictive version of the romantic *levée en masse*. It is marked by four characteristics. First, there is the absence of organization or structure. Second, there is the requirement that the *levée* occurs only with the 'approach' of enemy forces. Third, the resisters have to carry arms openly and comply with the laws and customs of war. And fourth, they are accorded laws-of-war status only when the resistance is directed at external enemies.

1998: a detour

This restrictive version of the *levée* was given some attention recently at the International Criminal Tribunal for the Former Yugoslavia in the Hague. On 30 June 2006, Trial Chamber II handed down its judgment in *Prosecutor v Oric* (case IT-03-68-T). The accused, Naser Oric, had been a commander of Bosnian forces in the municipality of Srebrenica. The prosecution alleged that between September 1992 and late-March 1993, Oric had been in command of military police at the Srebrenica police station where a group of Bosniaks (Bosnian Muslims) was accused of committing acts of abuse against Serb prisoners held in detention. Oric was charged, under the doctrine of command responsibility, with knowing or having reason to know that these abuses (rising to torture and murder) were taking place, and of failing to take the necessary measures to punish or prevent the acts of his subordinates (paragraphs 5–9). He also was charged with similar failures in relation to 'acts of wanton destruction' in hamlets around Srebrenica (Oric was alleged also to have participated directly in some of the attacks).

The defence argued that there were no organized fighting units around Srebrenica and that the Bosnian Muslim population had opposed the Serbian forces in a *levée en masse*. In its judgment, the trial chamber adopted the Geneva Conventions' conception of the *levée* as a makeshift uprising directed at occupying forces. It held that, for a short period in April and May 1992, Bosnian resistance could be characterized as a *levée en masse*. Thereafter, resistance was 'normalized'. The tribunal, though, appears divided on the nature of this process of 'normalization' and the meaning of the *levée en masse*.

On one hand, what we have is a temporal theory of resistance. As the trial chamber puts it:

> the concept by definition excludes its application to long-term situations.
>
> (paragraph 136)[11]

Uprisings may remain disorganized and ad hoc but they cease to be *levées* in prolonged engagements.[12] Article 2 of the 1907 Hague Regulations contains a single reference to this in its description of inhabitants taking up arms 'without having time to organise themselves' (paragraph 50).

But it is possible to imagine resistance that is both prolonged, *and* disorganized and non-hierarchical. And, indeed, in one curious footnote, the tribunal mentions that two of the witnesses acknowledge 'the existence of a *levée en masse* in Srebrenica during the period relevant to the indictment ... ' (fn. 330) before going on to say, 'however, the Trial Chamber reached its decision on the issue of the existence of a *levée en masse* in accordance with the aforementioned definition of the term in international law'. (At the very least, this suggests a split between the materiality of resistance and its formal position.) On the other hand, the tribunal does not wish to rely entirely on the temporal approach. It engages in an examination of the structure and behaviour of Bosnian forces. Here the trial chamber finds that after 20 May 1992, the Srebrenica *levée* had transformed itself into a coordinated and vertically integrated military unit (though, in a gesture to the Napoleonic *levée*, it states that 'no formal mobilisation was ever implemented').

The debate in *Orić* reflects, to an extent, a wider debate concerning the outlines of the *levée en masse* at conferences on international humanitarian law between 1874 and 1949 where the larger states consistently argued for a conception of the *levée* that required a command structure and strict geographic limits while smaller states supported a looser, less hierarchical definition (Nabulsi 1999: 44–60).

1871

The laws of war are built, then, on a relationship between normal and abnormal circumstances (war itself is a break with peace, and there are permissible and impermissible killings, ordinary and exceptional wars). The 'normal' war is conducted between conscripted or professional armies. We might say that the protagonists oscillate between the Napoleonic *levée* (mass mobilization) and its opposite (the small professional army). This 'normal' war is perpetually threatened and disrupted by outbreaks of abnormality. Civilians are conscripted as 'victims', and rebellious groups and figures have to be articulated through the laws of war as exceptional cases. The civilian-rebel (neither conscripted nor professionalized) is understood as a properly constituted warrior only if she can somehow mimic the regular soldier (by wearing insignia, by carrying arms openly, by organizing). The popular uprising (outside politics and outside law) is justifiable in only one case: the case of the spontaneous and ephemeral moment of rebellion against incoming occupiers. Once the occupation is in place or the resistance is organized or the resisters have been incorporated into regular armed forces or militia units, the uprising ceases to be a *levée*. At this point, resistance is either fully formalized or rendered outlaw.

The *levée*, then, is a moment (but just a moment) of rupture in the fabric of the international law of violence. Is it an event?

On 18 March 1871, with the Prussians outside Paris after the defeat of the French at Sedan and the French Government nervous about a possible workers' insurrection in the capital, French troops are ordered to seize weapons, provided in the previous year for the defence of Paris, from the National Guard (largely composed of the Parisian proletariat). These arms, we might say figuratively, are those first given to the Parisians in the first *levée* in 1793 and then furnished again in 1870.

But a remarkable act of resistance prevents the recovery of these weapons. French army contingents sent to retrieve the arms are surrounded by hundreds of Parisian women and withdraw. On the following day, the Paris Commune is inaugurated. The final defeat of the workers' uprising occurs on 21 May and is followed by a series of massacres in which 20,000 French citizens are killed.[13] This is, perhaps, the most romantic uprising in revolutionary history. Its brevity, its singularity, its purity and its fate have made it a sacred moment in Marxist–Leninist–Maoist thinking.[14] For Alain Badiou, it is a model of a political event, that is, a historical circumstance at once incapable of being characterized within the existing framework of norms and language, defying categorization or representation under that framework and constituting an irrevocable break with a hitherto dominant ontology. It is the moment when there is, prior to naming, the possibility of revelation.

The *levée en masse* is connected to the idea of the event in a number of tangential, obscure but potentially productive respects. Its Napoleonic version, of course, is linked historically with the Commune. The *levée* of 1793, as we have seen, is both the instrument of (it offers the possibility of the military mobilization of proletarian mass) and stands in contradiction to (it creates a regular army capable of squashing proletarian uprising) the Commune. The mass mobilization of the Parisian population against an external enemy is precisely what gives the Commune its military power and *some* of its sense of identity.

And in the end, the attempt, by the Government, to reverse the 1793 (or 1870) conscription *levée* precipitates the French Commune. But, of course, the result of the 1793 Napoleonic conscription *levée* is a regular army capable of being deployed later by the state to crush the Commune.[15] The Commune *levée* then, is, in some respects, a conceptual and historical inversion (and reversal) of the Napoleonic *levée*.

The *levée* of Geneva 1949 and of the contemporary international law of permissible killing in war, has, of course, a different relationship to the French Commune. This Geneva conception of the *levée* seems closely affiliated to the idea of the Commune. It may be the closest the law of violence gets to an 'event'. It is, as Simon Critchley puts it, something 'that is not' (Critchley 2007). It is a negative event in the rather literal sense that it may never have happened but, also, because it is the negation of a surrounding structure of war law that is otherwise dedicated to organization, co-option, bureaucracy, solidity and permanence. The *levée* promises spontaneity and evanescence in the face of organized violence. It also is an act 'outside the state'; the hierarchy and chain of command required in disciplined war are momentarily suspended for the short duration of the *levée en masse*. The Geneva Conventions mandate a return to the state (*Oric*) as quickly as possible. And, for Badiou, this is the story of the great revolutionary moments; everyday life is transformed but only for a brief period. Invariably, the state returns and begins the process of punishment, co-option, representation and democratic alignment. And the revolutionary (left) is left with the language of betrayal, failure and incapacity (Badiou 2007: 271).

Nasar Oric's lawyers were concerned to establish the existence of a transient event precisely in order to deny that their client could have had the sort of authority over subordinates necessary to sustain a finding of command responsibility. 'Command', after all, implies something to command and a structure of command. It is possible, then, to approach the *levée en masse* as a moment in which a people wills itself into existence in a local and provisional act of rebellion (an act of what Critchley calls 'political self-determination') grounded on the ideals of equality (there is no chain of command) and unanimity (there is no time for disagreement). International law wants to celebrate (by offering protected status) and nullify (by requiring swift assimilation) this moment of resistance.

But of course the romantic *levée*, as I have described it, hardly qualifies as an event in Badiou's admittedly rigorous terms.[16] For Badiou the resistance inscribed in events is generally directed inwards at a local constellation of ideas and forces, and not at an external enemy (though the repression of the Paris Commune was directed or at least authorized by the Prussians). But more importantly, the Communards act against the state (not with it) both formally and substantively, and enact a form of politics without leadership outside the state. The event provoked by their resistance is wholly new, ground-clearing and not-yet-imagined by the incumbent law and politics. In Terry Eagleton's phrase, 'it might also transform the very criteria by which we could identify it' (Eagleton 2003: 246).[17] It seems unlikely, then, that an act like the *levée en masse* – already described and anticipated in an existing legal order – could at the same time found a new order altogether or force 'an unheard-of transcendental evaluation of the political scene ... ' (Badiou 2007: 278). On the contrary, its articulation in law, and the requirement that rebels quickly become organized, may make it part of the centuries-long defence of the 'bourgeois' state against the threat of the popular, mass uprising (Badiou 2007: 259).[18]

For Badiou, everything turns on the capacity of the political moment to create a singular and transformative rupture with the previous circumstance.[19] An event cannot be recognized or registered by the existing conceptual–political order. On one hand, the *levée en masse* is pre-registered or already neutralized by its status in law.

But, and perhaps in a more interesting sense, the *levée*'s soldier-civilian-rebels sit at the edge of the void, between otherness and identity (Cox and Whalen 2001–2). And, famously, after all, international war law has been described as the vanishing point of the vanishing point (international law) of law.[20] The *levée en masse*, a brief moment of disordered, non-hierarchical rebellion against law and against the 'enemy' state, and, in the context of war law, an 'ontological particularity' (Badiou 2007: 279) lies at the vanishing point of a vanishing point of a vanishing point.

Notes

1 The *levée en masse* first appears, in a less elaborate form, at the Brussels Conference of 1874.
2 This law is most often called the law of war or, with varying degrees of sanitization, the 'law of armed conflict' or 'international humanitarian law'. I have tried to avoid these terms in this essay.
3 In *Heart of Darkness* (written by Joseph Conrad as the Hague Peace Conference Convention of 1899 was in session), the narrator, Marlow, remembers seeing, in one of the dark places on earth (the Congo), a group of six black men in chains with iron collars around their necks. It is a bleak scene: somehow, perhaps, related to war. These men are 'enemies', according to one of the Europeans he meets. Later he reflects on this 'war' as he witnesses a ship of war firing into the continent at, what one of the seamen has assures Marlow, also are 'enemies'. Marlow says: 'but these men could, by no stretch of imagination, be called enemies. They were called criminals and the outraged law, like, the bursting shells, had come to them, an insoluble mystery from over the sea' (Conrad 1902: 23). Before this they merely are 'unhappy savages' (Conrad 1902: 22). A little later he has two epiphanies: 'they were men, men, I tell you', and then in the end he sees, 'They were not enemies, they were not criminals, they were nothing earthly now … ' (Conrad 1902: 25). It is a motif, too, of *Heart of Darkness* that the European warships are always 'incomprehensible, firing into a continent' (Conrad 1902: 20).
4 See, too, Alain Badiou, 'The Cultural Revolution: the last revolution?', speech delivered at the Maison des écrivains in Paris, February, 2002 (Badiou 2007: 291–328).
5 A partial pre-Westphalian, but continuing, exception seems to have been the *postpolit ruszenie*, or Polish militia, founded around the thirteenth century and mobilized especially during the sixteenth and seventeenth centuries in the period of the Polish–Lithuanian Commonwealth.
6 Prior to this point, the professionalization of war meant armies in the field bore the brunt of the violence. Here is Vattel: 'At the present day, war is carried on by regular armies; the people, the peasantry, the towns-folk, take no part in it, and as a rule have nothing to fear from the sword of the enemy' (Vattel 1758: 283). Such conflicts were called, in the short eighteenth century (1715–92), 'cabinet wars' (see, too, Neff 2005: 114; Anderson 1988). See, too, Gat 2008: 502.
7 Anderson 1988: 184–85. Paul Virilio, in *Vitesse*, describes the *levée en masse* as a 'kidnapping of the masses'. See Bell 2004: 66–67.
8 This 'warring citizen' is also the newly crowned 'democratic citizen', replacing the royal subject. See Anderson 2007: 205.
9 Conscription has another romantic counterpart, this one harking back to the professionalism it had displaced and was later displaced by. A.E. Houseman honoured professional soldiers in 'Epitaph on an Army of Mercenaries' (Houseman 1922). Dying for money seemed more appealing than just dying. Hugh MacDiarmid, in a typically heartless response, denounced Houseman and professionalism in 'Another Epitaph on an Army of

Mercenaries': 'They were professional murderers and they took, Their blood money and died' (MacDiarmid 1935).

10 See, too, article 13, Geneva Convention I, article 13, Geneva Convention II.

11 'the site is a figure of the instant. It appears only to disappear' (Badiou 2007: 279).

12 'This [the *levée en masse*] is an extraordinary state of affairs ... for a short while and as an interim stage of fighting ... ' (Dinstein 2004: 42).

13 Or, as Badiou puts it: the government army entered Paris '*en masse*' (Badiou 2007: 260).

14 Marx 1933, Brecht 1978, Chinese Communist Party 1971. For a discussion, see Badiou 2007: 265–70.

15 Perhaps, to complicate this a little, the mobilizations of 1793 and 1870 are themselves quite distinct. In 1793 an army is created; in 1870, a specific force is held in reserve (to be later disarmed).

16 The Paris Commune seems to have been the first 'event'; the most recent contenders are the Cultural Revolution (in the period 1967–68) and, possibly, the 1968 student protests in Paris.

17 Certainly, 'something appears in a world which had not existed in it previously' (Badiou 2007: 285) but more than this, the world is incapable of describing this new something; it explodes the categories that might allow the world to give it meaning and changes the world. After the Commune, for example, the categories of political self-consciousness are transformed. It becomes impossible to think of the working classes as lacking a political identity. The consequence (upon which 'everything' depends) is two centuries of convulsive proletarian revolution.

18 Badiou, who does not seem to have much time for international humanitarian law and who has not fully appreciated the difference between the International Criminal Court and the International Criminal Tribunal for the former Yugoslavia, accuses the latter (or is it the former?) of being a 'pure servant to imperial military intentions' (Badiou 2007: 69). This, of course, says too little to be quite true. See my book-length elaborations around this (and other) themes: (Simpson 2007).

19 See, too, Cox and Whalen 2001–2.

20 'The logic of a site involves the distribution of intensities, around the vanishing point, in which the site consists' (Badiou 2007: 280).

References

Anderson, F.M. (ed.) (1908, 2nd edn) *The Constitutions and Other Selected Documents Illustrative of the History of France, 1789–1907*, New York: Russell and Russell.

Anderson, J.M. (1988) *War and Society in Europe of the Old Regime 1618–1789*, London: Fontana.

——(2007) *Daily Life During the French Revolution*, Westport, CT: Greenwood.

Badiou, A. (2007) *Polemics*, trans. S. Corcoran, New York: Verso.

Bell, D. (2004) *Real Time; Accelerating Narrative from Balzac to Zola*, Urbana and Chicago: University of Illinois Press.

Brecht, B. (1978) *The Days of the Commune*, trans. C. Barker and A. Reinfrank, London: Eyre Methuen.

Chinese Communist Party (1971) 'Long Live the Victory of the Dictatorship of the Proletariat! In Commemoration of the Centenary of the Paris Commune', editorial departments of *Renmin Ribao* (*People's Daily*), *Hongqi* (*Red Flag*) and *Jiefangjun Bao* (*Liberation Army Daily*), Peking: Foreign Languages Press.

Conrad, J. (1902) *Heart of Darkness*, Edinburgh and London: W. Blackwood and Sons.

Cox, C. and Whalen, M. (2001–2) 'On evil: an interview with Alain Badiou', *Cabinet Magazine*, winter 2001/2002.

Critchley, S. (2007) 'A Heroism of the Decision, a Politics of the Event' *London Review of Books* Vol 29 No. 18, 20 September 2007, pages 33–34 (reviews of *Polemics* by Alain Badiou, translated by Steven Concoran Verso, 2006).

Dinstein, Y. (2004) *The Conduct of Hostilities under the Law of International Armed Conflict*, Cambridge; New York: Cambridge University Press.

Eagleton, T. (2003) *Figures of Dissent*, Verso.

Gat, A. (2008) *War in Human Civilisation*, Oxford; New York: Oxford University Press.

Hazen, C.D. (1932) *The French Revolution*, 2 vols, New York: Henry Holt and Company.

Housman, A.E. (1922) 'Epitaph on an army of mercenaries', *Last Poems*, London: Grant Richards Ltd.

MacDiarmid, H. (1935) 'Another epitaph on an army of mercenaries', *Second Hymn to Lenin and Other Poems*, London: Stanley Nott.

Marx, K. (1933; 1st edn 1871) *The Civil War in France*, London: Martin Lawrence.

Nabulsi, K. (1999) *'Levée en Masse'* is Roy Gutman and David Rieff (eds) *Crimes of War*, New York: W.W. Norton.

Neff, S. (2005) *War and the Law of Nations*, Cambridge: Cambridge University Press.

Simpson, G. (2007) *Law, War and Crime*, Cambridge and Malden, MA: Polity.

Vattel, E. de (1758) *Law of Nations*, trans. C. Fenwick (1916), Washington, DC: Carnegie.

Chapter 7

Decolonization and the eventness of international law

*Sundhya Pahuja**

Introduction

Despite the heroic attempts by imperial mandarins to tell a coherent story about decolonization as an enlightened devolution of power (Darwin 1984: 188), it was actually a varied and heterogeneous series of events (Darwin 1988: 167–222). In the mid-twentieth century, during the formation of the key institutions of contemporary international law, much of the world was still under colonial rule. Even after the end of the Second World War, it was not evident to Britain and France that decolonization was necessarily to come at all, let alone at the speed at which it was ultimately to happen (Louis and Robinson 2003: 67). Within 18 months of the end of the Second World War the Cold War had begun, and despite its dislike of overt imperialism, the United States considered it to be in its strategic interests to support elements of the French and British empires if it was necessary to prevent communism and/or Sino-Soviet expansion (Louis and Robinson 2003: 49).

Notwithstanding the strategic imperatives of the 'Great Powers', however, anti-colonial resistance was on the increase, and agitation for independence was spreading. The struggle was happening on a number of fronts. Colonial people mobilized for independence, sometimes turning to arms, in Asia, Africa and the Middle East. In addition, as time wore on, the Cold War's relationship to decolonization became increasingly ambiguous, for while the United States had initially tempered its anti-imperial stance for reasons of Cold War strategy, by the end of the 1950s it was perceived by many, including Harold Macmillan, then prime-minister of Britain, that East–West rivalry over the Third World could have an enormous impact on the outcome of what was looking increasingly like an inevitability (Macmillan 1972: 203). Indeed, even by 1957, 'it was understood [by the Great Powers] that independence for co-operative nationalists was the best chance of saving Africa from communist subversion' (Louis and Robinson 2003: 63).

In this heterogeneous unfolding of decolonization, international law was both more and less significant than is often suggested. It was less significant than elite historiographies of human rights would have us believe, for it was by no means clear that the UN charter rendered colonialism unlawful, nor that it even intentionally provided for a regulated transition to self-government for most of the colonized world. Nor did the Universal Declaration of Human Rights (UDHR), whatever its own legal status at the time, prohibit imperialism. However, it was more significant than in the realist interpretation of events, for it was not simply epiphenomenal, whether to the struggle of the colonized or to the fatigue of the métropole. Its overlooked significance resides in it having a juristic monopoly, or in the fact that it was already the universal juridical frame covering the globe. This coverage meant that international law could provide a structure by which the heterogeneous movements for decolonization could be smoothed into a coherent story and 'be contained within the broader frameworks set by western interests' (Holland 1985: 112). Thus, on one hand while international law did provide a language in which claims for decolonization could gain a certain audibility, on the other it locked in nation statehood as the only way to claim legal personality. The price of audibility was thus the nation state form and, crucially, the universal historical narrative in which that form was situated. Beyond the nation state form, this narrative limited the possible outcomes of independence more generally, and opened the way for the project of the wholesale transformation of the decolonizing societies to be both internationalized and institutionalized through the concept, discourse and machinery of development.

The ambivalence of international law's role in the story of decolonization points to a complex duality of international law's character. Law has contradictory dimensions: it is both regulatory and emancipatory, both imperial and anti-imperial. In my argument, the duality hinges on a 'critical instability' at the heart of international law. The instability is 'critical' in both senses of the word – critical *of* and critical *to* – in that it both undoes and impels international law. It arises from the way in which international law first claims to be universal, and secondly, carries with it a certain promise of justice, whether that promise be symbolic or imaginative. In relation to the universal claim, law is the 'place' or 'moment' where the generality of rules meets the specificity of the facts to which they apply. And yet both 'law' and 'fact' are mutually reconstituted in that moment. In relation to the second, it is the place where positive rules or actual institutions meet and always fall short of the promise of justice; the enlightenment's legacy to positive law. And yet international law's failure to live up to its promise of justice continually breathes life back into it, as people continue to make demands for justice in the idioms of law and rights.

Arguably this critical instability, arising from the promise of justice and the claim to universality, is what attracts political battles to the language of international legality. My retelling of the decolonization story seeks to track at least one of these battles in that context. But in accordance with the purpose of this volume, I seek here to tell the story in an idiom influenced by current theoretical (re)conceptualizations of the 'event'. Accordingly, the emphasis here lies on what we might think of as 'the political' moment of law, or on a (re)discovery of the 'eventness' of international law itself. What such an idiom can bring to the theoretical observation about law's 'critical instability' is a way to highlight the moments of deliberation and choice, and ultimately contingency, in a story usually told as part of a historical unfolding of events in which international law serves in a straightforward way as a vehicle for a progression to a more equal world governed by law. Drawing on the new language of the event helps us to understand the way in which (international) law is involved in the produc-tion of common spaces or shared experiences, and institutions as a form of life. The moments of deliberation and choice that we wish to tease out are, therefore, not those presented as 'options' in an *already* institutionalized political discourse, but nor are they unconstrained by their context. In a sense, they are the situated but 'meta' choices that determine what paths will seem open to us at any given point. In other words, we are trying to get at both what is made possible and what is made invisible by the (legal) frame of the discussion itself.

In this retelling, we are thus challenging the 'smooth' story of decolo-nization sometimes told in the register of liberal internationalism. But we are also challenging aspects of the idiom of the event, particularly as pure irruption, for we see that the events around the struggles for independence, though politically radical, cannot be thought of simply as irruptions of the new. They are also part of a longer trajectory of resistance and repetition in (international) law. As we shall see, when the excess of law's categories irrupts through the ostensibly smooth surface of the law, that excess is quickly contained, in this instance by the discourse of development.

Retelling the story

In the context of decolonization, the 'political' moment in international law is repeated several times over. It occurs especially frequently during the formation of the contemporary institutions of international law, when Third World mass politics begin to enter international law. As Rajagopal has observed, by 1948 'many Third World countries had won independence – India, Pakistan, Iraq and Syria – and they began radicalizing international institutions, especially the UN, in order to quickly annihilate the colonial system. They actively used the UN fora, including the trusteeship council, to put an end to colonialism' (Rajagopal 2003: 72). The states that had gained access to the United Nations added international law to the tools of the struggle being waged against the imperial powers with other subjugated peoples fighting against colonialism, and with whom there was a strong sense of solidarity.[1]

In the context of this struggle, a particular series of documents created during a wave of decolonization and a short but intense moment of great activity at the UN provides us with an interesting insight into the contradictory dynamic of international law. The series begins in 1960 with the Declaration on the Granting of Independence to Colonial Countries and Peoples, an initiative taken by the Third World at the United Nations General Assembly (GA Res. 1514),[2] and ends (for our purposes) in 1961 with the Declaration of the United Nations Development Decade, an initiative of the United States (GA Res. 1710).

In the years before the Declaration on Independence, the status of colonialism in international law was ambivalent at best. Indeed, it is arguable that imperialism was not unlawful according to the key documents of the new international institutions. As remarked above, neither France nor the UK was willing to question the legality, or indeed the legitimacy, of colonialism during the establishment of the United Nations. The tight constraints on the trusteeship provisions,[3] the refusal to countenance 'independence' as a goal for non-self-governing territories and the attitude to the trust territories themselves all point to the understanding that the Charter was not intended to outlaw colonialism. Several 'eminent publicists' of the time endorsed this view. Kunz, for example, asserted that '[t]he Charter of the United Nations not only fails to permit the use of force to eradicate colonialism, but it expressly recognizes the legitimacy of colonialism in Chapter XI' (Kunz 1974: 82). Similarly, Dugard observes in response to the view that colonialism has been outlawed by the Charter, that '[s]uch a view is untenable, for Chapter XI in imposing the duty of accountability to the United Nations for the administration of colonies, recognizes the legitimacy of colonialism' (Dugard 1967: 16). The Universal Declaration of Human Rights is similarly circumspect, and whatever its own legal status at the time, did not outlaw colonialism. Instead, it strove 'to secure [the] universal and effective recognition and observance [of the rights contained in the declaration], both among the peoples of Member States themselves *and among the peoples of territories under their jurisdiction*' (GA Res. 217A: preamble – emphasis added)[4] and at best extended rights to everyone *regardless* of the 'political, jurisdictional or international status of the country or territory to which a person belongs, whether it be independent, *trust, non-self-governing or under any other limitation of sovereignty*' (GA Res. 217A: article 2 – emphasis added). These explicit acknowledgements of colonial rule, the exhortation that rights should be respected within the context of that rule and the failure to condemn it must surely ratify the historical evidence that when it was written, the UDHR was not intended to outlaw colonialism, especially given the political context. Even scholars who argued in the 1950s and 1960s that international law *does* prohibit colonialism generally concede that it is arguable that the Charter recognized the legality of colonialism at the time of its drafting (see e.g. Quaye 1991: 109).

Thus at the moment of the Declaration on Independence, under international law, and even according to the key documents of the new international institutions, imperialism was not unlawful. Accordingly at the time, in its refusal of this position the declaration was enormously significant. Indeed, it is sometimes referred to as the 'Magna Carta' of decolonization (Quayson-Sackey 1963: 111). But given that the UN General Assembly is not a legislature and has no direct capacity to make or change the law, the way the declaration engages with international law is salutary: it is a 'political' moment, in that what exceeds international law can clearly be felt. This moment arises through an engagement by the Third World with international law's 'critical instability'.

The declaration begins with an appeal to the universals in the UDHR. 'Fundamental Human Rights', the 'dignity and worth of the human person', 'equality', 'social progress' and 'better standards of life in larger freedom' launch the text. As Quaye observes, the preamble decries colonialism 'by observing the universal position against the perpetuation of colonialism and expressing belief in liberation from anything that is colonial' (Quaye 1991: 112). It reads:

> The General Assembly [...] Aware of the increasing conflicts resulting from the denial of or impediments in the way of the freedom of such peoples, which constitutes a serious threat to world peace ... *Recognising* that the peoples of the world ardently desire the end of colonialism in all its manifestations [...] *Convinced* that all peoples have an inalienable right to complete freedom, the exercise of their sovereignty and the integrity of their national territory [...] *Solemnly proclaims* the necessity of bringing to a speedy and unconditional end colonialism in all its forms and manifestations.
>
> (GA Res. 1514 – emphasis in original)

These appeals in effect ignore the legitimization of colonialism in the charter and UDHR and instead tap into the instability created by the assertion of what are said to be 'universal' rights even within a framework of documents that permitted continued colonial subjugation. This uncontainable aspect of rights derives from their universal orientation and symbolic valence. This quality offers to rights a restlessness not captured by a positivist conception of human rights which would limit them to human rights *law* as it exists in treaty and custom from time to time. This restlessness is what prevents human rights from being, as Arendt feared, either tautological or useless or, as Wendy Brown puts it, from 'build[ing] a fence' around the identity of the human rights victim at the site of violation, 'regulating rather than challenging the conditions within' (Brown 2000: 231). As the growing body of critical histories of human rights shows, that is simply not the history of human rights (e.g. Douzinas 2000; Cheah 2006). The paradigmatic example often given is Olympe de Gouges, who claims from the scaffold, in the name of the rights of man, that if a woman is entitled to go to the scaffold, she is entitled to go to the Assembly (e.g. Rancière 2004; Douzinas 2000; Scott 1996). The claim for decolonization has the same paradoxical quality, for it too brings to the universal arrogation of an extant right evidence in the claimant's own person of the right's particularity. In other words, the fact that the claim for independence must be made reveals that the ostensibly universal guarantees of freedom from oppression have only a partial, and not universal, application. An analogous dynamic applies to international law generally, which also makes a universal claim and which carries with it a symbolic valence in its imaginative link to justice (see generally Derrida 2002: 228). Thus here, the universal aspirations of the UDHR and the charter provided the symbolic ground for a claim made in legal terms against a practice which those documents had themselves arguably acquiesced in and regulated.

So on one level the uncontrollable or potentially radical aspect of international law is engaged in this example. International law's claim to be universal and its promise of justice facilitate this political moment of law. But if law's universal claim opens it up to that which exceeds it, it is the flip side of that universal claim which gives it an imperial dimension. Here, for example, the claims to justice and universality in the Declaration on Independence represent a resistant deployment of law against itself in relation to colonialism per se. However, in making that claim in a legal frame, the Third World cannot free itself from the sticky logic of international law's founding categories, and in particular, from nationalism.

Nation statehood, like international law, had its own paradoxical dimensions, of the potential inherent in the promise offered by its very assertion to universality, combined with the specificity of what was in fact being universalized (Fitzpatrick 2001: 127). If the nation is the universal form of collective political organization in the sense of being axiomatic, it is clearly not actually universal, either in the sense of every collective entity already existing as a nation state, nor in its cultural origins and form. The nation's universality is therefore a *claim*, and one which can be sustained only by rendering the non-nation somehow aberrant. This aberrance is narrated as a function of the passage of time; non-nations are not nations *yet*. Similarly, nation states which 'failed' were narrated away as not yet developed enough to achieve and maintain the nation state form, leaving unchallenged the orthodoxy that nation statehood was the natural form of collective politico-territorial organization. The story thus explains the actual existence of the non-nation in the face of the nation's claim to be universal by setting the non-nation on a path of transformation toward the (exemplary) nation state. In this way, both the putative universality of the nation state form and the need for the transformation of non-nations are rendered axiomatic. The price of finding an institutional language for the struggle for decolonization was therefore social transformation, and the internationalized project which ultimately came with it.

Indeed, in the Declaration on Independence itself, the critique of coloni-alism does not question the ostensibly axiomatic need for the transformation of colonized societies but instead argues that 'a backward nation could "modernize" *itself*' (Chatterjee 1993: 30 – emphasis added). The call for independence is based on the argument that colonialism 'prevents the development of international economic cooperation [and] impedes the social, cultural and economic development of dependent peoples' (GA Res. 1514). In other words, the civilizing mission is discredited and the alleged infer-iority of the colonized people is denied, *not* on the basis that the societies of colonized peoples are acceptable as they are, but because they can transform *themselves*, enhancing the naturalization of the necessity for transformation.

Similarly, the demand for independence cast in the frame of universal human rights requires an acceptance of the particular, European origins of human rights' putative universality. Even 'universal' rights still require an external particularity to secure themselves, for as Chatterjee has observed, if the universal really were universal, it would simply dissolve as a category (Chatterjee 1993: 17). Thus even as the colonized rely on the 'universality' of certain rights, the 'society', 'culture' and 'economy' of the 'dependent peoples' are offered up as the particularity which that universality must cut into. Relying on 'universal' rights to protect a 'particular' culture reinforces the particularity of one culture and sustains the universal claim of the other. Here this particularity is marked through a need for transformation, hence the framing of colonialism as an impediment to 'the social, cultural and economic development of dependent peoples' (GA Res. 1514). Thus once again, development, expressed here as a modernization narrative, opens that which is being protected to the need for transformation over time, rendering it vulnerable through its very mode of protection.

The paradox offered by the particular origins of universal rights to those claiming them was mirrored by the difficulty facing anti-colonial French intellectuals during the battle for Algerian independence, around the same time. As Le Sueur astutely observes, 'the French–Algerian war was the ultimate political litmus test for French intellectuals who were placed in the awkward position of defending the universal values of their personal, collective and national identities on the one hand, and on the other, siding with a people who largely denied this universalism. It was unques-tionably a cruel paradox: to affirm and subvert at the same time [...] To affirm by subversion, this was for intellectuals [...] the only truly orthodox anti-colonial position' (Le Sueur 2003: 115; Louis and Robinson 2003: 49).[5] But if the anti-imperial French intellectual had to affirm by subversion, then the Third World at the General Assembly had to subvert by affirmation, and what they tacitly affirmed was the need for their own transformation.

In making the Declaration on Independence, the Third World attempted to confine this sphere of transformation to a putatively distinct category of the 'economic' sphere. It then tried to subordinate economic development to the political sphere. Hence the declaration asserts the right of all peoples to 'freely determine their political status and freely pursue their economic, social and cultural development' (GA Res. 1514). Such an attempt was based on the idea that colonial peoples must 'seek first the political kingdom',[6] asserted here in the affirmation that 'peoples may, for their own ends, freely dispose of their natural wealth and resources' (GA Res. 1514). But no matter how many times the right to choose one's political and economic status was reiterated,[7] developmental orthodoxies and the institutional machinery would quickly make clear that the genie of development, and its concomitant demand for an ever-widening sphere of transformation, could not be contained.[8]

Several resolutions and declarations in the General Assembly followed, each attempting to reassert the 'political kingdom' and its supremacy over the economic.[9] Resolution 1515, for example, on Concerted Action for Economic Development of Less Developed Countries, made shortly after the resolution above, 'Reaffirms [the universal principles of the Charter] now when so many states have recently become members of the United Nations'. It urges the employment of international machinery for 'the promotion of the economic and social advancement of all peoples' but only through *voluntary programmes of the United Nations*' (emphasis added). It also asserts that '[t]echnical assistance and the supply of development capital [...] whether provided through existing and future international organizations and institutions or otherwise – should be of a kind and in a form in accordance with the wishes and recipients and should involve *no unacceptable conditions* for them, political, economic, military or other'.

This particular attempt to assert the power of self-definition ominously presages the extraordinary expansion of conditionality in World Bank and International Monetary Fund lending in the years to follow, but the seeds of that expansion are planted in the very same gesture. For like the Declaration on Independence before it and the nationalist movements before that, built into these resolutions was a belief that differences between the First and Third Worlds could be explained by the stage of a country's development and a faith in 'development' as the way to redress the global inequalities between rich and poor nation states, all the while trying to hold on to the possibility of difference and political sovereignty over the economic sphere. Resolution 1519 is a perfect example of this, for it recognizes 'that expansion of international trade between countries of *different social and economic systems* as well as of trade between countries at *markedly different stages of economic development*, is of real importance for the progress and welfare of all peoples, contributes to the strengthening of peace and constitutes one of the most *efficient means of accelerating the increase in the rate of development* of the less developed countries, many of which have recently become members of the United Nations' (emphasis added).

The context in which these resolutions were passed at the General Assembly was, of course, the wave of decolonization, particularly in the former French colonies of Africa, and the triumphant entry of those states into the United Nations in 1960 (Betts 1998: 99).[10] Britain too underwent a marked change in attitude towards decolonization from 1959 onwards (Darwin 1984: 203). Back at the United Nations, Cold War impediments to its security functions in the face of wars being waged by the 'Great Powers' by proxy in the Third World meant that it was an institution looking for something to do and a consensus within which to do it. Development as a nascently universal faith with a seemingly flexible content provided the perfect ground for agreement to be found and for institutional activity consequently to blossom (Rist 1997: 89). Thus at the tail end of this series of resolutions we have the Declaration of the United Nations Development Decade (GA Res. 1710). This declaration refers to the Declaration on Independence, as well as the related resolutions 1515, 1516, 1519 and 1526 mentioned above, and links decolonization and economic development in a seemingly unbroken continuum.

The idea for the declaration on a decade for development originated in a speech by the then US President, John Kennedy, to the US Congress followed up by a similar speech to the UN General Assembly in September 1961 (Rist 1997: 90). The development declaration followed in December of the same year. This declaration not only bound together decolonization and development with a firm yoke, but put forth a highly specific agenda for development which was to be echoed repeatedly in development discourse up to the present day (for the continuities of some aspects of the declaration, see Rist 1997: 90, 91). Indeed, the proposals have become part of development orthodoxy despite attempts to question their universal applicability regardless of the circumstances of different countries, the counter-factual evidence which emerged in the years to follow and their intrusive effect. The three key elements of the proposal were: to place economic growth at the heart of development, subordinating other domains to growth; to mediate the contradictory relationship between self-interest and welfare within development discourse; and to reassert development as the key horizon of hope for the future.

Growth subordinates other objectives of the decade such as '[m]easures to accelerate the elimination of illiteracy, hunger and disease', which are not put forward as worthwhile ends in themselves but as impediments to the greater goal of 'development' because they 'seriously affect the productivity of the people of the less developed countries' (GA Res. 1710: para. 4(d)). Both the centrality and primacy of growth are reiterated in the secretary-general's proposals for the programme made pursuant to the declaration, in which U-Thant observed that 'Development is not just economic growth.

It is growth plus change' (cited in Rist 1997: 90). As Rist observes, although this was meant to attack economic reductionism and question the sufficiency of growth as the content of development, the 'hard core' of development is still growth (Rist 1997: 90). The 'change' tacked on is both unspecified and additional. This adumbrates the way development was to balloon into the generalized transformation of society effected through economics as the master discipline.

The second key element of the proposal, to weave the self-interest of the developed world and the welfare of the developing world together into a single narrative, was achieved in part through the assertion that foreign direct investment was a 'development resource' (GA Res. 1710: para. 2(c)) and that 'international economic co-operation' (GA Res. 1710: para. 6) would foster 'improve[d ...] world economic relations' (GA Res. 1710: para. 6) and contribute to international peace and security. U-Thant's subsequent proposals elaborate on this idea further, asserting that '[t]he acceptance of the principle of capital assistance to developing countries is one of the most striking expressions of international solidarity as well as enlightened self-interest' (U-Thant 1976: 143). The idea that the development of the underdeveloped is in the global interest foreshadows the way that the political and economic teeth were removed from attempts to assert a New International Economic Order and to make a claim to Permanent Sovereignty over Natural Resources through a casting of those resources as somehow belonging to the 'international community' as a whole (Pahuja forthcoming; McVeigh and Pahuja 2010). However, the contradiction between an ostensibly disinterested solidarity and self-interest is already being mediated here, almost through simple incantation. As Rist points out, 'to say that one has an interest in being disinterested is to place oneself in a double bind' (Rist 1997: 91). He suggests that 'it would appear that the antinomy contained in such thinking gradually faded away by dint of repetition, as if one could get used to any nonsense in the end' (Rist 1997: 91). However, it is arguable that both the centrality of economic growth and the horizon of development play into how that contradiction was sustained.

But the last element is perhaps the most significant in the context of law's critical instability, its promise, and the new language of the event. This element is the way that development is posited as both process and horizon (see also Beard 2007: 1–2) such that it seems to be the only way to address global material inequalities. In other words, it stands in here as a proxy for 'justice'. Already in this declaration there is an elision between the search for 'social progress and better standard of life in larger freedom' and the 'economic and social development of all peoples' (GA Res. 1710: preamble). This is tied to the way development is still continually reiterated as a space of hope, despite the mountain of evidence of the violence, dislocation and immiseration brought in its name. As Easterley puts it almost 50 years later, reports on what development has achieved almost invariably begin with a more than sobering account of past failures, together with a reasserted hope in the horizon despite the failures, in the vein of 'catastrophic but improving' (Easterley 2006: 133). Already in the declaration on the development decade we find a 'recogni[tion] that during [the past decade] considerable efforts to advance economic progress in the less developed countries were made' combined with the tragic recognition that 'in spite of the efforts [...] the gap in [...] incomes between the economically developed and the less developed countries has increased ... ' (GA Res. 1710: para. 2). The resilience of development as a horizon is testament to what we might think of as its religious quality, or its existence in the realm of faith rather than 'science'. Such a position leaves it immune from attack, causing developmental failures in the years to come to be attributed to the insufficiency of the transformation of the 'developing' society rather than casting any doubt on the prescription. This is evidenced through the ever more tentacular expansion of developmental interventions and to the increased violence of the transformative logic that development sustains.

The overt link between 'larger freedom', 'social progress' or something we might call 'justice' and development is notable also for its failure to mention imperialism. Indeed, apart from the cross-reference to resolution 1515 (the Declaration on Independence), neither decolonization nor imperialism is explicitly mentioned at all. 'Poverty' and inequality are simply due to 'underdevelopment'. This both renders axiomatic the transition from former colony to developmental nation state and precludes a consideration of the causes of inequality as including imperialism or the ongoing dislocations of the globalization of capitalism (see generally Bagchi 2006) to be continued in the years to follow under the very mantle of development.

Conclusion

How then are we to understand decolonization as an event in international law? On one hand, much international law scholarship celebrates this period in retrospect as the moment when everything changed. In that body of scholarship, decolonization is understood as the end of imperialism and a purely European international law, and a key or originating moment of the 'real' or 'true' universalization of the international community and the reflection of that broader community in international law (see for example Jenks 1958; Röling 1960; Anand 1966. See also Garci-Amador 1983: 289). On the other hand, others, including many Third World scholars,[11] would question this assertion and argue that in this shift little, if anything, changed. According to that argument, a retrospective analysis requires that we see imperialism as continuing beyond this period under another name.

In contrast to both these positions, decolonization in my argument is not a moment of either/or, but rather a moment of both/and. It can be understood as a particularly *post-colonial* event. 'Post-colonial' in that it was neither still imperial nor newly liberatory, and yet it was both; formal sovereignty was forcefully claimed by and extended to the former colonies, but it did not bring the new equality it promised. But 'post-colonial' too in the sense that the 'universalization' of international law in this moment did effect a shift from the old rationality of rule to one which in the operative *mode* of that rationality was precisely the assertion of universality (Pahuja 2005: 459).

What then of the new language of the event, with its focus on the production of common spaces, and an institutional life? If the 'post-colonial' somehow marks a moment in which both the exercise of power and the struggle against it are conducted in the language of universality, then our thinking around the post-colonial *event* must be concerned with what happens to institutional life in that struggle. In this example, we see a 'political' moment of law, in which universals are in competition. This competition is 'evental' in that it marks the impossibility of absolute foundations. Indeed, if only at its most radical, the absence of a single universal implies the absence of a single international law. But this irruption of the new is limited by its coming into being in law. The event can be known through law's critical instability, but law still imposes limits on what can be known. In this moment of instability, the answer to every question quickly became development. A plurality – of meaning and institutions – could not itself be institutionalized. Much of the world did decolonize, but politically, international law itself needs ongoing strategies of decolonization – which highlight the contingency of its foundations and draw out what is lost and excluded in each actual founding – to minimize its imperial tendencies. Perhaps that then is the character of the post-colonial event in international law: a meshing of decision, deliberation and institution in which the event happens, but never quite takes place?

Notes

* The author wishes to thank Shaun McVeigh for comments on an earlier draft of this chapter.
1 The Bandung conference is a good example of this. There are many books on Bandung, but see generally Kahin 1956.
2 The resolution was passed by a vote of 89–0 with 9 abstentions. The abstentions included Britain, the US, France, Portugal and South Africa.
3 To territories of the former axis powers, former mandates and territories voluntarily included: see above.
4 Universal Declaration of Human Rights (1948).
5 Le Sueur goes on to observe that the political transformations of the period unleashed the intellectual and ideological processes and positions which heralded the advent of postmodernism.
6 This is of course a reference to Kwame Nkrumah's famous exhortation to 'seek ye first the political kingdom and all else will follow'.
7 This was also a significant part of the Bandung Declaration for example: 'Final Communiqué of the Asian-African Conference' (in Kahin 1956: 84).

8 And indeed, there were also self-preservational and rent-seeking reasons why many national elites accepted the constraints – and funding – that accepting the need for 'development' offered. The perceived twin imperatives of development and Cold War politics meant that such rent-seeking was legitimized more often than not by the 'international community'.

9 Notably Concerted Action for Economic Development of Economically Less Developed Countries (1960); Economic and Social Consequences of Disarmament (1960); Strengthening and Development of the World Market and Improvement of the Trade Conditions of the Economically Less Developed Countries (1960); Land Reform (1960).

10 1960 saw the independence of Senegal, Ivory Coast, Mauretania, French Sudan (Mali), Dahomey (Benin), Upper Volta (Burkina Faso) (all from French West Africa Federation); Chad, Gabon, Central African Republic, Congo Republic (all from French Equatorial Federation); Madagascar, Nigeria (Betts 1998: 99).

11 By this I mean, *inter alia*, the self-identified group of TWAIL, or Third World Approaches to International Law scholars, as well as several other scholars of international law with connections to or sympathies for the Third World (see generally Anghie *et al.* 2003).

References

Anand, R.P. (1966) 'Attitude of the Asian-African states towards certain problems of international law', *International and Comparative Law Quarterly* 15: 54–75.

Anghie, A., Chimni, B., Mickelson, K. and Okafor, O.C. (eds) (2003) *The Third World and International Order: Law, politics and globalization*, Leiden: Brill Academic Publishers, Martinus Nijhoff.

Bagchi, A.K. (2006) *Perilous Passage: Mankind and the Global Ascendancy of Capital*, New Delhi: Oxford University Press.

Beard, J.L. (2007) *The Political Economy of Desire: Law, Development and the Nation*, Abingdon, Routledge-Cavendish.

Betts, R.F. (1998) *Decolonization: The Making of the Contemporary World*, London, New York: Routledge.

Brown, W. (2000) 'Suffering rights as paradoxes', *Constellations* 7(2), 230–41.

Chatterjee, P. (1993) *Nationalist Thought and the Colonial World: A Derivative Discourse*, Tokyo: Zed Books. First pub. 1986.

Cheah, P. (2006) *Inhuman Conditions: On Cosmopolitanism and Human Rights*, Cambridge, MA: Harvard University Press.

Concerted Action for Economic Development of Economically Less Developed Countries (1960), G.A. Res. 1515 (XV), UN GAOR, 15th Sess., 948th plen. mtg, UN Doc. A/RES/1515 (XV) (15 December 1960).

Darwin, J. (1984) 'British decolonization since 1945: a puzzle or a pattern?', in R.F. Holland and G. Rizvi (eds), *Perspectives on Imperialism and Decolonization: Essays in Honour of A.F. Madden*, London: Frank Cass.

——(1988) *Britain and Decolonization: The Retreat from Empire in the Post-War World*, Basingstoke, London: Macmillan.

Declaration on the Granting of Indepence to Colonial Countries and Peoples (1960), G.A. Res. 1514 (XV), UN GAOR, 15th Sess., 947th plen. mtg, UN Doc. A/RES/1514 (XV) (14 December 1960).

Derrida, J. (2002) 'Force of law: The "mystical foundation of authority"' in J. Derrida *Acts of Religion* (ed. and trans. G. Anidjar), New York, London: Routledge.

Douzinas, C. (2000) *The End of Human Rights: Critical Legal Thought at the Turn of the Century*, Oxford: Hart.

Dugard, J. (1967) 'The Organization of African Unity and colonialism: an inquiry into the plea of self-defence as a justification for the use of force in the eradication of colonialism', *International and Comparative Law Quarterly* 16, cited in C.O. Quaye (1991).

Easterley, W. (2006) *The White Man's Burden: Why the West's Efforts to Aid the Rest Have Done So Much Ill and So Little Good*, Oxford: Oxford University Press.

Economic and Social Consequences of Disarmament (1960), G.A. Res. 1516 (XV), UN GAOR, 15th Sess., 948th plen. mtg, UN Doc. A/RES/1516 (XV) (15 December 1960).

Fitzpatrick, P. (2001) *Modernism and the Grounds of Law*, Cambridge: Cambridge University Press.

Garcia-Amador, F.V. (1983) 'Current attempts to revise international law: a comparative analysis', *American Journal of International Law* 77(2): 286–295.

Holland, R.F. (1985) *European Decolonization 1918–1981: An Introductory Survey*, London: Macmillan.

Jenks, C.W. (1958) *The Common Law of Mankind*, London: Stevens.

Kahin, G.M. (1956) *The Asian-African Conference: Bandung, Indonesia, April 1955*, Ithaca, NY: Cornell University Press.

Kunz, T. (1974) *Terrorism in International Law*, cited in C.O. Quaye (1991).

Land Reform (1960) G.A. Res 1526 (XV), UN GAOR, 15th Sess, 948th plen. mtg, UN Doc. A/RES/1519 (XV) (15 December 1960).

Le Sueur, J.D. (2003) 'Decolonizing "French Universalism": reconsidering the impact of the Algerian War on French intellectuals' in J.D. Le Sueur, *The Decolonization Reader*, London, New York: Routledge, 2003.

Louis, W.R. and Robinson, R. (2003) 'The imperialism of decolonization', in J.D. Le Sueur, *The Decolonization Reader*, London, New York: Routledge, 2003.

Macmillan, H. (1972) *Pointing the Way*, London: Macmillan; cited in J. Darwin 'British decolonization since 1945: a puzzle or a pattern?', in R.F. Holland and G. Rizvi (eds), *Perspectives on Imperialism and Decolonization: Essays in Honour of A.F. Madden*, London: Frank Cass, 1984.

McVeigh, S. and Pahuja, S. (2010) 'Rival Jurisdications: The Promise and Loss of Sovereignty', in C. Barbour and G.Parlich (eds) *After Soveregnity: On the Question of Political Beginnings*, Routledge.

Pahuja, S. (forthcoming) *Decolonising International Law: Development, Growth and the Politics of Universality*, Cambridge, UK: Cambridge University Press.

—— (2005) 'The postcoloniality of international law', *Harvard Journal of International Law* 46(2): 459–469.

Quaye, C.O. (1991) *Liberation Struggles in International Law*, Philadelphia: Temple University Press.

Quayson-Sackey, A. (1963) UN SCOR, 18th Sess., 1042nd mtg, para. 77, cited in C.O. Quaye (1991).

Rajagopal, B. (2003) *International Law from Below: Development, Social Movements and Third World Resistance*, Cambridge: Cambridge University Press.

Rancière, J. (2004) 'Who is the subject of the rights of man', *South Atlantic Quarterly* 297: 103(2/3).

Rist, G. (1997) *The History of Development: From Western Origins to Global Faith*, trans. P. Camiller, London, New York: Zed Books.

Röling, B.V.A. (1960) *International Law in an Expanded World*, Amsterdam: Djambatan.

Scott, J. (1996) *Only Paradoxes to Offer*, Cambridge, MA: Harvard University Press.

Strengthening and Development of the World Market and Improvement of the Trade Conditions of the Economically Less Developed Countries (1960) G.A. Res. 1519 (XV), UN GAOR, 15th Sess., 948th plen. mtg, UN Doc. A/RES/1519 (XV) (15 December 1960).

United Nations Development Decade: A Programme for International Economic Co-operation (I) (1961), G.A. Res. 1710 (XVI), UN GAOR, 16th Sess., 1084th plen. mtg, UN Doc. A/RES/1710 (XVI) (19 December 1961).

Universal Declaration of Human Rights (1948), G.A. Res. 217A (III), UN GAOR, 3rd Sess., 183rd plen. mtg, UN Doc. A/RES/217A (III) (10 December 1948).

U-Thant (1976) 'Foreword to the United Nations Development Decade: proposals for action' in A.W. Cordier and M. Harrelson (eds), *Public Papers of the Secretaries-General of the United Nations, Volume VI, 1961–1964*, New York and London: Columbia University Press.

Chapter 8

Post-war to new world order and post-socialist transition

1989 as pseudo-event

Scott Newton

For international law in 1989, the significance of the collapse of state socialism might initially have been imagined to be indifferent or trivial. International law had no 'position' to take on what ultimately was a series of individual domestic crises in a dozen European (Eurasian) states, remarkable only for their relative simultaneity. For international law, at least initially, 1989 betokened nothing more than an unusual temporal concatenation of succession and recognition issues, to be managed as they traditionally had been: case by case, with a fig leaf of doctrine to cover the obligatory political accommodation of regime change.

As things proceeded, '1989' (using the year as a kind of shorthand for the collapse of state socialism in Eastern and Central Europe and, after a further two years, in the USSR itself and the ensuing transformation of the geopolitical landscape; that is, the 'world-historical' 1989 rather than the calendrical 1989) rapidly assumed the dimensions of an epochal event, a demarcation and boundary which had the effect of definitively 'periodizing' the post-war international legal order, or 'Postwar' (Judt 2006), dividing it from an ostensible successor international legal order – the 'new world order', or globalization.

This event 1989 for international law, the implications of which are elaborated in the next section below, cannot well be analyzed in isolation from the aforementioned domestic crises which precipitated it, cumulatively now known as the 'transition'. Indeed the connection between the force of event in international law and *événement* in the classic Badiouvian sense of a mass mobilization or uprising is particularly tight for 1989, since the fall of the Wall, quite literally a result of direct popular action (brick by brick), and seemingly an event par excellence, set in motion (or at least carried forward) the train of events which brought in the new world order. The elusive and loaded nature of this domestic transition is explored in the concluding section. While both the 1989 new world order and the 1989 transition possess the trappings of a Badiouvian event, a supervenient and transformative rupture, upon closer inspection they each more closely resemble what one might venture to call a 'pseudo-event', staged or managed (or co-opted) by an existing configuration of power or authority, rather than spontaneously generating any new such configuration on the basis of new revolutionary subjectivities: full of sound and fury, but signifying a consolidation rather than a transformation. The new world order turned out to be an updated version of an old hegemony and the transition more of an assimilation.

1989 and the new world order

The emerging order of 1989 came swiftly to signify a reconceptualization and reconstruction of the post-war order: 1989 was 1945 reordered, the international system reimagined and reinvented. The so-called 'Peace of Paris' (Bobbitt 2003), which could be regarded as the Peace Treaty ending the Cold War (indeed the Peace Treaty for the War of the World, in Niall Ferguson's usage (Ferguson 2007)), resolved its principal internal legal questions (borders, sovereignty). But it also prepared the ground for a new international dispensation, premised on cooperation and the 'universal' adoption of a shared set of values and principles, the holy trinity of markets, democracy and human rights. Nineteen eighty-nine gave birth to the 'international community', united in purpose and programme as the United Nations had only ever been in embryo, as the wartime alliance. The new order issuing from the event of 1989 (and which reciprocally was held to confirm the status of 1989 as event) purported for the first time to be both global in scope and liberal in character, economically and politically the end of history, in the words of its enthusiasts (Fukayama 1993).

This new order would, however, preserve the inherited international institutional architecture, revitalizing and buttressing it and introducing some modest alterations (promulgation of new standards, creation of some new institutions). In the views of its champions, its chief features might be characterized as set out in the following sections.

I. Revitalization of international law and institutions

The disappearance of ideological polarity from international legal discourse and of the concomitant rote adversarial deployment of international legal argument heralded a new dispensation of harmony, and made possible the revitalization of multilateral institutions. This marked a mostly unlooked-for and serendipitous episode of renewalism, and made 1989 a chance to do 1945 again and get it right. The nations which had 50 years before successfully united for war and then much less successfully for post-war were now finally in a position to realize the abortive promise of perpetuation and universalization of the alliance, this time round as the 'international community'.

2. Economic liberalism and the creation of global economic space

Liberalism was enshrined as the organizing principle of the global economic order, and international economic law as its regulatory framework. The superiority of markets as the principle governing the allocation of social goods appeared beyond challenge, and the appropriate boundary between public and private became for the first time a matter of public international determination. International economic law, both the hard law of the GATT/WTO and the soft law of the IFIs (the international development law of the new age), supplied a functional regulatory framework for the new globally integrated economy.

3. Political liberalism and democratic proliferation/consolidation

For the first time the international legal order enshrined liberal-democratic governance as at least a regulative ideal, if not an actual standard or template. No longer would perversely surviving illiberal ideology exercise an artificial, irrational and anachronistic restraint on the universal valorization of constitutional governance and the rule of law, accompanied by international patronage and promotion, and leading to eventual general adoption.

4. The triumph of human rights

Human rights, which had been a struggling and marginal component of the previous international legal order, was elevated and made a pillar of the succeeding order. In collective humanitarian intervention, the human rights regime finally acquired an enforcement arm, even as it was rescued from its crippling political instrumentalization by the contending Cold War adversaries and from its sustained assault by their proxy wars. Delivery from evil was now something the international legal order was finally in a position to secure for violated populations.

5. Global collective security and the new emphasis on 'human security'

A functional global collective security regime was now in prospect, upon the overcoming of Cold War proxy conflict facilitation/fomentation. No longer would collective security remain a hostage to ideological rivalry, but would belatedly realize its promise as a safeguard against any and all threats to the peace, including gross and systematic human rights abuses and terrorism.

But that event could at the same time be read as masking continuity under the guise of change, completing a hegemonic project which long antedated it. Its promise of a rupture or departure was thus illusory from the start. Nineteen eighty-nine more appropriately qualifies as a pseudo-event and the new world order as but an edited version of the preceding order, an intensification of certain of its features at the expense of others, sooner a reduction or simplification than a reconceptualization or reinvention.

The Cold War was a geopolitical and international legal glaciation, which upon receding, unexpectedly and rapidly, might have opened up an entirely new zone for 'adaptive radiation', for a proliferation of innovative and imaginative approaches to so-called global governance (here borrowing the term 'adaptive radiation' from evolutionary biology, where it refers to the rapid proliferation of morphological diversity consequent on the exploitation of newly available ecological niches, e.g. by mammals after the extinction of ruling reptiles at the end of the Cretaceous period or upon the raising of a land bridge between separated continents: see Simpson 1984). The Cold War had constrained international legal implementation and innovation save for tinkering at the margins (the rise of Human Rights, the New International Economic Order (NIEO)) and artificially locked and aligned multiple other political currents (such as decolonization and anti-colonial struggles) within its frozen field. Its end promised to release a surge of international legal creativity and indeed, for a period in the immediate aftermath of 1989, established approaches and doctrines seemed in some sense to be up for grabs.

But the glacial recession marked by the end of the Cold War only made way for the colonization by the West of international institutional space. The international legal order, far from being augmented or enriched was, if anything, 'thinned out' and homogenized, suffering a loss of diversity as a vulgarized, reduced form of the normative institutional regime of Western industrialized democracies was adopted as the new global standard. The pseudo-event of 1989 carried a series of consequences for international law, which, evaluated from a position of political–critical awareness or by a metric of political imaginativeness or creativity, could only be deemed retrogressive. For each of the canonical claims enumerated above on behalf of 1989 as event, a counterclaim can be advanced on behalf of 1989 as pseudo-event.

1. Impoverishment of international legal discourse and the loss of counter-positions in international legal argument

The Soviet wager on international law was always a calculated one, designed to advance the interests of the Soviet state as defined by the Kremlin, interests which for ideological and strategic reasons came to coincide with a set of emancipatory interests (decolonization, social welfarism, etc.). But that wager had all sorts of highly interesting and creative and at least collaterally progressive features – from the rise of Third World solidarity to the enduring prominence of social and economic rights. In particular, the success of the NIEO and the Non-Aligned Movement was underwritten by the Soviet school of international law. The socialist bloc included powerful states in a position to interpret and apply international legal doctrines against the prevailing grain (Bowring 2008), on behalf of the former colonial world in its continuing struggle for international justice and equality.

During the Cold War there was no 'international community' in the sense of a community of common interests and values. There was rather a system of warring or contesting visions and ideologies and values. But the absence of an international community meant that international law itself was terrain for contestation and struggle; it was the common idiom of adversaries, not the agreed script of the like-minded. The pseudo-event that gave rise to the international community, that made of geopolitical space one church, pacified that contested terrain, making it a hegemonic field rather than a 'demilitarized zone'. And the hegemon in question was the familiar world sheriff, the USA, with its incomparable capacity to project (soft cultural/ economic and hard military) power globally and a justificatory ideology for doing so (amplified below).

2. Neoliberal orthodoxy and economic constitutionalism

The rise of international economic law betokened economic constitutionalism and the corseting of economic and social development options into the 'market-enabling' prescriptions of deregulation and privatization (Scheuerman 1999). The disappearance of the 'Second World' (or its assimilation into the First) afforded the opportunity to entrench and institutionalize the Washington Consensus on the international plane. At the same time, it cut the remaining legal ground out from under the now politically exposed Third World, even as international inequality became of undeferable urgency. Thus the extraordinarily swift delivery of the WTO after a gestation of 50 years became possible – indeed inevitable – once the triumph of capital was assured and the industrialized powers were uniformly market states.

3. Governance discourse, thin democracy and cultural hierarchies

Governance (or what in non-technocratic terminology was once called government, i.e. the political organization of society) became a focus of international standardization, regulation and concern. On the one hand, the coupling of markets with human rights and political liberalism resulted in a thinned-down, second-class version of democracy, largely procedural and formal, and centred around elections (Marks 1998–99). On the other, complex, situation-specific approaches to the challenges of societal pluralism and the political accommodation of cultural/ethnic difference were eschewed in favour of a state-centric insistence on sovereignty and borders, coupled with a reactivization of the colonial-era categories of civilization and barbarism.

Nowhere was retrogression more in evidence than in the transition zone itself, although its wider consequences were perhaps most pernicious in the global South. Here, in a context of shocking ethno-nationalist and regional violence in former Yugoslavia (Croatia, Bosnia-Herzegovina, Macedonia and Kosovo) and USSR (Tajikistan, Georgia, Azerbaijan, Chechnya) – 'events' themselves which might all serve as the perfect negation of the supposed event of 1989 – the response of international law was a dismal failure of imagination and a recursion to anachronistic norms and practices. The OSCE National Minorities regime effectively reintroduced Versailles-era conditional or earned sovereignty (Rasulov 2006). In a parallel move, the European Union, in the doctrine articulated by its Badinter Commission (see Pellet 1992; Radan 2000), reaffirmed a doctrine of simple external self-determination (political community defined by national boundaries) and revived-by-revising the decolonization doctrine of *uti possidetis*, allowing federal boundaries in the federal states of Yugoslavia, USSR and Czechoslovakia to become national boundaries, but insisting on their subsequent inviolability. At one stroke, international law found itself hamstrung in responding flexibly and creatively to vexing post-socialist self-determination claims and conflicts and accorded posthumous honour to socialist federalism, which had been derided in life.

4. The truncation and reduction of human rights

With the disappearance of the socialist regimes and their championship of social and economic rights, human rights have become reduced to the residual, now default category of political and civil rights: individual rights against overt coercion and violence, of the sort that grab headlines and pack benefit rock concerts, have eclipsed collective and solidary rights against structural coercion and violence. From a discourse against power, human rights in multiple respects appeared to have mutated into a discourse of power, manifested most tellingly by the invidiously applied doctrine of collective humanitarian intervention and its corollary, the responsibility to protect (Orford 2003: ch. 5).

5. Reactionary security regimes (employing anathematizing discourse and interdicting praxis) and the resurgence of imperialism

The advent of the newly solidary international community was anchored, if not engineered, by the US as hegemon, or hyperpuissance. The initial manifestation of a multilateral security system under unified command was the first Iraq War ('classic' chapter VII breach of the peace); its latest manifestation the second Iraq War (imperial prerogative behind a fig leaf of threat to peace). Over the intervening stages of collective humanitarian intervention (Haiti, Bosnia, Rwanda), selective humanitarian intervention (Kosovo), responsibility to protect (East Timor) and self-defence (Afghanistan 2001), the security regime appeared inexorably to revert to a familiar Great Powers scenario (Simpson 2004).

But the wider effects of the new security regime must be sought outside the UN Security Council, in the array of internationally institutionalized counter-policies and-strategies which have insidiously shifted in the direction of a police world, surely more daunting a prospect than a police state, by deploying 'globalized counterviolence' (Balibar 2001): counter-trafficking, counter-narcotics, counter-insurgency and, finally and culminatingly, counter-terrorism. All such policies and strategies have carried over into the new world order a moralizing and depoliticizing mix of the Manichaeism of the Cold War, the civilization–barbarism dichotomies of the colonial era and the penal categories of a pre-sociological criminology.

1989 and transition

The false dawn or pseudo-event of 1989 that was the new world order can only be adequately understood when grasped in conjunction with the pseudo-events of transition. That is, the reaffirmation and consolidation of the emergent hegemonic international legal constellation (in the succession of post-war to new world order) was paralleled and enabled (underwritten) by the rigid, overdetermined, ideologically loaded and politically strait-jacketed trajectories of transition: from plan to market, in canonical World Bank shorthand, or between any analogous set of fixed and fetishized start points and end points: collectivism to individualism, totalitarianism to democracy, tyranny to freedom. (Less gloriously but more accurately, the salient transition was from state bureaucracy to state democracy, in Badiou's terminology.)

The effort to proclaim the historical significance of transition was, from the off, an ideologically overdetermined one. The triumphalist narrative of the demise of state socialism and the vindication of free market democracy quickly assumed hegemonic and therefore unchallenged dimensions. But transition is an anodyne term for an ugly idea, which domesticates, de-fangs and de-claws, even neuters. To bracket a historical process as transition is precisely to empty it beforehand of any revolutionary import, to strip it of eventness: it does not erupt but flows, it is gradual not ruptural. Imagine the term transition in connection with revolutionary change: the 'Bolshevik transition' or, say, the 'Maoist transition', and the occult ideological vector of transition will immediately become evident. Formulated in the political science literature as a term for the shifts from authoritarian to democratic rule in the Latin American cone and southern Europe in the 1970s (see O'Donnell, Schmitter and Whitehead 1986), it betokened a movement back from excess to normalcy, a restoration of health after a pathological interval, a process of political detumescence or detoxification. So transition is vectoral, its direction and its destination already plotted: transitions are always to some posited status quo ante.

For Badiou, in stark contrast, an *événement* has the quality of an interruption or an eruption, a supervention, a break in the conventional, customary, quotidian, established: it comes from without, and once launched, it establishes its own logic of unfolding. Nineteen eighty-nine initially seemed to possess precisely this spontaneous, supervenient character, as analysts and theorists were quick to note. But if the unplanned nature of 1989 and its apparent deficit in agency is what conferred upon it the status of event, it at the same time is what rendered it susceptible to revocation of that status, to co-optation, pre-emption and interruption. Truth be told, 'radical contingency' of the Badiouvian variety was probably never in prospect in 1989, or perhaps only for a vanishingly brief moment. Indeed, it is difficult under these circumstances to treat transition as a failed event under one of the three heads of political evil for Badiou: simulacrum or the form without the content of truth (the cardinal Nazi sin), betrayal, and the 'unnameable' or absolutization (the cardinal Stalinist sin) (Badiou 2002: ch. 5). That is why transition is perhaps better understood as non-event or pseudo-event rather than abortive or failed event.

For lamentably, after the evacuation of the political–institutional space once occupied by state socialism, no 'third way', either hybrid or 'excluded middle'/alternative, was ever really in view or conceivable. The fall of the Wall was owing to implosion, not explosion; collapse, not overthrow; and hence led to capitulation, not production or regeneration. The real event, the moment of opening and release of possibility, of the removal of constraints on political imagination, thus preceded the transition itself, in the mass repudiation of actually existing socialism (AES) of 1989, facilitated and enabled by earlier elite efforts at its reinvention, notably perestroika.

Transition marked the collapse, or at least the dramatic eclipse, of a 150-year-old politically emancipatory project: the project that came to replace it was precisely *not* emancipatory or progressive or radical or innovative. From the right, it was represented as a belated liberation (or an awakening from a prolonged nightmare). From the left, it was represented as capitulation and a defeat, but not in a grudging or coerced manner (as might be supposed for the other objects of neoliberal demands to conform in the manner of IMF structural adjustment). It was more a failure or collapse of political imagination and energy, on the part of all and any potential subjects of the events. Offe has noted that this revolution lacked revolutionaries and any sort of revolutionary agenda or programme (Offe 1996). But surely the transition, damned in its very name, lacked political subjectivities as such: there were no subjects of the event; that is, the event never caught fire, captured the imagination, produced subjects capable of actualizing it or carrying it forward. What if they gave a revolution and nobody came? The exhaustion or depletion of revolutionary ambitions or energies defines transition – it could not be imagined otherwise. This is the foretold end of history, not as the triumphalists would have it, because liberal market democracy had arrived Muhammad-like, as the seal of the ideologies, immediately superseding and rendering obsolete all previous and all competing ideologies, but owing to a strange inertness or paralysis.

Indeed, it seems distinctly odd to employ the '68 term *'les événements'* to describe the upheavals of the transition period, even at its most dramatic – the opening and destruction of the Wall in Berlin, the gun battles with the Securitate in Bucharest and the execution of the Ceausescus, the Prague crowds celebrating the Velvet Revolution – the rare moments when the transitional approached the revolutionary. But 1989 was never going to be 1789, not even *in* 1989. The 'miraculous' occurrences of the autumn of that year, leaving Western observers delightedly astonished (and Eastern elites dismayingly astonished) at the swiftness of the collapse ('Can you play that again?' ran one famous end-of-year headline), were rapidly emptied of any utopian promise or potential, certainly for participants. They have therefore retrospectively come to signify not as political *'événements'*, but rather as clinical sequelae: the street-level manifestation of a systemic infarction. The suddenness with which endogenous East German reconstitution gave way to exogenous unification over the ensuing year can well stand as synecdoche for the whole arc of transition: the way in which transformation was overtaken by assimilation.

And indeed, it was precisely the absence of any prolonged turmoil or uncertainty regarding post-collapse systemic choice that reassured Western elites: the sequel to AES was not going to assume any threatening sustained mass or collectivist character. The crowds assembled in public squares throughout the bloc in the autumn of 1989 (Prague, Budapest, Berlin) were required decently and expeditiously to disperse and go home, once they had done their duty of delegitimizing the outgoing regimes, so as to clear political space for the incoming regimes. *Pouvoir constituant* was expected obligingly to yield (this time, without any fuss at all) to *pouvoir constitué*. The failure of socialism in its bureaucratic, ossified form was not going to mark a return to revolutionary plasticity and freedom of experimentation. It excluded any possibility of the renewal of socialist politics or reinvention of socialist forms and instead marked socialism's demise *tout court* as a practical political project. And that demise was greeted with relief as a sign of institutional maturity or realism, the surest bulwark against the resurgence of the tyranny and illiberality that had characterized AES.

However, the tyranny or illiberality which so offends the liberal sensibility and thus serves to damn the state socialist project *as such,* together with the series of events (of 1789, 1848, 1871, 1905, 1917) which engendered it, should be distinguished from the collectivist moment, which by definition informs any *événement* in Badiou's sense. Events are excessive; they exceed the liberal subjectivity and summon or generate precisely a subjectivity of another sort. Political subjectivity cannot be reduced to liberal subjectivity – liable, it seems, to offence at any mass mobilization, any getting out of hand, any departure from the institutional and the regulated and the ordinary. Revolutionary events must give that offence, precisely insofar as they are always excessive. The need to corral, cabin, channel and confine incipient events (as those of 1989) immediately into safe, known, institutional modes, categories and processes and away from threatening extra-institutional, or extra-ordinary ones is evidence of this elementary liberal/bourgeois allergy to radical moments.

However, AES had received perhaps its most trenchant critique not from the right but from the left, in the aftermath of *les événements* of 1968 (both those of Paris and Prague) and subsequently. The New Left – the avatar of Western Marxism of the 1960s and 1970s, with its diverse range of theoretical voices, from Habermas and Offe to Althusser, Marcuse and Negri – held no brief and spared no mercy for the tyrannical armature of AES. In 1968 the left turned its thunder on the USSR after the invasion of Czechoslovakia with none of the prevarication and equivocation that marked the stance of the Parti Communiste Français, for example, to the show trials of 15 years before, as indeed to Stalinism in general. The relation of that critique to the dissident movements of the East was, however, always problematic: the dissidents were not of the left, they were not even 'left deviationists', but neither were they of the right, or 'right deviationists' though many later found themselves happily on the right side of the political spectrum in post-socialist circumstances – they were antipolitical, champions of civil society as an expressly antipolitical thrust.

Indeed the left critique of AES was premised on disappointment in the face of failed promise – a failure to live up to ideals, ideals of examination and self-scrutiny as much as ideals of democracy. This was a performative as much as (or more so than) a conceptual critique: a critique of socialists in power rather than the AES they created, continuing and renewing a tradition of intra-left critique which dated from the debates of the Second International and its aftermath (Luxemburg's critique of Leninist authoritarianism). The critique was above all a critique of *the failure of critique*, its abdication and abortion by elites as an enabling condition of Stalinism: the combination of defensiveness, orthodoxy and violence. Badiou identifies this as the political evil of the totalization or absolutization of the truth of an event.

The gulf between Western and Eastern Marxism has thus proved wider than that between the fell and mighty opposites of the Cold War – that is, Western liberal capitalism and Eastern Marxism – as the stalwarts of the latter made for the most part untroubled accommodation of the former when the time came. But the absence of critique, of critical standpoints and critical discourse deprived the societies of transition states of the necessary resources for maintaining fidelity to an event, even supposing 1989 had constituted one. (Badiou's sin of the betrayal of the truth of an event). One positivist mode (capitalism and state democracy) succeeded another positivist mode (socialism and state bureaucracy), and the crack opened by the supreme critique that is the event was immediately sutured. The emergence thereafter of the new world order of globalized capitalism and resurgent imperialism was thus emphatically not event, enabled as it had been only by the foreclosure of event, or pseudo-event, which was transition.

References

Badiou, A. (2002) *Ethics: An Essay on the Understanding of Evil*, London: Verso.

Balibar, E. (2001) 'Outlines of a topography of cruelty: citizenship and civility in the era of global violence', *Constellations*, 8: 15–29.

Bobbitt, P. (2003) *The Shield of Achilles: War, Peace, and the Course of History*, London: Penguin.

Bowring, W. (2008) *The Degradation of the International Legal Order: The Rehabilitation of Law and the Possibility of Politics*, Oxford: Routledge-Cavendish.

Ferguson, N. (2007) *The War of the World: History's Age of Hatred*, London: Penguin.

Fukayama, F. (1993) *The End of History and the Last Man*, London: Penguin.

Judt, T. (2006) *Postwar: A History of Europe since 1945*, London: Penguin.

Marks, S. (1998–99) 'Guarding the gates with two faces: international law and political reconstruction', *Indiana Journal of Global Legal Studies*, 6: 457–95.

O'Donnell, G., Schmitter, P. and Whitehead, L. (1986) *Transitions from Authoritarian Rule*, vols 1–4, Baltimore: Johns Hopkins University Press.

Offe, C. (1996) *Varieties of Transition: the East European and East German Experience*, Cambridge: Polity.

Orford, A. (2003) *Reading Humanitarian Intervention: Human Rights and the Use of Force in International Law*, Cambridge: Cambridge University Press.

Pellet, A. (1992) 'The opinions of the Badinter Arbitration Committee: a second breath for the self-determination of peoples', *European Journal of International Law*, 3: 178–85.

Radan, P. (2000) 'Post-secession international borders: a critical analysis of the opinions of the Badinter Arbitration Commission', *Melbourne University Law Review*, 24: 50–76.

Rasulov, A. (2006) 'A legal realist critique of the new international law regime relating to the treatment of minority communities in Eastern and Central Europe (a dialectical theoretical inquiry)', Ph.D. dissertation, University of Hull, on file with author.

Simpson, G. (2004) *Great Powers and Outlaw States: Unequal Sovereigns in the International Legal Order*, Cambridge: Cambridge University Press.

Simpson, G.G. (1984) *Tempo and Mode in Evolution*, New York: Columbia University Press.

Scheuerman, W. (1999) 'Economic globalization and the rule of law', *Constellations*, 6: 3–25.

Chapter 9

The liberation of Nelson Mandela

Anatomy of a 'happy event' in international law

Frédéric Mégret

There are few enough happy events in international law that when one occurs it is likely to make a strong impression and likely that its memory will linger for a long time. The liberation of Nelson Mandela, as the symbolic end of the regime of apartheid (or at least the beginning of the end), was arguably such an event, and it is inseparable from a certain historical feeling that new horizons were opening up for international law and human rights. It is also inseparable from the history of international organization, and in particular of four decades of the issue of apartheid being in some form or other on the agenda of the United Nations (UN).

Not that a number of other events couldn't have qualified as similarly significant for the end of apartheid and for international law in the early 1990s. In terms of the end of apartheid, the constitutional transition of 1994 was clearly the turning moment. In terms of the definition of the era, the fall of the Berlin Wall probably outclassed most events. But both of these were large, structural events that perhaps lacked the individual poignancy of the release of Madiba (as Mandela is often affectionately known in South Africa). There was, in other words, something simultaneously particularly epochal and particularly personal about the slow emergence of that heroic figure on that heated and seemingly interminable afternoon of February 1990. The event was also an especially happy one because it had been awaited for so long – 27 years, no less.

A great event, therefore, but was it … an 'international law' event? There are, surely, more helpful characterizations. A personal, political, social event: all of these are, perhaps, more evident ways of seeing it. It was, moreover, a South African and an African event, perhaps before it could truly be described as an 'international' event. What are the ways, therefore, in which it might be described as an 'international', 'legal', and indeed an 'international legal' event?

There were certainly elements of 'law' in the liberation of Mandela: this was, after all, a liberation from prison. However purely political the decision to free him may have been, it did herald the demise not only of a political but an entire legal apparatus. Indeed, the apartheid regime had, like some racist or dictatorial regimes before it, been a powerfully *legal* regime. Maybe it was also *il*legal, but that did not prevent it from being very fond of the law, in its own perverse way. Mandela was not simply executed like so many victims of the South American 'dirty wars'; he was tried, sentenced and sent to jail. Apartheid was 'racism made law'. Furthermore, although primarily in some ways a South African event, the end of apartheid had a much larger global resonance. It fitted within a larger scenario of ending the Cold War. More generally, a considerable part of international public opinion had identified strongly with Mandela's plight over the years, and the apartheid regime was widely abhorred. But what did international law, a law traditionally thought to apply primarily to the relations between states, specifically have to do with this process?

The question may seem a strange one to raise given how much the fight against apartheid became an international and United Nations *cause célèbre* (see, for instance, United Nations Department of Public Information 1994). The international community certainly gives itself credit for substantially contributing to the downfall of apartheid. Boutros Boutros-Ghali (then UN Secretary-General) once spoke of the 'four decades' of UN involvement and the fact that universal organization 'has spearheaded the international campaign against apartheid'. Or, in a slightly more ornate style: 'The United Nations raised its flag against the evil of apartheid. The world joined against it. ... I pay tribute to the international organizations and the Member States who contributed and who stood together with you.'[1] In international organizations and human rights circles, the end of apartheid is widely seen as one of the great victories of international law, a 'model of international human rights change' (Black 1999). This is what might be described as the conventional 'internationalist' account of the end of apartheid, one rich with the echo of numerous General Assembly resolutions.

But the heroic story of the UN 'raising the flag of the anti-apartheid struggle' is maybe a little too self-serving to be entirely convincing. We should probably be wary of international law claiming too much for itself, as if to validate its particular narrative of justice. The temptation to 'personalize' international law as an autonomous force for progress is at best a simplification, at worse an unhelpful ex post reconstruction. What exactly, then, are we to make of this claim that international law was at the forefront of the demise of apartheid? What is the real link between international law and major domestic political change? Is international law cause or consequence of the 'event'?

A simplistic 'command-and-control' vision of international law would no doubt opt for causality. But the project of international law – and it has to be said that it is often misunderstood outside its limited sphere – is probably less a claim to be respected than a claim to *transform*. International lawyers know that their body of rules is not quite as established as they feign to treat it, and their project is not so much one of reigning as it is one of *taming*. It is less a system of rules than a process of programmatic change. It should come as no surprise, then, that the system relies even more on the occasional validation by 'happy events', or that this magic moment of liberation seems more defining of international law than four decades of blatant violation.

In that sense, however, there is always a risk that the international legal narrative will 'steal' the victory from some other, most likely non-international, actor. What might be excluded from international law's triumphant account of the end of apartheid? As it happens, there is little doubt that the greatest credit for the end of apartheid comes from forces *internal* to South Africa, often forgotten in accounts that focus on London, Washington and New York. The African National Congress (ANC), the Inkatha, the South African Communist Party, the Pan-Africanist Congress, the Azanian People's Liberation Army, the Black Consciousness Movement, the Black Sash, the National Forum, the United Democratic Front, the Liberal Party, the Armed Resistance Movement, the South African Indian Congress, the Organization of Coloured People, Poqo, Umkhonto, Isolera Sydafrika-Kommittén (ISAK), the Congress of South African Trade Unions (COSATU): all contributed in varying degrees to the collapse of the system they abhorred. Their crucible was the Defiance campaign, the Congress of the People, the Treason trials, the Sharpeville massacres, the Soweto uprisings and the Purple Rain protest. That narrative is, of course, an internally complicated one in that it was at times riddled with rivalries.[2] But what is obvious is that these movements were largely home-grown, and that apartheid would never have come to an end were it not for the relentless pressure they applied to the South African Government. Indeed, the 'international community' was occasionally happy to recognize this, as when Boutros-Ghali emphasized that, 'The destruction of apartheid is a tribute to the people of South Africa' (Boutros-Ghali 1994).

However, it would also be wrong to see the South African anti-apartheid movement itself as exclusively domestic. Although its roots may have been largely in South African reality, it was very adept at 'internationalizing' its struggle. The Congress of the People had, as early as 1955, evidenced a keen intent to put the world on notice:

> We, the people of South Africa, declare for all our country and the world to know: that South Africa belongs to all who live in it, black and white, and that no Government can justly claim authority unless it is based on the will of all the people.[3]

A small delegation of the ANC attended the All African People's Conference in Accra in 1958. After the party was banned from domestic politics, hundreds of ANC members went into exile, continually and successfully spreading the struggle abroad. It was the ANC which first called upon the United Nations to impose sanctions on the regime. In fact, by the 1980s, the ANC could successfully claim to be a sort of 'government in waiting', and was treated as such by many on the international stage. The home-grown struggle against apartheid did manage, therefore, to tap into a number of international resources that were made available by international law.

So international law probably did have something to do with the end of apartheid but not, one can speculate, merely as a resource waiting to be tapped into by non-state actors. International law arguably has a dynamic of its own, a dynamic that is both endogenous and exogenous, a product of the norms themselves and of those who produce and manipulate them.

The conventional starting point, then, would be to explore the norms. International law is, under at least one view, primarily about its norms (rather than, say, its institutions, its processes, its policy outcomes, etc.). On that level alone, the question of international law's attitude to apartheid is a little more complicated than it may seem at first. The Universal Declaration of Human Rights (UDHR), adopted by the General Assembly in 1948, proclaimed that 'all human beings are born free and equal in dignity and rights' (UDHR 1948: article 1). This was clearly incompatible with the then emerging regime of apartheid, which explains the abstention by the South African Government in signing the UDHR – although it also bears saying that the United States Government voted enthusiastically for the UDHR even as many of its southern states practised segregation. With the adoption of the human rights covenants and particularly the Convention on the Elimination of All Forms of Racial Discrimination (CERD), which specifically targeted apartheid, international law provided the basis for a fairly fundamental and continuous critique of the regime that held Mandela prisoner. Of course, the dominant view of the normative importance of human rights would become internalized by the South African Government, which adamantly claimed that apartheid meant 'separate but equal', or that it was merely privileging group rights over individual rights, or that the 'tribal homelands', or bantustans, were about honouring black South Africans' right to self-determination. That was, in a sense, a moderate tribute of vice to virtue by a regime that still otherwise belonged sufficiently to the Western tradition that it could not simply turn its back entirely on what that tradition was meant to stand for. Yet the fact that it fooled no one also showed that a norm of racial equality had gained enough traction that one could not deny its existence with total impunity.

At the same time, international law comes with a little more baggage than simply condemning racial discrimination; in particular, a strong norm of state sovereignty. That norm was one of the pillars of the UN charter, to the shaping of which, incidentally, Jan Christian Smuts, then Prime Minister of South Africa, had strongly contributed. For all the arguments that international law offered against apartheid, it also offered arguments not to intervene in South Africa, for example by imposing sanctions or an embargo. South Africa largely boycotted the United Nations, arguing that the universal organization was not respecting its own charter. Indeed, the regime sought to manipulate the norm of sovereignty itself in more or less transparent ways, for example by creating bantustans, which it claimed were sovereign (though no one believed this claim). Furthermore, other states occasionally came to the rescue, as when the US ambassador at the General Assembly argued that a country's 'policies' were not an appropriate matter for the credentials committee to consider.

What is more, the International Court of Justice, when given a historic opportunity to hear of the policies of the regime in South West Africa, stuck to a narrow understanding of who had *locus standi* before it, in what is still largely considered to be the court's biggest missed opportunity. In the South West Africa cases, in which Ethiopia and Liberia alleged various violations of the Mandate for South West Africa by the Republic of South Africa, the court decided by the President's casting vote that neither party had any legal interest in the subject matter of their claims and therefore did not pronounce on whether South Africa had contravened its obligations.[4] For every sovereignty-based argument, of course, international law could probably conjure its converse, or at least an argument that sovereignty was not involved either strictly (the repudiation of the existence of Transkei or Swaziland, and of the policy of 'grand apartheid') or broadly (the elevation of apartheid to the level of a crime made it much more difficult to argue that this was solely an internal matter). But at the very least the norms were initially not entirely determinative of the issue, and a modicum of clarity emerged only with the passage of time.

The story is less one of the content of the norms than of their dynamic interpretation. The key development in the decades leading to 1990 was the gradual rejection of the idea that violations as massive as that of apartheid could hide behind the shield of sovereignty. Early in the history of the UN, India had sought to bring the issue to scrutiny, only to be told that this was an issue that fell within the internal affairs of South Africa. However, as if to validate the international community's resolve, the South African regime, in addition to being internally repressive, also turned out to be externally adventurous and hegemonic, spreading its infectious brand of discrimination to other territories. The 1989 Declaration on Apartheid and its Destructive Consequences in Southern Africa would eventually make explicit the link between apartheid and the existence of a threat to international peace and security. Long before this, however, the Security Council had seized itself of the question. It considered, for example, that the Sharpeville massacre, on the face of it a major but nonetheless strictly domestic event by the classical standards of international law, was of a nature to cause major international frictions and was as such within its mandate.

This sort of development was certainly accompanied by international law, but did not simply emerge from the organic and continuous process of its interpretation. Rather, it sprang from very real political agendas which brought about new understandings of international law. It is clear that the metaphor of a benign 'international community' speaking with one voice – which is already questionable in ordinary circumstances – can be particularly misleading when used retrospectively to gloss over the elements of power play at work in achieving anything like a united front. The international system was always quite fragmented when it came to the issue of apartheid, both about how reprehensible the regime was and what could and should be done to facilitate a transition. Although South Africa had few open allies (Portugal and Israel were, at different points, the exception), it certainly had a measure of support from a small but powerful minority of states. A number of states which ultimately rallied strongly against apartheid were not always so adamant about change. Economic sanctions were for a long time opposed by South Africa's key trade partners and as a result remained non-mandatory. US President Ronald Reagan and UK Prime Minister Margaret Thatcher, in particular, were inspired by a belief that South Africa was the key to controlling a resource-rich continent and, moreover, that it was an ally in the Cold War whose regional power could not be totally undermined. South Africa was only too happy to play the anti-communist card, participating in the Berlin airlift in 1948, fighting in the Korean war and generally brandishing the spectre of Soviet regional domination. There was also scepticism in some quarters about the ANC and its ability to one day rule South Africa. It was, in fact, only by the second half of the 1980s (almost the dying days of the regime) that countries like Britain and the US adopted laws imposing trade sanctions on South Africa. Even then, several governments more or less explicitly called for the repeal of sanctions at the smallest sign of improvement in South Africa. This was in contrast, for example, to the Nordic countries, which proved steadfast in their opposition to apartheid, offering consistent support, including financial, to the ANC.

The challenge to the status quo imposed by these few but powerful states can be seen as having come through three routes. First, a 'pan-Africanist' or 'Third World solidarity' route. The resistance to apartheid bears a close affinity to African struggles of national liberation (even though what was at stake in South Africa was something more complex), and the fate of this resistance was closely tied to processes of decolonization elsewhere. Those significantly redefined the geopolitical reality of (notably) southern Africa and also helped swell the ranks of those who might support the ANC in international fora. African states were more directly and aggressively supportive of the role of black South Africans, particularly through the Organization of African Unity (OAU) (e.g. the Lusaka Manifesto or Mogadishu declaration). Some of these states provided the ANC and Pan Africanist Congress with bases. Nigeria had a pioneering role in promoting sporting boycotts against South Africa. The Afro-Asian group, formed in 1955, was also very influential at the UN, particularly the General Assembly. Even though it came at a substantial economic cost to some of South Africa's neighbours (Zimbabwe, Mozambique), the condemnation was largely consistent and unwavering.

A second very important contribution to the ending of apartheid was the mobilization of what might be described as domestic and transnational civil society. In the West, it proved a powerful shaming force to move governments to adopt sanctions and, essentially, treat the South African problem as one of human rights violations rather than as a geopolitical or economic issue. It was a diverse, bottom-up, informal type of civil society that was hardly restricted to formal human rights non-governmental organizations but also included students, trade unions, churches, city councils, sports associations, consumers ('Housewives, don't buy South African goods', began a famous British Anti-Apartheid Movement leaflet), artists and even schoolchildren. Perhaps most strikingly, in a move that was then unprecedented and which would not be replicated at any time soon, civil society successfully pressured many leading corporations to launch a policy of divestment vis-à-vis South Africa. Somewhere at the intersection of Third World solidarity and transnational civil society, the role of the African diaspora, particularly in the United States, deserves a special mention. There was a strong affinity between the civil rights movement, in particular, and efforts undertaken in South Africa to overthrow the systematic segregation that was apartheid. The American Negro Leadership Conference on Africa, the Black Caucus and Transafrica were important factors in getting Congress ultimately to pass the Comprehensive Anti-Apartheid Act in 1986, even against the will of Reagan.

Finally came the role of international organizations, and of the UN in particular. The aforementioned developments, for all their potency, remained very disparate and required formalization to become actual policies. International organizations or mechanisms, particularly those that were dependent on some sort of majoritarian decision making (e.g. the General Assembly), provided the appropriate venue. The first international calls for sanctions were made in the General Assembly (Resolution 1761, 6 November 1962) by African states, and led to the establishment of the Special Committee against Apartheid, which would become the focal point of efforts within the UN to marshal support against the South African regime. The Secretariat itself had responsibility for the Centre against Apartheid, which had a key role in publicizing the anti-apartheid cause and disseminating information about the nature of violations. A UN Trust Fund for South Africa was created to support the victims of apartheid. The existence of a strong universal normative condemnation of racial discrimination meant that the UN bound its hands normatively, as it were. In the event, its anti-apartheid stance managed to be both principled and interested. As Nelson Mandela put it, it was:

Because apartheid reduced and undermined the credibility of the UN as an effective international instrument to end racism and secure the fundamental human rights of all people, [that] its establishment and consolidation constituted a brazen challenge to the very existence of this organization.

(Mandela 1994)

Security Council involvement opened the way to the creation and gradual tightening of an embargo (voluntary from 1964, mandatory after 1977) on military goods, petroleum and raw materials, despite lukewarm support from the US, Britain and France. The council went so far as specifically to call for the liberation of Mandela and other political prisoners in resolutions. Other organizations also contributed, including the European Community, the Commonwealth (which pushed South Africa out in 1961) and the International Olympic Committee.

The liberation of Mandela, thus, must be retold as all these narratives at once, and not merely or strictly an international law one. The international system created huge pressures for the regime to reform, if only to show signs of goodwill and release some of the pressure. Each time it did so, however, it found itself on a slippery slope of pressing demands for ever more reforms. Locked in a widespread crisis of debt, employment, capital, budget, growth, credit, investment, balance of payment and trade, the South African Government eventually found that its economic and therefore political options were dwindling fast. The autocratic and defiant mood it sometimes sought to adopt was not economically viable, even if the regime thought it sustainable politically and militarily. The gradual marginalization and ostracization of the South African Government was the outcome.

This overall path of change was as much the product of actors and forces as it was the result of norms and processes. In the end, it was the convergence of a diversity of approaches that created an exceptionally united front against apartheid, even though motivations for wanting the end of the regime varied. Keen observers of the role of 'norms' in international relations have it right when they point to a 'spiral model' of human rights enforcement in which domestic struggles become transnationalized, internationalized and eventually supranationalized to ultimately come back and haunt the target government (Risse-Kappen et al. 1999). International law was essential to that process by both enabling and endowing it with a veneer of legitimacy. But the role of international law in precipitating the liberation of Mandela lay less in the strength of its injunctions than in its ability to point out the distance between norms and reality ... even as it was part of the production of that distance. International law, in brief, was more sounding board than orchestrator.

What made the event a 'happy' one for international law? Not simply the liberation of Mandela, nor the promise of the imminent breakdown of the apartheid regime, even though that certainly had something to do with it. The elation also lay in what the demise of apartheid meant – or could be understood as meaning – for international law itself. In ordinary times, at most times, international law can be said to be lingering in a chronic state of depression, torn between conflicting priorities: the promise of certainty and the reality of compromise; an overinflated humanist rhetoric and the depressing litany of violations. This made the liberation of Mandela a happy 'international law event' for three reasons.

First, it offered the prospect of some of international law's promises actually becoming real with the passage of time. The 'happy event' is precisely what momentarily and heroically breaks the cycle of repetition. Of course, the ambiguity remains as to how much 'international law' had to do with the outcome. But international law had clearly gone on the record stating that its norms were at stake; it could at least not be faulted for being on the wrong side of history. It provided at least a continuous forum for condemnation of the regime and a conduit through which anti-apartheid strategy could be channelled. It also probably helped to shape a peaceful transition by talking not only to the white Government but to the leaders of the ANC. Nelson Mandela may not have 'owed' his liberation to international law, but international law provided a powerful way to interpret that liberation as the symbol of something greater and as a signal for international law's own liberation of sorts.

Second, if one sees international law as a normative system constantly under strain as a result of the tensions within which it is embedded – human rights–sovereignty, progress–status quo, justice–order, peace–violence – then the end of apartheid offered, albeit briefly, an ephemeral resolution of the tensions. The event was 'happy' because it was unique, and it was unique precisely because it brought together actors and interests (Northern–Southern, Western–Eastern) that were otherwise often on opposite sides of the international system. It suggested that the interstate and the transnational, the supranational and the cosmopolitan, justice and security could all converge if not permanently, then at least temporarily to effect massive change. Nelson Mandela articulated it perhaps most clearly and succinctly when expressing his gratitude:

> [w]e stand here today to salute the United Nations Organization and its member states, both singly and collectively, for *joining forces* with the masses of our people in a common struggle that has brought about our emancipation and pushed back the frontiers of racism.
>
> (Mandela 1994)

Third, if international law helped in bringing about post-apartheid South Africa, it must also be said that the collapse of apartheid helped shape international law in a very positive way. The event is both arguably an outcome of the law and a powerful trigger for the law. In that respect, it is worth mentioning that it is not the international law of 1948 that defeated apartheid; apartheid changed, but so did international law in dealing with it. The international law of the 1950s afforded the South African Government every assurance that it could, by and large, maintain its project of racial domination. By contrast, the international law of the late 1980s was rich with the awareness of its past insufficiencies (at least as regards the treatment of that one particular issue) and was eager to seize the opportunity to redefine itself as a source of human rights and change. The end of apartheid therefore was not so much a product of 'international law' as it was an event that facilitated the *transformation* of international law.

The event, of course, also takes on a particular resonance with the passage of time. Today, with the Johannesburg suburbs still in abject poverty, the very unequal distribution of wealth in the 'rainbow nation' and the occasional bout of violent xenophobia, it can certainly seem like the transition has not quite delivered on its promises. The fragile silhouette of Mandela emerging from Victor Verster Prison remains a distant one. Yet perhaps the beauty of the 'event' is that it remains encapsulated in time, a moment disconnected at once from its cause and outcome, splendidly isolated from the ebb and flow of time, the reminder of a promise rather than of what went wrong.

The same is perhaps true of international law. The end of apartheid served to cement the new post-Cold War broad consensus on the need to promote human rights internationally. It showed that international law could reform, even reinvent itself under the early pressures of globalization. It redefined the frontiers between the domestic and the international, sovereignty and justice, international peace and security and human rights. Once the door into a state's domestic policies had been pried open by human rights, once core issues of treatment of a sovereign's citizenry had been internationalized for the entire world to criticize and condemn, that door would no longer be closed (although that would not prevent states from looking the other way). It showed the power of sanctions when used well (i.e. against a country that was conceivably vulnerable to them) – a lesson that wouldn't always be applied in the future – but also the attached political and moral dilemmas.[5] It bequeathed to the world a crime that would eventually make its way to the Statute of the International Criminal Court as a crime against humanity (despite the remarkable international reluctance to detect any instance of apartheid aside from the original). It showed, ultimately, the power of unity and resolve and, to no small extent, the power of principle to catch up with reality.

With its (big) sister event, the fall of the Berlin Wall, the end of apartheid also inaugurated the era that was to follow, in an extraordinarily auspicious way. This is by contrast with the era conventionally held to follow the post-Cold War (or 'globalization') era, namely the 'post 9/11 world', a sequence of history that began in such apparent fracas and destruction that it has sometimes seemed like nothing but destruction could come from it. In that

respect, the souvenir of the 'happy event' has lingered on long after its promise has been exhausted to the point of being fossilized, instilling a particular
mood of optimism about norm and institution building which not even
failure in Somalia, extermination in Srebrenica or genocide in Rwanda could
seemingly alter. The evocation of the event helped sustain the international
community through the long wait till the next event, and whose absence
would eventually leave us with only the familiar humming sound of efforts,
process, management, regulation.

In retrospect, however, it was easy to read too much into the demise of
apartheid and international law's role. For one thing, while the liberation of
Mandela told us something about what international law could achieve in
the best of cases, it did not provide us with a yardstick of success for the
future. In fact, the sort of epochal moment towards which all actors and
values converge is something that the post-Cold War world has sought to
emulate since, but with only limited success. This is partly because what was
right for Cold War politics was not necessarily what was needed for its
aftermath. The Cold War provided a particular geopolitical antagonism that
made human rights appealing as a prescription to transcend East and West
through a common challenge to sovereignty. In a sense, the post-apartheid
world is one where international human rights, although perhaps not dominant, have at least been ideologically and politically much more at home.
With power came the trappings of respectability, but also the familiar
doubts associated with its exercise. The international human rights movement has since made headway towards the triple promise of increased inter-
nationalization, institutionalization (from the High Commissioner to the
International Criminal Court) and enforcement. But in the process it has
arguably lost its more heroic ways. When it would come to Kosovo, China
or Zimbabwe, the lines would not always seem as clearly drawn, nor the
right policy prescription so evident.

One reason why it has been difficult to recapture the energy that led to
the liberation of Mandela is because the international human rights agenda
has never really managed to build itself into the sort of collective popular
movement found in the anti-apartheid struggle.[6] National liberation
and Third Worldism as collective, solidarist, totalizing ideologies probably
exercised a much more significant hold on the imagination of masses than
the comparatively bland promise of democracy and the rule of law could ever
hope for (see, for example, Houser 1992). Indeed, perhaps one of the dangers
is to read too much validation of the international human rights narrative
into the liberation of Mandela. Of course, international human rights law
had *something* to say about the incarceration for more than two decades of
an individual for his political opinions, not to mention the existence of a
regime based on racial discrimination and violence. But the intensity of the
fight against apartheid was linked primarily to its ability to associate itself
closely with the themes of national liberation struggles, anti-colonialism and

anti-imperialism (Black 1999). This Third World agenda never needed 'international human rights' to tell it that racial discrimination was wrong, and it remains to this day quite a distinct agenda from the more conventional and Western human rights narrative (indeed, the latter's reformist slant has come to dominate over the former's more radical aspirations).

Indeed, describing apartheid as *simply* an instance of systematic violation of the right to freedom from discrimination might curiously have diminished and de-contextualized that particular form of discrimination (white against black, in Africa, linked to the history of colonization and imperialism), by making it more an illustration of a universal than a concrete irreducibility. On the one hand, of course, it was precisely this constructive misunderstanding that made it possible for actors on opposite sides of the political spectrum to agree (for quite different reasons) on the need to dismantle the apartheid regime. On the other hand, the legacy of this misunderstanding arguably remains with us to this day, as when the successor of Mandela himself, Thabo Mbeki, could not find it in himself resolutely to confront fellow national liberation hero Robert Mugabe for his human rights violations (to Western consternation).

It was perhaps also, as a consequence, easy to read too much for the prospects of international law into that one event. Maybe what made it easy for international lawyers to speak so unanimously and vociferously against apartheid was that South Africa was so isolated. In a world where discrimination, racism and exclusion are otherwise rampant, the South African regime was perhaps uniquely at fault for inscribing its racism *in the law*. As such it had critically miscalculated the times and the degree to which, had it not been for the momentary paralyzing power of the Cold War, it was doomed to failure. Moreover, apartheid was a relatively easy issue to 'internationalize' legitimately, given the regime's external adventurism, its mishandling of its mandates and the resulting perception that it concretely rather than simply metaphorically threatened international peace and security. The international campaign against Khmer Rouge genocide did not fare nearly as well, even though this regime killed more than a million people. International law, in the end, worked to bring about Mandela's liberation, but it may have worked not so much thanks to itself as because it was mobilized by the right actors at the right moment, and for their own powerful motives.

Furthermore, there is all that the event does not capture, that the event cannot explain, and that it might indeed perniciously presume to be solved. It can be argued that in apartheid, international law had found a specifically legal target, and that this made the struggle against that regime an obvious *cause célèbre*. But it is obviously not as if the end of apartheid meant the end of racism in the world, or in South Africa for that matter. Factual, structural, systemic discrimination, specifically of the racial kind that international law so adamantly condemns, remains endemic and has led some to question whether a 'global apartheid' exists. Such challenges require international law to go beyond its traditional comfort zone of the public and the civil into the private and the economic. They were always bound to make progress more tenuous and less … 'eventful'. In that larger fight against racism, there will probably be fewer days like 11 February 1990, and one may question whether international law as a system of global regulation is not past its prime, even as it claims to have reached maturity. Maybe the challenge for international law will be not so much to understand itself in terms of a succession of 'events' presented as signposts in a linear progression as to understand why it is so dependent on 'events', and to understand its role in producing and celebrating them.

Notes

1 Remarks by the Secretary-General at the State Luncheon Following the Inauguration of Nelson Mandela as President of the Republic of South Africa, Pretoria, 10 May 1994.
2 Tension between different groups, particularly Inkatha and the UDF–ANC faction, provoked many deaths.
3 The Freedom Charter, Adopted at the Congress of the People, Kliptown, 26 June 1955.
4 *South-West Africa Cases (Ethiopia v South Africa; Liberia v South Africa); Second Phase*. International Court of Justice. 18 July 1966.
5 For example, as became apparent during the final years of apartheid, sanctions tended to affect poor black workers and businesses disproportionately. The domestic anti-apartheid movement nonetheless supported the sanctions as the only way of putting pressure on the Government, but there were clearly costs to the policy, which could probably only be efficient if it was effectively relayed domestically to supporters of the movement.
6 The international human rights movement has, of course, grown and is a significant force to be reckoned with today. But it remains in some ways elitist, linked to the law, and largely Western.

References

Black, D. (1999) 'The long and winding road: international norms and domestic political change in South Africa', in T. Risse-Kappen, S. Ropp *et al.*, *The Power of Human Rights: International Norms and Domestic Change*, Cambridge: Cambridge University Press, 1999.

Boutros-Ghali, B. (1994) 'Statement by Secretary-General Boutros-Ghali to the General Assembly plenary meeting on the resumption of South Africa's participation in the Assembly's work', A/48/PV.95, 23 June 1994 (Doc. 212).

Houser, G. (1992) 'The international impact of the South African struggle for liberation', in E.S. Reddy (ed.), *Struggle for Liberation in South Africa and International Solidarity*, New Delhi: Sterling Publishers.

Mandela, N. (1994) 'Address by President Nelson Mandela of South Africa to the forty-ninth Session of the General Assembly', 3 October 1994 (Doc. 216).

Risse-Kappen, T., Ropp, S. *et al.* (1999) *The Power of Human Rights: International Norms and Domestic Change*, Cambridge: Cambridge University Press.

United Nations Department of Public Information (1994) *The United Nations and Apartheid, 1948–1994*, New York: United Nations, Department of Public Information.

Universal Declaration of Human Rights (1948), G.A. Res. 217A, UN GAOR, 3d Sess., UN Doc. A/810 (1948).

Chapter 10

Political trials as events

Emilios Christodoulidis

After the revolutionary overthrow of the monarchy in France, the question of the fate of Louis XVI is posed before the Convention. The 'sublime' revolutionary Saint-Just dismisses in the following terms the Girondins' suggestion to 'appeal to the People' over the question of whether the deposed King should stand trial: 'Those who attach importance to the just punishment of a king will never establish a democracy.' Two weeks later, in his address to the Convention, Robespierre will seal the fate of Louis XVI:

> [p]eople doubt whether he is guilty, whether it is permitted to treat him like the enemy. The Constitution is invoked in his favour. I do not intend to repeat here all the unanswerable arguments developed by those who deign to answer objections of that sort. On this matter I will say a word for the benefit of those whom they have not convinced. The constitution forbade everything that you have done … You have no right at all to hold him in prison. He has the right to ask you for his release and for damages and interest. The Constitution condemns you: fall at Louis XVI's feet and ask for his clemency!
>
> Personally I should blush to discuss these constitutional quibbles any more seriously than that; they belong on school or palace benches, or rather in the cabinets of London, Vienna and Berlin. I cannot argue at length when I am convinced that deliberation is a scandal.
>
> Proposing to put Louis on trial … is a counter-revolutionary idea, for it means putting the revolution itself in contention …
>
> Louis cannot be judged; either he is already condemned or the Republic is not acquitted.
>
> (Robespierre [1791], this translation, 2007: 62, 58)

This famous incident in modern history confronts us with the perplexing link between the political, the trial and the truth; with an argument that pits political truth against any forum of law, and consequently the trial as a passage to political truth. In fact this incident invites a double quandary. First, it involves putting to question the givenness of the assumption that the courtroom is the forum for getting at the truth. Instead, a reflexive question is invited: is the trial the way to establish political truth? Second, it involves putting to question the appropriate addressee of this reflexive question. Not simply: are 'the people' to be entrusted with answering a question of such political importance? But more troublingly: *can they constitute the addressee* of the question if they are not *already* constituted as a Republic that invokes them as sovereign, this invocation and this constitution, in a crucial sense, having already answered the question over the fate of the King?

And that precisely is the reason why Robespierre says: *Louis cannot be judged; either he is already condemned or the Republic is not acquitted.* Against constitutional continuity, against any *droit commun* spanning the *ancien régime* and the republic (such fictions already debunked earlier by Saint-Just), Robespierre's disjunction aims to draw out the potentially disastrous implications of such forms of political accommodation of the revolution. At one level Robespierre's is an injunction against a constitutional containment of a revolution that would undercut it. In a later speech, when his own fate was on the line, he asks: 'Citizens, did you want a revolution without a revolution? ... Who can mark after the event, the exact point at which the waves of popular insurrection *should* break?' (Robespierre, this trans. 2007: 79). On a second level the stakes are even higher: here the injunction aims to claim a speaking position for the successful revolutionaries. As citizens of the Republic *only* can they claim the political subject position, and this in defiance of the previous distribution of speaking positions which must and can only (as per Robespierre above) 'already condemn' that which, with Alain Badiou, we might call the 'situation' of the *ancien régime*.

If we return now to these injunctions against these distributions, it is to explore whether, despite Robespierre this time, the trial itself might harbour, at its limits, the possibility of challenging existing distributions of subject positions and entitlements. In the next section we will look at how the trial establishes subject positions, delimits stakes and procedures and redeems these determinations by introducing a dimension of contestability to them according to the ideal of unconstrained discourse, as propounded by the Frankfurt School and which has acquired near-paradigmatic status in current normative theorizing of the trial (see, for example, Duff *et al.* 2006, 2008).

We will identify this determination and its legitimation through communicative openness, in terms of what Badiou calls a 'situation', and explore how the trial installs itself as one. After that we will look with the help of Badiou's concepts of *event*, *void* and *evental site* at whether the political trial might break out of its situational confinement. What does it mean to say that *resistance* to confinement, to the authorization, sanctioning and policing of statements in the courtroom as functions of the situation, might be generated *immanently*? We will explore these questions with the help of concrete examples and insist on the meaning of what constitutes *the event* of politicizing the trial.

The trial as 'situation'

The benign inclusion through discourse

What becomes possible through discourse theory is not just the containment of the trial but also the redemption of that containment through democratic categories. Containment and justification stand and fall together. The genius of the discursive turn is to ground the legitimacy of the trial in its openness and to conceive that openness as appropriate to the situation, in the double sense of a 'placing': a situating, and a delimitation of contours and alternatives.

Let us take this more gradually. If openness must bring with it an invitation to contest and challenge anything that is taken for granted, assumed or imposed, then one might reasonably object that what stands in the way of such openness in the situation of a trial is, on the one hand, a certain 'thickness' of the rules of evidence and procedure, of jurisdiction and standing, that delimit the ambit of all that can be contested in the trial; and on the other hand, the institutive rules and institutional categories that determine the who, the how and the when of courtroom interaction. How then does discourse theory explain, and also justify, the curtailment of open discourse in the institutionalization of proceedings?

To meet this kind of objection Robert Alexy argues that legal claims 'are not concerned with the *absolute* rationality of the normative statement in question, but only with showing that they can be rationally justified within the framework of the validly prevailing legal order' (Alexy 1989: 22). But why the concession? Alexy tells us that it is about remedying a 'weakness' that consists in the fact that these rules and forms define a decision-making procedure which in many cases leads to no result at all (Alexy 1989: 287). Therefore, for Alexy, what 'rationally justifies' the structural constraints imposed at the level of the trial against discourse theory's commitment to 'unfettered communication' is to redress the latter's 'weakness', which is its (occasional) inability to yield consensus and thus outcomes.

One must acknowledge the genius of the reversal effected here: structural constraints such as those identified above imposing limitations on or authorizing standing and jurisdiction, establishing finality through the principle of *res judicata* and rules concerning double indemnity and statutes of limitation are only perceivable as limiting from a position of open discourse, that is, from an external position. From the internal, functional, point of view that Alexy invites us to occupy, they are precisely *enabling* and thus structurally *constitutive* of the situation. The reduction of the range of discursive possibilities is specific to the law's structuring of the trial in allowing, to borrow briefly from Luhmann, the trial as a 'reduction achievement': where the institutive rules that map out and contain the world of legal meaning enable a form of communication (here: in the courtroom) that would have otherwise been impossible. In Badiou's language – and the proximity here between Badiou and Luhmann is worth remarking – the counting-as-one of the situation involves oper-ationalizing situation-specific criteria (those 'limiting' rules of procedure and conceptualizations) to assign meaning to elements in the world and allow them to be counted in. If law is a reduction achievement it is because what is limiting and what is constitutive stand in a mutually enabling relationship.

The reversal is now complete, and the trial receives its full immunity. If an external observer might object that every single aspect of the institutional achievement carries a serious cost in terms of what can be contested in the courtroom, our discourse theorists can justify this 'reducing of the range of discursive possibilities' in the name of rationality itself as appropriate to the function of law that informs the decisionism of legal, adjudicative procedures: that disputes *must be* resolved.

Let us pause to reflect on the power of the reversal effected by the dis-cursive understanding and redemption of the trial. To argue that limitations on discourse guarantee its 'well-groundedness' (Alexy 1989, 111, quoting Habermas) is of course no longer to ask for a concession. The urgency to reduce the openness of conflict and to resolve it is a functional imperative of law for which (discourse) theorists do not need to apologize. Both exigencies, to reduce and to solve, fold back into what Badiou will call the *situation* of the trial as imperatives of the situation itself rather than demands placed upon it externally or concessions extracted from it. In this way legal dis-course folds back upon itself to create a virtuous circle in which justificatory demands and legitimation are internalized without remainder. What might thus be presented by critics as silencing is simply what was not picked up, and not picked up for good reason: as selectivity-grids for particulars, legal criteria, generalizations, rules, categories, etc., *actualize situations* at the same time as they suppress alternatives (*to* them rather than *in* them). And it is precisely that deployment of selectivity underpinning the situation of the trial that lends to its well-groundedness and thus to its integrity.

We will now move to a discussion of what Badiou precisely identifies as a 'situation'. It gives us a framework to explain and expose the containment and confinement, respectively, of the trial as an instantiation of commu-nicative reason. There are two distinct moments in this that secure the con-tainment of new elements as elements *of* the situation. The first moment, of *naming*, picks out elements in the world to be 'counted'. To be identified, after all, as Peter Hallward puts it well, is to be 'enveloped by a dominant term' (2008: 114). The second moment has to do with *a setting itself in con-text*, which implies, ultimately, as I will attempt to show, the inclusion *in* the situation of all possible alternatives *to* it.

Defining 'situation'

'All thought supposes a situation, a structure, a counting-for-one, whereby the presented multiple is consistent, numerable,' says Badiou in his important work *Being and Event* (Badiou 1988: 44). With the idea of a 'situation' Badiou captures the moment of containment, of a certain gathering-in. And this gathering-in is effected through 'criteria that limit what is presented, that is, what qualifies for inclusion in the situation they describe' (Badiou 1988: 13).

If all these moves are moves of inclusion and delimitation, the intriguing moment here in Badiou's thinking is the contrast of the structuring function to what '*in-consists*' and the question over what it means to 'be' but *not* 'be counted-for-one', *not* situated, but in-consistent. The modality of that in-consistence goes to the heart of a discussion of what is potential, and thus also to what potentially resists ideological capture, which remains the stubborn cornerstone of critical theory, and of any critical theorization of the trial.

The reason why it is so difficult to discern potentiality in what 'in-consists' is because we are caught up in the 'always-already' of situations. Operations differentiate, order and stabilize elements *of* the situation. The operational 'reach' into that which we must assume to be an underdetermined multiplicity – the domain to be ordered, the 'beyond' of the situation – is always and can only be directed by, and thus contained within, the situation, as past memory, present options and future scope. And while structures are re-embedded and renewed (along given pathways) in this unfolding in time, it is always the situation that shapes and delimits the 'encounter': establishing in the process the very meaning of encounter, of *what* is situated and against what it is situated, establishing, that is, reference to self and other.

In a crucial way, only *after the event* might we say that what persisted as inconsistent, *despite* the situation, was being denied a register. It is the improbable, 'strange' persistence of the inconsistency that Badiou may help us think through by virtue of the notions of *void*, *event* and *evental site*. We will visit these soon. For now we remain with the situation – of the law and the legal trial – that, in providing criteria of intelligibility, establishes itself as register. What would it mean *in this situation* to say 'no' to the law?

The meaning of negation

Badiou's account of the situation, to begin with at least, presents us with closure that is totalizing. Similarly to Luhmann, for whom closure is a condition of openness, for Badiou the closure of situations is a condition of signification, of something counting-as *x*. In the face of such closure Badiou, like Luhmann, might speak of a certain improbability of resistance. Yet Badiou, this time in radical opposition to Luhmann, promises an *emancipatory* theory that claims *truth* for itself *if* the improbable surfacing of such truth is endorsed with a commitment to its promise, a commitment for which Badiou will reserve the term *fidelity*. But where, one asks, given the totalizing context that is the situation, might the incongruous event arise, let alone arise in a way that might command fidelity? Where is the register for the negation of the context, the meaning of being against it, to be sought?

The reason why the question of register is difficult is because it plays on a distinction of level and meta-level. For a negation of the situation to register it must operate at the meta-level (what it *means* to negate a situation) and yet Badiou reminds us that it can only appear *in* a situation. Refusal is caught up in a double bind here because while negation is crucially involved in breaking *out of* the confinement of a situation, yet it plays a functional role *within* the situation. The problem, of course, is that as the negative value in the dyad of exclusive alternatives, negation *confirms* the situation as much as affirmation does. Normative orders, after all, are not discredited through disappointment (of normative expectations) but in fact exploit negation as a means of immunizing themselves from challenge. Negating the situation thus forever runs the risk of slipping back into affirming it.

The key question which must remain unanswered for the moment is whether (and how) negation might lift itself to the meta-level, as a negation of the situation itself. This is what systems-theorists would call a 'rejection-value' of the system itself (Luhmann 1986, 1992), a third value that cuts across the yes–no computation of affirmation and negation that is of course no challenge to the situation but its very mode of operating in the world. Let us visit a practical instance of negation, and its attendant risk, while keeping the full potential scope in view: negation as functional; as contradiction; and as withdrawal.

The following is a short exchange between Andreas Baader and the judge on the 23rd day of the trial of the Baader-Meinhof group in August 1975.

BAADER: I find it hard to say anything at all here. It is my view that we ought not to talk to you or about you any more. Action is called for to deal with the antagonism of the state machine towards humanity, as it actually presents itself in …

JUDGE: You were not permitted to speak to make a declaration.

BAADER: You want to stop me speaking?

JUDGE: If you are not about to make a petition, then I can't allow you to speak.

BAADER: We are not on that plane any more. We are not on the plane of petitions made to this court, this rat-heap.

JUDGE: You are now forbidden to go on speaking for insulting the court.

(Aust 1987: 211)

I have argued at length elsewhere (Christodoulidis 2006) that Baader's refusal to engage with the court is an objection that cannot be heard. Baader's is a refusal to answer to the law: a refusal to '*talk to you {the Court} or about you any more*'. His is no longer an attempt to forge a contradiction in the law; it is instead an attempt at a withdrawal. Negation is here to be understood as a refusal to answer to the law and the speaking position is claimed *against* an idiom that includes him anyway *as* contemptuous of the court. Because, of course, in law's response there is no space for withdrawal from the law, only fulfilment of the conditions of an offence and thus affirmation of the law. In a previous case, in 1968, before a Frankfurt court, Gudrun Ensslin had refused to give any closing words before her sentencing: 'I do not want to give you the chance to create the impression that you were listening to me' (Klimke 2009: 27).

Using Badiou's idea of the situation we can conceptualize this distribution of speaking position and silencing in terms of a certain structuring of a multiple that provides (and polices) the criteria of what is to count, and count for what. The enfolding becomes total at the point of recursion, when a court is able to pronounce on the question of its own jurisdiction; that is, when it declares its competence to decide its competence. And this moment when self-reference becomes thus productive for it – the law answerable only to itself – discourse theory, as we saw above, offers this self-referential operation a democratic redemption. It invites the dissident of law to give his reasons *in* law, as the assumed addressee (in the court) of the laws he has given himself (as democratic citizen). The discursive turn underpins and sanctions the continuous recursive functionalization of democratic excess in institutions.

Against the form and force of this internalization, Badiou will insist here on an emergent truth that somehow takes place *within* the situation (here, of the trial) but is *not of* it. A counter-factual fidelity to the event of this emergent truth constitutes, for him, the subject of truth. If this calls for a 'wager' it is because no guarantee is offered that this will not be a tragic commitment. If Baader, Meinhoff, Raspe and Enslinn's was indeed the trajectory of a certain self-authorization, played out in the insistent claiming of a speaking position in a situation that afforded none, in confronting revolutionary to state violence, then with Badiou we could perhaps claim that they were the subjects of a bitter truth, their fidelity to the event of truth exacted in the white cells of Stammheim.

The trial as 'evental site'

Badiou's inventory: events, 'evental sites' and the 'void' of situations

Given a situation, where givenness overdetermines, structures and enumerates, what are the opportunities of putting the situation to question, and where might they be sought? What does it mean to step back from the givens of a situation to allow that questioning? The difficulty is, of course, this: that the situation – in the form of structures and states as we saw above – sets the conditions of what can be asked meaningfully. These are the *conditions* of the questions that can be asked, not their *object*. They determine what can be meaningfully counted-for and accounted in the situation, and in this they establish and guarantee a *finite* responsiveness.

'The central idea of my ontology', says Badiou, 'is the idea that what the state seeks to *foreclose* through the power of its count is the void of the situation, and the event that in each case reveals it' (quoted in Hallward 2003: 100). We will return to 'foreclosure' but let us remain briefly with the 'event'. For Badiou an event cannot be inferred from the situation. 'As something that cannot be recognized as one in the situation, an event is the presentation of inconsistency in the situation' (Hallward 2003: 115). 'From within the situation the existence of the event cannot be proved, it can only be asserted. An event is something that can only be said to exist in so far as it somehow inspires subjects to wager on its existence' (Badiou 1988: 214). What does it mean to 'assert' what is denied presence?

The event is 'unpresented and unpresentable' and its belonging to a situation is undecidable from within the situation itself (Badiou 1988: 199, 202). And yet the event must first be shown to have its site within the situation, what Badiou calls a 'site événementiel'. This, he argues, is a 'strict condition of immanence since the site is a part of the situation' (Hallward 2003: 116). As bridging concept, the evental site secures the location of the event – and thus any truth procedure – within the situation that it transforms. Žižek identifies it as 'what intervenes in the situation from the point of view of its symptom torsion' (in Hallward 2003: introduction). 'Point' is also the term that Badiou chooses to identify precisely how an event might fasten onto a situation to recast it, seeking the pivot in it, but crucially reconfiguring how the elements fall into place around it. Hallward puts it well. He says: 'We might say that every event is specific to, but not specified by, its site' (2003: 117). Sites are located at the limits of situations, conditions of immanence, names for a place which *a posteriori only* will have harboured the event. And retrospection will, of course, work the whole way back. The modification of an object in the world retroactively changes its history, for Badiou. In each case an event of rupture is presupposed that is impossible from the point of view of the situation, the circumference of which coincides with that of its evental site. For this event that irrupts in a space that has no place for it, Badiou insists that fidelity has a constitutive role to play, both for the occurrence of the event and the subject of truth. Why 'for the occurrence', though? What is the meaning of this fidelity to that which has not yet occurred, how can fidelity attach itself to that to which it is the precondition? Badiou's answer is this: in an important way fidelity carves out a space for the event in organizing its 'consequences'. Only in this way does *retroaction fully take effect*. In diachrony, rather than in the moment of emergence, does the event register as origin of something, as setting a certain sequence into action, as allowing causal links to be read into the run of time, patterns to emerge.

Might we not at this point return to Robespierre, to what Badiou might call his 'wager' in the notion of a fidelity to the revolution? It was the act of fidelity itself that created the space for the revolution, as it created – Saint-Just would claim this again and again – the subject position of the revolutionary. The point is not one about authorship of authorization, about who spoke for the revolution or could act in its name. The point is one about constitutive 'eventness', about a shift away from that which emerges-as from within, to that which endures-as in spite, and summons-as against.

If we have succeeded, with Badiou, in tracking a certain logic of rupture, of the emergence in a situation of an event that could not be counted-for from within the situation, and an opportunity that arises despite the opportunity structure available, we return now to the trial to look at the logic of that unfolding. What joins the two instances is the deployment of a defence structure that aimed at a form of rupture.

Strategies of rupture in the courtroom

The trial of the Algerian militants

In the way Jacques Vergès analyzes it in 'De la stratégie judiciaire', the defence strategy of the militants of the Algerian Liberation Movement (FLN) and their strategies of resistance against the French state consisted in iden-tifying and exploiting the core contradictions in the French Government's use of the criminal law. A radicalized successor of a long tradition of Algerian nationalist movements, the FLN militants sought, in their own words, to 'dégonfler les monsters juridiques', by which the French Government attempted to justify its sovereignty and repression. On the judicial plane the official French position is torn through by fundamental contradictions (Vergès 1968: 186) and the Algerian defendants fought to exploit these in the courtroom. Most strikingly, the declaration of a 'state of exception' con-tradicted the official position of the French Government, that what was involved in the clamping down of Algerian resistance was a simple police operation directed against French nationals. From the very beginning, says Vergès, 'the prisoners-combatants raised "l'exception d'incompétence" against the French justice in its entirety' – the jurisdictional objection that we encounter in its many forms across the landscape of political justice. 'Tactical exploitation' of the contradiction forged the emergence of the truth of an independent national Algerian identity, an affirmation which, with the escalation of resistance and the broadening of the repressive measures against the insurgents, became irrepressible. The broader claim was matched by a careful strategic use of the neutrality 'guarantees' of criminal procedure that aimed predominantly to force it into exposing its partiality. For example, when the 'double' massacre of El-halid occurred in which 35 Europeans and 700 Algerians died, but where the legal inquiry was only opened in respect of the Europeans' deaths, the FLN's legal strategy of derailment took the form of an insistent claim to perform autopsies on the corpses of all 700 Algerians. This 'forcing' (to use Badiou's term) articulated with two further moments of strategy. In the first, the defendants argued that the open, official and widespread use of torture marked the violation in the colony of basic rights that were protected in the metropolis. The act of denouncing torture in the courtroom was not limited to the stated aims of criminal procedure (as, for example, when used to rebut extracted admissions). Instead, the denunciation of its systematic use against the Algerians aimed again at transforming the exceptional into the ordinary to make torture the sign and signifier of the wrong of colonialism. Second, they argued, the sheer number of those interned gave the lie to the legal stipulation that they were a band of law-breakers. As numbers swelled and collective, markedly political, acts of defiance were organized in prisons, law-breaking ceased to be the 'pathology' in the healing of which a system of law fulfils its promise of justice and became a sign of systemic crisis as such.

The Milošević trial

Slobodan Milošević conducted his own defence in the Hague in 2002 as a cross-examination targeted at the West's legacy in the Balkans and the 'international community's' unwillingness to prosecute the NATO bombings of Serbia in 1999. Competing frames of explanation came to dominate the trial, intended as a prosecution of war criminals but increasingly presented by Milošević as a trial of the Serbian nation itself (see Boas 2007).

According to Martii Koskenniemi, 'in the Milošević trial the narrative of the "Greater Serbia" collided head-on with the self-determination stories of the seceding populations, while political assessments of socialism and nationalism competed with long-term historical and even religious frames of explanation' (Koskenniemi 2002: 12). If this was a history lesson it was one that continually came up against the limits of the legal medium. 'When a trial concerns larger political events,' writes Koskenniemi, 'it will necessarily involve an interpretation of the context which is precisely what is disputed in the individual actions that are the object of the trial' (Koskenniemi 2002: 16). Koskenniemi is surely right in this, difficult as it is sometimes to drive a clear line between frames of interpretation and controversial determinations they underscore. While it is arguably an achievement of the trial that it (sometimes) gave the lie to forms of denial (such as that described by Hazan: four years after Srebrenica, Serbs residing in the area proclaiming that 'nothing happened here ... It is all propaganda' (Koskenniemi 2002: 9)), on the other hand the selective prosecutions coupled with the discourse of victimhood that framed the official Croatian narrative of the conflict obfuscate, for example, the truth that the single most extensive act of ethnic cleansing was perpetrated by Croats against Serbs in Krajina.

But to return to Milošević and his strategy of defence. As is well known, he identifies and denounces the proceedings as a case of victor's justice, a partiality that for him frames and undergirds the trial. He makes maximum use of the *tu quoque* and the jurisdictional objection: why is he on trial, he repeatedly asks, and not Western leaders? If he is before the court to answer for war crimes, why not those who ordered the bombing of Serbia and who chose to fly the bombers at the relative safety of high altitudes that made precision bombing difficult and led to an unnecessary and vast destruction of civilian lives? And, of course, a trial that automatically vindicates the position of the prosecutor – if not his story – runs dangerously close to a show trial, was his message.

In each case the defence strategy attempts to exploit different elements of the situation and towards different strategic objectives. Let us analytically isolate certain trends of rupture, first in the direction of *forcing a certain displacement*, then in the more ambitious direction of the *forging of a new subject-position*.

Why displacement?

Vergès argues that the defence of 'rupture' aims at a confrontation with the *system* that is represented by the prosecution's case. In the confrontation with the law of the state, the main aim is to *derail* the process all the time *both* using *and* contesting it in a way best captured by the logic of immanent critique. He says: 'Rupture traverses the whole structure of the trial. Facts as well as circumstances of the action pass onto a secondary plane; in the forefront appears suddenly the brutal contestation with the order of the State' (Vergès 1968: 86–87, my translation). And perhaps most significantly the logic that is played out again and again is the logic of immanent critique, the attempt to 'place society in contradiction with its principles' (Vergès 1968: 44) in a way that 'excludes all compromise' (Vergès 1968: 17). Immanent critique, as is familiar, is tied to the logic of contradiction that is generated within the material reality of practices and institutions. The strategic tapping of contradiction aims to hold up the system to its own claims, force it to face up to its stated principles, to equality, to procedural fairness, etc., where this measuring up forces it beyond what it can possibly 'contain' within its economy of representation. And thus, here is something that the law cannot respond to; that it is *constitutively complicit* with. That this complicity isn't redressable is only a problem for *internal* critique, the promise of law's rational 'well-groundedness' and the promise of rational redemption. But from the point of view of *immanent* critique, the impossible redress is precisely the contradiction that invites political opportunity.

How did rupture as immanent critique register in the trials? It did so by forcing a displacement along three axes. This is clearest in the case of the

Algerian militants, where the mass incarcerations force a displacement from *individual* to *collective* responsibility and action, from the *exceptionality* of the suspension of procedural rights to the *normality* of a brutal police operation, and crucially from the *municipal* to the *international*, in this sense: that the prosecution's case could no longer be *rationally* contained within the context of the operations of the French municipal system of justice but was displaced onto a transcendent system – *of a cosmopolitan or international law*, Vergès calls it (187–88) – from which France's state of emergency could be seen for what it was: a facilitator of colonial brutality against an emergent people no longer subsumable to '*le peuple*'. The strategy invokes an international law as the only appropriate register for the continued (normal, not exceptional) state-perpetrated acts of colonialism (against a collective, not individuals) in which the state which presented itself as guarantor of the justice system could not at once also be the law-breaker. To exploit the contradiction was to force that displacement onto an (international) context that might harbour this emergent truth.

If this is a site of 'structural fragility' that the strategy exploits, as Badiou occasionally refers to it, is in some sense immaterial. It is, of course, by definition, only *a posteriori* a fissure or a fault line on which the event locates itself. The point is that this 'structural fragility' is only with hindsight, while from the forward-looking point of view of the situation it is invisible. What matters to strategy nonetheless is that the site of a truth is indicated by points of possible impasse or resistance to formalization that becomes apparent through this act of forcing. A new truth, says Badiou, emerges in the wake of an event that seems 'to displace the configuration of being under our own eyes ... The local collapse of its consistency, and so the provisional cancellation [résiliation] of all logic'. ... 'What then comes to the surface displacing or revoking the logic of place, is being itself, in its fearsome and creative inconsistency, or in its void, which is the without-place of every place' (quoted in Hallward 2008: 104). Let us keep from this: the reversal of the logic of placing, which is precisely what Badiou calls the situation; the disruption of this logic of placing that in the courtroom is activated through criteria that individuate relevant events and receives the full backing of rules of procedure and relevance; the displacement allows a reconfiguration of the elements of the situation excavated now as an evental site; a severing off from the interpretative framework, and its own reconfiguration of the field of reference in which it finds itself. Whether this reconfiguration can, if subjects remain faithful to it, generate a new truth in *law* is a difficult question, and perhaps for present purposes, immaterial. What it does, in any case, generate, if one remains with Badiou faithful to this new logic of the event, is political opportunity: a political opportunity that is not exhausted in 'being-against' but signals the arrival of a new political project.

But if the first strategic aim of rupture was in the direction of *forcing a certain displacement*, and a consequent seizing of what 'in-consists', a more ambitious dimension is that of the *forging of a new subject-position*, in a way that perhaps takes us back to Badiou's early work, *Theory of the Subject*. Let us return for this to the relentless use of the *tu quoque* objection by Milošević. For Milošević the '*tu*' – of the *tu quoque* – aimed at indiscriminately addressing both the international community and the 'West' that for centuries again and again tore the Balkan peninsula into pieces, throwing its people against each other in a ruthless game of European domination. Just as for Klaus Barbie's lawyers, notoriously in the trial in Lyon, the *tu* addressed the French Government as a colonial force that committed genocide against the races of Indochina and Africa. In each case the injunction removes legitimacy, withdraws the semblance of neutrality but most importantly collapses the constitutive role of the 'third' party in the trial that underpins the moment of institutionalization; from the complex systemic structure of the law that depends (in its social dimension, as Luhmann argues in the *Rechtssoziologie* (1972)) on the non-partisan, 'co-expecting third party' to a context of conflictual *interaction*, in which parties to the interaction set and negotiate its rules, and which thus queries law's institutional *achievement*. That is what the relentless use of the *tu quoque* as a ruptural device, as an exposure of the eventual site, achieves: it crucially undercuts the institutional nature of the law to re-situate the conflict not as occasion (for law's reproduction) but as context that precedes the identification of the stake and the identity of the parties to it. With the collapse of the third comes the exposure of the context of confrontation and with it *the two*. Subjects are no longer placed in relation, assumed and imposed, but subject-positions emerge as a stake of the struggle itself. As a moment of politicization of the trial this is both a deployment and a denial of the legal situation.

Conclusion

There is a crucial ambivalence in Badiou's work over the question of immanence, and more specifically to what extent critique and resistance to the orders of capital that we dwell under may proceed immanently, through the forcing of existing contradictions, or whether they come from outside. An ambivalence that is accentuated rather than settled with statements such as this: 'It is not from the world, in however ideal a manner, that the event holds its inexhaustible reserve, its silent (or indiscernible) excess, but from being unattached to it, its being separate, lacunary' (from Badiou's review of Deleuze, quoted in Hallward 2003: 115); or: 'The event reveals the "inadmissible empty point in which nothing is presented"' (Badiou, quoted in Hallward 2003: 115). An ambivalence which might also explain Antonio Negri's recent frustration with the insistence on a 'negative teleology', or 'the tragic limit of those [Negri refers explicitly to Badiou here] who see in an event, in transcendence, the determining of excess. An event, thus, without continuity, without institution and without any constituent positivity. Who knows why!' (Negri 2008: 342–43).

Can one perhaps begin to explain why in the following way? In his book on Badiou, Peter Hallward reminds us that 'a truth is something we make. It is declared, composed and upheld by the subjects it convokes and sustains' (Hallward 2003: xxv). It can be reached only through a process that breaks decisively with all established criteria of judging the validity of inter-pretations (Hallward 2003: xxiii). We explored in a trial situation how truth will concern its most indiscernibly or 'evasively included' groupings of ele-ments (Badiou 1988: 313). The process whereby such groupings might be assembled will take place in violation of all the usual ways in which ele-ments are grouped (Hallward 2003: xxiii).

With Badiou we have looked at the event of rupture in the courtroom, and the possibility to hold true to the in-consistency of what there is, against a structuring that overwhelms, and overwhelms more specifically presenta-tion with representation, forcing any excess to sediment into institutional forms that determine the modality of the questionable, and its opportunity. This is not dissimilar to an overwhelming that Negri himself struggled with and against in his early writings.

Isn't this then the crux of the radicalization sought by both communist theorists? One might suggest that in the context of the trial, the wager that Badiou invites us to assume, in all its ambivalence, is that the politicization of the trial involves the *creation* rather than the *realization* of an immanent possibility, which finds its expression not in that which it attempts to put to question, but in the space it clears for itself.

References

Alexy, R. (1989) *A Theory of Legal Argumentation*, Oxford: Oxford University Press.
Aust, S. (1987) *The Baader-Meinhof Complex*, London: Bodley Head.
Badiou, A. (1988) *Being and Event*, trans. O. Feltham (2008) London: Continuum.
Beasley-Murray, J. (1994) 'Ethics as post-political politics', *Research and Society*, 7: 5–26.
Boas, G. (2007) *The Milošević Trial: Lessons for the Conduct of Complex International Criminal Proceedings*, Cambridge: Cambridge University Press.
Christodoulidis, E. (2006) 'The objection that cannot be heard', in Duff *et al.* (2004–2008).
Duff, R.A. *et al.* (2004–2008) *The Trial on Trial*, three vols, Oxford: Hart.
Günther, K. (1988) *The Sense of Appropriateness*, trans. J. Farrell (1993) Albany: SUNY Press.
Habermas, J. (1987) *The Theory of Communicative Action*, Cambridge: Polity Press.
Hallward, P. (2003) *Badiou: A Subject to Truth*, Minneapolis: University of Minnesota Press.
——(2008) 'Order and event', *New Left Review*, 53: 97–122.
Klimke, M. (2009) '1968 and the courts', *German Law Journal*, 10: 261–74.
Koskenniemi, M. (2002) 'Between impunity and show trials', *Max Planck Yearbook of United Nations Law*, 6: 1–35.
Luhmann N, (1972) *Rechtssoziologie*, trans. E. King-Utz and M. Albrow (1985) *The Sociological Theory of Law*, London: Routledge and Kegan Paul.

——(1986): 'Distinctions Directrices: über Codierung von Semantiken und Systems', *Kölner Zeitschrift fur Soziologie und Sozialpsychologie*, 27: 145.

——(1992) 'The coding of the legal system', in G. Teubner and A. Febbrajo (eds), *State, Law, and Economy as Autopoietic Systems: Regulation and Autonomy in a New Perspective*, Milan: Giuffrè.

Negri, A. (2008) 'Philosophy of law against sovereignty: new excesses, old fragmentations', *Law and Critique*, 19: 335–43.

Robespierre, M. (1791) *Œvres Complètes, Paris: Ernest Leroux* (2007), vol. 10, trans. J. Howe, included in *Virtue and Terror*, London: Verso.

Vergès, J. (1968) *De la stratégie judiciare*, Paris: Minuit.

Chapter 11

The Tokyo Women's Tribunal and the turn to fiction

Karen Knop[1]

Introduction

These chapters are about events by which international law is marked, and through which it has registered and acquired force. At the outset, the editors asked contributors to explore some path not taken in international law's development, with a view to understanding its contemporary resonance. This could be a mental exercise: let us think how international law would look today if it had come to a fork in the road and taken the other road. Another way to go about the task would be to perform the act of going back in time and taking the other road. This chapter is about the Women's International War Crimes Tribunal for the Trial of Japan's Military Sexual Slavery, which did just that (TWT 2001).[2]

After the Second World War, the Allied powers established an International Military Tribunal for the Far East (IMTFE), the Tokyo counterpart of the better-known tribunal at Nuremberg, to determine the responsibility of high-ranking Japanese officials for Japan's initiation and conduct of military actions from 1928 to 1945 (Boister and Cryer 2008). The IMTFE tried a list of 'Class A' defendants for crimes against the peace together with war crimes and crimes against humanity, while 'Class B' and 'Class C' defendants were prosecuted at subsidiary trials held in the Asia-Pacific region (Piccigallo 1979). The Tokyo trial tends to be criticized as victors' justice imposed through a flawed legal process (Futamura 2008: 68–86; Minear 1971; Ōnuma 1986: 45), and indeed the IMTFE's split judgment provides support for such criticisms. Among 11 judges, there were three dissents of different kinds, one separate opinion and one concurring opinion. Judge Pal, from India, dissented completely from the findings of the majority and would have acquitted all of the accused of all of the charges. From the perspective of prosecuting sexual violence against women in war, however, Tokyo is more of a landmark than Nuremberg (Gardam and Jarvis 2001: 204–8; Sellers 2000: 278, 287–91). Unlike Nuremberg, the Tokyo judgment describes a number of instances and particularly the brutality and vast scale of the rapes by Japanese troops during and after the conquest of Nanking. Also unlike Nuremberg, there were prosecutions and convictions at Tokyo explicitly based on rape crimes (Boister and Cryer 2008: 604, 612).

But among the actions not addressed by the IMTFE was the Japanese military's institutionalization of the conscription and trafficking of women through force, coercion and deception, and their confinement to 'comfort stations' set up where Japanese troops were stationed to provide the troops with sexual services. In 2000, more than half a century after the Tokyo trial, various women's and human rights non-governmental organizations from across Asia created the Women's International War Crimes Tribunal for the Trial of Japan's Military Sexual Slavery (hereafter, the Tokyo Women's Tribunal) to remedy the failure to prosecute rape and sexual slavery as crimes against humanity based on the 'comfort women'[3] system.[4] The Tokyo Women's Tribunal chose a somewhat surprising identity for itself: it judged the crimes *as if it were* a reopening or a continuation' of the official IMTFE and subsidiary trials (emphasis added) – not as compensating for the IMTFE or similar to the IMTFE, but *as* the IMTFE. The fiction has scarcely been remarked upon by commentators, yet it is this feature that suits the tribunal to the editors' purpose.

In this chapter, I approach the Tokyo Women's Tribunal as an instance of performing the act of going back in time and taking another path. How did the tribunal accomplish this, what impact does it have on international law and what sort of critical bite does the tribunal's fiction of returning to international law's past offer? Because the tribunal acted out and thus inhabited the 'as if' fiction,[5] it did not address these sorts of questions. In its judgment, the tribunal explicitly used the fiction to solve a number of technical legal problems, but was silent on whether it intended the fiction to serve any other purpose and whether it recognized that the fiction might produce any other effect. My interest here is in exploring one type of other effect, namely on the past and thereby the present of international law.

While I thus do not take up the more familiar topics of the Tokyo Women's Tribunal's significance for the comfort women themselves and its legitimacy vis-à-vis those accused, my focus is not intended to minimize their importance. Authors, some with immediate knowledge of the tribunal, have written movingly about its meaning for the surviving comfort women, their relatives and others committed to achieving justice for them (Chinkin 2001; Dudden 2001; Matsui 2001; Sajor 2004; Sakamoto 2001), and I respectfully acknowledge this as the tribunal's paramount aim. There is also a critical and historical literature on people's tribunals in international law (for example, Klinghoffer and Klinghoffer 2002), and others have evaluated the tribunal from these perspectives (for example, Chinkin 2001, 2006). Instead, I investigate the Tokyo Women's Tribunal with an eye to its particular form of the 'path not taken'.

Turning to fiction

What did the Tokyo Women's Tribunal's 'as if' fiction mean, exactly? A trial about historical events ordinarily applies the law as it existed when the events took place, and the tribunal thus applied the international law of 1937 to 1945, when the comfort women system operated. The importance of the fiction emerges, however, when we see how the tribunal dealt with a series of legal obstacles, including amnesties, statutes of limitations and double jeopardy. Amnesties were irrelevant because the tribunal *was* the IMTFE as of the time the IMTFE sat (1946–48). Japan had accepted the IMTFE's judgments and those of other Allied war crimes courts within and outside Japan under the treaty of peace it signed in San Francisco in 1951 (San Francisco Peace Treaty 1951), so it had consented to the Tokyo Women's Tribunal. Statutes of limitations did not apply because the Tokyo Women's Tribunal was sitting *in the 1940s*, before the end of the limitation period. And so on.

In addition, the Tokyo Women's Tribunal relied on the evidence before, and the findings of, the IMTFE. It adopted the IMTFE's findings that Japan had waged aggressive war, that Japanese 'abuse of civilians and civilian internees was extensive and pervasive throughout the region, most commonly taking the form of murder, torture, rape, forced labour, and confinement under inhumane conditions', and that the vast scale and common pattern of the atrocities committed by the Japanese in all theatres of war was such that they must either have been secretly ordered or wilfully permitted.

The Tokyo Women's Tribunal's self-identification with the IMTFE distinguishes it from other 'people's tribunals'. Yet, oddly, the tribunal associated itself with this type of tribunal without including the fiction in its list of distinguishing features. In line with the international war crimes tribunal convened by the philosophers Bertrand Russell and Jean-Paul Sartre in the 1960s to judge US actions in Vietnam and with other people's tribunals (see Klinghoffer and Klinghoffer 2002), the Tokyo Women's Tribunal described itself as 'a Tribunal conceived and established by the voices of civil society' and authorized not by a state or intergovernmental organization like the United Nations, but by 'the peoples of the Asia-Pacific region, and indeed, the peoples of the world'. It also followed in the footsteps of earlier women's tribunals and particularly the ongoing Courts of Women project that originated in Asia in 1993 (Chinkin 2006: 212–13). These bodies, however, did not assume the identity of a specific state-authorized tribunal.

Perhaps this difference has attracted almost no attention because the tribunal's judgment did not rely on the fiction alone. That is, for holdings that depended on the fiction, it also provided alternative reasons and thereby enabled commentators to ignore the fiction as a fanciful exercise. More likely, though, is that the Tokyo Women's Tribunal fell within an existing debate over the legitimacy of this type of tribunal: people's tribunal or mock tribunal?

Apart from concern for the issues, much of the scholarly interest in people's tribunals comes from legal pluralists who argue that the state should not be thought to have a monopoly on law and adjudication (see, for example, Berman 2002: 508–9). People's tribunals are just as 'real' as a state's courts. Indeed, one of the judges on the Tokyo Women's Tribunal later commented on the tribunal's fiction accordingly: people's tribunals often seek to build legitimacy by modelling themselves on an official body, and the tribunal's authority was enhanced by relying on facts proven before the IMTFE (Chinkin 2006: 215–16). However, this account is not perfect – did it really help the tribunal be taken seriously to pretend that Japan consented to it in the 1951 peace treaty, or that it was the 1940s when it was really 2000? And, did it fully capture the tribunal's production of international law? Leaving aside the usual focus on the reality of people's tribunals, I argue that there is something to be gained by studying the fictionality of the Tokyo Women's Tribunal (compare Riles 2009).

'Fact-ion' and 'pre-quel'

To make this argument, I draw a parallel between the Tokyo Women's Tribunal and the turn to the past in literature. The English novelist A.S. Byatt, author of the historical *Angels and Insects* and *Possession*, has observed a move in literature away from describing social concerns of contemporary society, whether realist or experimental in form, towards fiction that takes the past as its subject. There is, Byatt says:

> a large body of serious and ambitious fiction set in the past, not for the pleasures of escapism or bodice-ripping, but for complex aesthetic and intellectual reasons. Some of it is sober and some of it is fantastic, some of it is knowing and postmodern, some of it is feminist or post-colonial rewritings of official history, some of it is past prehistory, some of it is very recent.
>
> (Byatt 2000: 92–93)

Among the authors she names are J.M. Coetzee, Italo Calvino, Jeanette Winterson and Toni Morrison, and a flip through the pages of almost any weekend's book reviews would reveal new serious historical novels.

To the legal side of the parallel we could add, for instance, several recent collective projects rewriting pivotal judgments of the past. Nine leading American constitutional law scholars have rewritten *Brown* v. *Board of Education*, the United States Supreme Court's 1954 landmark opinion ending the racial segregation of public schools (Balkin 2001), and others have subsequently rewritten *Roe* v. *Wade*, the Court's famous 1973 case on the right to abortion (Balkin 2005). Akin to the Tokyo Women's Tribunal, these scholars set themselves the task of writing, in hindsight, what the US Supreme Court 'should have said', using only materials available as of the date the original opinion was handed down. In 2004, a group of feminist activists, lawyers and academics constituted themselves as the Women's Court of Canada and embarked on rewriting, one by one, the Supreme Court of Canada's judgments on equality (Women's Court of Canada 2006), and a similar project is under way for England and Wales (Feminist Judgments Project 2007, 2009).

The Tokyo Women's Tribunal, I argue, parallels two particular forms of literary engagement with the past. One is what is sometimes called 'fact-ion' because it mixes fact with fiction; for example, authors set their fictional characters amidst real historical figures and events. The other is the 'prequel', as opposed to sequel, in which the author takes a character or storyline from a well-known novel and writes about what happened before the plot of the novel begins. Both are forms of fiction that operate within constraints. Observing the turn to true stories and facts in fiction, Byatt writes, 'Writers of fiction [have] become preoccupied with truthfulness and accuracy' (Byatt 2000: 99). Whereas the constraints imposed by faction are real people and occurrences in the past, the prequel is hemmed in by the original novel's characters and plot to come. Indeed, lawyers may already recognize the parallel between a judicial opinion and a sequel (in our case, a prequel) from the work of legal philosopher Ronald Dworkin, who used the idea of writing the next chapter in a chain novel to express how a judicial opinion should 'fit' the law and make it best (Dworkin 1986: 228–38; see also Suk 2002).

Through a comparison with faction and the prequel, I show how the 'as if' fiction of the Tokyo Women's Tribunal creates effects on the past. Yes, the fiction may help establish the tribunal's legitimacy in the present by associating it with an official tribunal and providing a consistent legal approach to disposing of legal objections such as statutes of limitations. My point, however, is that there are also effects for the original IMTFE, which may be purely fictional but are none the less important for that. Specifically, the tribunal is the factional story of the IMTFE trying the accused for rape and sexual slavery as crimes against humanity based on the comfort women system. It thereby also adds a prequel to the story of prosecution of gender-related offences in international law, a story often taken to begin only with the international criminal tribunals for the former Yugoslavia and Rwanda in the 1990s.

Following a brief introduction to the Tokyo Women's Tribunal, I explain how this initiative mixed fact and fiction in its locations, participants and prosecution. I then illustrate the ways in which the tribunal's judgment was structured and constrained by the work of the IMTFE and the international laws of that time, giving it the plausibility of faction. But if the tribunal's judgment therefore differs from the judgment a women's tribunal would now render, I show that it also differs from the judgment the IMTFE would have rendered had the issue of the comfort women been prosecuted at

Tokyo in 1946. Current historical fiction comes in many forms, as Byatt observes, and the purposes of its writer vary widely. As a type of faction between a freely feminist representation of the IMTFE's judgment that might have been and a judgment that channels the minds of the original judges, the tribunal's 'as if' device is, I suggest, a distinctive form of critique, and I conclude with some thoughts on the nature and limits of this form of critique.

Tokyo Women's Tribunal

A brief sketch

Prior to the 1990s, the existence of the Second World War comfort women was not unknown – in Japan, they turned up in memoirs, histories, novels and films – but their victimization was rarely recognized as criminal (Hicks 1994: 67–71, 180, 194–96; Kimura 2008: 13–15). This changed at the beginning of the 1990s, notably when Korean comfort women started to make their stories public and to demand an apology and compensation from the Japanese Government. These revelations led hundreds more comfort women throughout the Asia-Pacific region to speak out (Hicks 1994: 196–219). Although the Japanese Government has taken some steps to make amends (UN 1996a), lawsuits in Japan and elsewhere have been unsuccessful (Levin 2008; *Hwang Geum Joo* v. *Japan* 2005),[6] and United Nations recommendations (UN 1996, 1998; UN 2008: para. 22) and other forms of international pressure have also not yielded results (Chinkin 2006: 206–10; Hayashi 2001; UN 2008: para. 22).

Seeking a new forum, various women's and human rights non-governmental organizations across Asia created the Tokyo Women's Tribunal, which sat in Tokyo from 8 December to 10 December 2000. The tribunal's two lead prosecutors indicted a number of high-ranking Japanese military and political officials, including Emperor Hirohito, for rape and sexual slavery as crimes against humanity. Distinct from this issue of individual criminal responsibility, the prosecutors also submitted an application for restitution and reparations, asserting that Japan incurred ongoing responsibility as a state.[7] In addition to the common indictment, prosecution teams from 10 countries presented separate indictments: North and South Korea (which prepared a joint indictment), China, Japan, the Philippines, Indonesia, Taiwan, Malaysia, East Timor and the Netherlands. Sixty-four women from the comfort stations attended, and a number gave evidence. Others testified through video interview and by affidavit. The witnesses also included two former Japanese soldiers who had used the comfort women facilities. The prosecution presented documentary evidence and expert evidence on issues ranging from the structure of the Japanese army to international law to psychological and other sorts of trauma. As the Government of Japan was notified of the proceedings but did not appear, an *amicus curiae*, or 'friend of the court', presented the arguments of the individual accused and the state of Japan. The tribunal also considered Japan's submissions in related cases before its courts and elsewhere. In keeping with the tribunal's charter, the judges were four 'internationally renowned persons in the field of human rights' and reflected a diversity of regions (Africa, Europe, North and South America), expertise across relevant areas of domestic and international law, a combination of practitioner, judicial and academic experience and a gender ratio of three women and one man (a male judge from Asia was named, but could not attend due to illness).

The tribunal found Emperor Hirohito and the other nine defendants guilty of rape and sexual slavery as crimes against humanity. It also found Japan liable for the harm inflicted by the comfort women system and required the Japanese Government to provide a number of remedial measures, including a full apology and compensation for the victims. The preliminary judgment was given orally on 12 December 2000 in Tokyo before an audience of more than a thousand people, and the final judgment, more than 250 pages long, was delivered on 4 December 2001 in the Hague (Chinkin 2001: 336–38).

The tribunal as historical fiction

To see the Tokyo Women's Tribunal as 'fact-ion', consider Pat Barker's anti-war novel *Regeneration*, which combines real-life characters and events with fictional ones. At the centre of *Regeneration* is a true occurrence dating from 1917: during the First World War, Siegfried Sassoon, the poet and deco-rated British officer, protested against the continuation of the war. Rather than court martial him and thereby grant him the public forum he sought, the army declared him insane and sent him to a military hospital for the 'shell-shocked', where he came under the care of Dr William Rivers, a dis-tinguished neurologist and social anthropologist who was a captain in the Royal Army Medical Corps. In Barker's fictional plot probing the insanity of war, Sassoon's evident sanity troubles Dr Rivers and causes him to question his own role in 'curing' his patients only to return them to the slaughter of the battlefield. As one reviewer observed of the conversations between Sassoon and another real-life British war poet, Wilfred Owen, and the doctors at the hospital, they sound absolutely authentic. 'We are aware that she is invent-ing dialogue for her characters, but it is informed invention. If this isn't how they actually spoke, then it's surely how they might have' (Mitgang 1992).

Turning to the location of the tribunal and its participants, we can see a similar mixture of fact and fiction. Like the original IMTFE in 1946, the Tokyo Women's Tribunal sat in Tokyo. And in a nod to the future, the tribunal's final judgment was handed down in the Hague, seat of the International Criminal Court, the long-awaited permanent successor to the post-Second World War war crimes tribunals, which was then still on the horizon.

The victims and witnesses before the Tokyo Women's Tribunal, it goes without saying, were all too real. In contrast, though, among the tribunal's personnel there was a distinctive interplay of the real and the fictional, as well as present and past. Two of the four judges were judges by profession, switching from their regular role as official judge to that of unofficial judge on this 2000 grass-roots women's tribunal – and thereby taking on the part of official judge on the IMTFE in 1946. The presiding judge, Judge Gabrielle Kirk McDonald, was the former president of the International Criminal Tribunal for the Former Yugoslavia. Judge Carmen Argibay was a criminal law judge in Argentina and president of the International Association of Women Judges, and P.N. Bhagwati, formerly on the Indian Supreme Court, would have sat, but for ill health. One of the two lead prosecutors, Patricia Viseur Sellers, was with the Office of the Prosecutor, International Criminal Tribunal for the Former Yugoslavia. Whereas the surviving comfort women, and those who did not survive, could really have been at Tokyo, these judges and prosecutors obviously could not. In this sense, they are like *Regeneration*'s fictional characters among Sassoon, Rivers and Owen. They strike us, contemporary readers, as the kind of people who might have been involved in the original Tokyo Tribunal, had they been around then.

This past is also prelude. A number of the participants in the Tokyo Women's Tribunal, most notably Judges McDonald and Christine Chinkin and the two lead prosecutors, Sellers and Ustinia Dolgopol, have been central to the development of feminist approaches to international law or have played a role in the inclusion of crimes of sexual violence in the statutes of the Yugoslavia and Rwanda war crimes tribunals and the Rome Statute of the International Criminal Court, and in the prosecution of such crimes before the tribunals. These participants were, in effect, acting as their own predecessors. This is most striking at the moment in the judgment when the Tokyo Women's Tribunal referred to what current international law said about international law's treatment of rape at the time of the offences. In a double image, the judges circa 1946 (in fact, 2000) – who included McDonald and Chinkin – cited McDonald's and Chinkin's contributions to the explicit criminalization of rape in international law, along with those of Sellers, Dolgopol and other gender-oriented academics, activists and jurists dating from the 1990s (compare Riles 2002). By peopling and writing the 'pre-quel' to these late-twentieth century feminist initiatives in international law, the tribunal made these initiatives look like a continuation of the fact-ional Tokyo trial, rather than a change from the actual Tokyo trial. As I will discuss, this backfilling de-radicalizes the later developments, contributing to the impression that they were gradual next steps in the inclusion of women and issues of gender justice in international law and institutions.

The prosecution also mixes fact and fiction. The following facts appear in the Tokyo Women's Tribunal's judgment and indicate that charges could have been brought in 1946 for crimes committed against the comfort women. There is evidence that the Allies knew of them. The IMTFE's judgment even contains what has been read as a reference to the comfort women: in Kweilin, the Japanese forces 'recruited women labor on the pretext of establishing factories. They forced the women thus recruited into prostitution with the Japanese troops' (Boister and Cryer 2008: 540). Finally, crimes against Dutch comfort women were prosecuted by the Dutch in war crimes trials held in the Netherlands East Indies. At least two such trials took place in Batavia (now Jakarta) (*Trial of Washio Awochi* 1946; Yoshimi 2000: 163–76). The fiction is, of course, that the 'IMTFE' prosecuted crimes based on the comfort women system. And, more generally, the prosecution before the Tokyo Women's Tribunal, in effect, corrected several often-cited flaws in the original prosecution: the lack of significant Asian involvement in the prosecution, the non-indictment of Emperor Hirohito and the neglect of crimes committed against the Asian civilian population (Boister and Cryer 2008a: 203–4, 311–12; Paik 1986: 53–54).

The story

Unlike a historical hypothesis or a present-day people's tribunal dispensing historical justice, the Tokyo Women's Tribunal's fiction is a kind of time machine that enabled it to go back and convict *as* the IMTFE after the Second World War. According to the tribunal, the facts and the law demanded the conviction of Emperor Hirohito and the nine other high-ranking Japanese officials accused of rape and sexual slavery as crimes against humanity based on the comfort women system. The obvious 'fact-ional' effect is to add the tribunal's verdict to the number of post-war convictions for crimes of sexual violence and thereby to strengthen the pattern of prosecution. As well, the tribunal not only increased the total of the 'IMTFE's' accounts of sexual violence by Japanese troops; it effectively reconstituted the original IMTFE's accounts as part of a larger systemic problem which included institutionalized sexual violence in the form of the comfort women system – 'rape as part of the very engine of war' (Chinkin 2001: 340). There is a similarity here to *Regeneration*, in which Pat Barker placed Dr Rivers's treatment of Siegfried Sassoon within the novel's anti-war framework.

By analyzing rape as a tactic used strategically by the military despite its centuries-long prohibition by the laws of war, the tribunal also created a 'pre-quel'. In the 1990s, the recognition that rape was an instrument of ethnic cleansing in Yugoslavia and Rwanda led to the emergence of a global movement to end impunity for international crimes of sexual violence. In reality, the comfort women's public demands for an apology and compensation were contemporaneous with this movement and contributed to it significantly.

However, the fiction that the Tokyo Women's Tribunal *was* the IMTFE serves to backdate the tribunal's analysis of rape, thereby arguably defusing the novelty of 'later' feminist analyses of Yugoslavia and Rwanda that might otherwise seem extreme in characterizing the sexual violence in war as structural.

Perhaps most central to this chapter's task, the Tokyo Women's Tribunal itself tells us what broader impact its outcome would have had on the development of international law. It would have helped to change worldwide patterns of sexual stereotyping that continue to subjugate women, and it would have been a step, decades before Yugoslavia and Rwanda, toward 'ending impunity and reversing the blatant disregard of the bodily integrity, inherent dignity, and, indeed, the very humanity of women', particularly women of subordinated ethnicities.

Yet this is too simple because it understates the constraints imposed by faction, here in the form of the applicable law. On the one hand, the preamble of the Charter of the Tokyo Women's Tribunal refers to 'the principles of law, human conscience, humanity and gender justice that were an integral part of international law at the time of the offenses, and that *should have been* applied by, the International Military Tribunal for the Far East' (emphasis added). On the other, not all international laws of the time could be freed of their discriminatory assumptions about gender or race. For instance, the tribunal cited the 1907 Hague Convention IV Respecting the Laws and Customs of War and its annexed Regulations (Hague Convention IV 1907) to establish that sexual violence was prohibited by the laws and customs of war by the time of the Second World War. While the Hague convention and its regulations do not make express reference to rape, the article of the regulations on respect for family honour was and is generally understood to prohibit rape. Feminists have criticized the characterization of rape as an injury to honour, rather than an act of sexual violence (Charlesworth 1999: 386–87; Gardam and Jarvis 2001: 107–12; Halley 2008: 57–59). Indeed, the tribunal – in a sort of authorial aside – agreed that this characterization minimizes the crime's violent nature, ignores the egregious harm to the bodily integrity of the women and reflects as well as perpetuates the stigmatization of raped women. Nevertheless, given the provision's wording, the tribunal stuck to the legal sensibility of the time. By categorizing rape as a violation of family honour, the judges did not change the sexual stereotypes then embedded in international law or increase its regard for women's bodily integrity and inherent dignity. Rather, they applied these stereotypes even as they criticized them.

In taking a step towards reversing international law's disregard for women of subordinated ethnicities, the Tokyo Women's Tribunal also had to contend with the impact of colonialism on the international law of the Second World War period. The so-called 'colonial applications clause' in the 1921 International Convention for the Suppression of the Traffic in Women and

Children is a good example (LN 1922). The convention was among the sources of law used by the tribunal to establish that sexual slavery was an international criminal offence prior to 1937. Although Japan was a party, it had excluded Chosen (Korea), Taiwan and several Japanese territories, as was permitted by the convention's colonial applications clause. There is documentary evidence to indicate that the Japanese Government relied on this loophole in turning 'Korea and Taiwan into supply depots for military comfort women', while seeking to limit the recruitment of Japanese women from Japan in keeping with the anti-trafficking conventions (Yoshimi 2000: 157, 154–60). Indeed, the abduction and trafficking of Japanese women to a navy comfort station in 1932 had been prosecuted some years later. Although the wording of the clause clearly allowed Japan to exclude 'any or all of its colonies, overseas possessions, protectorates or territories under its sovereignty or authority', the Tokyo Women's Tribunal held that the convention nevertheless applied to Japan's territories in the case of the comfort women because the intention behind the clause was only to allow the imperial state to make allowances for local customs such as the payment of dowry, and the clause had to be interpreted narrowly in light of this intention.

The tribunal's reading of the colonial applications clause is possible (see Dolgopol and Paranjape 1994: 157–58), but the lack of any obvious sign of this intention in the League of Nations records (Robinson 2009)[8] as well as the wording make it seem more likely that a tribunal at the time would have upheld Japan's exclusion of its territories from the convention. In addition, the Tribunal's culturally sensitive story about the colonial applications clause effectively papers over the racialized history of what earlier anti-trafficking agreements called the issue of 'white slave traffic'. The popular push for these agreements came from a moral panic in various Western countries about white women who were deceived or tricked into becoming prostitutes abroad, and groups campaigning against trafficking adopted the term 'white slavery' to build on the success of earlier anti-slavery efforts (Demleitner 1994: 165–67; Doezema 2000).

Although the international anti-trafficking movement that developed and became institutionalized in the League of Nations extended to all women (LN Covenant 1919: art. 23(c)), it has similarly been criticized for ignoring women of colour or, conversely, for opposing their exploitation in the colonies out of fears of racial mixing (Limoncelli 2006: 60). The social purity reformers who made up one of the two major international associations behind the movement tended to concentrate on protecting women based on their nationality – 'our' women – and on increasing the state's control over sexuality in the process. In contrast, the feminist abolitionists who comprised the other major international association worked to outlaw trafficking as part of their agenda to abolish the state's regulation of prostitution worldwide, colonies included, and were motivated by universal concerns about gender exploitation and the individual rights of women. According to a comparative study, the relative influence of these two associations nationally was an important factor in whether a state applied the convention and other anti-trafficking agreements to its colonies or only to the metropole (Limoncelli 2006). This historical context of imperialism, race and gender is absent from the tribunal's treatment of the colonial applications clause.

It does not follow that the themes of colonialism and racism are altogether absent from the tribunal's judgment. The tribunal separated its description of the comfort women system by territory and nationality of the girls and women, and it noted, for example, that the Japanese treated many of the Dutch comfort women better.[9] However, the main theme was gender. The tribunal was a women's tribunal trying crimes against women and, unlike the IMTFE, did not ultimately have an Asian judge. It adjudicated the comfort women system as a whole, and the charges were crimes of sex-related violence. Indeed, the Korean women's movement had worked to shift the understanding of Korean comfort women away from a symbol of national shame, a nationalistic depiction that divided Korean victims from other comfort women (Sakamoto 2001: 51, 57; Ueno 2004: 92–94).

At the same time, in keeping with the scope of the IMTFE (Röling 1993: 59–60), the Tokyo Women's Tribunal did not venture into a gender analysis of the Allies' conduct during the Second World War. (Judge Pal, in marked contrast, measured Japanese war crimes against the decision of the Allied powers to use the atomic bomb (Boister and Cryer 2008: 1355).) In particular, the tribunal did not examine the issue of military-controlled prostitution during the Second World War apart from the Japanese comfort women system. Yuki Tanaka's controversial hypothesis is that the Japanese system did not give rise to charges in 1946 because the Allies saw nothing criminal about it (Tanaka 2002: 82–83, 87, 109). In addition to their treatment of non-Western women prior to the war, he grounds this theory in a demon-stration of the Allied countries' own practices of, and attempts to cover up, military-controlled prostitution during the war; and their complicity in the short-lived system that Japan created to service Allied soldiers during the post-war occupation of Japan.

As these various examples suggest, although the Tokyo Women's Tribunal's story was constrained by the fiction that the tribunal *was* the IMTFE in 1946, the tribunal's story might nevertheless not be the judgment the original IMTFE would have rendered had it adjudicated the comfort women issue. In the first place, the original IMTFE's treatment of the issue probably would have been less extensive. Relative to crimes against peace, it devoted little space in its judgment to the evidence of war crimes, which included mass rape – and the comfort women in Kweilin.

Even more to the point, we now have some idea of how the IMTFE itself might have dealt with the comfort women issue because research published since the judgment of the Tokyo Women's Tribunal challenges the common understanding that the IMTFE heard no evidence at all on the issue (Totani 2008: 179, 253). The overwhelming fact remains that the Allies did not prosecute crimes committed against comfort women in Korea and Taiwan, that is, in Japan's colonies (Totani 2008: 13–14), but the Chinese and the Dutch prosecution teams at Tokyo each presented evidence of the Japanese military's comfort women system in territories occupied by Japan. In particular, the Dutch sought to prove a widespread practice of what was characterized as enforced prostitution, and introduced four cases spanning a broad region in and around the Dutch East Indies and involving women of different racial and ethnic backgrounds (Totani 2008: 153, 174, 176–79). Besides the reference to the Kweilin comfort women in the majority judgment, however, the only other reference is found in Judge Pal's lengthy dissent; namely, that the prosecutors had led evidence that 'from early 1943 onwards throughout Western Borneo, Indian and Chinese women were arrested and forced into brothels' (Boister and Cryer 2008: 1348). Research has yet to explain why the IMTFE did not go further (Totani 2008: 185–86).

Lastly, even if the IMTFE had convicted, the reasons would probably not have been as progressive as in the tribunal's judgment, which gave as little play as possible to paternalistic assumptions about gender and race reflected in Second World War era international laws and legal sensibilities. The Dutch prosecutors at Tokyo and also at Batavia spoke in terms of enforced prostitution, whereas the charge before the Tokyo Women's Tribunal was sexual slavery – not recognized as an international crime until the 1990s (Oosterveld 2004: 607). The tribunal avoided fracturing its 'as if' fiction by maintaining, essentially, that sexual slavery was simply a more appropriate name for enforced prostitution (but see Oosterveld 2004: 616–22, 646). To call the crime 'enforced prostitution' or 'forced prostitution' was to obscure the crime's gravity: it tended to adopt the male viewpoint of the organizers, procurers and those who took advantage of the system to rape the women, as opposed to using the term 'sexual slavery' which better reflected the enormity of the women's subordination and suffering. The tribunal also objected to the term 'enforced prostitution' because it wrongly implied a level of voluntariness and branded its victims as immoral or 'used goods'. Nevertheless, the IMTFE likely would have adopted the Dutch prosecution's legal characterization of enforced prostitution; alternatively, it might have characterized the harms as slavery, but not as sexual slavery.

Conclusion

The nature of the Tokyo Women's Tribunal as both a 'real' people's tribunal sitting in the present and the 'fictional' extension of the post-war IMTFE means that the tribunal was simultaneously trying a case of justice delayed and creating an imaginary past in which the IMTFE tried the case. In creating this past, the tribunal did not distinguish between doing what the

IMTFE *could and should* have done, had the issue of the comfort women been fully addressed at the original Tokyo trial, and doing what the IMTFE *would* have done. The two are different critiques of international law, and I have suggested that the tribunal was engaged in the former. Its enterprise was textual more than sociological. The latter structuralist critique would have been to determine and criticize what would probably have occurred, taking into account the biases of the time reflected in the law, the Allied goals for the trial, different prosecutorial training and judicial backgrounds and so on. Instead, the tribunal's critique lay elsewhere: namely, in a painstakingly detailed technical legal demonstration that a different, more desirable past was possible and even plausible.

This brings us back to A.S. Byatt and the turn to historical fiction; this time, to what her novel *Possession* seems to tell us about her own approach to the genre. *Possession* is the story of a search by two literary scholars to uncover and trace the secret romance between two Victorian poets. Because it 'connects the scholars' transformation of their social identities to their growing knowledge about the lives and beliefs of the Victorian poets', the novel has been read as 'linking the imagination of alternative social identities to a historically accurate reconstruction of the past' (Su 2004: 687). But *Possession* has also been understood as expressing 'Byatt's apparent preference for what might be called a usable past over an absolutely accurate one' (Su 2004: 704). Similarly, we can interpret the Tokyo Women's Tribunal as offering a 'usable past' that depends on being true to the givens, but also seeks to consolidate feminist gains in current international law by constructing a fictional precedent.

The logical limit of the tribunal's style of critique is that it cannot judge the IMTFE because it cannot stand outside and judge 'itself'. The crucial structural question, almost implicit in the tribunal's *having taken* the other path and yet impossible to investigate within its parameters, is why crimes relating to the comfort women were not prosecuted at Tokyo (or not fully prosecuted, since we now know that some cases were raised).

However, much as a work of historical fiction can involve multiple forms of narrating the past, the Tokyo Women's Tribunal did not continue the logic that it *was* the IMTFE all the way through the judgment. Whereas the IMTFE tried and punished Japanese individuals for war crimes, the tribunal also went on to consider whether the state of Japan had a duty to prevent and repair the crimes committed against the comfort women and, if so, whether Japan's failure to fulfil this duty constituted a continuing breach of its responsibility as a state and inflicted additional harm upon the victims for which it was additionally liable. The tribunal thus implicitly set aside its institutional identity as the IMTFE in a sort of epilogue that returns us to the true narrative of the former comfort women since the Second World War.

In this context, the final pages of the judgment address the 'why not' question. Perhaps, in a sense, the tribunal's 'as if' fiction caused its own displacement: to perform the possibility of a better past is to all but ask why it did not happen that way in reality. The tribunal did not answer the question, but it recommended that the former Allied nations release the records necessary to determine why Japan's establishment and operation of the comfort women system was not prosecuted and acknowledge their own roles in this failure. Nevertheless, the tribunal also stated that it found persuasive the prosecutors' argument that the failure to address the issues of military sexual slavery and rape stemmed from women's lack of equal representation at the peace negotiations and the resulting gender bias of the peace treaty.

Of course, no one can say what would have happened, and it would have depended upon, among other things, which women, on what side, speaking for whom. The point I want to make is that here – in the 'nonfiction' part of the tribunal's judgment – is a gesture towards a further historical fiction: *had women been there* ... Ironically, though, the 'had women been there' theory obscures the reality of when they actually were. Perhaps women were not at the peace negotiations, but they helped to shape a number of international treaties prior to the Second World War, including some of the very treaties that figured in the reasons of the Tokyo Women's Tribunal. Historians of the British empire have argued that in the period between the two world wars, British imperialists' increasing attention to humanitarianism intersected with an emerging internationalism, and this intersection led women's groups previously concerned with domestic reforms to transform into international NGOs (Gorman 2008: 187–88). One has even dubbed this the 'maternalist moment' in imperial history (Pedersen 2001: 164–66). However, then as now, the women involved in the anti-trafficking movement were a mixture of feminists, social purity reformers, abolitionists, regulationists, and others. They were divided over the right approach to the problem, and these divisions were refracted through the power dynamics and social attitudes of colonialism (Limoncelli 2006). Much like social purity reformers in the West, the Japanese movement to abolish prostitution also 'stayed on friendly terms with imperialism' (Fujime 1997: 163). The effect of the 'had women been there' theory is to create a historical vacuum into which women *like those who participated in the Tokyo Women's Tribunal* could be fictionally inserted: had *they* been given an equal voice at the peace talks, the Allied powers would have prosecuted the war crimes based on Japan's military comfort women system. But this implicit filling of the vacuum neglects, to some extent, the real women who were active at the time on issues such as trafficking and prostitution and their diverse motives, beliefs and strategies.

On the one hand, then, 'had women been there' is simply an explanation for why crimes relating to the comfort women were not prosecuted at Tokyo. On the other, it implies a further 'path not taken', to quote from the editors' vision for these chapters. Although evoked only briefly, this path joins the path marked out by the Tokyo Women's Tribunal's principal fiction – that it *was* the IMTFE in 1946 – to help create a feminist past *manqué* for international law that reinforces its real present.

Notes

1 I am grateful to Annelise Riles, Christine Chinkin, Angela Fernandez, Janet Halley, Fleur Johns, Craig Martin, Valerie Oosterveld, Denise Réaume, Mark Selder and the members of the Women's Court of Canada for their comments on early versions of this chapter. My gratitude also goes to Robert Cryer and Tina Dolgopol for help with sources and to Cheryl Robinson for her unflagging research assistance.

2 Unless otherwise indicated, my analysis draws on the final judgment of the Women's International War Crimes Tribunal on Japan's Military Sexual Slavery (TWT 2001).

3 The term 'comfort women', which I follow the Women's International War Crimes Tribunal for the Trial of Japan's Military Sexual Slavery in using throughout, reflects the idea that sex provided Japanese soldiers with recreation that both fuelled them for battle and relieved their tensions. The principal reasons given for establishing the comfort women system, however, were to prevent Japanese troops from contracting sexually transmitted diseases and to counteract the anti-Japanese sentiment caused by Japanese soldiers' extensive sexual abuse of civilian women, particularly after the conquest of Nanking, as well as to eliminate the risk of spying and dissemination of army secrets if the soldiers went to local brothels.

4 The tribunal proceeded on the basis that the comfort women issue was not addressed at all at the original Tokyo trial. Research published since has shown that the prosecution did present some evidence, but I set this aside until later in the chapter because my interest is in the tribunal's project as it was understood at the time.

5 I use the term 'as if' as shorthand for the notion that Tokyo Women's Tribunal sat '*as if it were* a reopening or a continuation' of the official IMTFE and subsidiary trials, but 'as if' is also a philosophical term of art for knowledge that is consciously false and therefore irrefutable, unlike a hypothesis which can be disproven or a presumption which can be rebutted (Vaihinger 1924).

6 Nevertheless, the rulings in the Japanese cases have 'provided a modest degree of factual recognition of the historical record' (Levin 2008: 154).

7 Because the Tribunal's treatment of the state responsibility issue is implicitly not premised on its 'as if' fiction, I leave it until the discussion of the fiction's limits in the conclusion. A further charge, relating to the mass rapes inflicted upon the female population of Mapanique in the Philippines in November 1944, is not dealt with in this chapter.

8 To the contrary, authors writing around the time of the IMTFE identified local autonomy, rather than local customs, as Britain's stated rationale for insisting on a colonial applications clause in all international agreements capable of affecting the internal affairs of its colonies. The clause permitted Britain to exclude its colonies at the time of signature or ratification and to extend the agreement to them afterwards as consent was obtained (Fawcett 1949; Simpson 2001: 288–91, 476). In particular, this policy of self-government was the reason given by Britain for its efforts to insert a colonial applications clause into a later anti-trafficking convention (Liang 1951: 116–17, 124–25).

9 In contrast to the parts of the judgment in which the Tokyo Women's Tribunal dealt with individual criminal responsibility as if it were the IMTFE, the later parts on Japan's ongoing responsibility as a state, which do not employ this fiction, include the finding that Japan discriminated based on gender, race, nationality and/or ethnic origin. This shift in the tribunal's self-identification is addressed in the conclusion.

References

Balkin, J.M. (ed.) (2001) *What Brown v. Board of Education Should Have Said: The Nation's Top Legal Experts Rewrite America's Landmark Civil Rights Decision*, New York: New York University Press.

——(2005) *What Roe v. Wade Should Have Said: The Nation's Top Legal Experts Rewrite America's Most Controversial Decision*, New York: New York University Press.

Berman, P.S. (2002) 'The globalization of jurisdiction', *University of Pennsylvania Law Review*, 151: 311–545.

Boister, N. and Cryer, R. (eds) (2008) *Documents on the Tokyo International Military Tribunal. Charter, Indictment and Judgments*, Oxford: Oxford University Press.

——(2008a) *The Tokyo International Military Tribunal: A Reappraisal*, Oxford: Oxford University Press.

Byatt, A.S. (2000) 'True stories and the facts in fiction', in *On Histories and Stories. Selected Essays*, Cambridge, MA: Harvard University Press.

Charlesworth, H. (1999) 'Feminist methods in international law', *American Journal of International Law*, 93: 379–94.

Chinkin, C. (2001) 'Women's International Tribunal on Japanese Military Sexual Slavery', *American Journal of International Law*, 95: 335–41.

——(2006) 'Peoples' tribunals: legitimate or rough justice', *Windsor Yearbook of Access to Justice*, 24: 201–20.

Demleitner, N.V. (1994) 'Forced prostitution: naming an international offence', *Fordham International Law Journal*, 18: 163–97.

Doezema, J. (2000) 'Loose women or lost women? The re-emergence of the myth of white slavery in contemporary discourses of trafficking in women', *Gender Issues*, 18(1): 23–50.

Dolgopol, U. and Paranjape, S. (1994) *Comfort Women: An Unfinished Ordeal. Report of a Mission*, Geneva: International Commission of Jurists.

Dudden, A. (2001) '"We came to tell the truth": reflections on the Tokyo Women's Tribunal', *Critical Asian Studies*, 33: 591–602.

Dworkin, R. (1986) *Law's Empire*, Cambridge, MA: Belknap Press of Harvard University Press.

Fawcett, J.E.S. (1949) 'Treaty relations of British Overseas Territories', *British Year Book of International Law*, 26: 86–107.

Feminist Judgments Project (2007) Call for expressions of interest. Available online at: <www.dur.ac.uk/resources/law/research/feministjudgments.pdf> (accessed 9 August 2009).

——(2009) Feminist Judgements Project Available online at: <www.feministjudgments.org.uk> (accessed 9 August 2009).

Fujime, Y. (1997) 'The licensed prostitution system and the prostitution abolition movement in modern Japan', *Positions*, 5(1): 135–70.

Futamura, M. (2008) *War Crimes Tribunals and Transitional Justice: The Tokyo Trial and the Nuremberg Legacy*, London: Routledge.

Gardam, J.G. and Jarvis, M.J. (2001) *Women, Armed Conflict and International Law*, The Hague: Kluwer Law International.

Gorman, D. (2008) 'Empire, internationalism, and the campaign against the traffic in women and children in the 1920s', *Twentieth Century British History*, 19(2): 186–216.

Hague Convention IV (1907) *Convention Respecting the Laws and Customs of War on Land, with annexed Regulations*, 18 October 1907. Stat. 36: 227; Bevans 1: 631.

Halley, J. (2008) 'Rape at Rome: feminist interventions in the criminalization of sex-related violence in positive international criminal law', *Michigan Journal of International Law*, 30: 1–123.

Hayashi, H. (2001) 'The Japanese movement to protest wartime sexual violence: a survey of Japanese and international literature', *Critical Asian Studies*, 33(4): 572–80.

Hicks, G. (1994) *The Comfort Women: Japan's Brutal Regime of Enforced Prostitution in the Second World War*, New York: W.W. Norton & Co.

Hwang Geum Joo v. *Japan*. (2005) 413 F.3d 45, 367 US App. D.C. 45.

Kimura, M. (2008) 'Narrative as a site of subject construction: the "comfort women" debate', *Feminist Theory*, 9 (1): 5–24.

Klinghoffer, A.J. and Klinghoffer, J.A. (2002) *International Citizens' Tribunals. Mobilizing Public Opinion to Advance Human Rights*, New York: Palgrave.

Levin, M.A. (2008) 'Nishimatsu Construction Co. v. Song Jixiao *et al.*; Kō Hanako et al. v. Japan', *American Journal of International Law*, 102: 148–54.

Liang, Y. (1951) 'Notes on legal questions concerning the United Nations', *American Journal of International Law*, 45: 108–28.

Limoncelli, S.A. (2006) 'The politics of humanitarianism: states, reformers, and the international movement to combat the traffic in women, 1875–1960', Ph.D. diss., University of California, Los Angeles.

LN (League of Nations), Treaty Series (1922) International Convention for the Suppression of Traffic in Women and Children. 30 September 1921. *League of Nations Treaty Series*, 9, no. 269. Available online at: <http://treaties.un.org/doc/Treaties/1921/09/19210930%2005–59%20AM/Ch_VII_3p.pdf> (accessed 10 August 2009).

LN Covenant (Covenant of the League of Nations) (1919) Treaty of Versailles (Treaty of Peace Between the Allied and Associated Powers and Germany). 28 June 1919. *League of Nations Treaty Series*, No. 34.

Matsui, Y. (2001) 'Women's International War Crimes Tribunal on Japan's Military Sexual Slavery: memory, identity, and society', *East Asia: An International Quarterly*, 19(4): 119–42.

Minear, R.H. (1971) *Victors' Justice. The Tokyo War Crimes Trial*, Princeton: Princeton University Press.

Mitgang, H. (1992) 'Healing a mind and spirit badly wounded in the trenches', *New York Times*, 15 April.

Ōnuma, Y. (1986) 'The Tokyo trial: between law and politics', in C. Hosoya, N. Andō, Y. Ōnuma and R. Minear (eds) *The Tokyo War Crimes Trial: An International Symposium*, Tokyo: Kodansha Ltd.

Oosterveld, V. (2004) 'Sexual slavery and the International Criminal Court: advancing international law', *Michigan Journal of International Law*, 25: 605–51.

Paik, C. (1986) 'Comments', in C. Hosoya, N. Andō, Y. Ōnuma and R. Minear (eds) *The Tokyo War Crimes Trial: An International Symposium*, Tokyo: Kodansha Ltd.

Pedersen, S. (2001) 'The maternalist moment in British colonial policy: the controversy over "child slavery" in Hong Kong 1917–41', *Past and Present*, 171: 161–202.

Piccigallo, P.R. (1979) *The Japanese on Trial: Allied War Crimes Operations in the East, 1945–1951*, Austin: University of Texas Press.

Riles, A. (2002) 'The virtual sociality of rights: the case of "women's rights are human rights"', in Michael Likosky (ed) *Transnational Legal Processes*, Cambridge, UK: Cambridge University Press.

——(2009) 'Legal fictions', unpublished paper.

Robinson, C. (2009) 'The 1921 Convention for the Suppression of the Traffic in Women and Children and Colonialism', unpublished paper.

Röling, B.V.A. (1993) *The Tokyo Trial and Beyond: Reflections of a Peacemonger*, edited and with an introduction by Antonio Cassese, Cambridge: Polity Press.

Sajor, I.L. (2004) 'Challenging international law: the quest for justice of the former "comfort women"', in Sharon Pickering and Caroline Lambert (eds) *Global Issues, Women and Justice*, Sydney: Sydney Institute of Criminology Series No. 19.

Sakamoto, R. (2001) 'The Women's International War Crimes Tribunal on Japan's Military Sexual Slavery: a legal and feminist approach to the "comfort women" issue', *New Zealand Journal of Asian Studies*, 3: 49–58.

San Francisco Peace Treaty (Treaty of Peace with Japan). Signed at San Francisco, 8 September 1951; entered into force, 28 April 1962. *United Nations Treaty Series* 136: 45.

Sellers, P.V. (2000) 'The context of sexual violence: sexual violence as violations of international humanitarian law', in Gabrielle Kirk McDonald and Olivia Swaak-Goldman (eds) *Substantive and Procedural Aspects of International Criminal Law: The Experience of National and International Courts*, vol. 1, the Hague: Kluwer Law International.

Simpson, A.W.B. (2001) *Human Rights and the End of Empire. Britain and the Genesis of the European Convention*, Oxford: Oxford University Press.

Su, J.J. (2004) 'Fantasies of (re)collection: collecting and imagination in A.S. Byatt's *Possession: A Romance*', *Contemporary Literature*, 45 (4): 684–712.

Suk, J. (2002) 'Originality', *Harvard Law Review*, 115: 1988–2009.

TWT (Women's International War Crimes Tribunal for the Trial of Japan's Military Sexual Slavery) (2001) *Judgment on the Common Indictment and the Application for Restitution and Reparation*. Available online at: <http://www1.jca.apc.org/vaww-net-japan/english/womenstribunal2000/Judgement.pdf> (accessed 10 August 2009).

Tanaka, Y. (2002) *Japan's Comfort Women. Sexual slavery and prostitution during World War II and the US occupation*, New York: Routledge.

Totani, Y. (2008) *The Tokyo War Crimes Trial: The Pursuit of Justice in the Wake of World War II*, Cambridge, MA: Harvard University Asia Center.

Trial of Washio Awochi (1946) United Nations War Crimes Commission, Law Reports of Trials of War Criminals 8:122, No. 76 (1949).

Ueno, C. (2004) *Nationalism and Gender*, trans. Beverly Yamamoto. Melbourne: Trans Pacific Press.

UN (United Nations, Commission on Human Rights) (1996) *Report of the Special Rapporteur on Violence Against Women, Its Causes and Consequences, Ms Radhika Coomaraswamy, in accordance with Commission on Human Rights resolution 1994/45. Report on the Mission to the Democratic People's Republic of Korea, the Republic of Korea and Japan on the Issue of Military Sexual Slavery in Wartime*, E/CN.4/1996/53/Add.1.

UN (United Nations, Commission on Human Rights) (1996a) *Note Verbale Dated 26 March 1996 From the Permanent Mission of Japan to the United Nations Office at Geneva Addressed to the Centre for Human Rights*. E/CN.4/1996/137.

UN (United Nations, Human Rights Committee) (2008) *Concluding Observations of the Human Rights Committee: Japan*. Advance unedited version. 30 October 2008. CCPR/C/JPN/CO/5. Available online at: <www2.ohchr.org/english/bodies/hrc/docs/co/CCPR-C-JPN-CO.5.doc> (accessed 10 August 2009).

UN (United Nations, Sub-Commission on Prevention of Discrimination and Protection of Minorities) (1998) *Systematic Rape, Sexual Slavery and Slavery-Like Practices During Armed*

Conflict. Final Report, submitted by Ms Gay J. McDougall, Special Rapporteur, E/CN.4/Sub.2/1998/13.

Vaihinger, H. (1924) *The Philosophy of 'As If': A System of the Theoretical, Practical and Religious Fictions of Mankind*, trans. C.K. Ogden. London: Kegan, Paul, Trench, Trubner & Co., Ltd.

Women's Court of Canada (2006) 'Rewriting equality', special issue of *Canadian Journal of Women and the Law,* 18(1).

Yoshimi, Y. (2000) *Comfort Women: Sexual Slavery in the Japanese Military During World War II*, trans. Suzanne O'Brien. New York: Columbia University Press.

Chapter 12

Many hundred thousand bodies later

An analysis of the 'legacy' of the international criminal tribunal for Rwanda

Denise Ferreira da Silva

Two recent events indicate how state sovereignty underscores the political contradictions of the global present and suggest a revision of the left critical apparatus. Hidden in the midst of threats to the neo-liberal credo – calls for the return of state regulation in light of the 2008–9 collapse of the global economy – was another significant decision of global import, the International Criminal Court's (ICC) issue of a 'warrant of arrest' for the President of Sudan, Omar Hassan Ahmad al Bashir, in March 2009. Most of us in the left, I am guessing, celebrate the (even if weak) calls for the return of the state to the control room of economic affairs; many applaud the ICC's decision as a belated response to human suffering in Africa; while some, and of this I am sure, find the warrant of arrest for Bashir another expression of Western arrogance. For the critics of global juridical architecture and procedures – namely the human rights corpus, humanitarian law and humanitarian intervention – this later event constitutes a colonial act, a reinscription of Hegel's writing of Africa as the 'dark continent', where, according to this latest version, post-Enlightenment accomplishments, such as the democratic state and humanity, go to waste.

What this warrant signals, I think, is the shift in international law introduced by the International Criminal Tribunal for Rwanda's (ICTR) statute and decisions. The ICTR's main innovation was the elimination of the 'war nexus', that is, the requirement that the acts enumerated under genocide and crimes against humanity occurred in connection with an international conflict. That nexus appears in the 1945 London Declaration, which framed the Nuremberg Tribunal, and in the International Criminal Tribunal for Yugoslavia statute (Chesterman 2000 and Cerone 2008). After the establishment of the ICTR, and under the ICC's statute, on the other hand, the international forces of law enforcement and administration of justice have the authority – and, many claim, the obligation – to prosecute individual (state) officials even if their acts are not directly related to an armed international conflict.

This chapter reads the first decision of the ICTR, *The Prosecutor versus Jean-Paul Akayesu* (ICTR 1998), in light of these shifts. Then UN Secretary-General Kofi Annan celebrated this ruling as a 'landmark decision in the history of international criminal law' that 'brings to life, for the first time, the ideals of the Convention on the Prevention and Punishment of the Crime of Genocide' (Annan 1998). Because Kofi Annan does not provide any bases for this statement, it is all the more crucial that this 'landmark decision' should become an object of critical scrutiny. My goal here is to engage in such a task. More specifically, I frame a political 'legacy' of this decision, which is to consolidate the place of humanity in the books of international law through the particular deployment of cultural difference that sustains the chamber's decision to charge Akayesu with genocide and crimes against humanity. My reading of Akayesu's judgment considers the following questions: what happens after cultural difference is deployed to explain (as a scientific [truth] construct) why (the subjective grounds) many thousand persons were killed in Rwanda and to justify (as an ethical principle) the prosecution and punishment of other Rwandans for crimes against humanity (the universal ethical figure)? What sort of juridical subjects does this deployment produce? If they are among the first global (legal) subjects, what can an analysis of this particular juridical statement, in which they emerge, say about the political function of international law in the global present? More importantly, if the subject of crime against humanity is the latest refashioning of the global subaltern subject, what critical tool can help us to comprehend its conditions of emergence and effects of deployment?

My consideration of these questions is as follows. First, I begin with a critique of the prevailing critique of the human/humanitarian, which is encapsulated in what I call 'the racial "othering" thesis'. While this critical construct has been used in early analysis of colonialism and racism, I will argue that its deployment in the global present is limited because it does not examine the conditions of production of European/white superiority. Second, my analysis of the Akayesu decision tackles the necessary task. That is, it describes the effects of deployment of the tools of social scientific knowledge to reveal how they produce global subjects, which cannot be comprehended by the notion of humanity. Finally, the concluding section is more an invitation to consider a racial/global emancipatory project which does not fall in the trappings that haunt historical–materialist and anti-racist theoretical perspectives alike. Framed as a map of today's global political landscape, this chapter is not so much a critique or dismissal of the racial 'othering' thesis. What it does is suggest that post-Enlightenment ontological descriptors – such as self-determination (freedom), which the notion of ideology cannot but assume – cannot guide our critiques of the political work performed by the figure governing the global ethical–juridical vocabulary, namely humanity.

The racial 'othering' thesis

What are the conditions under which humanity (the post-Enlightenment ethical figure which is the embodiment of self-determination) becomes a powerful weapon in the global juridical arsenal? Perhaps it is unnecessary to return to the positivist delimitation of the field of law as beyond morality (natural law and moral rules) – and fully encompassed by the modern sovereign, the state – and to consider whether and how it is responsible for the ontological travails of international law (Austin 2000). Indeed, the positivist separation of law and morality has troubled the core of international law. Only a few events – the war-related mass killings in Nazi Germany, Japan and the former Yugoslavia – have yielded calls for justice in the name of humanity that quieted states' claims for sovereignty and opened the way for the criminal prosecution of their representatives and international military interventions in their territories. After Rwanda, humanity's ethical authority alone threatens to dissolve both the juridical and ethical boundaries of the nation state, potentially supporting unqualified international (juridical) intervention in domestic affairs. How did the ICTR craft a legal statement, the Akayesu decision, which renders international law both desirable and necessary?

Let us not forget the unevenness of global political terrain. Post-colonial polities of Latin America and the Caribbean, Africa, Asia and the Pacific have never been fully welcome in the community of the nations. The Western compound controls the United Nations and other international bodies and holds the chains of economic aid through its strongmen, namely the International Monetary Fund and the World Bank. More significantly, this juridical and economic unevenness has also a powerful symbolic companion. Many critics of global juridical architectures and procedures argue that colonial racial 'othering' is the ideological strategy deployed to separate the states charged with humanitarian crimes and those who control global juridical forces, such as the UN Security Council and ICC, and lead the forces of humanitarian intervention: NATO, UN forces (Mutua 2001; Mamdani 2009; Douzinas 2007).

For instance, Mutua argues that human rights mobilizations deploy a metaphor, 'savage-victim-saviour', that refigures the colonial trope through which Europeans justify domination of non-European polities in order to eliminate 'evils' authorized by their traditional (cultural) ways (Mutua 2001). 'Human rights', he argues, refer to 'a historical continuum', where one finds 'the impulse to universalize Eurocentric norms and values by repudiating, demonizing, and "othering" that which is different and non-European' (Mutua 2001: 210). While Christian missions advanced the colonial 'civilizing' task, in the global present it belongs to international non-government organizations (INGOs), such as Amnesty International and Human Rights Watch. In the human rights agenda and practices, Mutua argues, the 'savage-victims-saviour' metaphor produces a dichotomy within the non-European state, distinguishing between the 'savage' (the state and the cultural forms that sustain it) and the 'victim' (its faceless, helpless mass of citizens violated by the state and the 'evil' (cultural) tradition it enacts or fails to curb). The 'Euro-American' human rights 'warriors' then enter as mediators, the 'saviour', whose 'psyche reflects an intriguing interplay of both European superiority and manifest destiny over the subject' (Mutua 2001: 235). Liberalism, refigured in human rights and democratic forms, is the dominant political ideology, and global domination is marked by 'the imposition of the current dogma of human rights on non-European societies [which] contradicts conceptions of human dignity and rejects the contributions of the other culture in efforts to create a universal corpus of human rights' (Mutua 2001: 245). That is, according to Mutua, the problem with the 'savage-victim-saviour' is it inflects the human rights agenda and the notion of humanity with colonial hierarchies. For instance, Mamdani highlights this point when he argues that this 'othering' move, which now relies on constructs of cultural difference (in which gender violence plays a crucial role), is at work in the stark contrast between the number of activist and academic denouncements of the situation in Darfur and their (comparatively) virtual silence in regard to the US-led occupation of Iraq and, I add, the January 2009 Israeli attack on the Gaza Strip (Mamdani 2009).

While productively targeting the role of humanity in the global political vocabulary, critiques guided by the ideo-logic of racial 'othering' stop at the argument that representations of European cultural superiority justify global domination. Though concerned with a European subject whose political light has been redirected to the 'dark' moral mirror of humanity, Douzinas's rendering of racial 'othering' deploys the theme of a 'European I' projecting its undesirable traits onto the 'non-European other' (Douzinas 2007). He uses this strategy to describe how the human rights/humanitarian duo operates as a de-politicizing ideological form. For Douzinas, the category of 'crime against humanity' signifies a split, the 'moralist conception [that] both makes impossible and bars positive political visions and possibilities'. 'Human rights ethics', he proceeds, 'legitimize what the West already possesses' (Douzinas 2007: 88). He is not, however, calling for a dismissal of the humanitarian and the human; for him, '[r]adical humanitarianism aims to confront the existent with a transcendence found in history' (Douzinas 2007: 89).

Whether as a ruse of the unconscious or an articulation of Western arrogance, these critics claim, racial 'othering' is an ideological strategy that precludes articulations of the proper universal (political or moral subject), that is, self-determined humanity signified either in multicultural inclusion or in the figure of the radical humanitarian freed of rights. What they do not ask is why signifiers of the difference between European and non-European polities are deployed in the first place and how they manage to reinscribe 'universal' humanity in the political (ethical–juridical) architectures these polities inhabit.

Truth and consequences

The ICTR's definition of 'crime against humanity' includes the following requirements: it must be carried out (a) as part of a widespread or systematic attack; (b) against any civilian population; and (c) on discriminatory grounds (Chesterman 2000). Two moves then mark the ICTR's adjustment of international law and its particular inscription of humanity in the global juridical architecture. First, the inclusion of 'subjective intent' invites a consideration of why, against their better positivist judgment, the prosecutor and the chamber entered the murky terrain of interiority usually avoided in municipal criminal cases. That is, they took on the burden of proving what was in Akayesu's mind. Second, the positivist bind of the law and the state haunting international law disappears in another specificity of the ICTR statute, namely, the inclusion of 'discriminatory grounds' in the definition of 'crime against humanity' when genocide already refers to 'group discrimination'.[1] What this distinction between 'groups' and 'grounds' enables, I submit, is the possibility of dissolving the burden of proving intent into the diffuse notion of cultural (collective) 'grounds'. In the case of the Holocaust, racial 'group identification' provided the very definition of the crime of genocide, which is but the name of the Nazi state's actions and design. Lacking this exterior referent for action, the ICTR chamber needed to link actions to interior (cultural) representations in order to provide an objective explanation for the mass killings in Rwanda.

Here is the interpretive itinerary the Akayesu trial chamber follows to produce this link. The chamber did not have to decide whether or not the massacres occurred, or even if they constituted a crime, but whether the victims were killed as individuals or as Tutsi. Had it found that they were killed as individuals, neither international criminal charge, that is, genocide or crimes against humanity, would have held. The letter of the ICTR statute is unambiguous: these charges apply to crimes committed on the basis of 'group membership' and 'discriminatory grounds', respectively. The accused, Jean-Paul Akayesu, was the bourgemestre of the Taba Commune between April 1993 and June 1994, 'responsible for the execution of laws and regulations and the administration of justice, also subject only to the prefect's authority'.[2] He was found guilty of nine counts: one of genocide, seven of crimes against humanity (extermination, torture, murder [three counts], rape, other inhumane acts) and one of direct and public incitement to commit genocide. For the chamber, that the Tutsi massacre was a 'widespread or systematic attack against a civilian population on national, ethnic or racial grounds' was evidenced by the 'unusually large shipment of machetes into the country shortly before it occurred' and because, like in other parts of the country, the attackers first targeted teachers and intellectuals and used the media to encourage 'Hutu systematically to attack Tutsi' (ICTR 1998: para. 173). In short, the chamber decided that the massacres did constitute genocide and crimes against humanity – the latter finding was almost a matter of course because the finding of genocide immediately established the 'ethnic grounds' for the attack, as explained further below.

Let us look at the chamber's factual findings regarding the massacres of Tutsis. The difficult issue before the chamber was the fact that the Tutsi population does not fit any of the genocide classificatory terms, namely a 'national, ethnic, or a racial group'. 'The Tutsi population', the judgment reads, 'does not have its own language or a distinct culture from the rest of the Rwandan population' (ICTR 1998: para. 168). Further, the chamber notes the official (state's) indicators of ethnic differentiation – the identity card ('which includes an entry for ethnic group') and Rwanda's legal apparatus (the constitution and other laws) also refer to ethnic classification (ICTR 1998: para. 170). When describing its factual findings, the chamber relied on signifiers of Rwanda's cultural specificity, such as 'patriarchal authority' and linguistic ambiguities. These cultural signifiers would sustain the determination that Akayesu's actions resulted from an internal determinant (subjective intent) thoroughly constrained (outer-determined) by an exterior cultural context that represents the Tutsi as an ethnic group. The testimony of expert witness Alison Desforges, a historian and human rights activist, provided the basis for the following findings in the judgment:

> The primary criterion for [defining] an ethnic group is the sense of belonging to that ethnic group. It is a sense which can shift over time. In other words, the group, the definition of the group to which one feels allied may change over time. But, if you fix any given moment in time, and you say, how does this population divide itself, then you will see which ethnic groups are in existence in the minds of the participants at that time. The Rwandans currently, and for the last generation at least, have defined themselves in terms of these three ethnic groups. In addition reality is an interplay between the actual conditions and peoples' subjective perception of those conditions. In Rwanda, the reality was shaped by the colonial experience which imposed a categorization which was probably more fixed, and not completely appropriate to the scene. But, the Belgians did impose this classification in the early 1930s when they required the population to be registered according to ethnic group. The categorization imposed at that time is what people of the current generation have grown up with. They have always thought in terms of these categories, even if they did not, in their daily lives have to take cognizance of that. This practice was continued after independence by the First Republic and the Second Republic in Rwanda to such an extent that this division into three ethnic groups became an absolute reality.
>
> (ICTR 1998: para. 172)

Of significance here is how the statement that, in post-colonial Rwanda's self-representation, ethnic distinctions constitute an 'absolute reality', and the 'objective' context of Akayesu's actions, checks arguments based on the contingency of historical (the colonial origins and post-colonial usage of the distinction) and subjective (identity as a matter of self-representation) processes. Not surprisingly, the chamber never engages any other possible explanation for his actions, such as the defence that had he condemned or tried to prevent the killings and rapes Akayesu would have been killed. Instead, it based its findings on witnesses' accounts of 'customary rules in Rwanda governing the determination of ethnic group, which followed patrilineal lines of heredity' and concludes that '[t]he identification of persons as belonging to the group of Hutu or Tutsi (or Twa) has thus become embedded in Rwandan culture' (ICTR 1998: para. 171).

What formulation of cultural difference can displace contingency, that which, according to modern philosophers from Leibniz to Hegel, marks the cherished products of human history, distinguishes the human from any other existing thing, namely its being a subject and object of (cultural) self-representation? The anthropological rendering of cultural difference informing Desforges' testimony, which is continuously used in interpretation of events and actions in post-colonial (non-European) polities, refigures the formalizing (fixed/fixing as opposed to contingent) power of social scientific categories very effectively. For about 100 years, social and cultural anthropologists have been describing the kind of mind governed by custom, a concept which, as Fitzpatrick argues, has consistently been articulated to distinguish the very being of the law (Fitzpatrick 1992). To be sure, the notion of custom is ubiquitous in legal and social scientific theorizing (Durkheim 1965; Weber 1978). Read, for instance, Malinowski's rendering of the subject of custom:

> If we designate the sum total of rules, conventions and patterns of behaviour as the body of custom, there is no doubt that the native feels a strong respect for all of them, has a tendency to do what others do, what everyone approves of, and, if not drawn or driven in another direction by his appetites or interests, will follow the biddings of custom rather than any other course. The force of habit, the awe of traditional command and a sentimental attachment to it, the desire to satisfy public opinion – all combine to make custom be obeyed for its own sake. In this the 'savages' do not differ from the members of any self-contained community with a limited horizon, whether this be an Eastern European ghetto, an Oxford college or a Fundamentalist Middle West community.
>
> (Malinowski 1926: 52)

Notice that this statement highlights the continuities rather than discontinuities between Europeans and the 'savage'. When capturing distinct modes of human existence, the anthropological rendering of custom, as a signifier of cultural difference, foregrounds a common feature of human beings: the capacity to conceive of rules that guide individual conduct.

Recalling Claude Lévi-Strauss's, Margaret Mead's and Franz Boas's early twentieth-century demands for a focus on cultural difference to celebrate the gifts of human diversity (Silva 2007), the chamber's determination comprehends Rwandans in the ethical figure humanity. First, it names an expression of its *diversity*, in order to justify naming the mass killings genocide and crimes against humanity. That is, it highlights actions that hurt humanity's other distinguishing attribute, namely *dignity*, which is represented by particular persons (figurings of the liberal individual) but not by racial or ethnic collectives.

When tackling the same difficult task before the Akayesu chamber – to explain why common folks, Hutus who had no official charge, killed other Hutus and their Tutsi acquaintances, teachers, students, doctors, patients, employees, employers, neighbours or family members – Mamdani accepts the charge of genocide and moves to argue that it resulted from a political act, the colonial (Belgium's) and post-colonial (Rwanda's state) writing of Tutsi and Hutu as distinct 'racial groups' (Mamdani 2001). Decentring economic (historical–materialist) and cultural explanations, he argues that the mid-1990s mass killings resulted from state-led historical choices, which explain why Tutsi remained the enemy in post-colonial Rwanda and the civil war that constituted the political context for the genocide. 'If it is the struggle for power that explains the motivation of those who crafted the genocide', he argues, 'then it is the combined fear of a return to servitude and of reprisals thereafter that energized the foot soldiers of the genocide' (Mamdani 2001: 233). Fear of subjugation, a political factor, explains the events because 'the perpetrators of the genocide saw themselves as the true victims of an ongoing political drama, victims of yesterday who may yet be victims again' (Mamdani 2001: 233).

Precisely because the critical move here is not to counter the 'racial othering thesis' but to unpack the effects of the very categories deployed in the naming of the 'other' of Europe, I chose a distinct path. This analysis of the Akayesu judgment's reliance on an interpretation of the historical developments highlights how the judgment, because it 'naturalizes' the effects of those developments, produces a version of Rwanda's historical (cultural) specificity able to sustain the charges of genocide and crimes against humanity against representatives of that state. Put differently, I show how the anthropological construction of Rwanda's cultural particularity depoliticizes the killings, thus rendering them a crime, because it conveys the kind of (formal) universality that rewrites contingent (elusive) representations born out of historical trajectories into the kind of objective, 'absolute reality' demanded by the juridical text. Elsewhere I develop more extensively this argument regarding the effects of formalization of human difference (Silva 2007; Silva 2009). In this reading I provide but an instance of this kind of critical examination of the role of social scientific knowledge in the global political grammar. For as my reading of the

Akayesu decision shows, that which renders these international crimes and the juridical architectures in place to adjudge them powerful weapons of global subjugation is the fact that the tools of raciality, signifiers of racial and cultural difference, provide a formal ('universalizing') account that fissures the ethical figure of humanity's very core by instituting a descriptive (examples of human *diversity*) and a prescriptive (respect for human *dignity*) distinction at its core. In the Akayesu case, it happens when on the one hand, the judgment writes Rwandans as a whole as members of the human community, self-representing (cultural) subjects, while on the other hand it also criminalizes Rwandans as a whole by attributing the existence of ethnic distinction to fixed mental (cultural) attributes. Beyond depoliticizing the massacres and Akayesu's actions by writing them out of the political contexts of colonial domination and post-colonial violence, the chamber's findings have another, rather productive or positive political effect. For cultural difference produces a legal subject which, though part of humanity, cannot actualize humanity, because its cultural particularity refigures a prior moment of human history, of the self-revealing trajectory of Hegel's 'Spirit' – they have not and will never enjoy the gifts (rationality and freedom) universal reason has bestowed to post-Enlightenment Europe.

What I find in this ICTR decision is a political 'legacy', a reconfiguration of the global political terrain, in which the renaming of post-colonial political violence as culturally determined collective crimes threatens to remove the manta of sovereignty from post-colonial polities. Global juridical architectures and procedures of international criminal law seize these political events as examples of a state's failure to fulfil its ethical mandate or its protective role. Naming post-colonial massacres 'genocide' or 'crimes against humanity' pre-empts readings of state involvement as an exercise of self-preservation, for the associated requirement of 'group membership' or 'discriminatory grounds' immediately signifies a loss of legitimacy, or a loss of the state's capacity as the formal (universal) embodiment of its citizens' wills. Consistently, this undermining of the post-colonial state's ethical claims is a political–symbolic weapon that can only be justified in the name of the protection of an entity, humanity, the ethical figure that prefigures the moral bound embodied in the composite nation state. In sum, raciality – through cultural difference – works here not by writing Rwandans as non-human or less than human (as the racial 'othering' thesis suggests). Rather, it works by producing a body politic that fails to actualize universality because it lacks self-determination, the attribute reserved for polities found in post-Enlightenment Europe and its offshoots elsewhere.

Fetishism of ideologies

Reading recent leftist critiques of the global currency of cultural difference reminds me of Marx's famous passage on the fetishism of commodities, their 'mysterious' character, which can only be appreciated in the inversion they signify (Marx 1906). For while commodities are social products, resulting from relations among human beings established under the capitalist mode of production, that reality only appears in the moment of exchange as 'social relations' between things. At that moment, the social relations underpinning commodities appear as 'use value', which hides and signifies the 'material relations between persons' that give commodities their 'exchange value' (Marx 1906: 82). What would happen if political–symbolic strategies, such as signifiers of raciality, were the object of the same strategy framing Marx's critique of capitalism? What would happen if, instead of addressing them as ideology, as having solely 'use value'– 'objects of utility' that satisfy the 'wants' of the dominant or hegemonic class – we moved to examine the relationship between the 'use' and 'exchange value' of these representations?

Let me elaborate this point with a comment on Žižek's framing of cultural difference as a neo-liberal global capitalist ideological tool. Contra the multiculturalist liberal premise that inclusion (recognition via tolerance) would suffice to undo racial and cultural subjugation, he proposes that 'the way to fight ethnic hatred effectively is not through its immediate counterpart ethnic tolerance; on the contrary, what we need is even more hatred, but proper political hatred: hatred directed at the common political enemy' (Žižek 2000: 11). Like Douzinas, Žižek finds that moral arguments to justify military intervention, in the name of human rights, have a depoliticizing effect. For Žižek these 'cultural others' demands for justice are but as coercive deployments of the new dominant ideology of liberal multiculturalism. How can the oppressed recuperate their political attributes? '[I]n situation of forced choice', he prescribes, 'the subject makes the "crazy", impossible choice of, in a way, *striking at himself*, at what is most precious to himself', an act through which 'the subject finds himself by cutting himself loose from the precious object through whose possession the enemy kept him in check, the subject gains the space of free action' (Žižek 2000: 150, italics in the original). By severing the relationship, Žižek suggests, the (racially or culturally oppressed) returns to the proper place of the political subject, the scene of interiority, where individuals (in self-determination) and states (in sovereignty) thrive in the 'space of free action'.

What is at work here? A failure to consider exteriority renders Žižek's militant nightmare a rehearsal of the liberal calls for the ban of the concept of the racial calling it the fall of science, the death of rationality, myth and prejudice (Silva 2007). Let me return to the classical historical materialist text, where exteriority governs the critical programme even if it does not describe the political platform. In Marx's analysis of political economy, exteriority is crucial at two levels (Marx 1906). First, exteriority emerges in the defining statement regarding the social determinants of value: for the 'exchange value' of commodities derives from 'the fact that they are embodiments of abstract (averaged) human labour. That is, here Marx deploys labour as the formal ('universal') category that enables commodities to signify a particular social configuration, in this case capitalism. Second, exteriority is significant in the statement that labour is not an effect of human 'free will' (designs or desires), but of 'natural' needs for food and shelter. That is, modifying nature, productive activity, is just as necessary as the development of language. This indicates that 'exchange value' (labour expended), to the extent that it is a formal construct, comprehends the 'universals' (the laws of material production) that produce and govern human existence. Further, to the extent that the notion of human freedom, signified by the 'use value' of things, only comes into being under the capitalist mode of production, this representation of the human subject is also an effect of labour, the formal construct that comprehends freedom's (self-determination's) context of emergence.

Now the notion of freedom that emerges from Marx's work, as noted above, guides Žižek's critique of cultural difference and sustains his suicidal solution, which is the severing of the multicultural ideological bind which, from his point of view, determines racial subjugation. For Žižek racial subjugation would disappear if the racial subaltern subject would just sever the relationship by relinquishing life itself, as Sethe does in *Beloved*; that is, existence as determined by the relationship that cultural difference signifies (Morrison 1988). The problem with Žižek's solution is that it reads racial representation, refigured in racial and cultural difference, as ideology, or as having solely 'use value'. Without a consideration of their productive power, I contend, it is impossible to consider how exactly the tools of raciality institute political relationships and to recognize that their apparent 'social' (political) import ('use value') is contingent upon their ontological ('exchange value') role. Being formalizations of human difference, scientific 'universals', the tools of raciality are effective political–symbolic tools because they write an unsublatable difference at the core of humanity. That is, cultural difference does the work of global subjugation precisely because it produces human (ethical–juridical) figures, persons and states that do not actualize the principle of *dignity* which the human rights corpus has chosen from the post-Enlightenment symbolic reservoir, and which is now the letter of global legal texts. Today raciality's most effective tool, cultural difference, enables the articulation of humanity as an immanent and descriptive (ethical) universal, that is, one signified in the commeasurable fragments that humans' historical trajectory and scientific reason's formalizing tools have spread across the global space.

Notes

1 The full description of genocide and crime against humanity in the Rome Statute can be found at: <http://69.94.11.53/ENGLISH/basicdocs/statute.html> (accessed 28 September 2009).

2 The transcripts of the amended indictment, judgment and sentence are available at:
<http://69.94.11.53/ENGLISH/cases/Akayesu/indictment/actamond.htm>;
<http://69.94. 11.53/cases/Akayesu/judgement/akay001.htm>; and <http://69.94.11.53/
ENGLISH/cases /Akayesu/judgment/ak81002e.htm> (accessed 28 September 2009).

Bibliography

Annan, K. (1998) *Statement by UN Secretary-General Kofi Annan on the Occasion of the Announcement of the First Judgement in a Case of Genocide by the International Criminal Tribunal For
Rwanda*, Pretoria: UN Information Centre, UN doc. PR/10/98/UNIC, 2 September 1998.

Austin, J. (2000) *The Province of Jurisprudence Determined*, Amherst, NY: Prometheus Books.

Cerone, J.P. (2008) 'Much ado about non-state actors: the vanishing relevance of state
affiliation in international criminal law'. Available online at: <http://works.bepress.com/
john_cerone/1>.

Chesterman, S. (2000) 'An altogether different order: defining the elements of crimes against
humanity', *Duke Journal of Comparative and International Law* 10, 307.

Douzinas, C. (2007) *Human Rights and Empire*, London: Routledge-Cavendish.

Durkheim, E. (1965) *The Elementary Forms of Religious Life*, New York: Free Press/Macmillan
Publishing Co.

Fitzpatrick, P. (1992) *The Mythology of Modern Law*, London and New York: Routledge.

International Criminal Tribunal for Rwanda (ICTR) (1998) *Prosecutor v. Jean-Paul Akayesu*,
Case No. ICTR-96-4-T, 2 September 1998. Available online at: <http://69.94.11.53/
default.htm> (accessed 29 April 2009).

Malinowski, B. (1926, reprint 1982) *Crime and Custom in Savage Society*, Savage, MD:
Littlefield Adams Quality Paperbacks.

Mamdani, M. (2001) *When Victims Become Killers*, Princeton and Oxford: Princeton University
Press.

——(2009) *Saviors and Survivors*, New York: Pantheon Books.

Marx, K. (1906) *Capital: A Critique of Political Economy*, vol. I, trans S. Moore and E. Aveling,
New York: Modern Library.

Morrison, T. (1988) *Beloved: A Novel*, London: Pan Books in association with Chatto &
Windus.

Mutua, M. (2001) 'Savages, victims, and saviors: the metaphor of human rights', *Harvard
International Law Journal* 42, 201.

Silva, D.F. (2007) *Toward a Global Idea of Race*, Minneapolis: University of Minnesota Press.

——(2009) 'No-bodies: law, raciality and violence', *Griffith Law Review* 18(2): 212–236.

Weber, M. (1978) *Economy and Society: An Outline of Interpretive Sociology*, Berkeley, CA:
University of California Press.

Žižek, S. (2000) *The Fragile Absolute*, London: Verso.

Chapter 13

From the state to the Union

International law and the appropriation
of the new Europe

Patricia Tuitt

The European Union and the nomos of the earth

At first glance, the development of the European Union (or EU) would
appear to present the clearest illustration of the proposition advanced by
Carl Schmitt in *The Nomos of the Earth* (Schmitt 2006) that in post-war
political thought and practice, land appropriation has ceased to be a
condition precedent of a sovereign order. Instead, political theory would
have it that positive legal norms alone can confer upon a polity its constitutive force.

For many, the European Union can only be conceived of as a series of
international treaties, supranational institutions or bodies and exemplary
judgments of the European Court of Justice. Such legal norms, the novice
would be informed, set in train not a new European sovereign order – for
European law is thought of in terms of '"supremacy", in stark contrast to
"sovereignty"' (Everson and Eisner 2007: 54) – but rather the integration of
member states in Europe, initially over discrete economic sectors, such as
coal and steel, which were managed by 'rational technocrat[s]' (Lodge 1993:
xix) 'away from the foray of politics' (Craig and De Búrca 2007: 2).

In a no doubt unconscious affirmation of Schmitt's fear that political and
social systems consisting of 'norms without a nomos' (Schmitt 2006: 238–39)
would stand in substitution for a more *earthly* law, Curtin characterized the
European Union as a 'legal system' 'constructed' over several years, the 'true
world-wide significance' of which was its character as a 'cohesive legal unit
which confers rights on individuals and which enters into their legal systems
as an integral part of those systems' (Curtin 1993: 17). It was 'law', not
'politics', that created the European Union. So well rehearsed is this point of
view that it would be a task of enormous industry to gather references of
legal scholars who applaud the prevalence of 'law' over 'politics' in the
complex process of European integration.

It is the object of this study to show that it is land appropriation (in the
precise Schmittian sense), and not primarily legal innovations of the European
Court of Justice or, as neo-functionalist theories of integration suggest, the

manoeuvrings of political and legal elites, that gives the European Union its constitutive force.

The complex rearrangement of the European space which we have witnessed over the past 50 years or so follows the pattern of the land appropriation of the New World. Conceptually and analytically, the 'discovery' of the New World occupies an important place in this thesis, for, as with the development of the 'new' Europe, the particular challenge in that historical period was to effect radical constitutional change over territorial spaces that were both populated and governed. Discovery, for Schmitt, is 'not a timeless, universal, and normative concept' but rather 'is bound to a particular historical, even intellectual-historical situation: the "Age of Discovery"' (Schmitt 2006: 131). The argument presented here is that the constitution of the European Union shares the character of this earlier 'intellectual–historical situation'.

Here, I aim to elaborate the argument that the European Union does not *in fact* present a challenge to Schmitt's claim that 'land-appropriation precedes the order that follows from it' (Schmitt 2006: 48), by way of a re-evaluation of the function in the emergence of the European Union of the 'four freedoms' of the Rome Treaty, still indisputably the core or 'mainstay' of the 'new' European legal order.

In the Rome Treaty that established the 'common market' (now more often referred to as the internal market) we find not what most commentators would have us believe: an attempt at economic integration over closely defined avenues of competence, with the *expectation* but not the principal *objective* of political 'spillover', but, instead, a proclamation of free movement in connection with ostensibly economic objectives, which, like all similar historical projects with the goal of facilitating movement over a large geographical scale, had the *immediately political* objective of establishing a new European nomos by the appropriation of lands consisting of the old territories of Europe. Read in this light, the Rome Treaty sits alongside the royal charters, papal bulls and legal concepts or 'fictions' (such as the doctrine of terra nullius) which outline the rules and principles according to which land could be appropriated. Thus, any discussion of the European Union as a concrete order must begin with the Treaty of Rome, in which what have come to be known as the 'four freedoms' – the free movement of goods, services, workers and capital – were first enunciated. Attempts to locate the origins of the European Union before the assertion of the supreme virtue of the principle of free movement which the Rome Treaty represents – 'to Charlemagne ... to a fourteenth century treatise "on the way to shorten wars" by Pierre Dubois ... to pre- or proto-federalist writings by the likes of Kant, Rousseau, Bentham and Saint-Simon' (Douglas-Scott 2002: 7) – although no doubt of some interest, say little of the European Union's constitutive moment.

As I hope to establish, the 'freedom of movement of workers' 'secured' by article 39 of the treaty, the right of self-employed persons either to 'establish' themselves in another state by virtue of article 43EC or to 'provide services' under article 49EC, encourages and facilitates migration not merely in the interests of economic goals but with the intent of achieving at least one of the objectives that mass migration was designed to attain during the Age of Discovery between the sixteenth and nineteenth centuries. Then, the first objective was simply to extend the territories of a colonial power. The second, especially pertinent to our case, Catherine Hall describes as the 'destruction and/or transformation of other forms of social organisation and life' (Hall 2000: 5).

The movement of persons, above all other features of the development of the European Union, first *destroyed* then began to *transform* the obsolete economic and political forms characteristic of the arrangement of nation states in Europe. It was the movement of persons that undid the divisions and partitions that marked each territorial space in Europe as a separate nation state and that undid the divisions and partitions endemic to domestic markets.

The impact on the transformation of Europe of the 'negative integration of the European market' (Everson and Eisner 2007: 50) by the European Court of Justice in its heyday represented by decisions in cases such as *Van Gend en Loos* (1963) and *Costa v ENEL* (1964) pales in comparison to the impact of the movement of persons. As Ferguson rightly observes, even during the golden years of British command over land and sea, neither 'conquest' nor 'commerce' were sufficient to achieve 'empire' (Ferguson 2004: 52). It required the 'exodus' of people to 'change the world' (Ferguson 2004: 54).

Once we begin to accept that the European Union relies for its existence on modes of sovereign assertion that pre-dated (and made possible) the state system, we can begin to understand the uneven distribution of rights among the people of Europe.

I shall attempt to substantiate these claims through an analysis that seeks to re-evaluate how the free movement of persons and other factors of production figure within the framework of the European Union. I shall pay particular attention to the Single European Act 1986, which is generally thought to have brought a radical change in ideologies underpinning various methods of integration.

Free movement provisions

Treaty provisions governing the free movement of persons cover the right to move in search of work (article 39[2]), the 'right to establishment' (article 43) and the 'freedom to provide services ... in respect of nationals of Member States who are established in a state in the Community other than that of the person for whom the services are intended' (article 49). These freedoms, together with the free movement of goods and capital, form the original points of axis on which the internal market – 'an area without internal frontiers in which the free movement of goods, persons, services and capital is ensured ... ' (article 14(2)) – revolves. In later years, indeed almost immediately following the ratification of the Treaty of European Union in 1992 (which, among other things, subsumed the European Economic Community established by the Rome Treaty within the pillar structure of the European Union), further free movement rights were added to the treaty and existing rights strengthened. Article 18EC (part of the bundle of citizenship rights) provides that: 'Every citizen of the Union shall have the right to move and reside freely within the territory of the Member States ...' This right exists independently of the 'four freedoms' of the original treaty. A more recent measure governing the free movement of persons, directive 2004/38, establishes, among other things, a right of permanent residence in another member state of EU citizens and their family members after a continuous period of residence of five years and subject to certain limitations and qualifications that are beyond the scope of this enquiry. It is also beyond the scope of this chapter to chart the currents and tides attending the development of the free movement of the factors of production and of the internal market more generally. I turn instead to the Single European Act and its significance for this thesis.

In my view, although the Rome Treaty created the first step towards the appropriation of the European space, it was the Single European Act that made explicit the reliance of this aspirant new order on old land appropriation processes of 'exploration', 'discovery' and 'settlement'. Before I pursue this point, I need to briefly situate the Act within the development of free movement principles.

Few would deny that the Single European Act was designed to bring about, and largely achieved, the more rapid acceleration of the development of the internal market when compared with previous legislative and judicial initiatives aimed at its 'completion'. A Commission White Paper entitled 'Completing the internal market' (COM/85/310. 14.6.1985) explored the means through which to bring about the elimination of physical, technical and fiscal barriers that would otherwise obstruct the 'free movement of the factors of production' (Swan 1992: 11). Much of what the Commission recommended was adopted under the Single European Act, and, among other things, committees were set up to ensure the standardization of products and the 'approximation' of 'laws' and 'administrative provisions' (article 94). The ambition at legislative harmonization that article 94 expresses is now somewhat muted and harmonization is limited to matters like health and safety (article 100).

More importantly, the Act prompted a radical shift in the ideological presuppositions upon which EU 'integration' was to proceed. The 'new' ideology is expressed in the principle of 'mutual recognition'. The principle – which underlies all free movement principles, is observed by all institutions of the EU and has had an enormous impact on the recognition of professional qualifications, in particular – was first established by the European Court of Justice in its jurisprudence governing quantitative restrictions imposed on the movement of goods between states. *Cassis de Dijon* (1979) is the leading case on this point. According to the principle of mutual recognition, goods lawfully marketed in one member state should be available in all others, the hypothesis being that all member states share in equal part concerns over questions of health and safety, consumer protection and matters of that kind.

Exploration and discovery

The deadline set for completion of the internal market under article 14(2) warrants our particular attention. Article 14(2) reads: 'The Community shall adopt measures with the view of progressively establishing the internal market over a period expiring on 31 December 1992 ... ' Fearing that the provision might be construed as having binding legal force, member states attached a declaration to article 14, which effectively denied that the deadline had 'legal effect'.

I am not concerned with the question of whether or not the internal market objective was achieved in 1992 – indeed, no one seriously suggests that the deadline was to bring about the end of initiatives that would test the limits of a European market in goods and services. Several Commission reports since 1992 have served to review and expand the scope of the internal market in a way that belies its supposed pre-emptory completion. At the same time, the deadline of 1992 figures so explicitly in the fashioning of the market that it would be unwise not to explore the possibility that it has a deeper underlying significance than would at first appear. Its significance, I suggest, lies in how it captures the qualitative nature of the movement that European citizens would engage *before* and *after* 1992 and in so doing betrays the EU's reliance on old techniques of sovereign assertion.

Speaking of the land appropriation of the New World, Catherine Hall identifies three related activities associated with free movement, each being necessary to 'capture' a territorial space. These activities – 'exploration', 'discovery' and 'settlement' (2000: 5) – effect, to recall again her words, the 'destruction and/or transformation of previous forms of social organisation and life' (2000: 5). I would qualify her words further and say that 'exploration' and 'discovery' is the exercise of free movement that 'destroys' forms of social organization and life and 'settlement' that transforms these forms towards the vision of the emerging polity.

It is surely more than mere coincidence that free movement principles established by the Rome Treaty and in subsequent Community measures up until 1992 *discouraged* 'settlement' and actively *encouraged* 'exploration' and 'discovery'. One could put the point more unequivocally and say that these early initiatives permitted only 'exploration' and 'discovery' through mass migration. The purpose of the private journeys that individuals were encouraged by these principles to undertake was, as I hope to show in the ensuing analysis of ECJ jurisprudence on the free movement of workers, *destructive* rather than *reconstructive* – the aim was to erase, or at the very least disrupt, the supposedly degenerate systems of the old order in Europe. The limited nature of social assistance rights in the period before 1992 went a long way to ensuring movement was merely exploratory in nature and simply undid the divisions and partitions of the old order, without putting in place a concrete new social and political order. Post 1992 we see the addition of discrete rights aimed at the 'settlement' of persons and thereby the transformation of the social, political and economic order in Europe. Article 18 is one such initiative. In recent years free movement rights have been reformed in ways that enable them to be turned towards settlement – although the effects of these reforms are much less radical than the right of free movement which stems for European citizenship under article 18.

Of course the transition in rights that the deadline to the Single European Act marks has been noted and analysed by European legal scholars, but these two phases are quite wrongly construed as marking the transition from a 'market constitution' to a more 'politically oriented' one, or as the point is alternatively expressed: the slow accrual of social and political rights against the overwhelming impulse toward 'economic liberalization' (Moravcsik 1991). Such views point to understandings of these concepts, especially the concept of the *political*, which are wholly positivistic in nature. In truth, early so-called market-oriented free movement rights were more resolutely political than was the post 1992 preoccupation with citizenship and funda- mental rights, for they give practical and institutional expression to the most *primitive* and at the same time still most *decisive* means of fashioning a political community. This, with the assistance of Peter Fitzpatrick, I have described elsewhere as a crude and frenzied exercise of 'filling up spaces' so as to erase as quickly and finally as possible the 'previous condition' (Fitzpatrick 2001: 146–75; Tuitt (forthcoming: 2010)). It is against this understanding of the primary function of the 'four freedoms' of the Rome Treaty that I analyse, below, the principle of the free movement of workers.

How the European Union was 'discovered'

To begin with, the elucidation of the precise ambit and scope of the concept of 'worker' is one that, according to the ECJ in *Hoekstra* (1964), 'is not a matter for the competence of national law' (at 184). It is a concept of European law that is rightly applauded for its liberal breadth. A case often cited as exemplifying the liberal approach of the ECJ is *Levin* (1982), which concerned a British citizen living and working in the Netherlands in a part- time capacity as a chambermaid. The case came before the ECJ after Levin was refused a residence permit on the basis that since her part-time work did not provide sufficient income for her needs, she did not properly qualify as a 'worker' within the terms of the treaty. Disagreeing, the ECJ argued that there was a 'right of all workers to pursue the activity of their choice within the Community, irrespective of whether they are permanent, seasonal or frontier workers ... ' (*Levin* 1982: at 14). Specifically on the subject of whether part-time work was sufficient to invoke treaty rights, it held: '*part-time employment, although it may provide an income lower than what is considered to be the minimum required for subsistence, constitutes for a large number of workers an effective means of improving their living conditions*' (*Levin* 1982: at 14, my emphasis). Concluding that the Community concept of worker could not, consistently with the aims of the Treaty, be 'reserved solely to persons engaged in full-time employment ... ' the court provided the now familiar test for worker status:

> the rules on freedom of movement for workers ... cover only the pursuit of effective and genuine activities, to the exclusion of activities on such a small scale as to be regarded as purely marginal or ancillary ... those rules guarantee only the free movement of persons who pursue, or are desirous of pursuing a genuine economic activity.
>
> (*Levin* 1982: at 17)

The principles enunciated in *Levin* have been applied and adapted to support a number of important decisions: for example, *Kempf* (1986) in which it was decided that a music teacher whose earned income consisted of payment in respect of the provision of 12 music lessons a week was not precluded from enjoying worker rights merely because he was obliged to supplement his income through social assistance; and *Steymann* (1988), in which the applicant, in return for plumbing and the provision of general 'handyman' services to a religious community of which he was a member, received sufficient for his 'material needs ... including pocket-money ... ' (at 11). Seeming pro-migrant worker decisions like these would be familiar to every student of European law. Even the decision in *Bettray* (1989) that appeared to suggest that the Community concept of worker had been stretched to its limit by the applicant whose work was chosen in light of his 'capabilities' rather than, as would normally be expected, the person being 'selected on the basis of his or her capacity to perform a certain activity' appears to have been compromised in *Trojani* (2004).

What are we to make of these well-known cases? My argument is that they exemplify a line of authority that leaves little room for doubt that free movement rights were designed to encourage incursions on territory of the most transitory and (in terms of their effect on the old landscape of Europe) destructive nature. True it is that these judgments allow female workers, who make up a fair portion of the part-time workforce, to benefit from Rome Treaty provisions, but it is an equally significant fact that many individuals deemed to be 'workers' could not conceivably *settle* into work in a sense of ever forming part of a stable workforce – they become merely part of an itinerant working population.

Cases like *Levin* and *Kempf* entice the most marginal participants in the workforce to set out upon a voyage of exploration and discovery, with the lure of work providing the motivating force. Although work is certainly the *inducement* that is held out to private individuals to encourage them to migrate, it is not an *end* in itself. And so, people like Levin serve to undo entrenched ideas of what constitutes valuable labour. In other words, her role was to disrupt this particular aspect of social life and organization – something human migration can more effectively achieve than pronouncements of legal elites, sitting in the courts of justice.

Let's elaborate this point further with perhaps the most extreme example of the way the ECJ approaches the itinerant workforce in the European Union. Like *Levin, Raulin* (1992) also involved an applicant seeking to remain in the Netherlands as a worker. Raulin worked as a waitress in what appeared to be a very informal contract which did not guarantee a minimum number of working hours. This meant that she could go for days or weeks without work, and indeed after a period of eight months she had reportedly worked no more than 60 hours. The ECJ was not minded, even in the face of such limited *actual* labour, to conclude that such an arrangement could not ground worker status, although it did caution that:

> The national court may ... when assessing the effective and genuine nature of the activity in question, take account of the irregular nature and limited duration of the services actually performed ... the fact that the person concerned worked only a very limited number of hours in a labour relationship may be an indication that the activities exercised are purely marginal and ancillary. The national court may also take account, if appropriate, of the fact that the person must remain available to work if called upon to do so by the employer.
>
> (*Raulin* 1992: at 14)

These individuals, possessing or offering so little by way of sustaining skills, are unlikely to further the road towards European integration through *labour*, although undoubtedly their presence outside the territories in which they habitually resided was legitimated through the grant of worker status. It must then be asked in relation to *Raulin*, what, aside from the Commission of less than two days of work, was her precise function in the Netherlands? My question is not what in factual terms she was doing – that is entirely irrelevant for our purposes – but whether her time spent away from formal labour was idle time from the vantage point of the constituting of Europe. She was, an unsympathetic assessment of European worker movement might conclude, merely taking up space. Less pejoratively I would say she was 'filling up space' and thereby carrying on a necessary mode of sovereign land appropriation. The same point can be made of the category of 'jobseeker'. As the ECJ stated in *Antonissen* (1991) without, for at least a limited period, construing jobseekers as 'workers' for the purpose of European law, the '*actual chances that a national of a member state who is seeking employment will find it in another member state*' would be 'jeopardized' and the worker provisions would 'as a result' prove 'ineffective' (at 12, my emphasis). But *Antonissen* was but one-part jobseeker and three-parts explorer, whose hopeful journey is part of the process of 'capturing', in the interest of a new polity, the old territories of Europe.

Rights

So far I have spoken of free-movement principles as 'enabling', 'encouraging' or 'facilitating' the exploration, discovery and eventual settlement of European peoples. But such a weak choice of terminology simply perpetuates the presentation of migration as an exercise of free will and choice. Such a presentation does not sit comfortably with the claim that it is these movements that lend the European Union its constituent force. We know that some of the most politically powerful legal sovereigns were settled through migration and it need hardly be said that such could not be achieved through purely voluntary migration. So let it be understood that the migration that is tacitly exchanged for citizenship, as in the European Union, can never be truly voluntary, however much it may be stressed in official and academic discourses that such individuals who engage articles 39 or 49, for example, are exercising one or more of the 'four freedoms'. Those who argue that citizenship of the union is linked exclusively to market activity quite mistake the matter. Citizenship of the union – full citizenship (for there are gradations of citizenship, today as in every other epoch in history) – is a function of land appropriation and the greatest rewards, whether understood in terms of financial advantage or the legacies of history, belong to those who actively participate in the redrawing and reclaiming of lands. Post-1992 citizenship did not place the *static* individual on the same footing as the intrepid explorer. This point can be substantiated with reference to case law governing family reunion.

Not surprisingly, within a union composed of states that have accounted for a significant proportion of the world's diaspora, reunion with a non-national family member is a not inconsiderable exchange for the kind of migration needed to effect the eventual transformation of Europe. With one exception, EU law does not permit the reunion with a non-national family member unless the citizen is prepared to migrate.

It has always been the case that an individual exercising one or other of the Rome Treaty provisions governing the free movement of persons was entitled to have his or her 'spouse' and a certain category of family member reside with him or her, although until recently both the definition of 'spouse' and the class of family members benefiting from this particular 'social advantage' were limited. The rights of family reunion associated with the worker provisions have recently been consolidated and extended in article 23 of directive 2004/38, which replaced the previous article 10 of regulation 1612/68, which governed such rights. Furthermore, article 18EC provides a specific right to the Union citizen who is exercising his or her right to 'move freely and reside' in another member state also to be accompanied by a designated class of family members.

The leading case on the question of family reunion is *Singh* (1992), which concerned the question of whether an Indian national had a right to re-enter the United Kingdom after he had accompanied his British-born wife to Germany where she exercised her right to work under article 39. Concluding that the authorities of the United Kingdom could not repel his re-entry, the ECJ reasoned:

> A national of a member state might be deterred from leaving his country of origin in order to pursue an activity as an employed or self-employed person as envisaged by the Treaty in the territory of another member state if, on returning to the member state of which he is a national ... the conditions of his entry and residence were not at least equivalent to those which he would enjoy under the Treaty or secondary law in the territory of another Member State. He would in particular be deterred from so doing if his spouse and children were not also permitted to enter and reside in the territory of his Member State of origin under conditions at least equivalent to those granted them by Community law in the territory of another Member State.
>
> *(Singh* at 119)

Singh attests to the efforts made to encourage the movement of individuals. Later cases, such as *Baumbast* (2002), in which the non-national spouse virtually acquired a permanent right of residence in the United Kingdom, support the claim that I have made elsewhere to the effect that the 'four freedoms' 'hold the place within the exploration, discovery and settlement of Europe of the pot of gold or the opportunity to ensure a place in the Kingdom of God by bringing supposed savage, ungodly tribes to religion and civilization' (Tuitt, forthcoming: 2010) that were used to entice private individuals to migrate during the Age of Discovery of the New World. It is the citizen prepared to actively engage in the alteration of the previous forms of 'social life' prevalent in the old Europe and not the citizen per se who is valued. At least that is what the applicants in the more recent case of *Morson and Jharnjan* might reasonably conclude. Both applicants were Dutch nationals, living and working in the Netherlands. Relying upon their status as EU citizens, they sought to bring their Surinamese parents to reside with them. This they were unable to do because the question of the entry into the

Netherlands of Morson and Jharnjan's parents was deemed to be solely an issue of domestic immigration law. Cases like this are said to constitute wholly internal situations – meaning a situation that does not engage European law. Neither applicant was living or working in a member state other than that of their nationality and therefore the question was not one in which the ECJ or other EU institution was competent to intervene. Had the applicants been living and working in the United Kingdom or France, for instance, the conclusion would have been very different and the applicants would have been entitled to have their parents join them.

Free-movement principles do not simply enable or facilitate movement. As the cases on family reunion in particular illustrate, European citizens are placed under significant pressure to migrate in order to gain an advantage – one might say a fundamental human right – which citizenship *alone* ought to guarantee.

The distinctions between European citizens and resident non-nationals are legion. Balibar even goes so far as to predict the beginnings of a European 'Apartheid' (Balibar 2004: 31–51). But it is the uneven distribution of rights *between* European citizens that most clearly exposes the mechanisms through which the European Union constitutes itself.

Settlement

The Treaty of European Union and successive treaties have served to shift the function of free movement and now greater emphasis is placed on the settlement and reconstruction of the new, empty space through which the old Europe is imagined.

So, I would give a qualified answer to the question that legal scholars often pose in relation to the concept of European citizenship – that is, whether it produced substantially new rights for European citizens. Article 18 is undoubtedly the core of the concept of citizenship and thus migration continues to define the primary function of individuals in the fashioning of the European Union. It is for this reason that critics of the concept have concluded that it adds little to the bundle of rights that individuals could claim under the original Rome Treaty. On the other hand, citizenship and the development of a fundamental rights discourse that the concept spawned allowed migrants to settle in their 'chosen' territories of migration and thereby to begin the task of fashioning a community from the destruction wrought by the early phases of free movement. To put the point in more concrete terms, citizenship would soon transform the 'itinerant' members of the workforce, discussed above, who could only hope to have the most transitory of connections with another member state, into part of the settled, stable community. *Martinez Sala* (1998) is a case in point. At the time of her application to the ECJ, Sala, a Spanish national, had lived in Germany for 25 years and had worked there (although reports are vague as to the extent of economic activity she engaged in whilst living in Germany) and was receiving social assistance. Upon applying for a child-care allowance, she was asked to produce a residence permit (as evidence of entitlement to her claim for child allowance). This she was unable to do. She claimed that she had been discriminated against in the exercise of Treaty rights, contrary to article 12 (then article 6), which prohibits discrimination on grounds of nationality in the exercise of Treaty rights. It was established that German nationals were not obliged to produce a residence certificate when applying for the allowance in question. The national court rejected her claim. Article 12, it decided, was not a right that existed independently of the exercise of other Treaty rights. At the time of the application for child allowance, Sala was not in gainful employment and was thus not a worker within the meaning of the Treaty. The national court, therefore, concluded that Sala was not exercising a Treaty right and therefore that article 12 did not apply to her.

The ECJ rejected this line of reasoning. It stated that there was no need to determine whether or not Sala was a worker within the terms of the Treaty since article 18 (then 8) was a specific Treaty right available to all European citizens, irrespective of whether or not they were exercising any of the Rome Treaty free-movement rights. Consequently, Sala was entitled to rely upon article 12. The ECJ concluded: 'Article 8(2) attaches to the status of citizen of the Union the rights and duties laid down by the Treaty, including the right, laid down in Article 6 ... not to suffer discrimination on grounds of nationality ... ' (at 62).

That *Sala* was essentially concerned with entitlement to social benefits is significant, for as stated earlier, it was to some extent the limited nature of such entitlements that precluded settlement in the early phase of free-movement principles. This is not to suggest that EU law allows unlimited access to social benefits, for both *Sala* and the later case of *Trojani* (2004) are authority for the proposition that whilst an individual is lawfully on the territories of a member state, social assistance cannot be denied, but that member states can take steps to remove individuals who pose an unreasonable burden on the state. This position was later confirmed in *Baumbast*.

Despite this qualification, social assistance is now available to students (*Rudy Grzelczyk* 2001) and, consistently with the ECJ's approach to jobseekers, *Collins* (2004) decided that 'tide-over' allowances would be available for a reasonable period while work was being sought.

Conclusion

I would not venture to predict what kind of political community these two qualitatively distinct modes of exercise of free movement will bring about. Too often it seems that what is claimed to be a polity with a radically different set of ideologies and political ambitions than is evident in the nation state form it seeks to transcend simply replicates the exclusions and violence of that form. Ironically, this particular criticism is often levelled at the aspect of free movement that I argue here is designed more explicitly to effect the settlement of Europe – EU citizenship. As Carole Lyons argues, one might justifiably look with suspicion upon the EU for electing to introduce an idea of citizenship (Lyons 1998) since it is this political and legal concept that has engineered the violent divisions for which the nation state is famed.

References

Balibar, E. (2004) *We, The People of Europe? Reflections on Transnational Citizenship*, Princeton: Princeton University Press.

Craig, P. and De Búrca, G. (2007) *EU Law: Text, Cases and Materials*, Oxford: Oxford University Press.

Curtin, D. (1993) 'The constitutional structure of the union: a Europe of bits and pieces', *Common Market Law Review*, 30: 17–69.

Douglas-Scott, S. (2002) *Constitutional Law of the European Union*, Harlow: Pearson Education Ltd.

Everson, M. and Eisner, J. (2007) *The Making of the European Constitution*, Abingdon: Routledge-Cavendish.

Ferguson, N. (2004) *Empire: How Britain Made the Modern World*, London: Penguin Books.

Fitzpatrick, P. (2001) *Modernism and the Grounds of Law*, Cambridge: Cambridge University Press.

Hall, C. (ed.) (2000) *Cultures of Empire: A Reader*, Manchester: Manchester University Press.

Lodge, D. (1993), 'The European Community and the challenge of the future', in Pinder, J. *The Building of the European Union*, Oxford: Oxford University Press.

Lyons, C. (1998) 'Citizenship and alterity in the European Union', in P. Fitzpatrick and J. Bergeron (eds), *Europe's Other: European Law Between Modernity and Postmodernity*, Aldershot; Brookvield, VT: Ashgate Dartmouth.

Moravcsik, A. (1991) 'Negotiating the Single European Act: national interests and conventional statecraft in the European Community', *International Organisation*, 45: 19–56.

Schmitt, C. (2006) *The Nomos of the Earth in the International Law of the* Jus Publicum Europaeum, trans. G.L. Ulmen, New York: Telos Press.

Swan, D. (1992) *The Economics of the Common Market*, London: Penguin.

Tuitt, P. (forthcoming: 2010) 'The emergence of the European Union', in H. Lessard, R. Johnson and J. Webber, *Storied Communities: Narratives of Contact and Arrival in Constituting Political Community*, Vancouver: UBC Press.

Cases

C-292/89 *R v Immigration Appeal Tribunal, ex parte Antonissen* (1991) ECR1–745.

C-413/99 *Baumbast and R v Secretary of State for the Home Department* (2002) ECR1–7091.

344/87 *Bettray v Staatssecretaris van justitie* (1989) ECR 1621.

20/78 *Cassis de Dijon* (1979) ECR 648.

C-138/02 *Collins v Secretary of State for Work and Pensions* (2004) ECR1–2703.6/64.

Costa v ENEL (1964) ECR 585.

Hoekstra (1964) ECR 177.

139/85 *Kempf v Staatssecretaris van justitie* (1986) ECR 1035.

53/81 *Levin v Staatssecretaris van justitie* (1982) ECR 1035.

C-85/96 *Maria Martinez Sala v Freistaat Bayern* (1998) ECR1–2691.

35and 36/68 *Morson and Jhanjan v Netherlands* (1982) ECR 3723.

C-357/89 *Raulin v Minister van onderwijis en wetenschappen* (1992) ECR1–1022.

C-184-99 *Rudy Grzelczyk v CPAS* (2001) ECR1–6193.

C-370/90 *R v Immigration Appeal Tribunal and Surinder Singh, ex parte Secretary of State for the Home Department* (1992) ECR1–4265.

196/87 *Steymann v Staatssecretaris van justitie* (1988) ECR 6159.

C-456/02 *Trojani v CPAS* (2004) ECR1–7573.

26/26 *Van Gend & Loos v Netherlands* (1963) ECR 105.

Chapter 14

The emergence of the World Trade Organization

Another triumph of corporate capitalism?

Fiona Macmillan

Introduction

This chapter considers the establishment of the World Trade Organization (WTO) in the context of the rise of corporate capitalism and the structural effects of that ascent on the regulatory structure and institutional environment of the international trade regime. The chapter argues that the rise of corporate capitalism can be traced to at least the establishment of the English East India Company in 1600 and its Dutch counterpart, the Verenigde Oost-Indische Compagnie (VOC), in 1602. Thereafter it followed a trajectory that linked it irrevocably with the international regulatory strategies of the state that represented, as Arrighi (Arrighi 2002) has argued, the 'dominant agency of capitalist accumulation' in the relevant period. Focusing on the current period in which the United States has been the dominant state agency, the chapter traces the significance of the relationship between state strategy and corporate capitalism through to the Uruguay Round of trade negotiations and the emergence of the WTO as an intergovernmental institution.

The doctrine of comparative advantage

Arguing that there is a fundamental connection between the establishment of the WTO and the growth of corporate capitalism may seem to be what is popularly called 'a no-brainer'. Yet there is also a contradiction in this position, the acknowledgement of which provides a good taster for the rather muddy waters in which this chapter takes a short dip. The contradiction in question arises as a result of the fact that the commitment to a global free trade regime, which underlies the rhetoric – if not the reality – of the WTO system, is said to be based upon the doctrine of comparative advantage. This doctrine was developed in the work of nineteenth-century classical economists (for example, Ricardo 1817), building on the work of Adam Smith (Smith 1776).

Smith's insight was that economic gains would be produced where a nation concentrated on producing particular commodities and then traded its surpluses in these commodities. Smith argued that government interference in international trade would inhibit the development of such specialization (see Dunkley 2001: 108–9). Ricardo (Ricardo 1817) added the refinement that the ability to specialize was a consequence, not of so-called absolute advantage in the form of production costs, but of comparative advantage based on national tastes, technology and resources bases, as well as production costs. Thus, the modern version of the doctrine argues that optimal allocation of resources will be achieved if each country uses its comparative advantage to produce only the commodities that it can most efficiently produce and trades those commodities with other countries in order to obtain the commodities that it does not produce. Ultimately, it is argued that welfare will be maximized. It is also frequently argued that economic growth will be stimulated and everyone will be better off in economic terms. However, even some prominent free trade advocates are doubtful about this proposition (see, especially, Bhagwati 2002: 41–43). Non-economic benefits in the form of greater international cooperation and harmony are also postulated by adherents of the doctrine of comparative advantage and its concomitant of international trade free from government interference (as argued by both Smith and Ricardo: Alessandrini 2005).

Apart from a range of well-founded ethical concerns about the consequences of the doctrine of comparative advantage (see, for example, Gray 1998), there have been many criticisms of the economic assumptions upon which it is based (see Dunkley 2001: 110, for an indicative list). A serious problem concerning its current applicability, which is particularly relevant in the context of this chapter, relates to its assumption that capital, along with skilled labour, is largely immobile. The efficiency and welfare advantages predicted by the doctrine are based upon the movement of traded commodities, in the form of raw materials and manufactured goods, across borders. The twentieth century, however, marked an increase (that has continued unabated into the twenty-first century) in the movement of the means of production across borders. This generally occurs by means of foreign direct investment by multinational enterprises, which establish subsidiary undertakings in another country for this purpose. It seems clear that corporate decisions about the optimal destination of foreign direct investment are informed by a range of factors including 'raw materials, energy sources, markets, labor supply and costs, transportation availability and costs, capital availability, the potential for economies of scale, services and infrastructure (electricity, water supply, waste disposal, and so forth), governmental actions (taxes, incentives, regulations), and site costs' (Leonard 1998: 21). Disagreement exists about the relative weight of these factors, and it seems likely that their significance differs substantially from industry to industry (Leonard 1998: 21–26). The important point, however, is that the prevalence and pattern of foreign direct investment suggests that capital seeks absolute, rather than comparative, advantage (Dunkley 2001: 118; Gray 1998: 81–83).

This is likely to create welfare problems in countries that compete for foreign direct investment. Currently, such problems are most likely to be experienced in developing countries, the situation of which appears to pose particular problems for the vitality of the comparative advantage doctrine (see further Dunkley 2001: 118–99 and 145).

Of course, it is possible to sideline the contradiction between the WTO's appeal to the doctrine of comparative advantage as a justification for world market liberalization and the obstacles to the existence of comparative advantage that are raised by the growth of foreign direct investment by multinational corporations. This is because it is arguable that the WTO is incapable, in any case, of realizing the benefits promised by the doctrine because, rhetoric aside, it is not really concerned with removing barriers to international trade. Rather, the argument may be made that the WTO is a pretext for keeping up protectionist barriers in some areas. In particular, WTO rules show an unhealthy interest in keeping up protectionist barriers for the developed world so that enterprises based in the developed world have access to the markets they want, while enterprises of the developing world do not have access to the markets of the developed world that would be particularly valuable to them. Thus, Amin has remarked that 'the function of the IMF and the World Bank, and also the General Agreement on Trade and Tariffs (GATT), masquerading behind the discourse of free trade, is the protection of market control by the dominant transnational oligopolies' (Amin 1998: 97).

The rise of corporate capitalism

In their attachment to the doctrine of comparative advantage and its presumed concomitant of a world market economy under which economic welfare would be maximized, neither Smith nor Ricardo appear to have foreseen the meteoric rise of the multinational corporate entity. This is not particularly surprising. Like all of us, their intellectual horizons were shaped by their times and, in their case, by the prevailing pattern of capitalist development. It would, of course, have been impossible for the early theorists of comparative advantage to ignore the importance of the joint stock corporations in opening up lucrative avenues of foreign trade. Since at least the establishment of the English East India Company in 1600 and the VOC in 1602, these corporations had been features of the international trade landscape. The trade ascendancy of the VOC in the seventeenth century was, like the power of the Dutch Empire, on the wane by the middle of the eighteenth century (see Arrighi 2002: 139–44 on the VOC). At this time, as the British Empire superseded the Dutch, the English joint stock companies began their domination of international trade. This pattern was not a mere coincidence. As Arrighi has noted, the 'joint-stock chartered companies were highly malleable instruments of expansion of state power' (Arrighi 2002: 307).

In other words, these corporations were not just part of the trade landscape; they were also part of the political landscape in a way that directly allied them to the interests of their originating nation state.

Today's multinational corporate enterprise has a certain type of inter-dependence with the nation state, and this relationship has considerable political significance. However, despite its interdependence with the state, the modern multinational enterprise is not an instrument of state power. Rather, it has come to constitute 'the most fundamental limit of that power' (Arrighi 2002: 307). This is because, in many respects, the multinational corporation wields power quite independently of the state and of state constraints.

Viewed through the lens of the 'extroverted' national economy (Amin 1974: 599) that characterized the period of British dominance, during which both Smith and Ricardo were writing their influential works, this develop-ment in the nature of corporate power would have been far from predictable. It was the shift from Britain as the dominant global state power to the period of US dominance, associated with the move from a leading extro-verted national economy to a leading 'autocentric' national economy (Amin 1974: 599), that provided the conditions necessary for the flourishing of the multinational corporate enterprise:

> [i]n the US regime ... the autocentric nature of the dominant and leading national economy (the US) became the basis of a process of 'internalization' of the world market within the organizational domains of giant business corporations, while economic activities in the United States remained organically integrated into a single national reality to a far greater extent than they ever were in nineteenth-century Britain.
>
> (Arrighi 2002: 281)

The key feature of these new 'organizational domains' was vertical integra-tion, as a consequence of which the same corporate group controlled all aspects of innovation, production and distribution (see Chandler 1977: 244 on the significance of vertical integration in this context). This was the complete opposite of the approach taken by British trading concerns during the height of Britain's colonial and trade domination (Arrighi 2002: 283–300, especially 287).

With the advantage of increased historical perspective, Braudel enjoyed an insight denied to Smith, Ricardo and their ilk. He saw that the economy (in its broadest sense) was composed of three layers: the material life, the market economy and capitalism (Braudel 1982: 10–11). The first layer is 'an extremely elementary and mostly self-sufficient economy' (Arrighi 2002: 10), which Braudel also referred to as 'the non-economy' (Braudel 1982: 229). The second layer, that of the market economy, is characterized by 'its many horizontal communications between the different markets' where 'a degree of automatic coordination usually links supply, demand and prices' (Braudel 1982: 229). It seems likely that Smith, Ricardo and their fellow free trade enthusiasts were not only concerned with this second layer of the economy, but also would not have distinguished it from Braudel's third layer. As the market economy has its roots in the material life, so Braudel's top layer emerges from the market economy. This is 'the zone of the anti-market, where the great predators roam and the law of the jungle operates. This – today as in the past, before and after the industrial revolution – is the real home of capitalism' (Braudel 1982: 229–30). The real home of capitalism is, however, an unstable structure; and in its instability it threatens the stability of the lower layers of the economy, especially the market economy.

Arrighi argues that this inherent instability of the capitalist system has led to a cyclical series of paradigm shifts. When capital can longer be profitably employed by use in the development of new markets that expand the productive capacity of the existing markets, then a switch occurs and excess profits are ploughed into the trade in money. That is, a switch is made from trade to finance:

> [t]he switch is the expression of a 'crisis' in the sense that it marks a 'turning point', a 'crucial time of decision,' when the leading agency of systemic processes of capital accumulation reveals, through the switch, a negative judgment on the possibility of continuing to profit from the reinvestment of surplus capital in the material expansion of the world economy, as well as a positive judgment on the possibility of prolonging in time and space its leadership/dominance through a greater specialization in high finance.
>
> (Arrighi 2002: 215)

Of particular importance is the fact that the switch from trade to finance is fuelled by interstate competition for investment. Drawing on Weber (Weber 1978), Arrighi argues that interstate competition for mobile capital has been essential to the material expansion of the capitalist world economy. However, Arrighi's gloss to this proposition is that capitalist power has intensified during each period of capitalist accumulation (Arrighi 2002: 12ff.).

It seems that the modern multinational enterprise is very much a creature of this intensification of capitalist power. The precondition of the ascendancy of the multinational enterprise were the twentieth-century processes of vertical integration and internalization of international trade, but the dominance of multinational enterprises is crucially linked to interstate competition for investment. Gray notes:

> [t]oday's competition between states for investment by multinational corporations allows them to exercise a leverage they did not possess in a more hierarchical world order. At the same time such competition limits

the freedom of action of sovereign states. The leverage that states can exercise over corporations must be exercised in a global environment in which most of the competitive pressures that affect them work to limit the control of governments over their economies within a narrow margin.

Sovereign states remain the key arena of influence seeking by corporations. Multinationals exercise influence over the policies of sovereign states as well as exercising their ingenuity in eluding their jurisdiction. This is the typical interaction of sovereign states and business in the late twentieth century.

(Gray 1998: 70)

Little qualitative change in this interaction can be observed in the early stages of the twenty-first century. Thus, the evolution of the relationship between state and multinational corporate enterprise has been characterized by a move along the spectrum from an identity to an opposition of interest. The relationship remains interdependent, but the nature of that interdependence has altered.

The phenomenon of corporate capitalism, which has produced multinational corporate entities of considerable size and economic power (see, for example, Anderson and Cavanagh 2000), has also been responsible for structural change in the world economy. It is common to describe aspects of this under the rubric of economic globalization. Views on the meaning, depth, significance, inevitability and desirability of globalization are legion. Structurally speaking, important differences exist between those who perceive globalization as promoting diversity and those who perceive it as the harbinger of homogenization. Advocates of the former view often appear to be confusing the means of globalization with its ends. Arguments by those, such as Gray, that globalization is stimulated by *'differences* between localities, nations and regions' because '[t]here would not be profits to be made by investing and manufacturing worldwide if conditions were similar everywhere' (Gray 1998: 57–58) provide an example of this tendency. It may be that economic globalization is stimulated by difference, but its end result is homogenization. Ultimately, the ability to sell the same or substantially the same product or service in as many markets as possible seems not only to make the most economic sense for globalizing corporate interests, it also appears to be the obvious intention behind their worldwide marketing campaigns (see, for example, Levitt 1983). This is not to say that corporate interests do not routinely exploit their ability to isolate national markets in their drive for international homogenization (see, for example, Macmillan 1998). However, it is quite evident that the effect of this has been to produce international homogenization rather than diversity in the markets for the relevant forms of cultural output (see further Bettig 1996; Macmillan 1998; Macmillan 2002).

If homogenization of markets is the object or effect of economic globalization then it seems almost axiomatic that this will have an impact on cultural, social, legal and political life. Again, the precise nature of this impact is much disputed. It is, for example, common to perceive in globalization a threat to national sovereignty. However, the significance of this threat in terms of the exercise of sovereignty is much debated. For some commentators sovereignty has been relocated upwards to the supranational level and downwards to the sub-national level (for example, Jayasuriya 1999); for others, multinational corporations have usurped the role of the nation state; yet others argue that the global market 'has weakened and hollowed out' both nation states and multinational corporations (see, for example, Gray 1998: 63 and 74–77). Some consider the nation state to retain vitality and take the view that arguments to the contrary are propaganda for the proposition that complete globalization is inevitable (for example, Hirst and Thompson 1996). Many bemoan the decline in the power and autonomy of the nation state, but not all. There are those (for example, Hardt and Negri 2000) who, as Dunkley notes, 'see globalisation as allowing ... ideological diversity to combat narrow nationalisms, broad outlooks to supersede particularism or alternative models to rival European forms of modernisation' (Dunkley 2001: 16). In terms of the social, legal and political effects of globalization, Amin has argued that globalization has produced 'global disorder' because, amongst other things, the global system 'has not developed new forms of political and social organization going beyond the nation state – a requirement of the globalized system of production' (Amin 1998: 2). This is, of course, a consequence of the fact that the power of capital, and specifically of multinational corporate entities, has transcended the nation state while the exercise of political and legal power has remained trapped within its confines.

Despite all the competing views on the nature of the structural changes consequent on globalization, almost no one seems to deny that the rise of the multinational or transnational corporate enterprise is both a cause and a predominant feature of our globalized world. The power exercised by such enterprises is not appropriately characterized as simply economic. The self-reinforcing nature of corporate power has also conferred an explicitly political character on the exercise of this power. The political aspects of this power have a number of different dimensions. One manifestation of this political power is the way in which corporate interests are able to influence government policies in countries seeking foreign direct investment (FDI). The exercise of this power is a prevalent feature of twenty-first century political life precisely because of the importance of interstate competition for mobile capital. However, the leverage that such corporate interests are able to exert in this respect is obviously directly proportional to the needs of countries seeking FDI – the greater the need, the greater the potential power that may be wielded (see the argument advanced by China,

Cuba, India, Kenya, Pakistan and Zimbabwe in World Trade Organization 2002).

Another aspect of the political power of multinational corporate entities is the way in which they are also able to influence structural change and institution building at the supranational level. Because states are generally the formal actors at this level, corporate entities need to use their power and influence with states in order to achieve desired changes. The states implicated in this exercise of power are not only developing countries, the ability of which to influence political developments at the international level is perceived as comparatively limited, but are rather the most powerful states in the current world order (see Odell and Eichengreen 2000: 200–206 and Dryden 1995). For example, there is extensive evidence for the proposition that a powerful alliance of cross-sectoral multinational corporate interests operating under the auspices of the US Intellectual Property Committee procured both the inclusion of intellectual property as a trade issue within the Uruguay Round of trade talks and the eventual conclusion of the WTO Agreement on Trade Related Aspects of Intellectual Property Rights (Blakeney 1996: ch. 1; Sell 2003). In doing this, they exercised leverage not only with the US Government, but also on the governments of other powerful and influential states (especially those of the European Union and Japan) by mobilizing corporate interests based in those countries (Sell 2003: 46). This is not to say that the governments of these powerful states were reduced (entirely) to pawns in the hands of corporate interests. The US Government, for example, perceived a clear conjunction between its own interests and those of the corporate sector. Specifically, looking after the multinational corporate sector also involved addressing its own concern about the trade deficit and the increasing economic might of Japan (Sell 2003: 76). Further, the extent to which such direct corporate influence was responsible for the overall shape of the WTO and its covered agreements appears to vary qualitatively and quantitatively (see, for example, Sell 2003: chapter 7). Nevertheless, it is arguable that the general perception by the most powerful and influential states that there is a community of interest between state and corporation had a decisive influence on the outcome of the Uruguay Round.

The transition from GATT to the WTO

The new institution of the WTO was the final product of the long Uruguay Round of trade negotiations that commenced at Punta del Este in September 1986. A resounding chorus of commentators appears to embrace the view that the move from a regime predicated on an agreement to one predicated on an intergovernmental institution constitutes a quantum shift in the nature of multilateral trade relations. Looked at in the cold light of day, however, the differences might appear rather less monumental. By the time of the Uruguay Round, the GATT was considerably more than a mono-dimensional agreement governing tariff bindings on goods traded internationally. Rather, largely as a result of the Tokyo Round of trade negotiations, by the time the Uruguay Round came along, GATT was an umbrella agreement for a host of subsidiary agreements, some of which dealt with non-tariff issues. It had an established dispute resolution procedure; and, *de facto*, it had taken on the character of an international organization, the very well established bureaucracy (see Hoekman and Kostecki 2001: 37–41) of which simply transmogrified into the WTO bureaucracy. In a move that might similarly emphasize either continuity or the minimal nature of the shift from agreement to organization, the Agreement Establishing the World Trade Organization (hereafter, the WTO Agreement) contains a preamble that substantially reproduces the preamble of the 1947 GATT with the addition of some remarks directed towards the importance of sustainable development and of securing the economic development of the developing world. That constitutive agreement also makes it clear that important GATT principles, such as being member-driven and proceeding by consensus, have been carried over from GATT into the WTO. All this raises the question of whether any real significance can be attached to the movement in the multilateral trading regime from agreement to institution.

As is commonly noted, the Uruguay Round marked a move to a more focused concern with non-tariff barriers to international trade. This consolidated a trend that began during the Tokyo Round. As the post-Tokyo Round consequence of this was a plethora of smaller, often plurilateral, agreements there was considerable fragmentation in the legal system governing international trade. It seems clear that this created a pressure for consolidation, to which one possible response was the creation of an overarching institution. This seems to have been one of the factors that, in April 1990, motivated the suggestion by Canada's trade minister for the establishment of just such an institution (Hoekman and Kostecki 2001: 40; Odell and Eichengreen 2000: 188, citing Preeg 1995: 113), which was followed by the formal proposal of the European Communities in July 1990 for a so-called Multilateral Trade Organization (GATT Document MTN.GNG/NG14/W/42, 9 July 1990). There also seems to have been a strong view that the integration of the two new major areas of multilateral agreement, intellectual property and services, would be most efficiently achieved under the auspices of an institution (UNCTAD 1994: 8). These types of explanations for the emergence of what became the WTO may cast some light on immediately proximate pressures for the creation of an institution, although it is interesting that a number of GATT members found them less than compelling at the time. Switzerland, for example, preferred the option of retaining GATT and strengthening its links to the Bretton Woods institutions (GATT Document MTN.GNG/NG14/W/41, 17 May 1990), while the United States at that stage preferred a more gradual consideration of the need for a new institutional approach (GATT Document MTN.GNG/ NG14/W/45, 18 October 1990, and see UNCTAD 1994: 8–9 and 9n). It seems possible, however, despite the fact that an institutional approach was not contemplated in the Punta del Este Declaration, that there were longer-term systemic pressures behind the creation of the WTO as an institution. The creation of the institution may, in this sense, be no more than a recognition or legitimation of changes already occurring.

A problem in assessing the meaning and significance of the move from the GATT to the WTO is in distinguishing between proponents of the new institutional form and proponents of greater trade liberalization. While one might be tempted to argue that the quest to distinguish between the form of the organization and the content of its trade rules is difficult, if not impossible, it seems to be the case that this distinction did exist during the Uruguay Round negotiations. While it was the US Government that was pressing for greater trade liberalization and the inclusion of an agreement on intellectual property, the initial proposal for a multilateral institution did not emanate from the US, either formally or informally. Rather, as noted above, the formal impetus came from the European Communities following on from a Canadian proposal. Developing countries, which had become a significant presence in multilateral trade talks for the first time during the Uruguay Round, also seem to have supported an institutional framework on the basis that it would have greater potential to constrain aggressive US bilateralism – a consideration that was equally attractive to most of the developed world, including the European Communities (Odell and Eichengreen 2000: 188; Hoekman and Kostecki 2001: 34; UNCTAD 1994: 1). Possibly for connected reasons, the US seems to have been at first rather lukewarm in relation to the proposed new trade organization, preferring a more incremental approach to the establishment of any new overarching institution.

By the time of the 1991 Dunkel Draft, which formed the basis of the final agreement for the WTO, the US position appears to have solidified in favour of the proposed new institution. The European Communities, on the other hand, were having far more difficulty with the proposed content of the agreements that would make up the operating rules for the institution. The particular sticking point for the European Communities was the issue of agricultural liberalization, which was central to the US negotiating position (Odell and Eichengreen 2000: 188). Additionally, the French Government resisted services liberalization as a result of its fears about US cultural imperialism generally and its effect on the French film industry specifically (Odell and Eichengreen 2000: 188). In the end, it was the US that forced the issue (see further Odell and Eichengreen 2000: especially 187–94), demonstrating coalescence between pressures for trade liberalization and for the new institutional form. While this may have been, at least in part, a matter of strategic expediency, it suggests that ultimately there was no intrinsic contradiction between greater trade liberalization and the new institution of the WTO.

Given this final rapprochement between greater trade liberalization and the new institution of the WTO, it is tempting to argue that the greatest significance of the WTO lies in its free trade credentials. This argument gains strength from the fact that it was the US, consistently standing for the interests of trade liberalization in selected sectors, that drove the process that concluded the Uruguay Round. Given this US dominance, it does not seem unreasonable to go even further and suggest that, in its final form, the institution of the WTO serves the cause of the (sectorally selective) free traders, rather than free trade serving the cause of greater institutionalism in multilateral trading relations. If this is so, then we need to ask what motivated the free trade warriors of the late twentieth century.

It is notable that, rhetorically at least, considerable emphasis was placed on the economic benefits of trade liberalization. However, leaving aside the questions that have been raised about these above and (especially) the question of the distribution of these benefits, it seems that the WTO was not in any case essential to the expansion of world trade. As Bello remarks, on the basis of the WTO's own statistics, '[w]orld trade did not need the WTO to expand 87-fold between 1948 and 1997, from $124 billion to $10,772 billion' (Bello 2000: 104, citing World Trade Organization 1998, 12). Rather, as an explanation of the emergence of the WTO, it seems much more likely that the WTO was a response to that economic interdependence to which GATT had so successfully contributed. That is, the WTO was a response to the rise of so-called globalization in the form of corporate capitalism. Globalization as a vehicle of corporate capitalism was considerably inhibited by a range of non-tariff measures introduced after the 'exogenous shocks' (Hoekman and Kostecki 2001: 43), including the collapse of the fixed exchange rate system established under the auspices of Bretton Woods institutions and the OPEC crisis, of the 1970s and 1980s (Hoekman and Kostecki 2001: 41–44; Odell and Eichengreen 2000: 187–89). The rise of the WTO, therefore, with its emphasis on the removal of non-tariff barriers, is a response to the interruption of the process of corporate-led globalization.

Perspectives emerging from structuralist theory tend to reinforce the idea of an interdependent relationship between globalization, corporate capitalism and the emergence of the WTO as an institution. Sociological institutionalism (Nichols 1998: 482), for example, which focuses on the interaction of individual actors and institutions in the light of the political, social and cultural environment in which those interactions take place, posits 'that institutions are created or changed because the new institution will confer greater social legitimacy on the organization or its individuals' (Nichols 1998: 485). Indeed, this concern with legitimacy in the context of the wider cultural, political and social milieu is a key feature of sociological institutionalism. From this theoretical perspective, the mutually constitutive relationship between globalization and international organizations like the WTO can be explicitly recognized. It is also apposite to note that it is not merely the case that globalization has a legitimating effect on the WTO. The constitution of legitimacy is mutual so that the WTO has a legitimating effect on globalization. That is, there is a compelling argument that the legalization and juridicization of the trade regime through the framework of the WTO is a legitimization of the processes of globalization (Picciotto 2003: 386; Davis and Neacsu 2001: 737; compare Teubner 1997: especially 157).

Remaining within the structuralist tradition, post-Marxist accounts tend to build upon this type of approach by taking a longer and more nuanced view of the relationship between the structure of the world economy and the emergence of the WTO as an institution. Specifically, these accounts draw attention to a range of structures of varying depth and longevity. At the deep and long end, the structural development of capitalism is relevant to an account of the origins of the WTO. Occupying a median position is the birth of the Westphalian system and its relationship to the structure of international trade relations. The post-Second World War bifurcated system of international law, especially its management of international economic relations and the associated rise of corporate capitalism, occupies significant space at the shallower and shorter end of the spectrum.

Arrighi argues that a combination of structural changes has created a pressure to relocate state authority. These changes are 'the withering away of the modern system of territorial states as the primary locus of world power', 'the internalization of world-scale processes of production and exchange within the organizational domains of transnational corporations' and 'the resurgence of suprastatal world financial markets' (Arrighi 2002: 331; see also Jayasuriya 1999: 443):

> In recent years, the most significant pressure to relocate authority upward has been the tendency to counter escalating systemic chaos with a process of world government formation. In a wholly unplanned fashion, and under the pressure of events, the dormant suprastatal organizations established by the Roosevelt administration of the closing years of the Second World War have been hurriedly revitalized to perform the most urgent functions of world governance which the US state could neither neglect nor perform single-handed ... But the problems that has driven it to seek inter-statal forms of world governance remained.
>
> (Arrighi 2002: 331)

Following this account it might be argued that the creation of the WTO as an institution can be located as part of the escalating process of world government formation. This might account for the otherwise somewhat perplexing transition in the governance of the world trading system from agreement to institution. Going further and reflecting on the nature and ideology of the

WTO, do these represent an attempt on the part of the US, in its death throes as the dominant agency of capitalist accumulation, and its allies to control interstate competition for mobile capital? Certainly, the chronological coincidence between the phase following what Arrighi characterizes as a switch from trade to finance in the US cycle of capital accumulation and the Uruguay Round negotiations is striking. Similarly noteworthy is the fact that the two new Uruguay Round agreements, the TRIPs Agreement and the GATT, are quite conceivably conceptualized as being essentially concerned with investment (see further Macmillan 1999 and Macmillan 2005: 178–80). Added to this, a drive to control competition for mobile capital might explain the obsession with the conclusion of a global investment agreement (see further Macmillan 1999 and Macmillan 2004: especially 77–79).

Might we go even further than this and argue that at a more general level, during each turbulent post-switch phase (recalling Arrighi's cyclical account), the international community turns to international (economic) law making, perhaps as an alternative to war making, in order to manage conflict? Certainly, the post-switch period, from the 1870s onwards, of the British period of dominance was characterized by the intensive making of trade treaties (McGillivray et al. 2001). The multilateral free trade regime that was established in 1860 by the Anglo-French Treaty of Commerce was a dead duck by the end of the 1870s as a result of German protectionism (Arrighi 2002: 55). From around this time on, as the Germans vied with the British for economic and political dominance, the United Kingdom promoted or participated in a range of treaty obligations designed to keep its pre-eminent position afloat. While not all the 'trade' treaties are centrally concerned with the control of investment, it is possible to discern a new concern with aspects of investment during this period. In particular, the European nations turned their attention to the conclusion of multilateral treaties in relation to intellectual property. The Paris Convention for the Protection of Industrial Property (1883) and the Berne Convention for the Protection of Literary and Artistic Works (1886), the two founding conventions of modern intellectual property law, were negotiated in this period. Of course, it may be argued, as the dominant discourse of intellectual property still has it today, that these conventions were concerned with international innovation, not investment. And it is doubtless true that many of those involved in the negotiation of those conventions thought that this is what they were about (Ilardi and Blakeney 2004: 22–36 and 87–103). But looking at the corporate stranglehold over intellectual property today it seems difficult to contest the argument that it is as much about investment as it is about anything else. If this phase of multilateral intellectual property law making reflected a new concern about international investment, then we should not be surprised to see exactly the same concerns manifested in the Uruguay Round. This would explain the rather anomalous position of the Trade-Related Aspects of Intellectual Property Rights (TRIPs) Agreement within the suite of WTO agreements (Bhagwati 2002: 75–76), along with the privileged position of intellectual property obligations in the current spate of US bilateral investment treaties (see further Drahos 2002). Further, as has already been noted, the joined hands of the US Government and various powerful corporate sectors were fundamental to the existence and shape of the TRIPs Agreement (Blakeney 1996: ch. 1; Sell 2003).

Of course, the implications of this account are not happy. The unprecedented phenomenon of almost 100 years of European peace from the time of the Treaty of Vienna in 1815 was shattered by the onset of the First World War – the moment when the great European powers turned from law to war. The next 30-odd years of history marked an epoch of astounding horror that may have been focused on Europe but was certainly not confined to it. The idea, in the current period of economic turbulence, that we may be in danger of repeating the unsuccessful attempt to turn from war to law that characterized the end of the British period of economic dominance hardly bears thought – but it does require it.

References

Alessandrini, D (2005) 'WTO and current trade debate: an enquiry into the intellectual origins of free trade thought', *International Trade Law and Regulation* 11(2): 53–60.

Amin, S. (1974) *The Accumulation of Capital on a World Scale*, New York: Monthly Review Press.

——(1998) *Capitalism in the Age of Globalization*, London and New York: Zed Books.

Anderson, S. and Cavanagh, J. (2000) *Top 200: The Rise of Corporate Power*, Washington, DC: Institute for Policy Studies.

Arrighi, G. (2002) *The Long Twentieth Century: Money, Power and the Origins of Our Times*, London and New York: Verso.

Bello, W. (2000) 'Reforming the WTO is the wrong agenda', in K. Danaher and R. Burbach (eds), *Globalize This! The Battle Against the World Trade Organization and Corporate Rule*, Maine, ME: Common Courage Press.

Bettig, R. (1996) *Copyrighting Culture: The Political Economy of Intellectual Property*, Boulder, CO: Westview Press.

Bhagwati, J. (2002) *Free Trade Today*, Princeton and Oxford: Princeton University Press.

Blakeney, M. (1996) *Trade Related Aspects of Intellectual Property Rights*, London: Sweet & Maxwell.

Braudel, F. (1982) *The Wheels of Commerce*, New York: Harper & Row.

Chandler, A. (1977) *The Visible Hand: The Managerial Revolution in American Business*, Cambridge, MA: Belknap Press.

Davis, M.H. and Neacsu, D. (2001) 'Legitimacy, globally: the incoherence of free trade practice, global economics & their governing principles of political economy', *University of Missouri Kansas City Law Review* 69: 733.

Drahos, P. (2002) 'BITS and BIPs: bilateralism in intellectual property', *Journal of World Intellectual Property Law* 4: 791.

Dryden, S. (1995) *Trade Warriors: USTR and the American Crusade for Free Trade*, New York: Oxford University Press.

Dunkley, G. (2001) *The Free Trade Adventure: The WTO, the Uruguay Round & Globalism – A Critique*, London and New York: Zed Books.

Gray, J. (1998) *False Dawn: The Delusions of Global Capitalism*, New York: New Press.

Hardt, M. and Negri, A. (2000) *Empire*, Cambridge, MA: Harvard University Press.

Hirst, P. and Thompson, G. (1996) *Globalization in Question*, Cambridge: Polity Press.

Hoekman, B.H. and Kostecki, M.M. (2001, 2nd edn) *The Political Economy of the World Trading System: The WTO and Beyond*, Oxford and New York: Oxford University Press.

Ilardi, A. and Blakeney, M. (eds) (2004) *International Encyclopaedia of Intellectual Property Treaties*, Oxford: Oxford University Press.

Jayasuriya, K. (1999) 'Globalization, law and the transformation of sovereignty: the emergence of global regulatory governance', *Indiana Journal of Global Legal Studies* 6: 425.

Leonard, H.J. (1998) *Pollution and the Struggle for the World Product: Multinational Corporations, Environment and International Comparative Advantage*, Cambridge: Cambridge University Press.

Levitt, T. (1983) 'The globalisation of markets', *Harvard Business Review* 61: 92.

McGillivray, F., McLean, I., Pahre R. and Schonhardt-Bailey, C. (eds) (2001) *International Trade and Political Institutions: Instituting Trade in the Long Nineteenth Century*, Cheltenham: Edward Elgar.

Macmillan, F. (1998) 'Copyright & culture: a perspective on corporate power', *Media and Arts Law Review* 10: 71.

——(1999) 'Making corporate power global', *International Trade Law and Regulation* 5: 3.

——(2002) 'The cruel ©: copyright and film', *European Intellectual Property Review* 24: 483.

——(2004) 'If not this World Trade Organisation, then what?', *International Company and Commercial Law Review* 3: 75.

——(2005) 'Looking back to look forward: is there a future for human rights in the WTO?', *International Trade Law and Regulation* 6: 163.

Nichols, P.M. (1998) 'Forgotten linkages – historical institutionalism and sociological institutionalism and analysis of the World Trade Organization', *University of Pennsylvania Journal of International Economic Law* 19: 461.

Odell, J. and Eichengreen, B. (2000) 'The United States, the ITO, and the WTO: exit options, Agent Slack, and presidential leadership', in A.O. Krueger (ed.), *The WTO as an International Organization*, Chicago, IL and London: University of Chicago Press.

Picciotto, S. (2003) 'Private rights vs public standards in the WTO', *Review of International Political Economy* 10: 377.

Preeg, E.H. (1995) *Traders in a Brave New World: The Uruguay Round and the Future of the International Trading System*, Chicago, IL: University of Chicago Press.

Ricardo, D. (1817) *Principles of Political Economy and Taxation*, reissued as P. Sraffa (ed.) (1951), *The Works and Correspondence of David Ricardo*, vol. 1, Cambridge: University Press for the Royal Economic Society.

Sell, S. (2003) *Private Power, Public Law: The Globalization of Intellectual Property Rights*, Cambridge: Cambridge University Press.

Smith, A. (1776) *An Enquiry into the Nature and Causes of the Wealth of Nations*, reissued as E. Cannan (ed.) (1961), *An Enquiry into the Nature and Causes of the Wealth of Nations*, London: Methuen.

Teubner, G. (1997) 'Breaking frames: the global interplay of legal and social systems', *American Journal of Comparative Law* 45: 149.

United Nations Conference on Trade and Development (UNCTAD) (1994) *The Outcome of the Uruguay Round: An Initial Assessment – Supporting Papers to the Trade and Development Report 1994*, New York: United Nations, UNCTAD/TDR/14 (Supplement).

Weber, M. (1978) *Economy and Society*, Berkeley: California University Press.

World Trade Organization (1998) *Annual Report 1998: International Trade Statistics*, Geneva: WTO.

——(2002) Working Group on the Relationship between Trade and Investment, *Communication from China, Cuba, India, Kenya, Pakistan and Zimbabwe: Investors' and Home Governments' Obligations*, WT/WGTI/W/152, 19/11/2002.

Chapter 15

The World Trade Organization and development

Victory of 'rational choice'?

Donatella Alessandrini

Introduction

The establishment of the World Trade Organization (WTO) in 1995 is supposed to have signalled the 'rational choice' by so-called developing countries to abandon the failing economic policies and legal strategies they had pursued for more than three decades. To put it succinctly, trade scholars argue that by relying on trade protection as opposed to trade liberalization and insisting on unilateral measures on the developed countries' part, developing countries failed to obtain the liberalization of their competitive exports and consequently to 'develop' their economies by means of liberal trade. Conversely, by adhering to the same set of rules and the economic rationale those rules embody, namely the unquestionable belief in the universal beneficial role of trade liberalization, developing countries are finally able to demand and enforce compliance with WTO rules so as to enjoy the benefits its legal regime is supposed to generate.

The significance of the WTO in relation to development seems therefore to rest on the assumption that it brings to a close a past in which debates about the development dimension of the international trade regime have been informed by failing 'emotional', 'irrational' and 'ideological' claims. It is believed to inaugurate a new era in which past controversies, deriving from such ill-conceived claims, have been superseded by an international community founded on 'reason'. This chapter aims to challenge this linear reading of the neo-liberal transformation of the development dimension of the international trade regime. Indeed, the entry into force of the WTO was the outcome of a complex interrelationship between different factors that cannot be accounted for in terms of a rational and linear historic process.

Understanding how the 'consensus' on the trade and development rationale of the WTO emerged and consolidated would require a systematic account of the interplay among diverse and competing forces.[1] However, this chapter will focus on one particular aspect of this relationship, namely the 'scientific' authority the neo-liberal transformation of development thinking conferred upon the development agenda of the WTO. It is on the neo-liberal claim about the neutrality and rationality of its development analyses that this authority rests. This chapter makes two arguments in this respect: first, that neo-liberal theories and policies which have informed the WTO's approach to development since 1995 are based on political assumptions about Third World societies which belie their alleged neutrality; and second, that the conditions for their possibility need to be traced back to the 'scientific' authority, and a specific modality, with which 'development' was endowed since its inception. The 'science of development' is premised on the unquestionable need for developing countries to rely on a universal economic rationality in order to replicate the experience of developed countries. Accordingly, its means can be constantly transformed to both reconceptualize the 'failure' of development and posit anew the 'promise' of its overcoming.

The first part will therefore introduce the premises on which the development framework of the post-war period was established. A brief analysis of the mandate system under the League of Nations and the normative assumptions underlying its 'development mission' will serve to contextualize the subsequent discussion on the development enterprise of the post-war international community. These assumptions informed both early development theories and the development activity of the international trading regime. The second part will present an overview of the theoretical shifts in development thinking and will contend that, despite the qualitative difference from earlier approaches to development, neo-liberal thinking is both linked with, and has displaced, earlier development theories. The nexus is to be found within the terms of the development framework set up at the end of the colonial era.

Both the premise of development (that is, the representation of Third World societies as 'backward') and the consequent norm (namely the need for developing countries to replicate the successful experience of developed countries) remained unaffected by the so-called neo-liberal revolution of development thinking. Rather, that 'revolution' reformulated the means through which to achieve the undisputable goal. A reconceptualization of the 'nature' of Third World societies, however, was essential in order to replace earlier approaches to development with neo-liberal development. The uncovering of neo-liberal assumptions about Third World societies is crucial to emphasize the continuity of the 'development mission' in neo-liberal claims even when they seem to repudiate the paternalistic attitude of early development approaches. The aim is to provide a critique of the normative assumptions permeating the WTO's approach to development.

The development mission of the post-war period

Although the institutionalization and professionalization of the development enterprise occurred in the immediate post-war period (Escobar 1995: 45–46), its antecedents can be traced back to the mandate system under the

League of Nations. The League of Nations was the first major international institution managing the relationship between European and non-European peoples. As Anghie has pointed out, it was with the mandate system that the 'civilized–uncivilized' dichotomy of international law was reconceptualized in economic terms and development as a scientific discipline first emerged (Anghie 2000: 285). In particular, economic backwardness, rather than racial and cultural connotations, made the people of the mandate territories unable 'to stand by themselves under the strenuous conditions of the modern world' and, for the League's members, 'the well-being and *development* of such peoples form[ed] a sacred trust of *civilization* ... ' (Covenant of the League of Nations, art. 22).

Under the pragmatic 'new international law' of the interwar period, the League of Nations could be presented as a neutral institution as opposed to the self-interested nature of colonial powers (Anghie 2000: 283–85). The need for the former colonies to overcome their failure was premised on the universality of economics. The neutral character of the League was achieved through the resort to economic rationality and the establishment of a neutral body of experts, the Permanent Mandates Commission (PMC). The commission was given the task to gather, analyze and elaborate a vast amount of information regarding different territories and several subject areas (Anghie 2000: 280). The result was that the PMC could claim to be able to formulate neutral policies to be adopted in the different mandate territories. Once the failure of so-called backward societies was established in supposedly neutral terms, economic rationality, which happened to be the privileged domain of 'advanced' countries, was posited as the means through which mandate territories could overcome their inability to 'stand by themselves' and achieve equal status in the international community.

The 'development mission' of the post-war international community could thus be deployed. This enterprise relied on three assumptions borrowed from the experience of the mandate system: the positioning of a dichotomy between the status of developing and developed societies in terms of an economic gap; the reliance on economic rationality as the neutral terrain on which to bridge this gap; and the invocation of the help and expertise of the most 'advanced' members of the international community to facilitate this inevitable and desirable process. These three assumptions would set the terms within which it became possible to think about, speak of and reformulate 'development'.

Thus, in the immediate post-war period the basic underpinnings of development thinking were that the economic growth and progress experienced by industrialized countries were both desirable and inevitable. It was therefore a matter of identifying the most appropriate means for developing countries to replicate the industrialized countries' experience. Drawing on the practice of the mandate system, which had claimed to do away with the political interference of the past, the privileged terrain from which to articulate the 'development mission' was that of economics. Thus, the first preoccupation of development 'experts' in the 1950s was to overcome the fact that neoclassical economics was unable to explain the conditions of underdevelopment characterizing many Third World countries (see Escobar 1995: 55–89; Haque 1999: 53–79). With development economics and modernization theories, the so-called backwardness of Third World societies came to be theorized neutrally and development was made to coincide with the transition from backward and traditional to advanced and modern societies. As one major exponent of development economics put it:

> [w]e find a few industries highly capitalised, such as mining or electric power, side by side with the most primitive techniques ... We find the same contrast also outside the economic life. There are one or two modern towns, with the fine architectures, water supplies, communications and the like, into which people drift from other towns and villages which might almost belong to another planet. There is the same contrast even with people; between the few highly westernised, trousered, natives, educated in western universities, speaking western languages, and glorifying Beethoven, Mills, Marx or Einstein, and the great mass of their countrymen which live quite in other worlds ... Inevitably what one gets are very heavily developed patches of the economy, surrounded by economic darkness.
>
> (Lewis [1954] in Escobar 1995: 78).

The result of this representation of the so-called Third World was that the economic, social and cultural 'darkness' was to be replaced by new forms of societal organization which, in turn, were to be incorporated into the expanding world capitalist system. As development was identified with rapid economic growth, indiscriminate industrialization and capital accumulation, the radical transformation of Third World societies and their incorporation within the world capitalist system was posited as a necessary and desirable historic event to be achieved at the expense of other forms of societal organization with supposedly nothing to contribute to the development process.

The international trading regime played an important role in receiving and reinforcing this 'norm'. Modernization theories were predicated on an active role for the state. Thus, developing countries had to pursue economic growth and industrialization through injections of foreign capital and participation in the liberal trade regime whose rules had been established with the General Agreement on Trade and Tariffs (GATT). For its part, GATT received and further elaborated the development 'norm' of the post-war period through the institutionalization of the 'failure of developing countries to develop their trade as rapidly as that of the industrialised nations' (GATT 1958). This 'failure', established at the beginning of the 1950s, would inform the three-decades-long development-related trade activity of the international trading system.

Development economics and modernization theories were later challenged by dependency thinking, which rose to prominence in the 1960s. Most of the reformist dependency theories which impacted on the international trade regime hardly questioned the fundamental assumption that development was the necessary and inevitable result of a natural and linear historic process. However, they argued against the assumption that trade liberalization would automatically lead to greater growth and development for all countries, pointing out that the imbalances deriving from historical trading relationships and the rules of the GATT greatly limited the trade prospects of developing economies (see, for instance, Prebisch 1950; Furtado 1964). Dependency theorists' insights into the structural inequality of the international trading system contributed to the demands that developing countries articulated within the GATT between the 1960s and 1980s, which resulted in the formal recognition of their entitlement to maintain some flexibility from GATT legal strictures.[2]

This situation, however, was to change during the 1980s when the so-called counter-revolution in development thinking arrived. Writers such as Lal, Bauer, Balassa and Krueger refuted the basic assumptions underlying development economics and dependency theories (Lal 1983; Bauer 1981; Balassa 1982; Krueger 1993). As will be argued below, despite their differences, these authors shared several themes. First, the universality of rational economic behaviour was employed as the basis for arguing against the assumption that policy prescriptions deriving from neoclassical economics could not be extended to developing countries. Second, inefficient or failing institutional arrangements were identified as important factors precipitating developing countries' economic crisis. Third, a set of propositions was put forward to argue that inward-oriented policies and overextended public sectors were the causes of the economic inefficiency of developing countries. Finally, a series of comparative studies was used in order to assess the successes and failures of contrasting development policies employed by different developing countries.

The neo-liberal transformation of the 'science of development'

Neo-liberalism is a very complex system of thought whose origins and significance cannot be limited to the field of development thinking and the interaction between the developed and developing worlds. In what follows, however, the discussion will focus on a particular aspect of early neo-liberal theories, namely the way in which their economic analysis of development intersected with political representations of Third World societies.

The point made here is that these representations are central to the replacement of early development approaches with neo-liberal development. Neo-liberal analysis strongly rejected the underlying political assumptions of earlier development theories with respect to Third World economies and individuals. However, neo-liberal scholars simultaneously re-enacted a new and powerful construction of developing countries' 'backwardness'. Not only did this construction provide the basis for replacing earlier arguments about tariff flexibility with the WTO's emphasis on reciprocity. It also extended to areas previously exempted from trade regulation.

Rational choice-based approach ...

Development economics, as well as the dependency school of thought, had assumed that the existence of structural differences between developed and developing countries undermined the validity of neoclassical economic theories. Development economics had attributed these differences to the dual domestic structure of developing countries, whereas the dependency school had focused on the structural imbalances of the international trading system. Consequently, albeit for different underlying reasons, they all supported the central role of the state. These assumptions would become the target of the neo-liberal transformation of development thinking. Lal argued, for instance, that the major element of the dirigiste dogma is that:

> the price mechanism, or the working of a market economy, needs to be supplanted (and not merely supplemented) by various forms of direct government control, both national and international, to promote economic development ... [and] that the classical 19th century liberal case for free-trade is invalid for developing countries, and thus government restriction of international trade and payments is necessary for development.
>
> (Lal 1983: 5)

Therefore, the so-called dirigiste dogma (namely the belief in the active role of the government in promoting development) derived from the erroneous assumption that the differences in the structures of developing economies required separate economic analysis and policies from those applicable to the developed economies. The means on which Lal relies to show the fallacy of this assumption are the price mechanism and rational economic behaviour. The price mechanism is the principal organizer of economic activity, therefore the neoclassical analysis of human economic behaviour is not limited to agents operating in developed countries. Hence, the fallacy of the dirigiste dogma consists in denying the universality of rational economic behaviour to Third World individuals. This flaw derives from:

> a paternalist attitude born of a distrust of, if not contempt for, the ordinary, poor, uneducated masses of the Third World ... It is easy to

suppose that these half-starved, wretched and ignorant masses could not possibly conform, either as producers or consumers, to the behavioural assumption of orthodox neoclassical economics that people would act *economically*; when the opportunity of an advantage was presented to them they would take it.

(Lal 1983: 104)

This passage is relevant in that it seems to address the civilizing attitude of development economics towards so-called backward societies when, in actual fact, it is constructing a new vision of backwardness that extends beyond economics to include institutional and social arrangements. Lal denounces the paternalist attitude of development economics which had conceived of the 'masses of the Third World' as irrational economic agents. Simultaneously, according to Lal, these so-called uneducated masses are still in need of assistance in order to overcome their 'political and emotional resistance' to sound economic policies. As he points out:

the major benefit the developing countries derive from ... the multilateral trade institutions ... is the technical assistance built into the process of transferring the aid money to the recipient countries. Though often sound on general economic grounds, their advice is nevertheless resented for *political and emotional reasons* ...

(Lal 1983: 104, emphasis added)

The reformulation of the premises underlying the mandate system is fully accomplished. The mandate system, borrowing from the science of colonial administration, was based on the assumption that the inhabitants of the ex-colonies were 'not yet able to stand by themselves' and therefore needed guidance in order to pursue their material as well as moral and educational progress (Anghie 2000: 276). The result was the creation of a 'science of development' able to formulate universal policies by relying on the neutrality of economics. In the immediate post-war period, development economics would carry over precisely these assumptions: that 'backward societies' were characterized by an economic stage which was different from that of the advanced economies; that reliance on economic rationality would have paved the way to their development; and that this process would be facilitated through the assistance and guidance of the 'advanced' members of the international community. Lal claims to distance himself from the paternalist attitude of development economics by invoking the universality of rational economic behaviour. However, far from being removed, these assumptions are reformulated in his analysis in three main ways.

First, non-Western societies are still characterized as backward although, in contrast to the analysis of development economics, they do not require different economic analysis and policy prescriptions. The *modus operandi* of the Permanent Mandates Commission based on the collection, analysis and elaboration of a vast body of information from the mandate territories continues to operate. As Lal writes, 'there is by now a vast body of empirical evidence from different cultures and climates which shows that uneducated peasants act economically as producers and consumers. They respond to changes in relative prices much as neoclassical economic theory predicts' (Lal 1983: 105).

Second, reliance on neoclassical assumptions about rational economic behaviour and the price mechanism provides the premise for the replacement of development economics with the universality of neo-liberal economic laws. Therefore, the universality of neoclassical economics is invoked to argue for the applicability of market-based policies in developing countries. In other words, the means invoked to achieve development is once again the neutrality of economic laws, this time neo-liberal laws.

Third, developing countries are still in need of assistance in order to achieve development. The formal argument is that despite the fact that individuals in the developing world conform to the neoclassical model of rational utility-maximizers, their social and institutional arrangements are such that they will resist sound economic reforms. Lal is here referring to the second failure he imputed to development economics, namely the over-emphasis on physical capital formation as opposed to human capital formation. The latter needs to be encouraged through appropriate institutional arrangements both domestically and at the international level. Thus, it is necessary to make foreign aid conditional upon the adoption of sound, rational policies prescribed by the donors.

... and failing institutional arrangements

Lal's analysis can be read in conjunction with similar studies that emerged in the 1980s. Bauer, for instance, had already claimed that 'emergence from poverty [in the Third World] does not require large-scale capital formation' (Bauer 1981: 248). He was also sceptical of human capital formation, since his researches into the economic growth of the Malayan, West African and Indian economies had shown that their different economic performances could not be explained in 'terms of differences in human capital formation' but in terms of people's 'personal preferences, motivations and social arrangements' (Bauer 1984: 7). Thus, whereas Lal would argue for technical assistance and conditional aid in opposition to the overemphasis on physical capital formation, Bauer had anticipated the idea that institutional and social reforms in developing countries were necessary to stimulate growth. The theoretical basis for both, however, was a discourse about the Third World's societal organizations, which was presented as neutral, rational and technical rather than political.

The relevance of these theoretical constructions would gradually increase as their acceptance extended beyond traditional economic sectors. North, for instance, would argue that:

> transferring the formal political and economic rules of successful western market economies to Third World and Eastern European economies is not a sufficient condition for good economic governance ... as it is the informal norms that provide the essential legitimacy to any set of formal rules ... it is essential to change both the institutions and the belief systems for successful reform since it is the mental models of the actors that will shape choices.
>
> (North 1993: 6)

Technical assistance and conditional aid, together with institution building, would become crucial tools in the development arsenal of the international economic institutions for radically transforming institutional and social arrangements in developing countries. Thus, the neo-liberal transformation of the 'science of development' set out to effect a radical alteration of economic, political and social arrangements beyond the market, or, in other words, to reconceptualize in market terms all spheres of human interaction. The beginning of this shift can be traced in Lal's and Bauer's works, where all individuals are intrinsically rational economic agents able to seize any economic opportunity. It follows from this account that radical reforms are necessary for abolishing previous policies based on false economic assumptions such as those of development economics and dependency theories. Hence, the 'science of development' is transformed with regard to the means necessary to achieve the undisputed goal, namely catching up with the economic stage of the developed economies, so that the market, rather than the state, is posited as the crucial engine of development.

Outward-oriented policies and government controls

By positing the price mechanism as the principal organizer of human behaviour and economic activity, Lal defines direct government controls both at the national and international level as the major dogma of development economics. According to Lal, the economic crises developing countries experienced during the 1980s were the result of distortions induced by the economic policies pursued by their own governments. The major causes of the alleged distortions were to be found in the overextended public sectors and the inward-oriented policies developing countries had adopted in order to industrialize. Lal cites the studies conducted by Little, Scitovsky and Scott on the 'poor craftsmanship' of developing countries' economic controls as 'an impressive empirical validation of the case against protection, that, even though laissez-faire may be not justifiable, free trade remains the best policy for developing (and developed) countries' (Lal 1983: 27).

The tendency prevailing in development scholarship analyzing the economic crisis of developing countries in the 1980s is one that identifies the causes of the crisis in the adoption of the wrong development policies by developing countries. Integral to this tendency is the fact that the incidence of exogenous factors is greatly underestimated. Not only do insights into the structural imbalances of the international trading system gradually disappear from the development debate, but also, the impact of external phenomena such as the critical shortage of foreign exchange, the oil shock and the debt crisis is believed to have been magnified by the adoption of erroneous policies. For instance, in a comparative study on Argentina, Brazil, Chile, Mexico and Venezuela, Jaastad, Almansi and Hurtado argue that the origins of the debt crisis in Latin America preceded the inability of the Mexican Government to service its debt in August 1982 (Jaastad *et al.* 1986: 131–79).

Scholars who adhere to this tendency admit the presence of external factors such as falling world demand due to economic recession in industrialized countries, the rapid growth of external debt with the shortening of its maturity structure, the sudden rise in dollar interest rates accompanied by worldwide dollar deflation in industrialized countries and a consequent decline in developing countries' export capacity. However, the main problem is made to rest on the overambitious public investment programmes which led to uncontrolled and growing fiscal deficits and to trade policies with a bias against exports and domestic savings. Krueger, for instance, has argued that 'those countries that were unable to adjust and resume growth were those whose economic policies had been highly detrimental to growth' (Krueger 1993: 3–4). Balassa also links the adoption of outward-oriented policies to the improvement in the income distribution of developing countries (Balassa 1989: 95–96). In other words, the price mechanism in a liberal trade regime would not only contribute to an increase of growth but would also, concomitantly, work as an automatic mechanism of wealth distribution.

In this way, despite the recognition of various exogenous factors, the neo-liberal interpretation of the causes underlying the economic crises of the 1980s attributes the 'failure' to the development models adopted by developing countries. This is done through the invalidation of the theoretical underpinnings of development economics, as well as dependency theories, and by means of various comparative studies on different developing economies. Thus, the neo-liberal policy prescriptions that follow are based on the transformation of inward-looking, state-based economic structures into market-oriented economies, accompanied by reform of their institutional and social arrangements.

These analyses were to exert an enormous influence during the 1980s and 1990s, especially within the World Bank and the International Monetary

Fund. The 1985 *World Development Report* focusing on Latin American countries identified the causes of their economic crisis with their excessive expansionary fiscal and monetary policies impeding a sustainable external balance, overvalued exchange rates reducing the competitiveness of their exports and the low levels of savings during periods of high investment and consumption, leading to high external debt (World Bank 1985: 6–7). Similarly, in identifying the main areas on which scholars, politicians and technocrats of the international financial institutions in Washington agreed that developing countries needed immediate reforms, Williamson pointed to prudent macroeconomic policies, outward orientation and free-market capitalism (Williamson 1990).

The prescription put forward by the so-called Washington Consensus would become the template for policy reforms carried out throughout the 1980s and 1990s in the developing world. By relying on the 'scientific' authority of neo-liberal theories, these reforms aimed at the complete restructuring of the economic and institutional frameworks of developing countries. The establishment of the WTO in 1995 consolidated these reforms through the entry into force of its binding agreements and the creation of an effective dispute settlement system which would ensure compliance with its rules.

Unlike its predecessor, the WTO's competence extends to areas previously exempted from trade regulation. However, the legal, administrative and economic reforms required by the WTO in areas as disparate as services, investment and intellectual property rights do not merely involve exorbitant implementation costs, as trade scholars often point out. They also imply a profound rethinking and transformation of the way in which societies and governments have conceived of the nature of industrial policy, services provision, culture, creativity and invention. The WTO has constructed these practices, resources and processes as trade related and extended to them GATT-like disciplines which disregard their social, cultural, environmental as well as economic dimensions. By creating such a link between these many diverse areas and trade, the WTO has, in full neo-liberal mode, reconceptualized them in market terms. As market place objects, they are therefore made to enter 'a technical realm that is stripped of any social and political dimension' preventing 'other ways of perceiving them that might raise more objections' (Kelsey 2003: 267).

Conclusions

The entry into force of the WTO therefore consummated a significant shift in the development rationale that had prevailed since the immediate postwar period. The principle of reciprocity promoted by the WTO to replace the GATT's flexible approach to its legal rules and negotiations implies a view of the bargaining process as an exchange conducted by agents seen as rational utility maximizers. As a result, the international trade arena is transformed into a level playing field where state actors stand on an equal footing with one another and engage in trade-offs for the most efficient trade outcomes in a diverse range of areas that are constructed as trade related. The interpretation of this shift in terms of a rational choice for the most efficient trade policy is entirely congruent with the neo-liberal transformation of development thinking.

This transformation, however, cannot be accounted for in terms of neo-liberal theories alone. Indeed there were many other factors which contributed to such an outcome and which this chapter has not dealt with. Among the most important are those which neo-liberal scholars have easily dismissed: from the world recession to the monetarist responses of the industrialized countries, in particular the US decision to abandon the gold system, deregulate private finance and devalue the dollar; from the oil and debt crisis to the radical transformation of developing countries' economic structures imposed by the structural adjustment policies; from the negative discrimination suffered by developing countries under GATT to the pressure exercised by the 'developed' countries to bring in services, investment and intellectual property rights; these were each time political rather than rational and neutral choices.

However, the focus of this chapter on the role that 'development' has played within the international trading regime serves to emphasize the fact that its neo-liberal transformation and effects were made possible thanks to the framework established at the end of the colonial era: the need for developing countries to overcome their 'failure' and replicate the successful experience of developed countries remained the premise for the transformation and continuous authority of 'development'. In the immediate post-war period, the so-called failure of development was imputed to the dual economic structures of the ex-colonies so that their capitalist transformation through an interventionist state would deliver the promise of development. In the 1980s, the persistence of this failure is attributed to the adoption of erroneous economic policies and legal claims by developing countries so that the reliance of market forces would have delivered the development promise. With the WTO the failure is extended to developing countries' institutional and social arrangements, which are posited as the ultimate obstacles to development. Thus, the current development promise with which the WTO is imbued rests on the developing countries' integration into the global economy to be achieved through harmonization of regulatory practices in addition to trade liberalization. As former WTO Director-General Moore puts it:

> [t]rade is one component of a policy framework for growth, poverty reduction and development. Trade must be part of the equation, but it is only a part of that framework. Sound macroeconomic policies, debt

reduction, capacity building and good governance are critical to any programme of development and poverty reduction.

(WTO 2001:1)

However, the analysis carried out in this chapter shows that the WTO's adoption of the language of technical assistance, institution building and good governance to promote development is informed by the political representations of Third World societies advanced by neo-liberal theories. The political nature of such analyses challenges the claims of neutrality, objectivity and rationality on which the WTO purports to promote 'development'. At a more general level, however, it has been argued that the whole WTO development apparatus relies on the three normative assumptions permeating the 'science of development'. Recognizing how the 'development mission' of the international trading regime has operated since its inception is therefore crucial to challenge both the inevitability and the desirability of the WTO's development agenda.

Notes

1 These factors include: the end of the Cold War; the crisis of capital accumulation, the oil crisis of the 1970s and the political decisions made to address these events; the impact of these decisions on the debt crisis and the consequent structural adjustment policies disseminated by the World Bank and International Monetary Fund; the consequent transformation of developing countries into export-led economies and the persistent GATT discriminatory practices against their competitive exports.
2 This notwithstanding the fact that the actual gains deriving from GATT's legal reforms were limited since developed countries often circumvented the scope of these provisions and adopted several GATT inconsistent measures contradicting the spirit of the development agenda they claimed to promote.

References

Anghie, A. (2000) 'Time present and time past: globalisation, international financial institutions, and the Third World', *New York University Journal of International Law and Politics* 32: 243.

Balassa, B. (1982) *Development Strategies in Semi-Industrial Countries*, Baltimore: Johns Hopkins University Press.

——(1989) *New Directions in the World Economy*, Basingstoke: Macmillan Press.

Bauer, P.T. (1981) *Equality, the Third World and Economic Delusion*, London: Methuen.

——(1984) *Reality and Rhetoric: Studies in the Economics of Development*, London: Weidenfeld & Nicolson.

Covenant of the League of Nations (1924) *Covenant of the League of Nations*. Available online at: <http://avalon.law.yale.edu/20th_century/leagcov.asp> (accessed 30 April 2009).

Escobar, A. (1995) *Encountering Development: The Making and Unmaking of the Third World*, Princeton: Princeton University Press.

Furtado, C. (1964) *Development and Underdevelopment*, Berkley, CA: University of California Press.

GATT (1958) *Trends in International Trade: A Report by a Panel of Experts*, Geneva: GATT Publications.

Haque, M.S. (1999) *Restructuring Development Theories and Policies: A Critical Study*, Albany, NY: State University of New York Press.

Jaastad, A., Almansi, A., Hurtado, C. (1986) 'The debt crisis in Latin America', in D. Lal and M. Wolf (eds), *Stagflation, Savings and the State: Perspectives on the Global Economy*, Oxford and New York: Oxford University Press.

Kelsey, J. (2003) 'Legal fetishism and the contradictions of the GATS', *Globalisation, Societies and Education* 1(3): 267.

Krueger, A.O. (1993) *Political Economy of Policy Reform in Developing Countries*, Cambridge, MA: The MIT Press.

Lal, D. (1983) *The Poverty of 'Development Economics'*, London: Institute of Economic Affairs.

North, D.C. (1993) 'The new institutional economics and development', Smithian Forum, Working Paper.

Prebisch, R. (1950) *Economic Development of Latin America and its Principal Problems*, New York: United Nations.

Williamson, J. (1990) 'What Washington means by policy reform', in J. Williamson (ed.), *Latin American Adjustment: How Much Has Happened?*, Washington, DC: Institute for International Economics.

World Bank (1985) *World Development Report 1985*, Oxford and New York: Oxford University Press.

WTO (2001) *Integrated Framework (IF) Joint Core Agency Seminar on the Policy-Relevance of Mainstreaming Trade into Country Development Strategies: Perspectives of LDCs*. Statement by M. Moore, 17 January 2001.

Chapter 16

Protesting the WTO in Seattle

Transnational citizen action, international law and the event

*Ruth M. Buchanan**

Introduction

> The raison d'etre of politics is freedom and its field of experience is action ... Since all acting contains an element of virtuosity and because virtuosity is the excellence we ascribe to the performing art, politics has often been described as an art.
>
> (Arendt 2000: 444/446)

> Now everything seems possible. Anything could happen. An infinite number of new dimensions open up. What does it feel like to be inside one of these events, to be a time traveller and leap from one time line to another? And what are these possibilities? These might seem like daft or impossible questions, but we're not the only people asking them.
>
> (Free Association 2005: 569)

There is a growing recognition within international law of the significant role played by actors from civil society, mostly non-governmental organizations (NGOs), both in the creation of international norms and in the work of international institutions (Charnovitz 2006). However, significant obstacles to the integration of civil society into international law remain, such that it is quite difficult, for example, to consider social movements as actors in relation to international law or its institutions. Yet contemporary social movements, with increasing frequency and impact, function to mobilize citizens beyond state boundaries explicitly in the service of international goals and objectives (Della Porta and Tarrow 2005; Drache 2008). This chapter takes up the example of street-level social mobilizations directed against particular international institutions or regimes, such as the 1999 mobilizations in Seattle against the World Trade Organization (WTO), in order to consider how they might be understood as direct interventions into ongoing legal debates over the legitimacy and accountability of that institution. In so doing, it aligns itself with existent and ongoing scholarly work that has begun to consider the constitutive role of resistance in international law and to develop, on that foundation, a methodological approach to the study of international law 'from below' (Santos and Rodriguez-Garavito

2005; Rajagopal 2003). This chapter builds on that work both conceptually and historically.

Its central insight is that in order to account fully for the constitutive role played by acts of resistance, one's account of international law must also be able to take into consideration the performative, and hence unpredictable, eruption of 'events'. The argument proceeds in four parts. The first part identifies two approaches to thinking about the role of civil society actors in relation to international law, which I describe as modern/cosmopolitan and critical/diverse. The second part will aim to contribute to the critical/diverse approach by articulating a twofold conception of the 'event'. The third part applies this conception in the course of providing an alternative or 'people's' historical account of the Seattle mobilizations against the WTO in 1999. The chapter concludes with a 'postscript' – a discussion of *Battle in Seattle*, a Hollywood feature film starring Woody Harrelson and Charlize Theron that purports to both fictionalize and re-enact the events of those five days. The film's release in late 2008 reignited fierce debates over the political meaning of the events in Seattle that had taken place nearly nine years previously.

Two ways of thinking about international law and civil society

In recent years, the need to understand the many ways in which people have sought to engage directly with international law and institutions, across or beyond nation state boundaries, has become increasingly evident. One useful frame of reference for contemplating the advocacy efforts of individual activists, social movements and civil society organizations in this realm is the notion of citizenship, although there are, admittedly, significant hurdles to a clear conceptualization of 'transnational citizenship' (Fox 2005). Some of these obstacles can be more clearly identified if we first distinguish between two main approaches to thinking about citizenship in these contexts. James Tully has provided a very helpful and comprehensive elucidation of these two traditions in the final chapter of his recent two-volume treatise, *Public Philosophy in a New Key*, which I have adopted here (Tully 2009: 243–309).

Following Tully, we can identify these two approaches as 'modern' and 'diverse'. The modern, liberal way of thinking about global citizenship predominates most academic discussions. This is perhaps especially so among international lawyers, as it is closely associated with the modern form of the nation state and the process by which that European construct has been universalized; that is, brought to the non-West through historical processes of colonialism, decolonization and development (Tully 2009, Vol II: 247). Indeed, that international law is a modernist enterprise can hardly be questioned. Among its chief characteristics are that it is 'animated by a progressive and universalistic spirit, [and] firm confidence in the ability of liberal political institutions to transform the world into a democratic and rule-governed Kantian *Volkerstaat*' (Koskenniemi 2008: 30).

Modern citizenship is conceived in both institutional and universal terms. It presupposes a particular set of institutional, legal and economic arrangements, including constitutional rule of law, representative government and 'free' (capitalist) markets. Within that context, citizens are understood as possessing a defined set of entitlements, most importantly, civil liberties and some procedural rights to be consulted and to participate in the public sphere of decision making. Participatory rights in this modern model of citizenship are limited, however, to forms of engagement and discourse which are compatible with existing legal and institutionalized mechanisms of governance. In the international context, modern citizenship becomes equated with cosmopolitan citizenship (Tully 2009: 256). So while the predominant account of international law's engagement with civil society is both progressivist and institutional in orientation – that is, it is a story of international law becoming ever more cosmopolitan and inclusive through the expansion of NGO participation in a variety of institutions and forums – this account refers only to participation understood in this liberal sense (Rajagopal 2003: 291). While the institutions and forms of international law may have adapted over time to incorporate more input from civil society groups, the groups thus engaged and the forms of engagement are circumscribed by the conception of modern citizenship itself. Tully describes this as 'low-intensity' citizenship (Tully 2009: II, 265). Only those 'transnational citizens' that are sufficiently organized, modernized and technocratic are cognizable within this model (Buchanan 2003; Christodoulidis 2003).

In contrast to the singular conception of modern cosmopolitan citizenship, diverse citizenship is associated with a plurality of citizenship practices. In this model, 'citizenship is not a status given by the institutions of the modern constitutional state and international law, but negotiated practices in which one becomes a citizen through participation' (Tully 2009: 248). The ongoing process of negotiation is key to understanding this approach, as is attentiveness to the particularity and diversity of citizenship practice emanating from both the West and non-West. This form of citizenship is premised on an understanding of individuals as 'free' in the sense of freedom of action and freedom of participation with fellow citizens in the ongoing re-creation of relations of governance (Arendt 2000; Tully 2009: Vol II, 272). Of course, civic or diverse citizenship practices must be enacted on a field that is already structured, and indeed dominated, by modern institutions of international law and economic governance such as the WTO. While unequal relations of power in our contemporary society may significantly diminish the range and scope of possible action, it is an article of faith for critical (civic) citizens (as we will see in our discussion of the events in Seattle) that they can never fully eliminate the human capacity for 'acting otherwise', enacting, covertly or explicitly forms of political resistance (Tully 2009: II, 278).

Several other re-orientations are also implicated in the turn from a modern or cosmopolitan to a diverse or critical orientation towards the conceptualization of transnational citizen action. A critical approach is one that grants 'a certain primacy to practice' in the sense of being a 'practical philosophy' (Tully 2009: 16). This approach, then, requires that we reject at the outset the assumption that there can be a clear division of labour between thought and action; that is, one must reject the idea that activists are not engaged in theory production or that scholars are not practical. As Gayatri Spivak insists, 'the world suffers too much from that binary opposition between philosophy and the practical, from banishing history as mythopoesis into the philosophical or the pre-political ... ' (Butler and Spivak 2007: 118). Or, as Tully puts it, 'every reflective and engaged citizen is a public philosopher in this sense, and every academic public philosopher is a fellow citizen working within the same broad dialogue with his or her specific skills' (Tully 2009: 4).

Further, it becomes evident that in recounting a critical history of citizen action in any given context, such as the mobilizations around the 1999 WTO ministerial meeting in Seattle, one also must engage with the problem of how to think about history, without implicitly resorting to a modernist teleology. However political struggle is instantiated or articulated – as interruption, disruption, even eruption – it is immersed in temporality. 'Political and cultural struggles are all, in some sense, directed to bringing into existence futures that dislocate themselves from dominant tendencies and forces of the present' (Grosz 2004: 14). Yet most contemporary discourses of international law and politics seem almost unavoidably progressivist in their orientation. That is, time is only imagined in terms of the homogenous, empty time of capital, and the future can only be imagined in terms of a projection of the past (Chatterjee 2004: 6). In contrast, a critical conception of citizen action needs to think of history as 'in the process of becoming' (Butler and Spivak 2007: 118).

A final dimension of politics for which liberal accounts of cosmopolitan citizenship fail to account is the 'affective'. What is important about the 'affective turn' in contemporary critical theory is that it directs our attention to what is 'produced' by an event (be it a mobilization, a text or a film), at a material level or the level of bodily sensations, vibrations, resonances (Buchanan and Johnson 2008; Massumi 2002). In contrast to a discussion of the meaning of 'Seattle' that would confine it to a disembodied (and hence, abstract and universalizable) realm of ideas, a critical approach attends to the particular, embodied, affective dimension of the events as they were experienced by participants. In so doing, it resists the reduction of the plurality of the event to any fixed or definable meaning or representation.

To reiterate, an important point of departure for this chapter is the observation that conventional narratives of expanding civil society participation in an ever more inclusive international legal order simply fail to account for periodic eruptions of activism and mobilization such as we saw in five days in Seattle in late 1999 (as described below). While the alternative approach to thinking about citizen engagement, 'diverse' or 'critical', brings us much closer to an understanding of what might be at stake in this and other such events (that is, an understanding of them as instantiations of practices of diverse citizenship), it does not yet fully explain their status as political events. How we conceptualize the 'event' is, however, a crucial dimension of the turn to a critical perspective, as it is implicated in both a theory of human action as freedom and with non-linear conceptions of 'history as becoming'. In the effort to carve out a place within theoretical accounts of international law for the resistant politics of a transnational public mobilizing in a site like Seattle, the Arendtian line that seeks to reground politics in a deterritorialized and pluralized conception of a political community of action (rather than will) seems very promising.

Two aspects of the 'event'

I want to argue that there are two aspects that are crucial to thinking about the event in a way that allows us to come to terms with our condition as embodied and affective beings that manifest freedom by acting in the world. The first is what I might describe as the element of surprise; that the event marks a break or rupture from what we have come to expect, and thus from a certain kind of linear narrative of history (Grosz 2004: 257–58). The second aspect is its irreducible plurality, that is, that the event can never be reduced to the view from a single vantage point, nor assigned a fixed, unitary meaning.

To elaborate on the first aspect, a political event is an action that counter-actualizes; rather than affirming established meanings, it reveals something new in the world. That is, political action 'breaks into the world as an infinite improbability', in Hannah Arendt's terms (Arendt 2000: 459). Arendt continues:

> It is because of this element of the 'miraculous' present in all reality that events, no matter how well anticipated in fear or hope, strike us with a shock of surprise once they come to pass. The very impact of an event is never wholly explicable; its factuality transcends in principle all anticipation.
>
> (Arendt 2000: 459)

A more contemporary formulation of this idea of the event as something that erupts onto a system, generating change, upheaval and asystematicity

(Grosz 2004: 8), comes from a text called 'Event horizon', written as a pamphlet for a counter-mobilization against the Group of Eight (G8) summit in Gleneagles in July 2005. The anonymous authors of the collective that called themselves the Free Association connect the element of 'surprise' that attaches to events with a non-linear account of history:

> We're used to thinking of time as a straight line. When we look back at history it seems like all past events only existed to lead us to this point. And when we think about the future we can only imagine that line continuing. The future we imagine is really only the present stretched out ahead of us ... But, history isn't a straight line. It moves in a series of uncontrolled breaks, jolts and ruptures. Every now and then we get events that seem to have popped out of an alternate dimension.
>
> (Free Association 2005: 568)

The collective authors of 'Event horizon' are more interested in politics than history. That is, they are less interested in offering genealogical accounts that reveal history as 'unstable assemblages of faults, fissures and heterogeneous layers' (Foucault 1984: 82) than in what political possibilities the 'openings along faultlines' might accommodate in the future. 'Such events also seem to carry their own alternate future ... Things that seemed impossible a day or two before seem irresistible now' (Free Association 2005: 568). The activist authors of 'Event horizon' write themselves into these multiple histories, drawing a line of connection between themselves and the events in Seattle 1999 and May 1968, connecting them together in their 'semi-conscious' effort to engineer another such rupture in time.

> These moments go down in history under a flattening name. Seattle 1999. May 1968. Kronstadt 1917. They eventually get tamed and forced into the history books but their alternate futures never totally disappear. You read about these events and you can still feel the tug of the future they thought they had. You still feel their potential welling up. Events like Gleneagles are semi-conscious attempts to engineer such ruptures in time, attempts to shatter any orderly 'progression' of history.
>
> (Free Association 2005: 568)

As a text that is also a political action, 'Event horizon' articulates and puts into play its own vocabulary of mobilization and resistance for the current moment. The form of writing itself – its occasional or ephemeral nature – is an extension of the visceral and collective experience of mobilization, of being part of an 'event':

> It's a physical thing. The hairs on the back of your arms stand up. You get goosebumps. There's a tingling in your spine. Your heart is racing.

Your eyes shine and all your senses are heightened: sights, sounds, smells are all more intense. Somebody brushes past you, skin on skin, and you feel sparks.

(Free Association 2005: 569)

Reading Arendt alongside the Free Association gives us a better sense of the first element: surprise understood in this embodied way as 'spark' or intensity. And this understanding is intimately connected to the second crucial element of this way of thinking about 'event': its irreducible plurality. For if we try to understand events in this way, as physical, embodied, interactive, it follows that they are as diverse as their participants. To put it another way, the 'significance engendered by an event is not passively received by individuals but actively constructed in and through the individual that senses it' (MacKenzie 2008: 16). That is, events are made by the individuals who experience them.

A question that then arises, because it is so central to most of our usual ways of thinking about politics, is how can we ever fully account for the meaning of an event? The response from within the critical or diverse perspective is that we simply can't. There is no ultimate or final interpretation that can be assigned to something like Seattle. To endeavour to do so would displace the meaning of event itself to another level (the hermeneutic plane, if you will), beyond our capacity to sense an occurrence and, through our sense of how the relations of intensity changed in that moment, to make meaning out of it. In the place of a singular metaphysical conception of the significance of a given political event, the critical approach (here in its Deleuzian formulation) gives us 'a series of essentially contested conceptual constructions of the relationship between the occurrence and the event it embodies' (MacKenzie 2008: 17).

Although more could be said, this preliminary sketch of the 'event' can now be put to work. That is, I want to use this concept of the event to extend the type of critical or diverse approach to thinking about citizen action that was developed in the previous section into the particular context of the street-level mobilizations in Seattle in 1999.

How might we understand Seattle as a 'political event'?

The Seattle mobilizations are a daunting subject for investigation, because of the sheer magnitude of accounts that are available, in text, audio and video, through conventional media as well as online (Cockburn *et al.* 2000; Thomas 2000; Gill 2005; Indymedia/Big Noise Film 2000). The diversity of accounts that we can access of the event in Seattle in late 1999 are themselves a form of evidence of its irreducible plurality. This rich documentation is itself also part of what was surprising about Seattle; what it revealed to be new about the political landscape in which we now live.

The eyewitness with a video camera who in some senses emerged in Seattle has become ubiquitous at least in the developed world. Part of this is due to the fact that this 'event' took place just at the moment when the widespread availability of digital video began to democratize multimedia. Alternative media (such as the online media collective Indymedia) emerged in Seattle as a forum for documenting the occurrences from a variety of perspectives not seen or under-represented in the mainstream media. Shortly thereafter, the emergence of YouTube has made it possible to disseminate some of this film much more widely, and a lot of it is available online even now, nearly a decade later.

But for those who may not have had the inclination or wherewithal to access this rich multimedia landscape of representations, the occurrences in Seattle, if they are recalled at all, tend to evoke images of tear gas and street riots. Mainstream media coverage of the 'event', and hence, public memory, has emphasized its violence – both the violent response of the police to the non-violent (and surprisingly effective) efforts of the direct action groups to shut down the meeting, as well as the violence of a small group of window-smashing youths (erroneously described in media reports as 'anarchists from Oregon'). It became known as 'the Battle in Seattle', a label which was picked up, along with the emphasis on its violent elements, by a Hollywood film released in 2008. Although one of the characters in the film observes of its title that it 'Sounds like a monster truck show', the passing remark does little to disrupt the film's reproduction of the dominant understandings encapsulated in the phrase.

The effect on public debates of the 'story' of Seattle becoming reduced to the 'battle' is profound. The law-breaking activities of a few were extrapolated and effectively overcame in the public's consciousness the effect of the non-violent mobilization of the many, while the substantive messages of those attending the various workshops, mobilizations and marches were minimized or forgotten. From the modern/cosmopolitan perspective, by impeding the orderly course of business of an international institution and impugning its legitimacy from the outside, the protestors had effectively ruled themselves 'out of order'. Unfortunately, the most significant consequence of Seattle from the perspective of the mainstream can be seen in the heightened attention to security arrangements and corresponding constriction of civic freedoms in subsequent international meetings. The next WTO ministerial meeting, held in late 2001 but planned well before 11 September, was in Doha, Qatar: an absolute monarchy in which political parties are banned and freedom of expression severely restricted.

However, from a critical/diverse perspective, the political 'event' in Seattle – that which could not have been anticipated or extrapolated from prior occurrences – was not the 'battle' but the organized non-violent mobilization of solidarity among a wide variety of movements and affinity groups in opposition to the WTO that both preceded and postdated the police crackdown. One contemporaneous activist account of the happenings in Seattle summarizes them as follows:

> On November 30, 1999, a public uprising shut down the World Trade Organisation and took over downtown Seattle, transforming it into a festival of resistance. Tens of thousands of people joined the non-violent direct action blockade that encircled the WTO conference site, keeping the most powerful institution on earth shut down from dawn until dusk ... Longshore workers shut down every West Coast port from Alaska to Los Angeles. Large numbers of Seattle taxi drivers went on strike. All week the firefighters union refused authorities' requests to turn their fire hoses on people. Tens of thousands of working people and students skipped or walked out of work or school.
>
> (Solnit 2008)

Several days of workshops, teach-ins and conferences organized by a variety of civil society organizations both preceded and coincided with the dates of the WTO ministerial meetings. Thompson (2000) provides a useful timetable of these various activities. On 30 November 1999, non-violent direct action coordinated by a number of groups, including DAN (Direct Action Network) and the Ruckus Society (and preceded by a series of training and education sessions in the fundamentals of non-violent direct action protest), led to a successful non-violent blockade of the streets around the conference centre on the first scheduled day of the WTO ministerial meeting. Also on 30 November, a peaceful labour march of at least 40,000 people proceeded through the streets of downtown Seattle ending in a rally. A peaceful protest vigil of many thousands outside the lock-up in which several hundred arrested protestors were being held also contributed to their eventual release, without charges, several days later.

Among the elements of surprise in Seattle were the creativity, organization and scale of the non-violent mobilization. The street action in Seattle, one that had affinities with the UK Reclaim the Streets movements, reflected a shift from oppositional to 'compositional' social movement strategies. As well, the organization of the activities was networked, organized through a series of smaller affinity groups, coordinated on the fly through the internet and a network of cellphones (de Armond 2001). At times, the streets were turned into a 'festival of resistance', with giant puppets, an enormous green condom that entreated the WTO to practise safe trade, 200 people dressed in sea turtle costumes and an enormous inflatable killer whale.

> One of the environmental groups (Greenpeace, perhaps? Or the Humane Society?) brought a giant inflatable killer whale. Huge, perhaps 30' long. The police were charging up a hill to clear an area and the environmentalists laid the whale in the street and pushed/rolled it down the

hill into the police charge, completely breaking it up. The police just didn't know what to do when facing a giant, inflatable killer whale ...

(Paik 2008)

The whale incident illuminates something about what made Seattle politically significant. It was not the size of the marches or the panicked and violent response of the police, but the creativity, the improvizational forms of organization, the commitment to non-violence and solidarity among the vast majority of people who were there. These are linked to an affective dimension that is perhaps more difficult to capture, though it is revealed in many other first-person accounts of the events, the sense that people who had participated were moved, transformed by that experience.

A documentary film made by independent journalist Rustin Thompson entitled *30 Frames a Second: The WTO in Seattle* illustrates this transformative dimension (Thompson 2000). A short illustrative excerpt is posted on YouTube. It opens on a scene of police in full riot gear with gas masks, and a burning dumpster in the otherwise empty street. A voice-over narration states matter of factly, 'I think the police had intended to clear this intersection, but the wind was moving in the wrong direction, blowing the tear gas away from the protestors, so they began to sit down'. As the protestors are seen sitting down, some holding up peace signs, some praying, an activist can be heard speaking to the crowd: 'We have every right to be here. This is a peaceful protest, unprovoked.' The voice-over then says, over a low drumbeat and the voices of protestors claiming their right to be in the public streets of Seattle, 'Finally, I understood what it was all about'.

People's vs. Hollywood histories

Nine years after the protestors returned home from the streets of Seattle, in late 2008, a feature film entitled *Battle in Seattle* was released in the US. The film provides a 'fictionalized re-enactment' of the occurrences of those five days in 1999. A number of well-documented scenes, such as the unfurling of banners from a construction crane, the lock-down of the intersections outside the convention centre and the solidarity rally outside the jail where some 600 arrested protesters were detained for several days, were re-created for the film, and almost seamlessly mixed with historical footage. The story is told through the creation of a number of 'fictional' characters, complete with overly dramatized back stories that are invoked to 'explain' their actions. Two of the main characters are an activist whose brother had been killed in an antilogging protest and a cop (Woody Harrelson) whose pregnant wife (Charlize Theron) is kicked in the belly by police on her way home from work during the protests and miscarries.

A number of activists involved in the mobilizations in Seattle, some of them as organizers, protested the making of the film, and lobbied for a number of changes to the script. Some minor changes were made but the impact was limited, as the director was already filming by the time the activists had been contacted (Solnit 2008).

Why would the activists who had been involved in the protests be troubled by a big-budget Hollywood movie about it? The film begins with an account of the WTO and a (sympathetic) explanation of why it evoked the concern of so many. It might have been seen as an opportunity for more people to learn about the WTO, or at least 'that it was bad', to quote a character in the film. In my view, however, the film fails both aesthetically and politically in two main ways. First, as I've already suggested, the film emphasizes, both narratively and visually, the element of violence of the protests. It is clear that violent assaults by the police on uninvolved bystanders (and, in one instance, an official delegate who happened to be black) did occur, but my objection is not about historical veracity. Rather, my observation is that the way in which the violent response of the police to the non-violent protests dominates the film replicates the way in which it dominated contemporaneous media coverage of the Seattle protests, and perhaps for the same reasons; this is the type of story that most easily captures public attention in our crowded media landscape.

The second shortcoming of the film relates to what I would describe as the overwrought fictionalization of the protagonists. What cannot be told, in this fictionalized account, is the ways in which thousands of ordinary citizens were politicized by this event, some only for a few days or weeks, perhaps, others more profoundly. The activist characters in the film speak to each other of an irresistible drive to activism, a drive that is akin to a compulsion, which again, sets it and them apart from the thousands of ordinary people who found themselves acting politically in the streets during those days. In the perceived need to create fictional activists who are somehow extra-ordinary, the film-maker not only detracted from (in my view) the aesthetic value of the film itself, he also undermined its ability to offer an evocative account of the event itself. What is lost in this re-enactment is the 'affect' of the event – the essence of the event as it was experienced by actual people. In purporting to retell the story from the perspective of these various fictionalized characters, *Battle in Seattle* ends up telling the story from nowhere. This is not a film that will change anyone's life – it does not surprise or counter-actualize. Rather, in 're-enacting', it serves to confirm the ways in which 'the battle in Seattle' had already been understood within dominant, linear historical narratives.

To invoke the language of 'Event horizon', if the 'alternate futures' of Seattle can't be found in the Hollywood film version, it is not because they don't still exist (Free Association 2005: 568). In my efforts in this chapter to redirect our attention to the proliferation of documentary and first-person accounts that reveal the transformative experiences of so many on the streets of Seattle, I have been invoking a larger argument about politics and history.

That is, to the extent that activist and scholarly struggles against international economic institutions are seeking to bring about meaningful political change, they may need to draw on a different conception of time and history – not as a predictable extension or continuation of the past, but as a leap or rupture. 'It is an unexpected shift, the shift produced by the unexpectedness of events, which reorients the past ... in a continuity which is also a discontinuity, a becoming' (Grosz 2004: 257–58). The accounts I have described here, in their affective and embodied diversity, both reveal to us a conception of history 'as becoming' and solicit our complicity in that process. That is, we are invited to join these activists in their efforts to 'induce the untimely ... rupturing the continuity of processes through the upheaval posed by events' (Grosz 2004: 14). Rereading or rewatching these accounts, even nine years later, is politically inspiring in a way that, notwithstanding the best intentions of its director, *Battle in Seattle* is not.

Note

* Versions of this chapter were presented at the annual meeting of the Association for the Study of Law, Culture and Humanities in Boston and at the annual meeting of the Law and Society Association in Denver, CO. The author would like to thank the co-panellists and audience members at those events for their questions and comments.

References

Arendt, H. (2000) *The Portable Hannah Arendt*, ed. Peter Baehr, New York: Penguin Books.

Armond, P. de (2001) 'Netwar in the Emerald City: WTO protest strategy and tactics', in J. Arquilla and D. Ronfeldt (eds), *Networks and Netwars: The Future of Terror, Crime and Military,* Santa Monica, CA: Rand.

Buchanan, R. (2003) 'Global civil society and cosmopolitan legality at the WTO: perpetual peace or perpetual process?', *Leiden Journal of International Law*, 16: 673–99.

Buchanan, R. and Johnson, R. (2008) 'Strange encounters: exploring law and film in the affective register', *Studies in Law, Politics and Society*, 46: 33–60.

Butler, J. and Spivak, G. (2007) *Who Sings the Nation-State? Language, Politics, Belonging,* New York: Palgrave Macmillan.

Charnovitz, S. (2006) 'Nongovernmental organisations and international law', *American Journal of International Law*, 100: 348–72.

Chatterjee, P. (2004) *The Politics of the Governed: Reflections on Popular Politics in Most of the World*, New York: Columbia University Press.

Christodoulidis, E. (2003) 'Constitutional irresolution: law and the framing of civil society', *European Law Journal* 9: 401–32.

Cockburn, A., St Clair, J. and Sekula, A. (2000) *Five Days that Shook the World: Seattle and Beyond*, New York and London: Verso.

Della Porta, D. and Tarrow, S. (2005) *Transnational Protest and Global Activism: People, Passions, and Power*, Lanham, MD; Toronto: Rowman & Littlefield.

Drache, D. (2008) *Defiant Publics: The Unprecedented Reach of the Global Citizen*, Cambridge, UK and Malden, MA: Polity.

Foucault, M. (1984) 'Nietzsche, genealogy, history', in P. Rabinow (ed.), *The Foucault Reader*, New York: Parthenon, 1984.

Fox, J. (2005) 'Unpacking "transnational citizenship"', *Annual Review of Political Science* 8: 171–201.

Free Association the (collective) (2005) 'Event horizon', *Ephemera* 5: 4: 568–79.

Gill, S. (2005) 'Toward a postmodern prince: the battle in Seattle as a moment in the new politics of globalisation', in L. Amoore (ed.), *The Global Resistance Reader*, London and New York: Routledge.

Grosz, E. (2004) *The Nick of Time: Politics, Evolution and the Untimely*, Durham, NC: Duke University Press.

Indymedia/Big Noise Film (2000) *This is What Democracy Looks Like*.

Koskenniemi, M. (2008) 'What should international lawyers learn from Karl Marx?', in S. Marks (ed.), *International Law on the Left: Re-examining Marxist Legacies*, Cambridge: Cambridge University Press.

MacKenzie, I. (2008) 'What is a political event?', *Theory and Event*, 11: 3.

Massumi, B. (2002) *Parables for the Virtual: Movement, Affect, Sensation*, Durham, NC: Duke University Press.

Paik, A. (2008) 'The whale' (posted 10 October 2008), Seattle WTO People's History Project. Available online: <www.realbattleinseattle.org/node/123> (accessed 28 March 2009).

Rajagopal, B. (2003) *International Law from Below: Development, Social Movements and Third World Resistance*, Cambridge: Cambridge University Press.

Santos, B.S. and Rodrignez-Garavito, C.A. (eds) (2005) *Law and Globalization from Below: Toward a Cosmopolitan Legality*, Cambridge, UK: Cambridge University Press.

Solnit, D. (2008) 'The battle for reality', *Yes Magazine*. Available online: <www.yesmagazine. org/other/pop_print_article.asp?ID=2850> (accessed 11 February 2009).

Sousa Santos, B. de and Rodriguez-Garavito, C. (2005) *Law and Globalization from Below: Towards a Cosmopolitan Legality*, Cambridge: Cambridge University Press.

Thomas, J. (2000) *The Battle in Seattle: The Story Behind and Beyond the WTO Demonstrations*, Golden, CO: Fulcrum.

Thompson, R. (2000) *30 Frames a Second: The WTO in Seattle* (documentary film) White Noise Productions, distributed by Bullfrog Films. Available online: <www.youtube.com/watch? v=SJbRJuXDe4w& NR=1> (accessed 21 May 2009).

Tully, J. (2009) *Public Philosophy in a New Key, Volumes I and II*, Cambridge: Cambridge University Press.

Chapter 17

Globalism, memory and 9/11

A critical Third World perspective

Obiora Chinedu Okafor*

We can only speak to these critical events ... as they unfold before our own eyes, from our own unhappy situatednesss; the Clio's couch, the disengagement that only distance may bring, is not for us the gift of time. We have to struggle, as best we can, to make sense of current developments, amidst ever menacing forms of infliction of traumatic human suffering. This struggle is necessary, especially in an emergent global milieu rife with what early Habermas was to name as 'systematically distorted communication'.

(Baxi 2003: 31)

The September 11 attacks on the United States have become the pretext for the renewal of a world order centred on ... domination.

(Mutua 2002: 1)

Nolumus [the refusal to learn from foreigners and from the past] is a self-defeating response.

(Head 2002: 2)

Introductory remarks

As articulated by its editors, the organizing ambition of this volume centres on the offering of stylistically much more accessible, if no less profound or articulate, 're-readings (or indeed first readings) of a series of events by which international law is marked, and through which it has registered and acquired force, all with a view to understanding its [i.e. international law's] contemporary resonance [or perhaps the lack thereof?]'.[1]

That broad thematic raises many important, challenging and interesting questions, a number of which have been raised and addressed in the other chapters of this book. But other possibilities leap to the eye. From the ranks of these other possibilities, I have decided to focus my own contribution to this important volume on two intimately interrelated issues that, in my mind, define and dog the dominant understandings of, and reactions to, the events of 11 September 2001. My decision to focus on these particular issues is grounded in their importance in helping to frame, shape and even transform our understandings of the nature of the times in which we now live; the necessity or lack thereof of a number of the suggestions for international law reform that have been made by certain actors; and of the appropriateness or otherwise of certain measures that have been justified by particular readings or pictures of the character of this so-called post-9/11 world. This chapter also pays attention to a number of insights arising from my approach to those issues. The entire discussion is approached from a critical Third World perspective.[2]

The first main issue examined in this chapter relates to the insufficient attention paid to the need for much more *geographical globalism* in post-9/11 argumentation about human rights and national security. The second issue concerns the deliberate or mistaken marginalization of *memory* in so much of the relevant discussion. These issues are discussed seriatim, if in a necessarily brief way, but not before a consideration of what is meant in this chapter by the expressions 'Third World' and a 'critical Third World perspective'.

The 'Third World' as a contingent but useful category

Given that the arguments made in this chapter, and the insights it offers, are largely derived from training a set of critical Third World lenses on the issues at hand, it is important that the familiar (though vexed) question of the coherence of the 'Third World' category is addressed at the outset. This section is devoted to that preliminary but key task.

The immediate post-Cold War era intensified pre-existing debates about the location, even existence, of the 'Third World'. At the time, many commentators, who mostly lived outside the societies that self-identify as 'Third World', were quick to proclaim the death of that expression as a useful analytical category (for example, see Otto 1996: 353). In their view, the category no longer had much purchase or relevance in a post-Cold War world.[3] Moreover, they argued, given the huge disparities in resources and power within the 'Third World', how could countries like China, Taiwan and Singapore continue to be lumped in the same general international political category as Bhutan, Mauritania and Jamaica (see Mittleman and Pasha 1997: 23)? Many sceptics have also averred that there is a 'Third World' within the 'First World', and vice versa (Mittleman and Pasha 1997: 23). The sceptics are not completely wrong. Their argument that diversity exists within the category is, of course, correct. They are also right about the existence of some 'Third World-like' communities within the First World.

The whole argument is wrongly *framed*, however. The point is not the existence and validity of an unproblematic and monolithic 'Third World' category. Rather, the point is the existence of a group of states and populations that have tended to *self-identify* as such, that coalesce around the historical and continuing experience of subordination at the global level that they feel they share. That much is undeniable. Now, if these states tend to complain about similar things and tend to speak to similar concerns, it is, of course, undeniable that, contingent and problematic as any style they wish to assign to their grouping is or can be, that grouping – that *sense* of shared experience – does exist and has been repeatedly expressed. What is more, there is nothing even remotely strange about coalitions being built or carrying on their work under a certain style, even one that has been mostly assigned to them (for example, global women's movements), and even while *themselves* recognizing the contingency of that style or category.[4] And since categories and the words that represent them only serve as contingent signifiers which can shelter many meanings depending on the context, if various peoples tend to continue to self-identify under the banner 'Third World', it is difficult to ignore that category without ignoring to a large extent the *shared* experience of subordination that it has come to represent, as well as the strategic deployment of that expression that is obviously entailed.

As long as the inevitable contingency of this expression is understood, and the expression is not *inflexibly* moored to a fixed geographic space – but rather to a self-expressed and shared sense of subordination within the global system – it does retain much relevance even today, even in this moment of ferment, even in this 'postmodern' world. I am thus in agreement with Balakrishnan Rajagopal that although the expression needs to be thought of with a slightly more flexible geographic sensibility, it need not be abandoned (see Rajagopal 1998–99). That said, self-identification is heavily influenced by experience, and the sorts of experience of global subjugation that often marks Third World coalitions will often reveal and entail certain kind of maps – certain 'geographies of injustice' (see Baxi 2003: 46).

As such, there is a sense in which states or societies or even scholars must *choose* whether or not to self-identify as 'Third World' (Nyerere 1983). As Karin Mickelson has aptly put it, Third World voices are best imagined as 'a chorus of voices that blend, though not always harmoniously, in attempting to make heard a common set of concerns' (see Mickelson 1998: 361). While there will be some tenors in that chorus, there will also be some sopranos, basses and altos. These important differences in pitches, resources and capacities are not usually sufficient to deny coherence or relevance to a chorus or orchestra. And so for me, and almost all other TWAIL scholars, the 'Third World' remains an important, indeed crucial, analytic category; one which suffices to ground a scholarly perspective.

What is meant by 'a critical Third World perspective'?

The main exponents of this perspective in international law have been a group of scholars writing in the idiom and style that is popularly referred to as the critical Third World approaches to international law, or TWAIL, school. As such, in order to understand what is meant by a critical Third World perspective, and how such a perspective is developed and articulated, the nature of the broad approach taken by these TWAIL scholars, including their analytic sensibilities and techniques must first be understood.

On a general level, the TWAIL movement within the discipline of international legal studies is best viewed as a broad dialectic of opposition to the generally unequal, unfair and unjust character of an international legal regime that all too often (not always) helps subject the Third World to domination, subordination and serious disadvantage (see Mutua 2000). Just like the Third World on which it focuses, TWAIL is not a monolithic school of thought. No unanimity can be found within its ranks, and no complete and compulsory liturgy directs its engagement with the international order. Some strains of TWAIL are more oppositional than reconstructive, while others are more reconstructive than oppositional.[5] Some TWAIL scholars are avowed socialists (e.g. Bhupinder Chimni), but many are not (see Chimni 1999). Some can be seen as leaning towards post-structuralism (e.g. Rajagopal and Nesiah), but many do not accept the post-structuralist label (see Rajagopal 1998–99; Nesiah 2003: 133). Some are feminists (e.g. Nyamu, Tamale and Nesiah), but many may not make bold to claim that prize. TWAIL is therefore not even close to a theology. Just like the Third World itself, it may be considered 'a chorus of voices' rather than a simple monolithic collegium (see Mickelson 1998: 361).

However, despite their healthy differences and the variegation within the 'school', TWAIL scholars (or TWAILers) are solidly united by a *shared ethical commitment* to the intellectual and practical struggle to expose, reform or even retrench those features of the international legal system that help create or maintain the generally unequal, unfair or unjust global order. They are united by a commitment to 'centre the rest rather than *merely* the West', thereby taking the lives and experiences of those who have self-identified as 'Third World' much more seriously than has generally been the case.

Thus, TWAIL scholars agree that the:

> international law that was shaped in the colonial era was not a neutral discipline but an instrument of naked power *skillfully dressed up so as to hide its objective* of controlling the colonized world for the benefit of the colonial powers [and that] ... though the projection of power may be the object of the law [that is, international law], hiding such projection is a necessary one as it would otherwise provoke dissent and contempt for the rules so fashioned.
>
> (Sornarajah 2001: 285, emphasis added)

As such, TWAIL scholars are also convinced of the need to understand and expose the technologies and devices through which international law has so often facilitated the achievement of the goals of more powerful societies and states. Understanding the means by which that law was extended throughout the globe as a result of the colonial encounter is crucial to achieving an understanding of the nature of the current international legal regime (see Anghie 2000: 245–46).

In this sense, Mutua is correct to say that 'TWAIL is not a recent phenomenon' (see Mutua 2000). Rather, it is part of a long tradition of critical internationalism (see Gathii 2000). Its intellectual and inspirational roots stretch all the way back to the Afro-Asian anti-colonial struggles of the 1940s to the 1960s, and even before that to the Latin American decolonization movements (Gathii 2000). It is also deeply connected to the New International Economic Order/G77 movements that were launched in the 1960s, carried on into the 1970s and stymied by powerful global forces in the 1980s and 1990s (see Mickelson 1998: 362–68). Thus, an earlier generation of TWAIL scholars (like Baxi, Bedjaoui, Mbaye and Weeramantry) did foreground most of the very same concerns now expressed in contemporary TWAIL scholarship (see Baxi 2003; Bedjaoui 1979; Mbaye 1972).

However, contemporary TWAIL scholarship has benefited much from sustained engagement with other schools of critical international legal scholarship, such as feminist, critical legal studies (CLS), new approaches to international law (NAIL), Marxian, post-structuralist and critical race approaches to international law and global politics. Thus, many of the analytic techniques/sensibilities that TWAIL scholars deploy in their scrutiny of the international order will be familiar to other critical internationalists.

The first such technique/sensibility that I discuss in this article is TWAIL's deep commitment to taking *world* (as opposed to merely Western) history much more seriously than most internationalists tend to. TWAIL scholars agree that a historical perspective is key to understanding current features of and debates about the international system.[6] TWAILers are thus concerned to map the continuities and discontinuities in the historical development of international legal norms, structures, claims or rules in order to understand better the ways in which they facilitate the serious disadvantages that Third World peoples now suffer. By mapping the techniques and devices used by the global powers of yesteryears, TWAIL scholars can recognize similar techniques in contemporary international relations. They can then reveal how those techniques, morphed or not, continue to work today to sustain or create global injustice. Of necessity therefore, TWAIL takes extremely seriously the history of the colonial subordination of the rest of the world to European power. TWAIL is concerned to understand and reveal the ways in which international law facilitated this colonial encounter, and the extent to which its role in that encounter is too often replayed and repeated, even to this day, to the disadvantage of most Third World people. In this sense, a key TWAIL technique/sensibility is to seek to write the Third World's shared historical experiences into the processes and outcomes of international thought and action. That the development of this kind of historical sensibility in international legal analysis is critical even today is underscored by the way in which the occlusion of the earlier history of US involvement in Iraq more or less worked to allow a particular sense and version of US–Iraq relations to take hold – one that seems to have legitimized the latest invasion of Iraq in the minds of far too many observers (see Bisharat 2003: 2–15).

Another key TWAIL technique/sensibility is to take the equality of Third World peoples much more seriously than conventional approaches, to insist that all thought and action concerning international law and relations should proceed on the assumption that Third World peoples deserve no less dignity, no less security and no fewer rights or benefits from international action than do the citizens of Northern states. And so, claims that international law should allow the 'consensual' transfer of toxic waste from the North to the Third World are rejected when viewed through this kind of equality optic (e.g. see Gwam 2003–4). And claims that states (in practice the powerful states) ought to enjoy, or already enjoy, a unilateral right to intervene in Third World societies, when the converse is virtually impossible in practice, are viewed by most TWAILers with much (deserved) suspicion (see Chimni 2003: 64; Anghie 1996). Thus, the TWAIL vision of equality, in this connection, extends well beyond formal equality to include a rejection of international norms or decisions that operate like Anatole France's law that 'equally' prohibits the rich and poor from sleeping under bridges (see Trachtman 2002: 984–85).

Informed by their deep attentiveness to the fact that 'universality' and 'common humanity' claims have long facilitated and justified Europe's colonial subjugation and continuing exploitation of much of the Third World, TWAIL scholars recognize the need to beware of glib assertions of universality that tend to elide or mask underlying politics of domination. As Sornarajah put it, 'a lesson to be learnt [from Third World history] ... is that one must beware of self-proclaimed universalists ... [their] reasons for taking universalist stances must be constantly scrutinized' (Sornarajah 2001: 285).

The last key TWAIL technique/sensibility discussed here is the insistence on thinking through the various ways of offering epistemic and ideational resistance to the global hegemonies that their work often unearths or explains (see Chimni 2003). TWAIL scholars have also explored and analyzed the myriad ways in which international law and global institutions have, over time, responded to the resistance posed to them by Third World actors, more especially social movements, and the effects that such resistance has had on law and institutions (see Rajagopal 2003).

It is the application of these key TWAIL techniques/sensibilities that allow a critical Third World perspective to be deciphered, applied and offered. Some of these techniques/sensibilities are utilized below to expose (albeit in brief) the debilitating blind spots in the dominant readings of the post-9/11 world and suggest ways of re-reading our current global circumstance.

Insufficient attention to geographical globalism

What, we could ask, are the implications of seeing the events of 9/11 and its aftermath through a much less localized and more geographically *global* optic? Might we thereby see a significantly different picture of those events and their aftermath? Shorn of their detail (for example, details regarding the particular vehicles of destruction and techniques used in this case by the terrorists), how unique do they seem after being situated in this expanded and more realistic geographical context? Not very, I would suggest. The overwhelming global (as opposed to United States or Western) evidence points to many similarities with as many instances of the perpetration of terror – and not always by non-state actors. In my view, then, only through a deliberate or mistaken displacement of the experience of most of the globe, i.e. the Third World, can the arguments of those who now suggest and defend the legitimized (re)turn to torture and such other acts of barbarism even seem plausible enough to be taken as seriously as they often have. This is especially true when we consider what Third World peoples have experienced in hundreds of terror-style assaults (either direct or by proxy) on civilians, and what Western states and commentators have often said about the attempts by many of these regimes to justify their resort to torture and the like in the name of grave national security threats.

And so once a critical Third World perspective is brought to bear on the idea that post-9/11 terrorism is so new that it must be taken to have inaugurated a significantly new era of world history, the severe weakness of that argument becomes palpable. Also debunked in this way is the argument that this supposed newness of the post-9/11 world necessitates a form of international legal reform that authorizes (and even celebrates) torture, assassinations (in the name of targeted killings) and unilateral (Iraq-style) invasions. Thus, the seeming force of the 'security relativism' of the Bush doctrine (that makes or suggests the aforementioned arguments) withers in the critical gaze of a Third World perspective.

The marginalization of memory

What are the implications of an insufficient historicization in the discussion about the post-9/11 security threat? Without sufficiently accounting for the past, do we not also run the risk of exaggerating the newness or uniqueness of this post-9/11 world? For example, have the West and the Rest, either separately or collectively, not faced down even more dangerous situations in the past? During the Cold War, the West and East each faced certain anni-hilation from threats posed to the one by the other. It was a threat that was posed by a certainly more powerful source than al-Qaeda. Were torture and unilateral pre-emptive invasions justifiable then? I think not. Some have, of course, argued that al-Qaeda is different; that unlike the Soviets, it operates from no fixed address. This is true. However, agreement on this basic point does not point one inexorably in the direction of the necessity or legitimacy of the use of torture. Despite the stealth and guerrilla tactics that make it somewhat harder to fight with old-style battle formations and techniques, do the different (though historically commonplace) tactics adopted by al-Qaeda *necessarily* entail a resort to torture, unilateral invasion, targeted killings and the like? I think not. The gap between agreement on al-Qaeda's use of stealth tactics and the legitimization of the use of torture in the fight against that group is a very large one; one that arguably no commentator or policy maker has so far successfully bridged.

In any case, al-Qaeda and other guerrilla-style groups have existed for a long time. There is little that is new about their capacity to wreak havoc on innocent people. What is different today is that they can with some difficulty reach the US mainland. Yet the fact that they possess that capacity does not necessarily offer us a cogent basis for legitimizing torture, etc. in fighting them.

Moreover, when certain powerful Western states waged wars (by proxy or otherwise) in the Third World that led to the death of millions of civilians, did they not pose very serious threats to the security of the peoples of the relevant Third World countries? Should the operatives of these Western states have been legitimately subjected to torture and targeted killings by these Third World regimes? I think not.

The history of the West's behaviour in this connection should humble us as we debate and ponder these difficult questions. It is perhaps because an appreciation of that history can be so humbling that it has so far played very little role in the mainstream debates in the West about the appropriate response to the post-9/11 security threat. For the larger that unhappy memory of Western complicity looms, the less justifiable the very notion of newness or uniqueness that grounds most of the arguments that have been made in favour of resorting to extreme measures of torture and targeted killings.

Thus the key point here is that the plausibility of the kind of post-9/11 security relativism discussed above is seriously challenged by the demarginalization of memories of Third World suffering at the hands of largely non-Third World terrorists; once these particular kinds of Third World suffering are foregrounded (rather than backgrounded as usual) significantly different and more accurate pictures emerge. Such pictures belie the rather crude security relativism of the exponents of the necessity of the legitimization post-9/11 of torture, assassinations, unilateral invasions and the like.

Security relativism: dead or alive?[7]

In the end, the argument made above is that the more we fail to factor global and especially Third World (as opposed to merely US or Western) social experience into arguments about appropriate responses to the post-9/11 security threat, and the more we marginalize historical memory in the calculus that seeks to determine how unique our post-9/11 world is, the more we construct, sell and buy an inaccurate picture of the nature of this historical moment and the severity of the kinds of international or domestic reform measures that are required in response.

As evil as terrorism and terrorists are, the argument that we ourselves must stoop as low as them, that we must ourselves become monsters in order to confront their monstrosities, must be rejected once globalism and memory are accorded their rightful place in the relevant calculations. So does the sister argument that if Western states perpetuate torture, theirs is a sort of 'kind hearted' torture; and that as kind hearted torturers, Western countries in that position must seek to democratize the practice of torture, for example by insisting that it be approved by judges before it occurs. Surely, democratized evil is no more inspiring or legitimate than authoritarian evil?

To be clear, my argument is not that a certain balancing of the relatively more minor rights against the demands of national security (what one can refer to as security relativism) should never be undertaken. My point is that such security-related curtailments of our more minor rights must be shown to be *warranted* (through rigorous assessment) before they are undertaken. In any case, it should never be permissible to violate certain core human rights (such as the right to be free from torture and arbitrary deprivations of life) that touch upon our very essence as human beings, and the violations of which turn us into barbarians. There are a large number of other non-monstrous measures that can be taken, short of resorting to barbarisms. So, I am not talking of wire taps and email intercepts here. I speak about torture and the like. There is a significant difference.

In holding this view, I associate myself with the behaviour of US Senator John McCain when running for office in the US. His introduction of a legislative amendment in the Senate initially led to a capitulation to him on this question of US President George Bush, and dealt a serious blow to proponents of US resort to or continuation of the practice of torture in the name of national security. I am also proud of the excellent job performed by the British House of Lords over the years on this subject, and more especially since 9/11. In *A (FC) & Ors v Secretary of State for the Home Department*,[8] a decision handed down in late 2005, that court (per Lord Bingham of Cornhill, *et al.*) affirmed quite robustly that not only should the British Government not itself participate in the infliction of torture, it is also illegal for that Government to rely on information obtained by others through the infliction of torture.

This said, is security relativism (the view that even core human rights should give way in the face of national security threats) dead or dying? As I have shown, despite the serious blow dealt by the McCain amendment and the British House of Lords' decision, security relativism is still very much alive. And there is reason to suspect that it will outlive the author. For throughout human history, governments have relied on that approach to pursue their political agendas. As such a convenient political tool, it is likely to be propped up and kept on life support by many governments, including many of the more democratic ones. What is more, under the right level of national security pressure, governments – even liberal democratic ones – do tend to bare their fangs! It is therefore tempting to conclude this chapter by stating, somewhat tongue in cheek, that 'security relativism is dead; long live security relativism!'

Notes

* I am grateful to Sundhya Pahuja, Fleur Johns and Richard Joyce for inviting me to con-tribute this chapter. The ideas expressed in this chapter are heavily influenced by my previous work on the subject, in particular Okafor 2005 and 2006. I am grateful to the relevant publishers for permission to reproduce parts of those articles.

1 See email communication between the editors of this volume and this author as part of the original brief to authors (on file).

2 The perspective that animates the work of critical Third World approaches to inter-national law (TWAIL) scholars. This approach is explained in more detail in the next section of this chapter. For descriptions of its nature and brief histories of its intellectual origins and foundations, see Gathii 2000 and Mickelson 1998.

3 For overviews of these kinds of objections, see Rajagopal 1998–99 and Mickelson 1998.

4 For example, as far back as 1983, even before much of the scholarly debate gained currency, Julius Nyerere, former President of Tanzania and a key leader of the Third World movement of his time, wrote about this very issue. See Nyerere 1983. Feminist scholars are also aware of the contingency of 'women' as an analytical category. Many of them have recognized the political practices involved in using or abandoning that category. See Oloka-Onyango and Tamale 1995: 697–705.

5 For instance, while Bhupinder Chimni is an avowed reconstructionist, Joel Ngugi is more sceptical of the viability of the reconstructionist effort. See Chimni 2003 and Ngugi 2002.

6 See Mickelson 1998: 406–11 (noting that this deep concern for world history is 'the feature most fundamental to anything one could label a Third World approach to inter-national law').

7 This is to paraphrase Baxi's interesting question about the nature of cultural relativism in our time (see Baxi 2002: 91–118).

8 (2005) UKHL 71 (delivered on 8 December 2005).

References

Anghie, A. (1996) 'Francisco de Vitoria and the colonial origins of international law', *Social and Legal Studies*, 5: 321.

——(2000) 'Time present and time past: globalization, international financial institutions, and the Third World', *New York University Journal of International Law and Politics*, 32: 243.

Baxi, U. (2002) *The Future of Human Rights*, Delhi: Oxford University Press.

——(2003) 'Operation Enduring Freedom: toward a new international law and order?', in A. Anghie, B. Chimni, K. Mickelson and O. Okafor (eds), *The Third World and Inter-national Order: Law, Politics and Globalization*, Leiden: Martinus Nijhoff, at 31.

Bedjaoui, M. (1979) *Towards a New International Economic Order*, Paris: UNESCO.

Bisharat, G.E. (2003) 'Facing tyranny with justice: alternatives to war in the confrontation with Iraq', *Journal of Gender, Race and Justice*, 7: 1.

Chimni, B.S. (1999) 'Marxism and international law: a contemporary analysis', *Economic and Political Weekly* 337 (6 February issue). Available online at: <www.multiworld.org/m_versity/articles/chimni.htm> (accessed 9 January 2005).

——(2003) 'Third World approaches to international law: a manifesto', in A. Anghie, B. Chimni, K. Mickelson and O. Okafor (eds), *The Third World and International Order: Law, Politics and Globalization*, Leiden: Martinus Nijhoff, at 47.

Gathii, J. (2000) 'Alternative and critical: the contribution of research and scholarship on developing countries to international legal theory', *Harvard International Law Journal*, 41: 263.

——(2000a) 'Rejoinder: TWAILing international law', *Michigan Law Review*, 98: 2066.

Gwam, C.U. (2003–4) 'Travaux preparatoires of the Basel Convention on the Control of Transboundary Movements of Hazardous Wastes and their Disposal', *Journal of Natural Resources and Environmental Law*, 18: 1.

Head, I.L. (2002) 'Our global circumstance', unpublished paper delivered at the Joint Study Institute, in Victoria (Canada), 22 May 2002 (on file with the author).

Mbaye, K. (1972) 'Le droit au développment comme un droit de l'homme', *Revue des Droits de L'Homme*. 5: 505.

Mickelson, K. (1998) 'Rhetoric and rage: Third World voices in international legal discourse', *Wisconsin International Law Journal*, 16: 353.

Mittleman, J.H. and Pasha, M.K. (1997) *Out from Underdevelopment Revisited: Changing Global Structures and the Remaking of the Third World*, New York: St Martins Press.

Mutua, M. (2000) 'What is TWAIL?', *American Society of International Law Proceedings*, 94: 31.

——(2002) 'Terrorism and human rights – power, culture, and subordination', paper presented at International Meeting on Global Trends and Human Rights – before and after September 11, 12 January 2002, Geneva (on file with the author).

Nesiah, V. (2003) 'The ground beneath her feet: TWAIL feminisms', in A. Anghie, B. Chimni, K. Mickelson and O. Okafor (eds), *The Third World and International Order: Law, Politics and Globalization*, Leiden: Martinus Nijhoff, at 133.

Ngugi, J. (2002) 'Making new wine for old wineskins: can the reform of international law emancipate the Third World in the age of globalization?', *University of California Davis Journal of International Law and Policy*, 8: 73.

Nyerere, J.K. (1983) 'South–South option', in A. Gauhar (ed.), *The Third World Strategy*, New York: Praeger.

Okafor, O.C. (2005) 'Newness, imperialism, and international legal reform in our time: a TWAIL perspective', *Osgoode Hall Law Journal*, 43: 171.

——(2006) 'Globalism and memory in post-9/11 human rights and national security argumentation', *Proceedings of the Raoul Wallenberg International Human Rights Symposium*, 17–18 January 2006, York (Canada), at 69.

Oloka-Onyango, J. and Tamale, S. (1995) '"The personal is political" or why women's rights are indeed human rights: an African perspective on international feminism', *Human Rights Quarterly*, 17: 691.

Otto, D. (1996) 'Subalternity and international law: the problems of global community and the incommensurability of difference', *Social and Legal Studies*, 5: 337.

Rajagopal, B. (1998–99) 'Locating the Third World in cultural geography', *Third World Legal Studies*, 1998–99: 1.

——(2003) 'International law and Third World resistance: a theoretical inquiry', in A. Anghie, B. Chimni, K. Mickelson and O. Okafor (eds), *The Third World and International Order: Law, Politics and Globalization*, Leiden: Martinus Nijhoff, at 145.

Sornarajah, M. (2001) 'The Asian perspective to international law in the age of globalization', *Singapore Journal of International and Comparative Law*, 5: 284.

Trachtman, J. (2002) 'The law and economics of global justice', *American Journal of International Law*, 94: 984.

Chapter 18

Provoking international law

War and regime change in Iraq

John Strawson

Perhaps the only service that George W. Bush performed for the international community was raising the profile of international law. The Iraq War of 2003 ensured that international law was forced out of the seminar room and the library and onto the streets. Demonstrators and political activists demanded law not war. The assumption that the war was contrary to international law was shared by some specialists who regarded military action against Iraq without the explicit approval of the United Nations Security Council as an outrageous breach of well-established principles of international law (Sands 2005; Bowring 2008). This chapter will reflect on these assumptions. It will begin by interrogating the principle of the non-use of force and suggest that its effect on states is more limited than popularly believed. It continues by arguing that the long reach of colonialism has bequeathed doctrinal ambiguities on the use of force, occupation and regime change, the key issues at stake over Iraq. It concludes by recalling the debates over the Indian occupation and annexation of Goa four decades earlier, where the same doctrines were invoked but where war was seen as a means to enforce law.

The non-use of force in international law

The principle of the non-use of force in international law should not be interpreted as a general prohibition on the use of force by states. I will argue that there is no foundation to the popular view that Security Council approval is required before states take lawful military action. It is noticeable that after the Iraq War neither the Security Council nor the General Assembly questioned the legality of the war. The Security Council rather set about providing a legal framework for the occupation (UNSC resolutions 1483 (2003); 1511 (2003)). The General Assembly was silent on the matter, unlike its reaction to the 1983 US invasion of Grenada, when it deplored 'the armed intervention in Grenada, which constitutes a flagrant violation of international law' (UNGA resolution 38/7 (XXXVIII), 1983). The silence over the Iraq War requires us to look more closely at the legal doctrine on the use of force.

The starting point for contemporary law on the use of force is paragraph 176 of the International Court of Justice's judgment in the Nicaragua case. Critically, the Court determined that there are two sources of law that govern the use of force, including the right to self-defence: the UN Charter and customary international law. In that case the United States had argued that the United Nations Charter 'subsumes and supervenes' all other sources of law on the doctrine (*Nicaragua* 1986: 428). In dealing with this question that Court turned to interpret article 51 of the Charter, which states that '[n]othing in the present Charter shall impair the inherent right of individual or collective self-defence if an armed attack occurs against a Member of the United Nations'. The Court construed the article as follows:

> Article 51 is only meaningful on the basis that there is a 'natural' or 'inherent' right to self-defence, and it is hard to see how this can be other than of a customary nature, even if its present content has been confirmed and influenced by the Charter. Moreover the Charter having recognized the existence of this right, does not go on to regulate directly all aspects of its content. For example it does not contain any specific rule whereby self-defence would warrant only measures which are proportional to the armed attack and necessary to respond to it, a rule well established in customary law. Moreover, a definition of 'armed attack,' which if found to exist, authorizes the exercise of the 'inherent right' to self-defence, is not provided in the Charter, and is not part of treaty law. It cannot therefore be held that Article 51 is a provision which 'subsumes and supervenes' customary international law. It rather demonstrates that in the field in question ... customary international law continues to exist alongside treaty law. The areas governed by the two sources of law thus do not overlap exactly, and the rules do not have the same content.
>
> (*Nicaragua* 1986: 428)

As a consequence of this finding, article 51 can only be understood in the light of customary international law, which established that to rely on self-defence a state had to determine that force was necessary, proportionate to the threat and confined to the purpose of self-defence. It is thus the threatened state and no other entity that makes this determination. The Court endorsed the view that the use of such force does not require prior approval of the Security Council.

Despite popular sentiments, the United Nations Charter has rather sparse references to the use of force by states. Other than article 51, article 2(4) is the only other article to address the issue. Here, the Charter states that 'all Members shall refrain in their international relations from the threat or the use of force against the territorial integrity or political independence of any state, or in any other manner inconsistent with the purposes of the

United Nations'. There has been much academic debate about the scope of this article, but the focus here will be on the significant contribution the United Nations General Assembly has made to its meaning. The General Assembly has elaborated the principle of the non-use of force in international law through a series of resolutions adopted over four decades. The high point of this process was reached in the late 1980s when it commissioned the Special Committee on Enhancing the Effectiveness of the Principle of Non-Use of Force in International Relations to draft a comprehensive resolution. The result was the 1987 General Assembly resolution 4222 (XXXXII) which while reiterating the obligation to refrain from the threat or the use of force, insists that 'nothing in the present declaration shall be construed as enlarging or diminishing in any way the scope of the Charter concerning cases in which the use of force is lawful' (clause 33(2)). This formula had been used in many other General Assembly resolutions (such as the key declaration on international law, UNGA resolution 2625 (XXV), 1970), and therefore one has to assume that it is a considered view. The implication must be that the General Assembly assumes that the Charter provides for several 'cases' in which the use of force by states would be legal. This appears to undermine those who argue that self-defence is the single exception to the principle of the non-use of force.

General Assembly resolution 4222 highlights one such case: the situation of self-determination. Referring to the principles articulated in resolution 2625, the General Assembly declared that 'nothing in the present Declaration could in anyway prejudice the right to self-determination, freedom and independence ... of peoples forcibly deprived of that right' (clause 33(3)). It continues that 'peoples under colonial and racist regimes or other forms of alien domination' possess the right to 'struggle ... and to seek and receive support' for that struggle. The resolution therefore grants peoples with legitimate claims to self-determination the right to use force against the colonial power and permits states to use force in support. Two situations are thus indicated where states can use force without the approval of the Security Council: in self-defence and for self-determination. The text is silent on whether there are other situations but the elliptical formulations seem to offer that possibility.

Within the legal doctrine then, there appears much latitude allocated to states on the use of force. On the question of the Iraq War this latitude is compounded by the UN Security Council resolutions that apply to Iraq. After 1990 the Security Council invoked its powers under chapter VII. Of particular significance was resolution 678 (1990), later incorporated into resolution 1441 (2002), which in turn formed the backdrop to the war. Resolution 678 did not specifically authorize the use of force against Iraq over its invasion of Kuwait. Rather, it authorized the 'states cooperating with the Government of Kuwait ... to use all necessary means to uphold and implement' the resolutions calling on Iraq to withdraw from Kuwait, 'and to restore international peace and security in the area'. Thus the Security Council transferred to states the power to take the decision as to what means would be necessary to make Iraq comply with Security Council requirements. This formula is repeated in resolution 1441, and it was this that formed the basis of the United Kingdom's Attorney General's opinion that the war would be legal (Attorney General's Advice 2005). Resolution 1441 found that Iraq was still in 'material breach' of obligations to demonstrate to the United Nations that it had destroyed all weapons of mass destruction and categories of delivery systems required by UNSC resolution 687 (1991). By incorporating the terms of resolution 678, the Security Council opened the way for the US and Britain to claim that international peace and security had not been 'restored' in Iraq and that they could use force to do so. As a consequence both states were able to portray Iraq as a threat and so make the case that a combination of Security Council resolutions and the general law on self-defence offered a legitimate basis for military action.

Such arguments were quite consistent with the manner in which the principle of the non-use of force had been formulated during the formative period of the United Nations. The creation of the United Nations might have been against the background of the Second World War but its institutions and practices were shaped by the combined impact of the East–West conflict and the rise of national liberation movements. It was a period, as Mikhail Gorbachev aptly observed, in which the United Nations was 'a propaganda battlefield and a scene of political confrontation' (Gorbachev 1988: 15). International law, enmeshed as it was within this 'confrontation', lost any appearance of singularity, which is why Gorbachev saw the end of the Cold War as an opportunity to reach an accord on a 'uniform understanding of the principles and norms of international law' (Gorbachev 1988: 21). What this attractive appeal underestimated was the difficulty of overcoming both contingency and indeterminacy (and consequent dependence on sovereign state determination) in delivering international law from the 'propaganda battlefield', as the arguments about the Iraq War demonstrate.

The 1960s saw the transformation of the scale of the international community as former colonies became independent states. This, together with entry to the UN of many of the states of the Eastern bloc, created a new balance in international relations as a coalition between the 'socialist states' and the newly independent countries gained a majority within the General Assembly. The addition to the international community of the former colonies combined with a powerful Soviet Union to influence the course of international law. While the Soviet Union sought to elaborate the legal aspects of peaceful co-existence (Tunkin 1974), the former colonies sought to become part of the international law-making process. In the West this process saw many responses but the most significant was that of the New Haven school, for which international law was considered a tool of policy and a mode of intervening in international affairs (McDougal and Feliciano 1961).

Whatever the differences in world-view, all three camps shared an attachment to the doctrine of sovereignty. But while all formally referred to sovereignty in classical legal terms, there were fundamental differences between them on questions of how sovereignty could be acquired, exercised and maintained.

In the 1950s and 1960s states of the three camps deployed their sovereign rights to justify the use of force. In the Suez War, the invasion of Hungary and the Goa intervention, each political project was justified through an appeal to legal doctrine. The British and French justified their military action against Egypt as upholding the principles of international law and the UN Charter on the grounds that force was being used to end the Israeli–Egyptian war. These legal niceties were a cover for an attempt to regain control of the recently nationalized Suez Canal. The Soviet Government claimed that its invasion of Hungary during the same period in 1956 was also consistent with the UN charter's prohibition on aggression. The invocation of law in this instance was to justify forcibly keeping Hungary in the Communist bloc and to secure the strategic interests of the USSR. In 1961 the Indian Government invoked a combination of self-defence and just war to explain the legal basis of the use of force to attack and then annex Portuguese Goa to India – we will return to this issue.

Each camp enshrined the sovereign state at the centre of its system. For the Eastern bloc non-interference in internal affairs became the legal shield of socialism. The newly freed states sought to consolidate self-determination behind the walls of sovereignty. In the West international legal doctrine was seen as a protective cordon against the spread of communism and attempts to undermine its economic system. The competing political camps tended to vie for the appropriation of international law's dominant narrative rather than attempt to replace it. The next section of this chapter will consider the way in which this dominant narrative is produced and reproduced. Subsequent sections will then explore how its colonial origins continue to influence attempts at its appropriation and work towards the reinscription of sovereign discretion at the heart of the principle of the non-use of force.

Voices of the dominant narrative

> The sovereignty of territory may be acquired by occupation, prescription, cession, conquest and accretion.
>
> (Brierly 1963: 163)

In reviewing the literature of the 1950s and 1960s it is striking how the method of production of key international legal texts exercises an influence on the construction of the narrative itself. The practice of regarding certain texts as authoritative and ensuring their continuing circulation through reissuing new versions under new editors was at its high point. Through this process the core text remains and this ensures that the authentic voice of colonial past is encoded within the contemporary discourse. This is a form of legal grafting in which new ideas, principles, cases and other sources are attached to an existing body. This occurs in three different ways. First, statements such as Brierly's merely offer authoritative opinions of law that were originally written during the colonial period itself. Second, citations draw on the authority of even older works, many dating from the nineteenth century, which also connects the reader to the colonial period. Third, the legal methodology itself, through which the effort to create a systematic jurisprudence deploys a series of techniques, such as analogy, distinction making and the notion of authority, all of which reinscribe the legitimacy of past positions. Brierly's *Law of Nations* first appeared in 1928. The 1963 (sixth) edition was edited by the eminent international lawyer Humphrey Waldock, who was at the time Chichele Professor of Public International Law at Oxford and who was to become a judge of the International Court of Justice. In his preface Waldock explained much of this methodology. He acknowledged the drastic changes that had taken place:

> the world community itself has undergone a radical change through the transformation of many colonial, protected, and mandated territories into independent states. The process of transformation, it is true, was under-way in 1954, when the previous edition went to press; but its tempo quickened dramatically after that date, and the emergence of new African and Asian states has fundamentally affected the structure, politics and work of the United Nations ... As a result of these and other develop-ments the United Nations and the Charter have acquired a significance in relation to international legal order that was not yet fully apparent in Brierly's lifetime ... Much as he would have preferred to leave Brierly's own text largely intact, the present editor has not thought this to be a possible course to adopt.
>
> (Brierly 1963: vii–viii)

He continued that the book would lose its value if it:

> did not reflect the present rather than the past state of international law. The editor accordingly has decided that he must displace the original text with new material, wherever necessary, to prevent the book from falling behind the quickening march of international law and inter-national institutions. The present edition in consequence contains not only additions to cover new developments but also, in some places, quite extensive submissions of new material for Brierly's text.
>
> (Brierly 1963: viii–ix)

For example, Waldock said that the sections on colonies had been 'substantially revised' (Brierly 1963: ix). While this may have been the case it is extraordinary that the revisions did not include any reference at all to the then emerging right to self-determination contained in the two 1960 General Assembly resolutions on the question (UNGA resolutions 1514 and 1541). The book rather dwelt on the way in which colonies were acquired and the legal distinctions between colonies, protectorates, mandates and trusts. Such assumptions about the legitimacy of colonialism are not, however, merely the reflections of jurists who are writing from the location of a major colonial power. In the edited *Manual of Public International Law*, consciously developed as an international project by the Carnegie Endowment for International Peace, the colonial acquisition of territory was also regarded as quite legitimate. In discussing title to occupation of territory, Milan Sahovic and William Bishop wrote:

> An attempt was also made to recognize notification as a constitutive element of occupation. Thus with the adoption of the General Act of the Congo Conference in 1885, the colonial powers agreed that notification to other states of the decision to occupy a definite region in Africa should be one of the required conditions for the recognition of title by occupation. This measure was a direct consequence of agreement reached by the colonial powers for their division of the colonial world.
>
> (Sahovic and Bishop 1968: 322–23).

However, for the authors this is a record expressed in the past tense and they do explain that such methods of acquiring territory would now be contrary to the UN Charter and the principle of self-determination (Sahovic and Bishop 1968: 323–24). Brierly is thus not alone in the manner in which colonization enters the mainstream discourse of international law. The past use of force to acquire territories and to shape their internal regimes appears legally unquestioned. Sahovic and Bishop comment that 'in contemporary conditions the right of self-determination of peoples deserves special attention in the process of territorial changes, since the application of all modes of acquisition or loss of title to territory should depend on the will of its people' (Sahovic and Bishop 1968: 324). They do not discuss the validity of the original title nor whether the people possessed the capacity to challenge the consequences. It is, however, significant that the two books, while clearly having quite different origins and purposes, treat colonial conquest and colonial regimes as legitimate foundations for international law.

Colonialism and regime change

It is this colonial heritage that embeds a particular view of the right of states to inquire into the legitimacy of the regimes of other states or territories. The extent to which this view formed part of the established canon despite the changes brought by decolonization can be seen from the contents of the *Manual of Public International Law* (1968). This text has an extensive bibliography and clearly attempts to offer a multicultural list, with works in different languages and traditions. This perhaps makes all the more significant the inclusion of so many works that date from the nineteenth and early twentieth centuries. Oppenheim (Oppenheim 1905, 1906), perhaps one of the most authoritative commentaries, is regularly cited and engaged with. This is a work which has been repeatedly re-edited now for a century and thus is very much a work of legal grafting. Another cited work is Charles Hyde's *International Law* (Hyde 1922), which contains an entire section subtitled 'Countries Not Possessed of European Civilization'. For Hyde, 'what are known as the States of International Law, notwithstanding the sharp differences between some of them, resemble each other in the possession of what is called European civilization' (Hyde 1922: vol. 1, 49). In cases where European civilization is lacking, 'the States of International Law demand and secure ... the yielding of important rights of jurisdiction which are never relinquished by the territorial sovereign of a full-fledged and independent member of the family of nations' (Hyde 1922: vol. 1, 50). However, it should not be thought that European civilization is 'beyond the reach of any country which is zealous to meet it' (Hyde 1922: vol. 1, 51). The two examples that Hyde gives of countries passing this test are Japan and Turkey. I do not suggest that Max Sørensen, the editor of the *Manual*, in any way would have endorsed such sentiments, but merely draw attention to the way in which international legal discourses circulate. The frequent citation of works such as Hyde within international legal literature nourishes canonical sources which, as with orientalism generally, leave their imprint on the discourse (Said 1978).

The reference to civilization as the basis of international law – with and without the prefix European – is common in the work of the period. Georg Schwarzenberger's approach was based on the 'civilization principle' (Schwarzenberger 1968). In his *International Law* he pondered the application of international humanitarian law to 'the position of the Occupying Power in the territory of an enemy who has relapsed into a state of barbarism' (Schwarzenberger 1968: vol. II, 195). He continued that in exceptional situations the occupying power may be forced to abrogate the law of a 'barbarous system' so as to restore 'a minimum civilized life in the occupied territory' (Schwarzenberger 1968: vol. II, 195). The idea of civilization was to make a marked return in political and legal discourses following 11 September 2001, and was used to characterize Saddam Hussein's regime in the run-up to the war. Civilization was now used as a signifier of whether or not a state was a 'terrorist state' or a 'failed state', both denoting a loss of sovereignty. Thus while civilization could be gained during colonialism, it could be lost in the post-colonial period.

'New international law'

The creation of the new states did, however, initiate a discussion of international law from their new perspectives. For example, Arnand in the early 1960s surveyed the impact of the new states on what he called 'present' international law. He attempted to grapple with the problem of at once advocating new developments in international law while maintaining its continuity. As he explained:

> [t]he present body of international rules applicable between states, so-called international law, was developed among the West European countries during the last four centuries and is basically the outcome of, or is dominated by, their influence. Though in the beginning these rules derived from Jus Naturale and Jus Gentium of the Roman legal system, and were thought of as applicable between all the countries of the world, during the nineteenth century there developed a spirit of provincialism in Europe.
>
> (Arnand 1962: 386)

Arnand then contrasted this universalism of Vitoria, Suarez, Gentili, Grotuis, Pufendorf, Bynkershoek, Wolff, Vattel with the provincialism of Wheaton, Phillimore, Hall, Oppenheim, Fauchille, Westlake who, 'declared it [international law] only applicable between European powers' (Arnand 1962: 388). He then quoted Hall, another major canonical text dating from 1917, as saying, 'States outside European civilization must enter into the circle of law governed countries ... with the acquiescence of the latter' (Arnand 1962: 389). In distinguishing the classical writers on international law from those who emerge from the late nineteenth century, Arnand's position initiated an analysis that has become popular in debates about international law. In this account, international law begins as universal but becomes tarnished by colonialism and injustice and stands in need of restoration to its true self (see, for example: Weeremantry 2004; Strawson 2004). (There are quite different accounts of the work of the classical writers which indeed suggest that colonialism was a central concern of theirs: see, for example: Anghie 1999.) But while the discussion on what was 'new' in international law became a theme of the debates of the 1960s, for example in the *American Journal of International Law* (Jessup 1964; McWhinney 1966; Fenwick 1966), the colonial origins of international law were rarely challenged head-on. What is important to register is the way in which even those who want to argue for a new departure in international law do not challenge its origins but rather claim them as their own. There is a process of competitive appropriation – a process which certainly continues to the contemporary period.

Goa

It was perhaps the Goa incident in 1961 that critically exemplified the reinscription of classical international law although apparently dressed in new clothes. On 18 December 1961 Indian armed forces attacked the Portuguese enclave of Goa and occupied it. The Indian Government then annexed Goa, which at the time had the status of overseas province of Portugal. The use of force, occupation and drastic regime change all raised fundamental questions for international law. The international community was unable to find a united response to the Indian action and the Security Council was unable to adopt a resolution (Wright 1962: 617–19). However, the statements at the Security Council provide an instructive example of the competitive appropriation of international law.

The Indian Ambassador, C.S. Jha, argued a combination of justifications for the action. His starting point was that Portuguese control of the territory was illegitimate as it had been acquired by force some 450 years before. As a result, he argued, 'the idea that the territories could be integral parts of Portugal was a remarkable myth' (as quoted in Wright 1962: 619). In this account, if the territories were not part of Portugal then they 'were integral parts of India' (Wright 1962: 619). As a consequence of this status, 'there could be no question of aggression against one's own frontier, against one's own people' (quoted in Wright 1962: 619). This argument suggests that all India was doing was redeploying armed forces within its own territory – an argument to be repeated by Saddam Hussein when his forces invaded Kuwait in 1991 (see Moore 1992). This central argument was supplemented by claims that Portuguese armed forces had attacked India owing to a border incident in which two Indian fishermen had been killed. This should be put in the context of a Portuguese total armed force of 12,000 which possessed neither tanks nor air cover and the Indian deployment of a well-armed 30,000-strong force which completed the operation within 36 hours. In addition, India invoked the 'just war' doctrine due to the refusal of Portugal to decolonize the territory. This position was supported by the Soviet Union, which, referring to the key terms in the UN Charter, claimed that Portugal in refusing to decolonize 'created a threat to international peace and security in various parts of the world including Goa' (quoted in Wright 1962: 619). Ceylon echoed this invocation of the Charter in supporting the Indian position that as Goa had been conquered by force, India had the right to assist in its liberation and that 'it had not used force for territorial aggrandizement' (quoted in Wright 1962: 619).

India based its claims in relation to self-determination on the 1960 General Assembly resolution 1514, arguing that from the moment the resolution was adopted, Portugal's continuance of its colonial regime was illegal. In an effort to assert the 'new' international law, India further argued that Portugal's 1510 conquest of Goa had been illegal and that force in 1961 was justified in rectifying this situation. This, of course, also assumed that decolonization could only mean union with India. However, reflecting a more dominant view, Quincy Wright commented that 'four and a half centuries of uncontested occupation and general recognition had established good title' (Wright 1962: 622). But for India its historical claim was central and at the time was widely accepted by the Soviet camp and the new states.

However, thornier than the question of the merits of India's historical claim was undoubtedly the issue of whether it could use force to enforce it. The discussion on the use of force came in the wake of the failure of the United Nations to define aggression, perhaps the central concept within the UN Charter. The UN Charter itself does not include a definition of aggression or indeed of those acts regarded as less than aggression – threats to the peace and breaches of the peace. In the 1950s the key tests for the international community had been the Korean War and the Suez and Hungarian crises. While the United Nations had through both the Security Council and the General Assembly found North Korea the 'aggressor' and had called on states to assist in resisting aggression, there were no such determinations on Suez and Hungary five years later. It was significant that the UN Special Committee on the Definition of Aggression had had its final meeting between 8 October and 9 November 1956 – the Soviet invasion of Hungary began on 24 October and the Suez War on 29 October. Against this dramatic background the committee concluded that 'no general consensus was attainable, either as to whether the definition is possible or desirable' (quoted in Stone 1958: 1). Despite the attempt of the General Assembly to define aggression in 1974, it still remains undefined and the Assembly of State Parties of the International Criminal Court still grapples with the question. Thus the condemnation of aggression is a rhetorical device rather than a legal determination. In Goa and with Iraq, much debate turned on the meaning of UN Charter article 2(4). In the decade before the Goa incident Stone had argued that the scope of article 2(4) did not include a broad prohibition on the use of force:

> the extreme view asserts that resort to force by a Member is unlawful regardless of wrongs and dangers that provoked it, and that if no collective United Nations relief is available, the Member may still have to submit indefinitely without redress to the continuance of these wrongs and dangers.
>
> (Stone 1958: 95)

Indeed he continued, 'article 2(4) does not forbid "threat or the use of force" *simpliciter*; it forbids it only when directed "against the territorial integrity or political independence of any state or in any other manner inconsistent with the purposes of the United Nations"' (Stone 1958: 95).

Stone's propositions would be supportive of the Indian position, summed up by Wright as that 'colonialism was such an evil that the use of force to eliminate it should be tolerated' (Wright 1962: 624). As the debate about self-determination persisted throughout the decade, the issue of the use of force was part of the thrust of the 'new' international law advocated by the 'new' states. As we have seen, this was codified in the UN Declaration on the Principles of International Law (UNGA resolution 2625 (XXV), 1970). The apparent right of states to use force in support of peoples forcibly denied their right to self-determination necessarily raises the issue of what this means. For India it was clear that the mere continuation of a colonial regime constituted forcible denial. The 'new' international law thus opened a wide front in which the sovereign state would be able to use force. However, this 'progressive' use of force would be a two-edged sword as the period of formal colonialism came to an end and as the content of self-determination came into focus, especially with the discussion of democratic entitlement. This issue was to be prominent in the US and British policy which tried to suggest that the Iraq War was a war of liberation (Strawson 2008).

In the 1960s the view that colonialism was based on an initial aggressive use of force and that the subject peoples were entitled to use self-defence became common amongst the new states (see Dugard 1967). It is interesting, however, that as a result of the discussions held in the sixth (legal) committee of the General Assembly this position became somewhat more nuanced by the time of the adoption of resolution 2625. From the point of view of the UN Charter the issue of the use of force in connection to colonialism was moved from the area of self-defence under article 51 to the more general provision on the use of force under article 2(4), suggesting that Stone's arguments indeed had some force. The significance of this process lies in the way in which rather old ideas about sovereign states and the right to use force are reasserted in the guise of a 'new' international law. However universal the values articulated in the instruments, any application or implementation of them is returned to the command of the sovereign state.

Quincy Wright observed this problematic in the Goa incident. While he viewed the legality of India's use of force to be highly questionable having regard to both what he called 'general international law' and the UN Charter, his view nonetheless was that whatever the basis of the legality of the action itself, the results – the annexation to India – would stand. He was right about Goa's status but perhaps erroneous about international law.

Conclusion

The stance of many in the Iraq War debate has been that international law has been violated. It has been suggested that clear and precise norms on the use of force, the powers of the United Nations Security Council and territorial integrity were broken with impunity by the Bush Administration.

The reflections here are not to provide an apologia for the devastation that has been inflicted on the people of Iraq and the Middle East. The purpose is rather to serve as a warning that legality, rather than illegality, is the issue. Much work remains to be done in addressing current international legal doctrine which still enthrones the sovereign state at every critical moment. This work cannot be done if we remain entranced by the myth of a golden age of international law.

References

Anghie, A. (1999) 'Francisco de Vitoria and the colonial origins of international law', in E. Darian-Smith and P. Fitzpatrick (eds), *Laws of the Postcolonial*, Ann Arbor, MI: University of Michigan Press, 89–107.

Arnand, R.P. (1962) 'The role of the "new" Asian-African countries in the present international legal order', *American Journal of International Law*, 56: 383–406.

Attorney General's Advice on the Iraq War: Resolution 1441 (2005) *International and Comparative Law Quarterly*, 54: 767–78.

Bowring, B. (2008) *The Degradation of the International Legal Order?*, Abingdon: Routledge-Cavendish.

Brierly, J.L. (1963) *The Law of Nations*, Oxford: Clarendon Press.

Dugard, C.J.R. (1967) 'The OAU and colonialism: an enquiry into the plea for self-defense as a justification for the use of force in the eradication of colonialism', *International and Comparative Law Quarterly*, 16: 145–90.

Fenwick, C.G. (1966) 'International law: the old and the new', *American Journal of International Law*, 60: 475–83.

Gorbachev, M. (1988) *Address to the United Nations*, New York: 7 December 1988, Moscow: Novosti Press Agency Publishing House.

Hyde, C.C. (1922) *International Law as Chiefly Applied by the United States*, Boston: Little, Brown & Co.

Jessup, P.C. (1964) 'Diversity and uniformity in the law of nations', *American Journal of International Law*, 58: 341–58.

McDougal, M.S. and Feliciano F.P. (1961) *Law and Minimum World Public Order: The Legal Regulation of International Coercion*, New Haven and London: Yale University Press.

McWhinney, E. (1966) 'The "new" countries and the "new" international law: the United Nations Special Conference on Friendly Relations and Cooperation among States', *American Journal of International Law*, 60: 1–33.

Moore, J.N. (1992) *Crisis in the Gulf: Enforcing the Rule of Law*, New York: Oceana.

Oppenheim, L.F.L. (1905, 1906) *International Law: A Treatise*, London: Longmans.

Sahovic, M. and Bishop, W. (1968) 'The authority of the state: its range with respect to persons and places', in M. Sørensen (ed.), *Manual of Public International Law*, London: Macmillan, 311–80.

Said, E.W. (1978) *Orientalism: Western Conceptions of the Orient*, Harmondsworth: Penguin.

Sands, P. (2005) *'Lawless World': America and the Making and Breaking of Global Rules*, London: Allen Lane.

Schwarzenberger, G. (1968) *International Law: as Applied in International Courts and Tribunals*, London: Stevens & Son.

Sørensen, M. (ed.) (1968) *Manual of Public International Law*, London: Macmillan.

Stone, J. (1958) *Aggression and World Order: A Critique of United Nations Theories of Aggression*, London: Stevens & Sons.

Strawson, J. (2004) 'Book review: *Universalizing International Law* by Christopher Weeramantry', *Melbourne Journal of International Law*, 5(2): 513–18.

——(2008) 'Britain's democratic vision for Iraq: strategic interest or contingency?', *International Journal of Contemporary Iraqi Studies*, 2: 351–73.

Tunkin, G.I. (1974) *Theory of International Law*, trans. W. Butler, London: George Allen & Unwin.

Weeramantry, G.S. (2004) *Universalizing International Law*, Leiden: Martinus Nijhoff.

Wright, Q. (1962), 'The Goa incident', *American Journal of International Law*, 56: 617–32.

Case

Military and Paramilitary Activities in and against Nicaragua (Nicaragua v United States of America), Merits, Judgment, ICJ Reports 1986, 14.

Chapter 19

The torture memos

*Fleur Johns**

Something happened to international law between 2004 and 2009. It
happened in fits and starts and was largely unforeseen. At various moments
during that period, classified legal memoranda were released that analyzed
and sought to affirm the legality of the United States' programme of detention, interrogation and surveillance in connection with global anti-terrorism
initiatives and military operations in Iraq and Afghanistan. Through these
memos' release, international law encountered itself and found the encounter
troubling. This chapter explores prospects for deciding to name that
encounter an 'event'. It does so with regard to the work of Alain Badiou
(Badiou 2007). Nonetheless, this chapter's probing of the 'evental' potential
of the torture memos' release seeks to adopt a perspective internal to the
international legal situation of which it is part. That is, it will remain,
more or less, within the vocabulary of international law by way of preventing
the passage of a 'philosopher king' (Badiou) being received as one or other
exit route out of the discipline's troubles.

Introduction

The phrase 'torture memos' has come to serve as a collective shorthand for
many hundreds of pages of legal memoranda and correspondence produced by
White House counsel, US Defense Department counsel, assistant Attorneys
General and other officials and legal advisers of the US Government and the
US military between 2002 and 2005 (Danner 2004, 2009; Greenberg and
Dratel 2005; Sands 2008a; American Civil Liberties Union 2009).
The documents in question addressed the status of prisoners detained during
US military operations in Afghanistan and Iraq, as well the lawfulness
of certain counter-insurgency techniques used, or considered for possible use,
in connection with anti-terrorism initiatives of the US administration.
International legal commentators have focused particular attention on a few
of these memoranda, especially one written in August 2002 that adopted a
highly permissive reading of international legal prohibitions on torture
(Bybee 2002).

Media disclosure of some of these documents occurred in 2004, sparking a series of investigations official and otherwise (Brazin 2004; Rosen 2004). A further round of disclosures occurred in 2009, prompted by freedom-of-information requests made by the American Civil Liberties Union (Mazzetti and Shane 2009). These documents circulated in the context of widespread allegations of detainee mistreatment and torture levelled at the United States and its allies; a number of these have been substantiated in investigative reports (ICRC 2004, 2007; Amnesty International 2006; Human Rights Watch 2006a, 2006b; Physicians for Human Rights 2005; Taguba 2004; DAIG 2004). In some accounts, a direct causal link has been posited between the permissive legal architecture the memos inscribed and the subjection of detainees to inhuman treatment (Brazin 2004; Sands 2008a). Other accounts point to incidents of alleged torture predating the legal memoranda in question (Leopold 2009). Whether or not a direct causal link along these lines can be maintained, the memos in question enacted, for international lawyers, a profoundly destabilizing equation of international law with that which it customarily took as its opposite: unmitigated, self-interested violence without rational justification in coherent, plausible terms.

Detailed critiques of the legal content and reasoning of these memoranda have been published elsewhere (see, e.g., Paust 2007; Nowak 2006). This chapter does not speak to that content or reasoning. Instead, this chapter is concerned with the reactions that the torture memos' publication (alongside the aforementioned reports of ill-treatment) have engendered among international lawyers, as recorded in print. As will be demonstrated in this chapter, the torture memos and related reports generated an opportunity for the renewal of international legality. To that extent, international legal scholarship's assimilation of the memos can be read as a rallying of familiar dispositions as well as a reaffirmation of established positions and relations. Yet something more might have emerged in the torture memos' release: a dislocation of international legal authority; a breakdown in the discipline's claim to conscience. This chapter seeks to elucidate both that reaffirmation and its failure.

Beginning with the reaffirmation engendered by the torture memos, the first part of this chapter explores four moods through which international legal scholarship 'responding' to the torture memos has cycled erratically. Each of these moods revolves around the reassertion of a claim to authority on the part of international law and international lawyers, and a re-placement of international law in relation to violence. As such, these comprise four dimensions of a particular international legal 'situation', the presentation of which the torture memos occasioned (Hallward 2003: 93–100). Together, they bring to light a constitutive link between international law's degradation (or the perception thereof) and its force. The force of the threat or steepness of the decline that the torture memos are perceived to embody seems to underwrite, through its inversion, the force of authority with which international law and the international legal profession are to be invested anew.

Rather than reading the torture memos and related reports as instances of international law's abandonment or corruption, they are read here as constitutive enactments of international legal authority of a sort vital to the discipline's continued purchase in legal, social and political discourse. This comprises the operational domain to which Badiou gives the name 'the state' of a situation: the metastructure whereby that which is presented as a historico-social situation is represented in apparent completeness and 'a clause of closure and security' is proposed (Badiou 2007: 98). In the four different registers identified, the relationship of legal expertise to violence is to be stabilized 'such that consistent belongings be preserved' (Badiou 2007: 109).

The second part of this chapter will explore the torture memos' release as a breakdown in international law's customary representation of itself to itself; that is, the failure of the affirmational and representational claims outlined above. That breakdown cannot be attributed to the traditional sites and processes through which the discipline is thought to change. It marked, instead, international law's openness to collective change unnameable as reformist programme. That opening occurred at sites characterized in international legal terms as devoid of promise, definitionally unrecognizable: that is, sites marked by the seemingly unrepresentable figure of the 'unlawful combatant' held in one or other 'legal black hole' (Johns 2005). There, the existence of an evental site might be identified with the following statements: the detention centres which the torture memos seek to structure are locations at which law is being and has been made in abundance – law that is partly unrecognizable to prevailing international law on torture and inhuman treatment. Further, the detainee is actively and combatively engaged in making law at this site, and in so doing inhabiting anew the name 'combatant': a name the ethical and legal coordinates of which are in increasing disarray (e.g., McMahan 2009). It is in this context that we might decide to name the torture memos' release an 'event' by way of intervention.

The international legal situation re-presented

Let us begin, however, in the field of the non-evental statement: amid the anxious outpouring of reassuring words engendered by the torture memos' release. Among international lawyers, and others invoking international law, the unexpected public emergence of these documents provoked appeals to hope, correction, community and conscience. In a variety of ways, the writings in question have sought to reassert configurations of state/individual and law/ violence familiar to the discipline in which they work: configurations in which the international lawyer necessarily remains a central mediating figure.

Hope

> In describing abuse of his family by US prison guards, a disabled Iraqi man told US army investigators that guards pulled him around by his penis and then sodomized him with a water bottle.
>
> (Jackson 2006: 149)

So begins one law review article on the torture memos. This is a familiar opening gesture from an international legal text. The sexualized body of a 'victim' is offered up for ritual consumption. That body is called upon to shock and to school (Orford 1999: 697).

It is, however, another sacrificial body that is offered up most regularly by the international legal literature surrounding the torture memos: the body of the law. Throughout this literature, international lawyers critical of the torture memos and alarmed by the revelations of detainee mistreatment in official reports have struggled to transpose international law itself onto the rack of moral trial and thereby to stage its deliverance. Consider the words of Scott Horton, chair of the Committee on International Law for the Association of the Bar of the City of New York:

> In the War on Terror, law and legal ethics have been sacrificed to a misguided notion of political expedience. We are suffering the consequences of those mistakes now, and our country is likely to suffer them for some time to come.
>
> (Horton 2005: 301)

US Supreme Court Justice Louis Brandeis has been hauled from the grave, repeatedly, to reissue a warning (from his dissent in the 1928 wire-tapping case of *Olmstead v United States*): that governmental contempt for law 'would bring terrible retribution' (Bilder and Vagts 2004: 695; Bilder 2006: 145). Theo van Boven, former UN Special Rapporteur on Torture, has worried about the effect on international human rights and humanitarian law of the United States attempting to 'argue[] away [its] real cornerstone[s]' (van Boven 2006: 151). Leila Sadat has warned of 'serious consequences … for the … stability of all the [international] institutions established … after the Second World War' (Sadat 2007: 1248). And 'what will be the spiritual cost, the overall damage to the character of the nation?' lamented Karen Greenberg, editor of *The Torture Papers* (Greenberg 2005: xviiii).

So framed, legal analysis of the (im)propriety of torture promises to perform one seventeenth-century sense of the term 'limit': to delineate the 'comely' contours of the human form (OED 1989). As the torture memos purported to do away with legal limits upon torture at the expense of mostly unnamed detainees, legal scholars recorded the threat that they posed as a danger to *themselves*: to the contours of their nation, their discipline, their profession and their faith. Jeremy Waldron's observation that the torture memos 'shook [his] faith in the integrity of the community of American jurists' seems characteristic of the reaction among legal scholarly readers of these documents, within and beyond the United States (Waldron 2005: 1687).

Thus international lawyers, among others, have reacted to the degradation of international legal limits (and, secondarily it seems, the degradation of detainee bodies) that they attribute to the torture memos by reinscribing the integrity of the human form in a number of metaphoric representational modes: as the body of the law, the body politic and the professional corps. Through this act of transposition, international lawyers' confrontation with what one commentator has termed law 'in the cause of evil' has offered many participants in the field hope (Lewis 2005: xiii). In anticipation of the US Supreme Court's 2004 decision on Guantánamo Bay detainee claims in the consolidated case of *Rasul v Bush*, George Fletcher invoked the corpus of the nation as a wellspring of hope:

> The hope remains that the Supreme Court will assert its judicial authority and redeem the American commitment to principles of liberty and individualised justice.
>
> (Fletcher 2004: 132; see also Mayerfield 2007: 124)

Discussing, among other matters, the US Government's 'use of cruel, inhuman and degrading interrogation methods at Abu Ghraib and elsewhere', Richard Bilder derived similar hope from the prospective realignment of a professional corps:

> Hopefully, international lawyers and others are succeeding in moving us gradually towards a better and more peaceful world – one in which law *does* speak to power.
>
> (Bilder 2006: 146)

In each case, this hope is, it seems, for a disentangling (correction), a rebinding (community), and a renewal of belief (conscience). Let us explore each of these dimensions in turn.

Correction

For all the genuine expressions of horror and distress that they have provoked among international lawyers, the torture memos' publication, and the release of reports attributing responsibility for torture to US and coalition forces, have elicited a thrill – a frisson palpable in international legal scholarly accounts of the same. This, it seems, could be a Nuremberg moment for the noughties: a moment of clarity and distinction. Finally, it has appeared to many, international law's anti-formalism might be disentangled once and for all from the moral relativism it *knows* itself not to be. 'The constructive value of these memos and reports', Karen Greenberg wrote in the opening pages of *The Torture Papers*, 'is to enable open-minded reflection and self-correction' (Greenberg 2005: xx).

The 'self-correction' of which Greenberg has written is to proceed from a *redoubled* anti-formalism. The problem, we have been told, is not politics, but imprudence. Recall Scott Horton's words: the decomposition of law and legal ethics emanated from a '*misguided* notion of political expedience' (Horton 2005: 301, emphasis added). The answer, for many, is to do more or less what international legal pragmatists already do, only better. '[T]here is much these memos overlook', Greenberg has tutored, highlighting a number of legal, policy and strategic considerations missed (Greenberg 2005: xviii). Harold Koh has labelled the advice contained in the memos incompetent (quoted in Liptak 2004) and a 'stunning failure of lawyerly craft' (Koh 2005: 649). Kathleen Clark has suggested that 'assertions about the state of the law [made in the 2002 Bybee memorandum] are so inaccurate that they seem to be arguments about what the authors (or the intended recipients) wanted the law to be rather than assessments of what the law actually is' (Clark 2005: 458). Philippe Sands has expressed horror at the 'awful' legal advice provided by one lawyer stationed at Guantánamo Bay (Sands 2008b: 372). The problem, Sands suggests, was a combination of lack of expertise and the influence of a pernicious ideology distorting and derailing the 'normal' operations of international law:

> [R]eal responsibility centres on a small group of politically-appointed lawyers, adhering to a particular ideology as to America's place in the world and its relationship with norms of international law. The lawyers who knew the rules, who had lengthy experience on these issues, were circumvented. The military lawyers were cut out of the process ... The normal checks and balances were avoided, with care and deliberation.
>
> (Sands 2008b: 376)

Nonetheless, through careful effort, 'normality' might be restored, legal scholars report. 'Lawyers and public officials need to be instructed, in school and on the job, to be cognizant of the real-life consequences of their policy choices', Joshua Dratel has written (Dratel 2005: xxiii). Others provide instruction on the ways in which the office of the White House Counsel might be reformed (Jackson 2006; Lopez 2005). New Zealand, Aaron Jackson has suggested, yields a useful example (Jackson 2006: 153, 179–81). In this state of tropic inversion, international lawyers of the North must look to the South (albeit no further than the white Commonwealth) for tutelage in anti-corruption.

Community

Next, the rebinding: there follows a call to courage and loyalty. 'American lawyers still honour ... courage, integrity, and fidelity to the law', insist Richard Bilder and Detlav Vagts, citing noble lawyerly conduct against Watergate-era Nixon and among German military lawyers in the face of Nazi policy (Bilder and Vagts 2004: 695). 'We as lawyers', writes Scott Horton, 'have a sacred duty to ensure [the Nuremberg] legacy is upheld' (Horton 2005: 305). So, international legal responses to the torture memos could be read as an effort to restore the sanctity of the human as such, after the fall and after a virtual (virtual for these commentators, that is) descent into hell. The lawyers responsible for the torture memos, Joshua Dratel writes, 'all too willingly failed to act as a constitutional or moral compass that could brake their client's descent into unconscionable behaviour' (Dratel 2005: xxii).

Yet the *denouement* in this morality tale has been not a scene of humanitarian triumph, but one of self-immolation. The culmination of *this* reformation was to be, as before, a reconnection with the commons (Broadhead 1996). There would be no miracles here. Richard Bilder and Detlav Vagts have urged international lawyers to get back in touch with 'ordinary morality and common decency' (Bilder and Vagts 2004: 695). They cited an American Bar Association committee report on the role of the government legal adviser as follows:

> [s]ome members think that the international law community's good judgment and the public's common sense can generally be relied on to tell responsible arguments from those which are patently unfounded.
>
> (Bilder and Vagts 2004: 694, n. 31)

In a similar vein, the publicly released 'Lawyers' statement on the Bush Administration's torture memos' looked to the 'public outcry' with which the torture memos' publication was greeted as confirmation of their 'original lawless[ness]' (Ackerman *et al.* 2004).

Here, in this egalitarian gesture, one is reminded of the link between doctrines of equality and prohibitions on torture in the genealogy of liberalism. 'The same collective intelligence which brings in the doctrine of equality before the law, ... will instantly put an end to torture', wrote the nineteenth-century anthropologist James Welling, for it was the 'mean and plebeian' who tended to be tortured (Welling 1892: 211). John Langbein has suggested a historical connection to egalitarianism of a more procedural kind (Langbein 2004).

The problem, recent commentaries imply, was one of elevation and insulation. 'Hand-picked political appointees collaborated secretly on the

Torture Memo', wrote Cornelia Pillard, 'driving directly to a desired bottom line' (Pillard 2006: 1297). Philippe Sands suggested likewise in his reference to 'a small group of politically-appointed lawyers' (Sands 2008b: 376). It is this elevation and insulation against which Bilder and Vagts have railed when insisting 'these memoranda cannot in themselves insulate or immunize persons engaging or complicit in torture' and against which Horton inveighed in warning '[t]here is no immunity for those who craft opinions' (Bilder and Vagts 2004: 694; Horton 2005: 303). The turn these lawyers have attempted to take, by way of response, is outwards, towards transparency, weightlessness, dissolution.

The sensation of this turn is a vertiginous one: 'there may be no "safety net"', Bilder and Vagts have cautioned, 'other than these attorneys' own competence, care, integrity, and good faith' (Bilder and Vagts 2004: 693). And yet there *is* a certain safety to be found in numbers, for the qualities cited here are cast as professional qualities. Here is the rest of the Bilder and Vagts quote: 'it is only these professional qualities that protect against legal advice or advocacy that might undermine the national interest in respect for law, or subvert or erode the international legal order' (Bilder and Vagts 2004: 693).

Appeals are made, again and again, to the public. Cornelia Pillard, for instance, lauds the salutary effects of publicity for legal decision making: '[a]fter the public, the press, and other independent commentators had a chance to analyze and critique the executive's legal analysis, its flaws became clear', she writes (Pillard 2006: 1301). Yet it is primarily to *each other* that international lawyers would be made transparent. The collectivity among whom legal judgment is to be dispersed, and from whom norms of 'common decency' are to be drawn, is a *professional* fraternity in most accounts. The 'professional obligations' of the torture memos' authors are those most frequently cited as the norms they violated, and by which they must be held to account (Johnson 2009; Koh 2005: 654–55; Weisberg 2004: 300). As to the defensibility of the government attorneys' actions, Bilder and Vagts concluded that 'a final verdict on these matters is likely to emerge only out of the collective sentiment of the professional legal community' (Bilder and Vagts 2004: 694). The original substitution has been reinstated. It is the *discipline*, remember, that is suffering on the rack. It is the *profession* under thumbscrews. And it is the professional legal community (above all the community comprising international law specialists) that is imagined to emerge all the worthier for the ordeal. The turn outwards has rapidly become an encircling or gathering in.

Conscience

The call to an ethical commons is, nonetheless, one chastened by a Hobbesian suspicion of antinomian conscience (Andrew 1999). After all, critics have acknowledged that the lawyers concerned apparently believed themselves, and the cause for which they were working, to be right. Their affliction, those critics have reported, was not a lack of inwardness, but its excess. '[T]he torture debacle', Cornelia Pillard has written, was born in part of 'ideologically driven myopia' (Pillard 2006: 1297–98). The policies inscribed and endorsed in these memos were, according to Joshua Dratel, 'distorted by only a single, subjective point of view' (Dratel 2005: xxiii). Their vice, in Bradley Wendel's account, was one of 'ethical solipsism' (Wendel 2005a: 126). These memos were written, it seems, by the men of chapter 7 of *Leviathan*: 'men, vehemently in love with their own new opinions ... and obstinately bent to maintain them, [that] gave those opinions also that reverenced name of conscience, as if they would have it seem unlawful, to change or speak against them' (Hobbes 1651 [2005]: 51).

So, for all their appeals to ethics, outraged international lawyers have sensed the way of (Protestant) conscience to be paved with peril for their rule of law. And the rule of law itself has inspired ambivalence in this context. For the shock of these memos, for some, is the diligence, competence and Ivy League provenance of those whose names they bear (Weisberg 2004: 303). Karen Greenberg recited the credentials of the authors in *The Torture Papers*: these were Harvard men, Yale men. Their writings 'do not', she has noted, 'overlook basic ethical and legal questions'. Rather, their memos evidenced a search for 'legally viable argument' (Greenberg 2005: xvii). These would-be torturers' accomplices, José Álvarez has observed, are 'distinguished, accomplished, highly credentialed ... [and employed as] current or former professors of law at famous law schools' (Álvarez 2006: 176). Their memos enacted some 'clever' manipulation of legal norms (Wendel 2005b: 1210). International lawyers have long regarded as fraught the way of a legalism too 'punctilious' (Dratel 2005: xxii). Sensing these dangers, international lawyers draw the 'con' – the 'with' – of the conscience to which they would lay claim with circumspection.

So what would international lawyers invoking transparency against the 'darkness' of the torture memos have us see? What is the effect of this 'original lawlessness' by which international law is so transported? What is to emerge, it seems, is a Hobbesian 'public conscience', hoarded as a professional cache. Sensing contamination, international lawyers respond auto-immunely, to protect themselves against their own protective mechanisms (Borradori 2003: 93; Derrida 2005: 45). Faith *in* and *as* professionalism seeks to return law to its professional fold in order that it might be inoculated against excesses both of law and of conscience.

Witnessing torture, international lawyers respond with 'mineness', saying: let this suffering be mine that I might be saved (e.g., Horton 2005: 301). Witnessing a destructive faculty seemingly in charge of its decisions – will-to-power worn as conscience – international lawyers respond by disavowing the mine, saying: let this be dispersed that we might be saved (e.g., van

Boven 2006: 151). Witnessing law stinking of cruelty, international lawyers respond with a veil, saying: let this be lawlessness that we might be saved (Johns 2005). Witnessing the hordes rushing to judge, international lawyers respond with professionalism, saying: let us be the judges that we might not be judged (e.g., Bilder and Vagts 2004).

Hope, correction, community and conscience: in each mood, legal scholarly commentators writing about the torture memos and related reports have urged us towards international law's redemption. The route to redemption most favoured is one of learning to manage better international law's relation to that which it is not: that is, to one or other quasi-naturalized domain 'outside' or 'beyond' international law, greeted with both awe and anxiety (e.g., Paust 2007). In many of the foregoing accounts, that outside is the world of 'the Washington policy makers' or their counterparts in the executive branches and defence departments of other governments (van Boven 2006: 151; European Parliament 2007). Elsewhere, it is the secret, 'black[ened]' world of intelligence operatives and military personnel (Ross 2007: 587).

In so doing, legal scholars have reordered the international legal field to 'reinforce the position of its dominant parts', as if to structure every possible arrangement of its elements (Hallward 2003: 96; see generally Badiou 2007: 104–111). Yet that which could only partially be refused by international legal scholarship surrounding the torture memos' release was the unpresentable idea that the interactions between torturer and tortured of which it spoke might have been law-making acts and, moreover, that in those interactions detainees – as 'detainee-combatants' – might have begun to enact their radical inconsistency with the situation of which they would otherwise be presented as part.

The torture memos' release as event

For all the obsessive attention and regulatory fervour international lawyers and military policy makers alike have devoted to the figure of the terror-suspect detainee or 'unlawful combatant', this figure still seems to elude representation in international law. Despite its prevalence in domestic policy making, international lawyers have repeatedly insisted that the identity 'unlawful combatant' does not belong in or to international humanitarian law (Sassoli 2006; Zachary 2005). Similarly, decades of debate in international legal circles have failed to yield global agreement on how to define terrorism or the terrorist for legal purposes (Saul 2006). Awareness of these doctrinal failures or resistances, plus the fact of such figures being afforded relatively limited access to judicial review, have loomed much larger in international lawyers' vision than the many, overlapping layers of transnational and national regulation deployed with a view to these figures' containment. Their sense of such detainees as singularly and peculiarly lacking (the benefits of) law has also tended to impede international lawyers' attentiveness to the numerous ways in which access to judicial review is routinely compromised elsewhere and otherwise (by plea bargaining, constraints upon publicly funded legal aid, three-strikes-and-you're-out laws and the like). As a result, the person of an 'unlawful combatant' or terror-suspect detainee – one of the globe's most intensely regulated sites – is still widely perceived as one whose belonging international law has so far failed to ensure.

It is tempting to read this incongruity, as I have elsewhere, as symptomatic of international law's deployment of the sort of law–non-law distinctions on which it routinely relies to affirm its renewability and its relevance (Johns 2005). In this chapter, however, I have decided to venture another reading of international law's insistence upon this vacuity. In its feature of not being amenable to stable arrangement or classification with other elements of the international legal order, the multiples terror-suspect detainees or 'unlawful combatants' comprise what Badiou would call an 'evental site' within (but not a part of) international law (Badiou 2007: 173–77).

The void indicated by naming an event at this site would not be the fact of these detainees' supposed non-representation in or by international law at a particular point in time (the notion that they currently occupy a 'legal black hole' or a falsely fabricated legal category), but rather the persistence of their 'unpresentable errancy' (Badiou 2007: 110). The torture memos' release inscribes terror-suspect detainees as more errant than their being non-represented (or inadequately represented) would suggest. Scholarly commentary on and official military reactions to the torture memos have sought to place the figure of the terror-suspect detainee in some reliable way, whether as a figure of abject, mute suffering or as 'a faceless enemy whose hatred of the United States knew no limits' (Jones 2004: 12). Yet these efforts have failed. Like the proletariat or the category 'undocumented migrants', those detained in the war on terror (unnamed doctrinally as well as routinely unnamed as a matter of military record) occupy the absent centre of international legal debate surrounding torture, inhuman and degrading treatment practised in the name of the war on terror (Hallward 2003: 14).

International legal texts can draw near to the figure of the terror-suspect detainee in a posture of empathy, but cannot embrace him or her for fear of his or her agency; for fear, that is, of contamination by whatever deadly desires and faith-based motivations he or she might bring to bear. Hence, commentators vie to place themselves at the greatest possible remove from the prospect of aiding 'the' cause of terrorism. For international lawyers, it is those who would rewrite legal norms who risk conceding a 'victory for terrorism' (Dekker 2003: 327). So too, empathy is quickly redirected towards an embrace of, and lamentation for, the familiar: for Harold Koh, for instance, the 'American soldiers [at risk of being] tortured by foreign captors' and the 'soul' of the United States 'as a people' (Koh 2005: 659, 661). The 'world without torture' that Koh has sketched is, by implication, all the more reassuring by virtue of its banishment of the anxiety-producing figure of the tortured detainee (Koh 2005). Each drawing close to this figure triggers a drawing away, such that international law remains unable to redress the apparent unbonding from the international legal order that was, for international lawyers, one of the most alarming aspects of the torture memos' release. The repeated attempts at substitution described above – seeking to transpose the law itself into the role of mute suffering intended for the terror-suspect detainee – indicate the profound and persistent unrecognizability of the latter for international law.

The happening to which we might give the name 'event' at the site edged by the errant detainee or 'unlawful combatant' would be a realisation (or forcing) of the possibility that some of international law's primary representations – its claims to stand opposed to unquestioned and unquestionable violence and to be capable of managing the processes of its own making – might not be sustainable. This was precisely the happening signified by the torture memos' public release, an occurrence both exceptional (experienced as an unexpected shock) and universal (Hallward 2003: 107). The claims identified above were exposed in their failure by the torture memos' release because the torture memos documented a process of law making saturated with violence. Through the torture memos, international lawyers were invited to see the site of violent detention as a law-making site. Moreover, the law making happening there could in no way be described or circumscribed through any standard arrangement of international legal elements.

For the international law on torture, inhuman and degrading treatment, the tortured must remain prostrate; needy of protection and little else. The limits of legality have been designed for interpretative realization above or around the body of the tortured, but that body is to remain inert in the process. The definition of torture set forth in the 1984 Convention against Torture and Other Cruel, Inhuman or Degrading Treatment or Punishment, for instance, concerns itself wholly with the purposes of the torturer and the official consent or instigation granted to the torturer. The tortured is vested indirectly with rights, but those rights' sum total is no more than the status of being recognized as the person upon whom torture has been inflicted. All that registers of that person is his or her 'severe pain or suffering, whether physical or mental' (Torture Convention 1984).

The torture memos, however, revealed international law as a field of combat within which detainees were far from inert. Rather, detainees were actively resistant to and participating in a process recognized by all involved as law making: a violently embodied process entailing the promulgation of norms readied for application to other people and in other settings. Acting on contradictions latent within the multiples 'unlawful combatants' and terror-suspect detainees, detainees have assumed the configuration of a detainee-combatant by way of intervention in the international legal situation. One such detainee-combatant, Abu Zubaydeh, reported the following:

> I collapsed and lost consciousness on several occasions. Eventually the torture was stopped by the intervention of the doctor. I was told during this period that I was one of the first to receive these interrogation techniques, so no rules applied. It felt like they were experimenting and trying out techniques to be used later on other people. At the end of this period two women and a man came to interrogate me. I was still naked and, because of this, I refused to answer any questions. So they again repeatedly slapped me in the face and smashed me against the wall using the towel around my neck.
>
> (ICRC 2007: 31)

In Zubaydeh's account, he 'refuse[d] to answer questions' out of protest at his continued deprivation of clothing, mindful that these were 'techniques to be used later on other people'. Elsewhere, reports reveal recurrent techniques of resistance, each marking an attempt to subvert and reorder the law-making routines and relations in which they were called to participate. Affidavits of those reporting violent abuse, for example, document the efforts of detainee-combatants to recall and record publicly each others' names as well as those of the soldiers occupying the sites of their abuse: efforts some-times verging on the obsessive. The naming of names was, of course, vital to the evidence-gathering exercise in which detainee-combatants invited to give sworn statements understood themselves to be assisting (on the significance of detainees' naming as a site of struggle otherwise, see Schmitt 2009). Yet the ritual incantation of names in these statements seemed, at times, to exceed the requirements of evidentiary precision. By these methods, detainee-combatants sought, it seemed, to fill the space of their detention with a singularity and a collective agency that their captors would refuse them. The sworn statement of Nori Samir Gunbar Al-Yasseri is indicative in this respect:

> [a]fter this they make Hashim ... stand in front of me and they forced me to slap him in the face, but I refused cause [sic] he is my friend. After this they asked Hashim to hit me, so he punched my stomach. I asked him to do that so they don't beat him like they had beaten me when I refused to hit Hashim. Nori Samir, Hussein, Mustafa Mahadi Saleh, Hashim, Hiadar, Hathem, Ahmed Sabri; those are the names of the people who were there at this night which felt like 1000 nights ... I don't know the soldiers names, but I know what one of them looks like and this was their supervisor. The reason why I know him [is] because I saw him every single night I spent there.
>
> (Al-Yasseri 2004)

Shalan Said Alsharoni's sworn statement revealed a similar insistence upon proper names as markers in a setting otherwise disorienting and lifted, as it were, out of time:

> [o]ne of those days the guards tortured the prisoners. Those guards are Grainer, Davis and another man. First they tortured a man whose name is Amjid Iraqi ... And after that they beat up an Iraqi whose name is Assad ... Grainer beat up a man whose name is Ali the Syrian ... This is what I saw and what I remember to be true.
>
> (Alsharoni 2004)

Other statements recorded detainee-combatants straining to register, with their every sensory power, the exact details of what was happening to them, including faint clues as to their locale, as though they might, by this means, have been able to undo the conditions of sensory deprivation and profound isolation to which they were subjected. A sworn statement provided by Kasim Mehaddi Hilas that detailed abuse to which he had been exposed as a detainee included the following statement: 'Not one night for all the time I was there passed without me seeing, hearing or feeling what was happening to me' (Hilas 2004). A detainee-combatant named Khaled Shaik Mohammed reported, of one location, that '[d]uring my time at this place of detention I could hear planes taking off and landing', which led him to suggest, 'I think the place was Bagram' (ICRC 2007: 33). Later in the same report he remarked:

> I could see at one point that there was snow on the ground ... I think the country was Poland. I think this because on one occasion a water bottle was brought to me without the label removed. It had an email address ending in '.pl'. The central-heating system was an old style one that I would expect only to see in countries of the former communist system.
>
> (ICRC 2007: 34–35)

Like other detainee-combatants, Khaled Shaik Mohammed also insisted upon assuming the power of naming and at least a nominal power of repositioning in his account:

> [i]t was here that the most intense interrogation occurred, led by three experienced CIA interrogators, all over 65 years old and all strong and well trained. They were 'emirs'. Although of course they never revealed their own names, I gave them names by which I could refer to them, all beginning with 'Abu'. I think that 'Abu Captain' was of South American origin, whereas 'Abu Hannan' was perhaps of Moroccan origin and 'Abu White' was of Eastern European descent.
>
> (ICRC 2007: 35)

Other techniques too were used to enact the incongruent subject-position 'detainee-combatant' within international law. Through hunger strikes and suicide attempts, detainee-combatants reclaimed and reactivated bodies that international law would render torpid (McDonald 2005: 222–23).

For these detainee-combatants, the sites of their torture were not devoid of transnational norms surrounding their treatment and the treatment of others similarly categorized. Rather, they were engaged in a violent struggle over those norms' formation, a struggle to which they brought every means of resistance and every possibility of reoccupation available to them. It was this violent, novatory struggle that surfaced for international law in the torture memos and rendered them 'absolutely supernumerary to all that we [were] in the habit of counting' in the international law surrounding torture (Hallward 2003: 78). In seeking to assemble a novel legal regime around the sites of detainees' torture and abuse, the lawyers who wrote the torture memos were framing those sites in one sense just as the detainee-combatants quoted above had done: as sites for international law's profound remaking and violent reassertion. They were acknowledging, furthermore, that the processes of law making ongoing at these sites were being vigorously contested and that, accordingly, they were not processes over which either torturer or tortured (let alone the international law on sources as habitually known (Koskenniemi 2000)) had anything like complete control.

At the very point of their most insistent erasure by or within the international legal order (including scholarly understandings of it), detainee-combatants' agency punctured the surface of that order. The effectiveness of this happening so far has not been mediated by what it means to those whom it affects; rather, it has arisen from a failure of international legal meaning indicated by the unrepresentability of which I wrote above (Hallward 2003: 17, 24). It remains to be seen, but this may amount to an intervention comparable to Sigmund Freud's rendering of childhood as event; '[s]omething has happened, it cannot be erased, and the constitution of the subject depends upon it' (Hallward 2003: 113) – the subject being a law-bearing 'detainee-combatant' previously unknown to international law.

Conclusion

Badiou calls, upon the naming of or 'wager[ing]' on an event, for a division of those elements of the situation that fit the naming of this event and those that do not (Badiou 2007: 201, 232). To the former, I would assign all those initiatives and forms of activism that strive to grasp the 'not yet' that a politically embodied torture-victim-detainee-combatant might bring to the fore: among them, experiments in political organization in and around endemic, normatively encoded violence (Bailey 2009), as well as efforts to take account of, and engage politically with, the multiplicity of 'terrorists' and those who laud them, the discontinuity and fractile complexity of the 'networks' and 'cells' in which they are incessantly grouped, the diversity of projects in which they are engaged and the range of ways in which this multiple articulates with others – 'the poor' and 'the displaced', for instance. To the latter set, I would allot all those efforts – scholarly and otherwise – whereby the encounter that the torture memos' release occasioned is to be corrective, salutary or redemptive for international law as habitually known. According to Badiou's prescription:

> [i]t is not from the world, in however ideal a manner, that the event holds its inexhaustible reserve, its silent (or indiscernible) excess, but from its being unattached to it, its being separate, lacunary.
>
> (Badiou 1990: 180)

If the torture memos' release is to be an 'uncountable zero of a new time (a new calendar, a new order of history)' (Hallward 2003: 115), then the law-making detainee-combatant, and figures of fidelity to its emergence, must yet make it so.

Note

* My thanks to Richard Bailey, Emilios Christodoulidis and Jacqueline Mowbray for their generosity in reading and commenting on earlier drafts of this chapter.

References

Ackerman, B. *et al.* (2004) 'Lawyers' statement on Bush Administration's torture memos' (4 August 2004). Available online at: <http://physiciansforhumanrights.org/library/documents/non-phr/lawyers-statement-on-bush.pdf> (accessed 21 August 2009).

Alsharoni, S.S. (2004) 'Translation of statement provided by Shalan Said Alsharoni, detainee # 150422' (17 January 2004). Available online at: <www.washingtonpost.com/wp-srv/world/iraq/abughraib/150422.pdf> (accessed 1 September 2009).

Álvarez, J. (2006) 'Torturing the law', *Case Western Reserve Journal of International Law* 37: 175.

Al-Yasseri, N.S.G. (2004) 'Sworn statement – Al-Yasseri, Nori Samir Gunbar' (17 January 2004). Available online: <http://media.washingtonpost.com/wp-srv/world/iraq/abughraib/7787.pdf> (accessed 1 September 2009).

American Civil Liberties Union (2009) 'Index of Bush-Era OLC memoranda relating to interrogation, detention, rendition and/or surveillance' (3 May 2009). Available online at: <www.aclu.org/pdfs/safefree/olcmemos_2009_0305.pdf> (accessed 11 May 2009).

Amnesty International (2006) 'Beyond Abu Ghraib: detention and torture in Iraq'. Available online at: <www.amnesty.org/en/library/info/MDE14/001/2006> (accessed 1 September 2009).

Andrew, E.G. (1999) 'Hobbes on conscience within the law and without', *Canadian Journal of Political Science* 32: 203.

Badiou, A. (1990) 'Le pli: Leibniz et la baroque', in F. Wahl (ed.), *Annuaire Philosophique 1988–1989*, Paris: Seuil; trans. T. Sowley (1994) as 'Gilles Deleuze, the fold, Leibniz and the baroque' in C. Boundas and D. Olkowski (eds), *Gilles Deleuze: The Theatre of Philosophy*, New York: Columbia University Press.

——(2007) *Being and Event*, trans. O. Feltham, London, New York: Continuum.

Bailey, R. (2009) 'Up against the wall: bare life and resistance in the camp', *Law and Critique* 2:2. Available online at: <www.springerlink.com/content/l456v46062617731/fulltext.pdf> (accessed 3 September 2009).

Bilder, R.B. (2006) 'On being an international lawyer', *Loyola International Law Review* 3: 135.

Bilder, R.B. and Vagts, D.F. (2004) 'Speaking law to power: lawyers and torture', *American Journal of International Law* 98: 689.

Borradori, G. (2003) *Philosophy in a Time of Terror: Dialogues with Jürgen Habermas and Jacques Derrida*, Chicago, IL: University of Chicago Press.

Brazin, J. (2004) 'Pentagon report set framework for use of torture', *Wall Street Journal*. Online posting. Available online at: <www.wsj.com/> (accessed 9 July 2009).

Broadhead, P.J. (1996) 'Guildsmen, religious reform, and the search for the common good: the role of the guilds in the early reformation in Augsburg', *Historical Journal* 39: 577.

Bybee, J.S. (2002) 'Memorandum for Alberto R. Gonzales, Counsel to the President, from Jay S. Bybee, Asst. Atty. General, standards of conduct for interrogation under 18 USC. 2340–2340A', 1 August 2002, reprinted in K.J. Greenberg and J.L. Dratel (2005) *The Torture Papers: The Road to Abu Ghraib*, Cambridge: Cambridge University Press.

Clark, K. (2005) 'Ethical issues raised by the OLC torture memorandum', *Journal of National Security Law and Policy* 1: 455.

Convention against Torture and Other Cruel, Inhuman or Degrading Treatment or Punishment (Torture Convention) (1984) 'G.A. res. 39/46, annex, 39 UN GAOR Supp. (No. 51) at 197, UN Doc. A/39/51 (1984)'. Available online at: <www2.ohchr.org/english/law/cat.htm> (accessed 1 September 2009).

Danner, M. (2004) *Torture and Truth: America, Abu Ghraib, and the War on Terror*, New York: New York Review of Books.

——(2009) 'The Red Cross torture report: what it means', *New York Review of Books* 56:7. Available online at: <www.nybooks.com/articles/22614> (accessed 9 July 2009).

Dekker, I. (2003) 'Declaration on the fight against terrorism and the protection of human rights – a resolvable conflict', *Helsinki Monitor* 14: 327.

Derrida, J. (2005) *Rogues: Two Essays on Reason*, Stanford: Stanford University Press.

Dratel, J. (2005) 'The legal narrative', in K.J. Greenberg and J.L. Dratel (eds), *The Torture Papers: The Road to Abu Ghraib*, Cambridge: Cambridge University Press, 2005.

European Parliament (2007), *Report on the alleged use of European countries by the CIA for the transportation and illegal detention of prisoners*', Eur. Parl. Doc. A6–0020/2007.

Fletcher, G.P. (2004) 'Black hole in Guántanamo Bay', *Journal of International Criminal Justice* 2: 121.

Greenberg, K.J. (2005) 'From fear to torture', in K.J. Greenberg and J.L. Dratel (eds), *The Torture Papers: The Road to Abu Ghraib*, Cambridge: Cambridge University Press, 2005.

Greenberg, K.J. and Dratel, J.L. (2005) *The Torture Papers: The Road to Abu Ghraib*, Cambridge: Cambridge University Press.

Hallward, P. (2003) *Badiou: A Subject to Truth*, Minneapolis: University of Minnesota Press.

Hilas, K.M. (2004) 'Translation of statement provided by Kasim Mehaddi Hilas, Detainee #151108' (18 January 2004) Available online: <http://media.washingtonpost.com/wp-srv/world/iraq/abughraib/151108.pdf> (accessed 1 September 2009).

Hobbes, T. (1651) *Leviathan*, ed. A.P. Martinich (2005) *Leviathan: Parts I and II*, Peterborough, Ontario: Broadview Press.

Horton, S. (2005) 'Legal ethics and the war on terror: the role of the government lawyer: ethics lawyers and the torture memoranda', *American Society of International Law Proceedings* 99: 301.

Human Rights Watch (2006a) 'By the numbers'. Available online: <http://hrw.org/reports/2006/ct0406/> (accessed 11 May 2009).

——(2006b), '"No blood, no foul": soldiers' accounts of detainee abuse in Iraq'. Available online: <http://www.hrw.org/reports/2006/us0706/> (accessed 11 May 2009).

Inspector General of the US Department of the Army (DAIG) (2004) 'Detainee operations inspection' (21 July 2004). Available online: <www.4.army.mil/ocpa/reports/ArmyIGDetaineeAbuse/> (accessed 11 May 2009).

International Committee of the Red Cross (ICRC) (2004) *Report of the International Committee of the Red Cross on the treatment by the coalition forces of prisoners of war and other persons protected by the Geneva Conventions in Iraq during arrest, internment and interrogation.* Available online: <www.globalsecurity.org/military/library/report/2004/icrc_report_iraq_feb2004.htm> (accessed 11 May 2009).

——(2007) *ICRC report on the detention of fourteen 'high-value detainees' in CIA custody.* Available online: <www.nybooks.com/icrc-report.pdf> (accessed 11 May 2009).

Jackson, A.R. (2006) 'The White House Counsel torture memo: the final product of a flawed system', *California Western Law Review* 42: 149.

Johns, F. (2005) 'Guantanamo Bay and the Annihilation of the Exception', *European Journal of International Law*, 16(4): 613.

Johnson, C. (2009) 'Judge invited to testify about role in interrogation memos', *Washington Post* (30 April 2009), A07.

Jones, A.R. (2004) 'Article 15–16 investigation of the Abu Ghraib Prison and 205th Military Intelligence Brigade' (23 August 2004). Available online: <http://slate.msn.com/features/whatistorture/pdfs/FayJonesReport.pdf> (accessed 28 August 2009).

Koh, H.H. (2005) 'A world without torture', *Columbia Journal of Transnational Law* 43: 641.

Koskenniemi, M. (ed.) (2000) *Sources of International Law*, Aldershot; Burlington, USA: Ashgate/Dartmouth.

Langbein, J.H. (2004) 'The legal history of torture', in S. Levinson (ed.), *Torture: A Collection*, Oxford, New York: Oxford University Press.

Leopold, J. (2009) 'CIA interrogation tapes predated torture memo'. Available online at: <www.pubrecord.org/torture/827-court-docs-suggest-detainees-tortured-before-cia-received-legal-ok.html> (accessed 9 July 2009).

Lewis, A. (2005) 'Introduction', in K.J. Greenberg and J.L. Dratel (eds), *The Torture Papers: The Road to Abu Ghraib*, Cambridge: Cambridge University Press, 2005.

Liptak, A. (2004) 'Legal scholars criticize memos on torture', *New York Times.* Available online at: <www.nytimes.com/2004/06/25/politics/25LEGA.html> (accessed 9 July 2009).

Lopez, M. (2005) 'Professional responsibility: tortured independence in the office of legal counsel', *Florida Law Review* 57: 685.

McDonald, A. (2005) 'The year in review', *Yearbook of International Humanitarian Law* 8: 221.

McMahan, J. (2009) *Killing in War*, Oxford: Oxford University Press.

Mayerfield, J. (2007) 'Playing by our own rules: how US marginalization of international human rights law led to torture', *Harvard Human Rights Journal* 20: 89.

Mazzetti, M. and Shane, S. (2009) 'Interrogation memos detail harsh tactics by the CIA', *New York Times.* Available online at: <www.nytimes.com/2009/04/17/us/politics/17detain.html?_r=1> (accessed 9 July 2009).

Nowak, M. (2006) 'What practices constitute torture?: US and UN standards', *Human Rights Quarterly* 28: 809.

Orford, A. (1999) 'Muscular humanitarianism: reading the narratives of the new interventionism', *European Journal of International Law* 10: 679.

Oxford English Dictionary (OED) (2nd edn, 1989) *OED Online*. Oxford: Oxford University Press. Available online at: <http://dictionary.oed.com> (accessed 9 July 2009).

Paust, J.J. (2007) *Beyond the Law: The Bush Administration's Unlawful Responses in the 'War' on Terror*, New York: Cambridge University Press.

Physicians for Human Rights (2005) 'Break them down: systematic use of psychological torture by US Forces'. Available online at: <http://physiciansforhumanrights.org/library/report-2005-may.html> (accessed 11 May 2009).

Pillard, C. (2006) 'Unitariness and myopia: the executive branch, legal process, and torture', *Indiana Law Journal* 81: 1297.

Rosen, J. (2004) 'The struggle over the torture memos', *New York Times*. Available online at: <www.nytimes.com/2004/08/15/weekinreview/15rose.html> (accessed 9 July 2009).

Ross, J. (2007) 'Black letter abuse: the US legal response to torture since 9/11', *International Review of the Red Cross* 89: 561.

Sadat, L.N. (2007) 'Extraordinary rendition, torture and other nightmares from the war on terror', *George Washington Law Review* 75: 1200.

Sands, P. (2008a) *Torture Team: Rumsfeld's Memo and the Betrayal of American Values*, Hampshire: Palgrave Macmillan.

——(2008b) 'Torture team: the responsibility of lawyers for abusive interrogation', *Melbourne Journal of International Law* 9: 365.

Sassoli, M. (2006) 'Is there a status of "unlawful combatant"?', *International Law Studies Series. US Naval War College* 80: 57.

Saul, B. (2006) *Defining Terrorism in International Law*, Oxford: Oxford University Press.

Schmitt, E. (2009) 'US shifts, giving detainee names to the Red Cross', *New York Times*, 23 August 2009, A1.

Taguba, A.M. (2004) *Article 15–6 investigation of the 800th Military Police Brigade* (March 2004). Available online at: <www.npr.org/iraq/2004/prison_abuse_report.pdf> (accessed 11 May 2009).

van Boven, T. (2006) 'The torture papers: the road to Abu Ghraib', *Netherlands International Law Review* 53: 149 (book review).

Waldron, J. (2005) 'Torture and positive law: jurisprudence for the White House', *Columbia Law Review* 105: 1681.

Weisberg, R.H. (2004) 'Loose professionalism, or why lawyers take the lead on torture', in S. Levinson (ed.), *Torture: A Collection*, Oxford, New York: Oxford University Press, 2004.

Welling, J.C. (1892) 'The law of torture: a study in the evolution of law', *American Anthropologist* 5: 193.

Wendel, W.B. (2005a) 'Legal ethics and the separation of law and morals', *Cornell Law Review* 91: 67.

——(2005b) 'Professionalism as interpretation', *Northwestern University Law Review* 99: 1167.

Zachary, S. (2005) 'Between the Geneva Conventions: where does the unlawful combatant belong?', *Israeli Law Review* 38: 378.

Index

actually existing socialism (AES) 113–15
Adorno, Theodor 24, 26
Afghanistan 260
aggression 256
Akayesu trial 165–66, 169–73
Alexander VI, pope 22
Alexy, Robert 132
Alfonso V of Portugal, king 22
Algerian militants 97, 138–39
Almansi, A 216
al-Qaeda 240–41
Alsharoni, Shalan Said 273
Álvarez, José 268
Al-Yasseri, Nori Samir Gunbar 272
Americas *see* New World; United States
Amin, S 193
amnesties 157
Anderson, S 196
Anghie, A 209
Annan, Kofi 165–66
antinomian conscience 267–68
apartheid 117–29
Aquinas, Thomas 32, 47
Arendt, Hannah 93, 225, 227
Argibay, Carmen 152
Aristotle 32, 50
Arnand, RP 254
arrest warrants 165
Arrighi, G 191, 193–95, 203
Ayala, Guamán Poma de 33–34, 37–40

Baader, Andreas 135
Baader-Meinhoff trial 135–36
Badiou, Alain 6–7, 86–87, 106–7, 114–15,
    131–36, 138, 141–43, 260, 262, 270,
    274–75
Balassa, B 211, 216
Balibar, E 187

Barbie, Klaus 142
Barker, Pat 151, 153
Bashir, Omar Hassan Ahmad al 165
Battle in Seattle film 230–32
Bauer, PT 211, 214–15
Bello, W 201
Benjamin, Walter 18–21, 27, 32, 40
Beaulac, Stéphane 57–58
Bhagwati, PN 152, 192
Bilder, Richard 264, 266, 267
Bishop, W 252
Boas, Franz 172
Bosnian resistance 84–85, 87
Boutros-Ghali, Boutros 118, 119
Brandeis, Louis 263
Braudal, F 194–95
Brierly, Ian 73, 251–52
Brown, Wendy 95
Burgos debates 29
Bush, George W 242, 257–58, 266
Butler, Judith 23–25
Byatt, AS 148, 150, 158
Bynkershoek, Cornelius van 254

Calvino, Italo 148
Catholic Church, universal jurisdiction
    of the 21–22
Cavanagh, J 196
Charles V of Spain, king 30
Chatterjee, P 97
China 81
Chinkin, Christine 152
Christian and non-Christian
    world 21–24, 49
Christianity 21–24, 49, 52
chronology of events 3, 4
citizenship 185–89, 223–24
civil society 123, 221–25

civilized and uncivilized 24, 33, 36, 63, 97, 209, 253
Clark, Kathleen 265
Coetzee, JM 148
Cold War 92, 108–10, 118, 122, 126–28, 249
collective humanitarian intervention 108, 111–12
colonialism and imperialism *see also* New World
Christianity 52; civilizing mission 63, 97, 253; Declaration on Independence 94–98, 101; decolonization 24, 91–102, 122, 253, 255–57; dominant narrative 251; International Criminal Tribunal for Rwanda 166, 173; Iraq, war and regime change in 253; nation states 51–52; Peace of Westphalia 1648 18, 21–24; post-colonial states 24–26; regime change 252–53; Spain 51; state socialism in 1989, collapse of 109, 110; textbooks 251–52, 253; Third World 237–39; Tokyo Women's Tribunal and fiction 154–56; United Nations 93–98, 101, 249; Valladolid events 32–33, 36–37; violence 18, 21; World Trade Organization 213
Columbus, Christopher 22, 26
comfort women 146–47, 150–60
command responsibility 84, 87
conditional aid 214–15
conscience 267–68
conscription 82–83, 86
Cornell, Drucilla 38–39
counter-positions in international legal argument, loss of 109–10
creation of international law 44–45
crimes against humanity 126, 166, 168–69, 172–73
Critchley, Simon 86–87
critical Third World perspective 236–37
culture 24, 166, 171–74
Curtin, D 177
customary law 2, 76, 247

de Gouges, Olympe 96
decolonization; Algerian War 97; civilizing mission 97; Cold War 92; Declaration on Independence (UN) 94–98, 101; development 98–101; eventness of international law 91–102; Goa incident 1961 255–57; human rights 94–97; institutions, radicalization of international 93; international law 91–94; Iraq, war and regime change in 253; Mandela, Nelson, liberation of 122; nation states 24, 96–97; New International Economic Order 100; Permanent Sovereignty over Natural Resources 100; post-colonial event, as 101–2; resistance movements 92; role of international law 92–93, 100; United Nations 93–95; United States 92, 94–99; Universal Declaration of Human Rights 94–95; universality 92–99, 101–2
Deleuze, Gilles 227
democracy 108, 110–11
dependency 52, 211
deregulation 110
Derrida, Jacques 7–8, 45, 47, 66
Desforges, Alison 170, 171
determinacy 46, 51, 75–77, 78
developing countries 98–101, 193, 199–200, 207–19 *see also* Third World
development 207–19
diplomacy 59
discipline 1, 2, 4, 6
discourse theory 132–33
discovery 21–27, 29–30, 178, 181–87
discrimination 117–29, 166–68, 172, 188
Dolgopol, Ustinia 152
Douzinas, C 168, 174
Dratel, Joshua 265, 266, 268
Dubois, Pierre 178
Dugard, J 94
Dunkley, G 197
Dutch East India Company 191, 193
Dworkin, Ronald 149

Eagleton, Terry 87
economics; constitutionalism 110; crises 215–17; developing countries 210–11, 215–17; liberalism 108
English East India Company 191, 193
Ensslin, Gudrun 136
equality 237, 266
ethical commons 267–68
ethno-nationalist and regional violence 111
European Union 177–89; citizenship 185–89; discovery 181–85, 187; exploration 181–82; family reunion 185–87; free movement of workers

178–79, 182–84; freedom to provide
services 179; freedoms 178–89;
integration 177–80, 184; internal market
179–80; land appropriation 177–78,
184–85; nationality discrimination 188;
norms 177; qualifications, recognition of
professional 180–81; rights 185–86;
Rome Treaty 178, 185–87; self-
determination 111; settlement 187–88;
Single European Act 179–80; social
benefits, access to 188–89; state socialism
in 1989, collapse of 111; supremacy 177;
World Trade Organization 200
'Event Horizon' 224–25
event of the event 47–51
evental moments 5–8
evental sites 5–8
eventing international law 1–4
expertise 30–31, 38–41, 269–74
exploration 181–82

family reunion 185–87
Fanon, Frantz 36
Fauchille, P 254
feminism 237, 238
Ferdinand, king 22
Ferguson, Niall 107, 179
fetishism of ideologies 173–75
fiction see Tokyo Women's Tribunal
and fiction
First World War 71–72
Fitzpatrick, Peter 66, 171, 182
Fletcher, George 264
force, use of see use of force
foreign direct investment 192–93,
197–98
Foucault, Michel 64
foundations 5–6, 18–21
France 59–60
France, Anatole 239
Free Association 226–27
freedoms, European Union and 178–89
Freud, Sigmund 274

G77 238
GATT 193, 198–204, 210–11, 217–18
General Assembly (UN) 246, 247–48,
252, 255–57
Geneva 1949 87
Geneva Conventions 81, 83–84, 87
genocide 165–75
Gentili, A 254

globalization 106, 108–9, 116, 126–27,
196, 201–2, 240
Goa incident 1961 255–57
God; divine violence 21; natural law
43, 47–48
Gorbachev, Mikhail 249
governance 110–11
government legal advisers, role of 266–67
Gray, J 192, 195–96
Greenberg, Karen 263, 265, 268
Gross, Leo 58, 62
Grotius, Hugo 26, 36, 43–44, 50, 254
groundlessness 5–6
group survival 30–31

Hague Convention 1907 154
Hague Regulations 81, 84
Hall, Catherine 179, 181
Hall, William 254
Hallward, Peter 133, 137, 142–43
Harrelson, Woody 222, 230
Hegel, GWF 165, 171, 173
hegemony 110, 112
Henkin, Louis 1
Hilas, Kasim Mehaddi 273
Hirohito, emperor 150–51, 153
Hobbes, Thomas 267–68
Hollywood 230–32
Holy Roman Empire 69
Horton, Scott 263, 265, 267
human rights; decolonization 94–97;
Mandela, Nelson, liberation of 126–28;
September 11, 2001, terrorist attacks on
the United States 242; state socialism in
1989, collapse of 107, 108, 111–12;
truncation and reduction 111–12;
United States 112; Universal Declaration
of Human Rights 94–95, 120;
universality 97
humanitarian intervention 108, 111–12
humanity, crimes against 126, 166,
168–69, 172–73
Hungary, invasion of 250, 256
Hurtado, C 216
Hussein, Saddam 253, 255
Hyde, Charles 253

ideologies, fetishism of 173–75
imperialism see colonialism and
imperialism
impoverishment of international legal
discourse 109–10

industrialization 210–11
instability of international law 92–93, 100
intellectual property treaties 203–4
international community, advent of
   107, 110
International Court of Justice (ICJ)
   121, 247
International Criminal Court (ICC),
   arrest warrants issued by 165
International Criminal Tribunal for Rwanda
   (ICTR) 165–75; *Akayesu* trial 165–66,
   169–73; colonialism 166, 173; crimes
   against humanity 166,168–69, 172–73;
   culture 166, 171–74; fetishism of
   ideologies 173–75; Genocide Convention
   166; human/humanitarian 166–67; racial
   other 166–68, 172; savage-victims-
   saviour metaphor 166–67; subjective
   intent 169; truth and consequences
   168–73; war nexus, elimination of 165
International Criminal Tribunal for the
   former Yugoslavia 84–85
international financial institutions, soft
   law of 108
International Monetary Fund (IMF) 216–17
international organizations 60–61, 123
international relations; origins 55;
   mythical, as 38–41
Iraq, war and regime change in 246–58;
   civilization 253; colonialism 246,
   251–54; customary law 247;
   decolonization 253; dominant narrative
   250–52; General Assembly 246, 252;
   International Court of Justice 247;
   international law 246–50, 254; Kuwait,
   invasion of 248–49, 255; new
   international law 254; *Nicaragua* case
   247; non-use of force 246–50; resolutions
   248–49; self-defence 247; self-
   determination 248, 252; Third World
   239; UN Charter 247–48, 252; UN
   General Assembly 247–48, 252; UN
   Security Council 246–49, 257–58;
   universalism 254; use of force 246–50
Isabella of Spain, queen 22
ius gentium 18, 35–37, 48–49
ius inter gentes 48

Jaastad, A 216
Jackson, Aaron 265
Japan *see* Tokyo Women's Tribunal
   and fiction

Jha, CS 255
joint stock companies 193–94
Jonas, H 35
just war 33–34, 250, 255

Kamen, H 51
Kant, Immanuel 178, 223
Kennedy, D 41, 76
Kennedy, John 99
Koh, Harold 265, 270–71
Korean War 256
Koskenniemi, Martii 76, 139
Krasner, Stephen 55, 58, 60
Krueger, AO 211, 216
Kunz, T 94
Kuwait, invasion of 248–49, 255

Lal, D 211, 212–15
land appropriation 177–78, 184–85
Las Casas, Bartolomé de 32, 39
Latin America, economic crises in
   216–17
law-making violence and law-preserving
   violence 19–20
Le Suer, James D 97
League of Nations 208, 209
legitimacy 21, 23, 78, 132, 142, 149
Leibniz, Gottfried 36, 38, 171
levée en masse 81–84; arms, carrying 84;
   Bosnian resistance 84–85, 87;
   characteristics 84; China 81; command
   responsibility 84, 87; conscription
   82–83, 86; enemy forces, approach of 84;
   Geneva 1949 86; Geneva Conventions
   81, 83–84, 87; Hague Regulations 81,
   84; International Criminal Tribunal for
   the former Yugoslavia 84–85; lawfare 82;
   organisation or structure, absence of
   84–85; Paris 1793 81, 83, 86; Paris
   1949 81; Paris Commune 1871 85–88;
   prisoner of war status under Geneva
   Conventions 83–84; Second World War
   83; total war 83; war, laws of 84, 85;
   warlaw 82; Warsaw Uprising 1955 83
Lévi-Strauss, Claude 172
liberalism 108, 211–12
liberalization 199–201, 207, 211
Little, Ian 215
logic of international law 44–47
Louis XVI, trial of 130–31, 138, 140
Luhmann, Niklas 132–34, 142
Lyons, Carole189

Macmillan, F 196–97
Macmillan, Harold 91
Malebranche, Nicolas 47
Malinowski, B 171
Mamdani, M 168, 172
Mandela, Nelson, liberation of 117–29;
    ANC (African National Congress)
    119–22; apartheid 117–29; civil society,
    contribution of 123; Cold War 118, 122,
    126–28; crime against humanity,
    apartheid as 126; Declaration on
    Apartheid 1989 (UN) 121;
    decolonization 122; globalization
    126–27; human rights 126–28; internal
    forces 119; International Court of Justice
    121; international law 117–21, 124–26,
    128–29; international organizations 123;
    national liberation movements 122,
    127–28; pan-African or third world
    solidarity 122–23; sanctions 120, 122,
    123–24; state sovereignty 120–21;
    United Nations 117–24; United States
    122; Universal Declaration of Human
    Rights 120
Marchart, O 5
Marxism 115–16, 173–75
mass uprisings see levée en masse
Mbeki, Thabo 128
McCain, John 242–43
McDonald, Gabrielle Kirk 152
Mead, Margaret 172
memory, marginalization of 240–41
Mickelson, Karin 236
Milošević trial 139–40, 142
Minkkinen, P 75
modernization theories 210–11
Mohammed, Khaled Shaik 273
Moore, Mike 218–19
Morrison, Toni 148
multinationals 193–98
Mutua, M 167, 238
myths; international law 38–41;
    international relations 38–41;
    New World 22–23; origin myths 56,
    64–66, 67; Peace of Westphalia as a
    myth 1, 57, 63–66, 67; power 20;
    universal law, mythical belief in 24, 26;
    violence 20–21

names and naming 272–73
nation states see also state sovereignty;
    colonialism and imperialism 24, 51–52;

commonality 44, 46; creation of
    international law 44–45; decolonization
    24, 96–97; definition 45; dependency
    52; emergence 55–58, 61; international
    law 44–45, 51; multinationals,
    interdependence with 193–98; origins
    44–45; Peace of Westphalia 1648 18,
    20, 24, 44, 50–51, 55–56; recognition
    44–45
national liberation movements 92, 122,
    127–28
nationality discrimination 188, 249
nationalism 50, 51–52, 111
nations, law of (ius gentium) 18, 35–37,
    48–49
natural justice 23
natural law 19–21, 32–33, 36, 43,
    48–50
natural resources 100
Negri, Toni 142
neo-classicalism 214
neoliberalism 110, 207–8, 211–12,
    214, 218
New Haven School 2, 249–50
New International Economic Order
    (NIEO) 100, 110, 238
New Left 115
New World; anger 23–24; Catholic
    Church, universal jurisdiction of the
    21–22; Christian and non-Christian
    world 21–24, 49; civilized and barbaric
    24; commonality 23; delegitimization of
    difference 23; discovery, event of 21–27,
    29–30, 32–36, 178, 186; donation of
    Americas 34–35, 37; force of law 22;
    global justice 23; imperialism 48–49;
    justification for violence 19; myth
    22–23; nationalism 50; nations, law of
    (ius gentium) 49; natural justice 23;
    objectification 18; papal bulls 22;
    patriarchal protection 34; Peace of
    Westphalia 1648 18–19, 21–22; perfect
    communities 29–30; salvation 22–23
self-governing capacity of Amerindians 32,
    37; unification of humanity 23;
    universality 24–26; Valladolid events
    29–41; violence 18–27, 32
new world order 106–7, 112
Nicaragua case 247
Nicolas V, pope 22
Nietzsche, Friedrich 50–51
Nomos of the Earth. Schmitt, Carl 177

non-governmental organizations
(NGOs) 221
norms 24–25, 120–21, 125, 177, 210

Offe, C 113
Oppenheim, LFL 253, 254
Oric, Nasar 87
OSCE National Minorities 111
opinio juris 75
origin myths 54, 65–66, 67
Owen, Wilfred 151

Pal, Radhabinod 157
Paris 1793 81–83; Committee of Public
Safety 81, 83; conscription 82; *levee en
masse* 81, 83, 86; mass recruitment
81–82; Napoleonic France 82–83, 86;
violence in war, regulation of 81
Paris 1949 81–88
Paris Commune 1872, *levee en masse* and
85–88
past in literature, return to the
148–50, 151
past international law, fiction of 146–47
PCIJ article 38 and doctrine of sources of
international law 69–79; adoption of
Article 69; Advisory Committee of
Jurists 71; content from form,
distinguishing 73–74; correctness 75–77;
customary law 76; definitions 76–77;
determinacy 75–77, 78; event of article
38 70–72; First World War 71–72;
formalization 72, 74–75, 77–78;
hierarchy 76; legitimacy 78; open and
closed lists of sources 73, 77; *opinio iuris*
75; relevance 75–76; sources of
international law, doctrine of 69–72;
standardization 72–74, 75, 77–78; state
practice 75, 76; textbooks 73; treaties
77; types of sources 72–73; universality
73, 78
Peace of Westphalia 1648 1, 55–67;
autonomy 60; balance of power 19;
before Westphalia, sovereignty before 55,
58–59, 61; Catholic Church, universal
jurisdiction of the 21–22; centralized
authority before Westphalia, existence of
55, 58–59, 61; challenges to sovereignty
60–61, 67; civilized and non-civilized
nations 63; colonization 18, 21–24;
consolidation of notion of sovereignty
55–56, 57–59; definition of modern

sovereignty 56; diplomacy 59; emergence
of nation states 55–58, 61; France
59–60; historical and memory 56,
57–63; Holy Roman Empire 59–60;
law-making violence 19–20; law-
preserving violence 19–20; modern
international relations, origin of 55;
modern sovereignty, Peace as origin of
55, 60, 64–67; myth, Peace of
Westphalia as a 1, 57, 63–66, 67; nation
states 18, 20, 24, 44, 50–51, 55–56;
nations, law of 18; New World 18–19,
21–22; norms 24–25; origin myths 56,
64–66, 67; overlapping authorities 61;
positive law 19–21; post-colonial states
24–26; power 20, 25–26; religious
settlement 61–63; sovereignty 20,
55–67; supranational authority 61;
Sweden 60; territorial settlements 59–60;
universality 24–27, 56; violence 19–21,
24–26
people, law governing relations between
(ius inter gentes) 48
perfect communities 29–31, 33, 36, 50
Permanent Court of International Justice
see PCIJ article 38 and doctrine of
sources of international law 69
Permanent Mandates Commission 209, 214
Permanent Sovereignty over Natural
Resources 100
Philip II of Spain, king 32
Phillimore, R 254
Philpot, Daniel 55–56, 58, 60, 62–63
Pillard, Cornelia 267–68
political trials as events 130–43; Algerian
militants 138–39; Baader-Meinhoff trial
135–36; containment and confinement
132–34; discourse theory 132–33;
displacement 141–42; emancipatory
theory 134; eventual site, trial as 131,
136–38; foreclosure 137;
institutionalization of proceedings
132–33; legitimacy 132, 142; Louis
XVI, trial of 130–31, 138, 140;
Milošević trial 139–40, 142; negation,
meaning of 134–36; openness 132;
resistance 131, 138; rupture in
courtroom, strategies of 138–43;
situation, trial as 131, 132–38, 140;
structural fragility 141; truth 130–31,
134–35, 138; void of situations 131,
136–38

politics 5–7 *see also* state socialism in 1989, collapse of
Portugal, Goa incident 1961 and 255–57
positive law 19–21, 115–16
post-colonial states 24–26
post-foundational scholarship 5–6
post-structuralism 237, 238
power 2, 20, 25–26, 30
prisoner of war status under Geneva Conventions 83–84
privatization 110
professional qualifications, recognition of 180–81
protectionism 193
Pufendorf, Samuel 254

Quaye, CO 95

racial other 166–68, 172
racism 117–29, 166–68, 172
Rajagopal, Balakrishnan 93, 236
rape crimes 145–47, 149–60
Raspe, Jan-Carl 136
rational choice 207, 212–14
raw material, events as 2–3
Reagan, Ronald 122
realism 38–40
recession 109, 214
reciprocity 40–41
recognition, constitutive and evidentiary theory of 44–45
regime change 246–58
Reisman, Michael 2, 3
relativism 240–43, 265
religious settlement 61–63
renewal 2, 107
resistance movements 92, 122, 127–28, 249
revitalization of international law and institutions 107
Ricardo, D 193–95
Rivers, William 151
Robespierre, Maximilien de 130–31, 138, 140
Roman law 35
Rousseau, Jean-Jacques 178
rule of law 268
rupture 4, 138–43, 226
Russell, Bertrand 147
Rwanda *see* International Criminal Tribunal for Rwanda (ICTR)

Sadat, Leila 263
Sahovic, M 252
salvation 22–23
sanctions 120, 122, 123–24
Sands, Philippe 265, 267
Sartre, Jean-Paul 147
Sassoon, Siegfried 151
savage-victims-saviour metaphor 166–67
Schmitt, Carl 177–78
Schwarzenberger, Georg 253
Scitovsky, Tibor 215
Scott, Maurice 215
Seattle protests against the World Trade Organization 221–32
Second World War 83, 145–60
Security Council (UN) 112, 246–49, 255, 257–58
security relativism 240–43
self-defence 12, 247
self-determination 248, 252, 255–56
Sepúlveda, Juan Ginés de 32, 35
September 11, 2001, terrorist attacks on the United States from; Third World perspective 234–43; al-Qaeda 240–41; geographical globalism 240; human rights 242; memory, marginalization 240–41; security relativism 240–43; torture 241–42
sexual slavery 146–47, 149–50
Shaw, MN 3
Singh Mehta, Uday 36–37
situations; definition 133–34; political trials 131, 232–38, 140; void of situations 131, 136–38
slavery 32, 146–47, 149–50, 155
Smith, A 191–95
Smuts, Jan 120
social benefits, access to 188–89
socialism 237 *see also* state socialism in 1989, collapse of
Sørensen, Max 253
Sornarajah, M 239
sources of international law *see* PCIJ article 38 and doctrine of sources of international law
South Africa *see* Mandela, Nelson, liberation of
sovereignty *see* state sovereignty
Spain 51
Spivak, Gayari 224
state practice 75, 76

state socialism in 1989, collapse of 106–16;
actually existing socialism (AES) 113–15;
Badouvian events 106–7; Cold War 108,
109–10; collective humanitarian
intervention 108, 111–12; colonization
109, 110; counter-positions in
international legal argument, loss of
109–10; cultural hierarchies 110–11;
democracy 108, 110–11; democratic
proliferation and consolidation 108;
deregulation 110; economic
constitutionalism 110; economic
liberalism 108; ethno-nationalist and
regional violence 111; European Union
111; global collective security 108–9;
global economic space, creation of 108;
globalisation 106, 108–9, 116;
governance 110–11; hegemony 110,
112; human rights 107, 108, 111–12;
human security 108–9, 112;
impoverishment of international legal
discourse 109–10; international
community, advent of 107, 110;
international financial institutions, soft
law of 108; interruption, as 113;
Marxism, gulf between Western and
Eastern 115–16; neoliberal orthodoxy
110; new international economic order
(NIEO) 110; New Left 115; new world
order 106–7, 112; Non-Aligned
Movement 110; OSCE National
Minorities 111; political liberalism 108;
positivism 115–16; privatization 110;
pseudo-event, as 109, 112; renewalism
107; revitalization of international law
and institutions 107; self-defence 12;
subjectivity 114–15; thin democracy
110–11; transition 112–16; UN Security
Council 112; United States 110, 112;
WTO/GATT 108, 110
state sovereignty; autonomy 60;
centralized authority before Westphalia,
existence of 55, 58–59, 61; challenges to
sovereignty 60–61, 67; civilized and
non-civilized nations 63; commonality
44; conditional sovereignty 111;
consolidation of notion of sovereignty
55–56, 57–59; definition of modern
sovereignty 56; diplomacy 59;
emergence of nation states 55–58, 61;
France 59–60; historical and memory 56,
57–63; Holy Roman Empire 59–60;

Mandela, Nelson, liberation of 120–21;
modern sovereignty, Peace as origin of
55, 60, 64–67; myth, Peace of
Westphalia as a 57, 63–66, 67;
origin myths 56, 64–66, 67; OSCE
National Minorities 111; overlapping
authorities 61
Peace of Westphalia 1648 20, 55–67;
religious settlement 61–63; supranational
authority 61; Sweden 60; territorial
settlements 59–60; universality 56;
use of force 250; World Trade
Organization 197
state succession 3
Stone, J 256–57
Suarez, F 254
subordination 236–39
Suez, invasion of 256
supremacy of EU law 177
supranationalism 61
Sweden 60

technical assistance 214–15
territorial settlements under Peace of
Westphalia 59–60
terrorism; September 11, 2001 attacks on
United States 234–43; torture of
suspects 269–74
textbooks 3, 73, 251–53
Thant, U 99–100
Thatcher, Margaret 122
Theron, Charlize 222, 230
Third World see also developing countries;
colonialism 237–39; critical Third
World perspective, meaning of 236–39;
equality 237; feminism 237, 238; G77
238; Iraq, invasion of 239; New
International Economic Order 238;
pan-African or third world solidarity
122–23; post-structuralism 237, 238;
September 11, 2001, terrorist attacks on
the United States 234–43; socialism 237;
subordination, shared experience of
236–39; Third World, use of term
235–36; TWAIL (Third World
approaches to international law) 236–39;
United States 238–39; universality 239
Thompson, Rustin 229–30
Tokyo Women's Tribunal and fiction
145–60; amnesties 157; colonialism
154–56; comfort women 146–47,
150–60; 'fact-ion' 148–50, 153;

Hague Convention 1907 154; historical
fiction 151–53, 158; international law
145; legitimacy 149; past in literature,
return to the 148–50, 151; past
international law, fiction of 146–47;
'pre-quel' 148–50, 152–54; rape crimes
145–47, 149–60; sexual slavery 146–47,
149–60; sexual stereotyping 154; statute
of limitations 147; Tokyo Military
Tribunal 145, 147, 149, 151–54,
156–60; trafficking 155–56, 159;
victor's justice 145; white slavery 155
torture 260–75; Afghanistan 260;
antinomian conscience 267–68; causation
261; community 266–67, 269;
conscience 267–69; correction 264–65,
269; detainee-combatants 274; equality
266; ethical commons 267–68; event,
release as an 269–74; expertise to
violence, relationship of legal 262;
government legal advisers, role of
266–67; hope 263–64, 269;
international law 261–71; Iraq 260;
lawyers, involvement and response of
260–70; media disclosure 261; memos
260–75; 'mineness' 268–69; moral
relativism 265; names and naming
272–73; professional qualities 267;
publicity, effect of 267; rule of law 268;
September 11, 2001, terrorist attacks on
the United States 241–42; substitution
271; terrorists-suspects-detainees
241–42, 269–74; Torture Convention
271; United States 260–75; unlawful
combatants 269–73
trafficking 155–56, 159
treaties as sources of law 77
Treaty of Osnabrück 62
trials see political trials as events
TRIPs 203, 204
truth 130–31, 134–35, 138, 168–73
Tully, James 222–23
TWAIL (Third World approaches to
international law) 236–39

United Nations (UN); apartheid,
declaration on 121; Charter 247–48,
252, 256–57; Cold War 249; colonialism
93–98, 101, 249; decolonization 93–95;
General Assembly 242, 247–48, 252,
255; Goa incident 1961 255–57;
intervention as challenge to sovereignty
60; Iraq, war and regime change in
246–50; Mandela, Nelson, liberation of
117–24; national liberation movements
249; resolutions 248–49, 256–57;
Security Council 112, 246–49, 255,
257–58; Soviet Union 249–50; state
socialism in 1989, collapse of 112; state
sovereignty 60; use of force 246–50
United States; Cold War 92; decolonization
92, 94–99; hegemony 110; human rights
112; Mandela, Nelson, liberation of 122;
September 11, 2001, terrorist attacks on
the United States 234–43; state socialism
in 1989, collapse of 110, 112; Third
World 234–43; World Trade
Organization 198–201, 203
Universal Declaration of Human Rights
94–95, 120
universality; Catholic Church, universal
jurisdiction of the 21–22; culture 24;
decolonization 92–99, 101–2; ethos
26–27; human rights 97; Iraq, war and
regime change in 254; mythical belief in
universal law 24, 26; New World
24–26; PCIJ article 38 and doctrine of
sources of international law 73, 78; Peace
of Westphalia 1648 24–27, 56; power
26; state sovereignty 56; subjects 26;
Third World 239; violence 23
unlawful combatants 269–73
uprisings see levée en masse
use of force; collective violence 26–27;
colonialism 18, 21; critique of violence
19–21; divine violence 21;
ethno-nationalist and regional violence
111; Goa incident 1961 250, 256–57;
Hungary, invasion of 250; Iraq, war and
regime change in 246–50; justification
19, 20–21; law-making violence 19–20;
law-preserving violence 19–20; mythical
violence 20–21; New World 18–27, 32;
positive law 19–20; regulation of
violence in war 81; state sovereignty
250; Suez, invasion of 250; United
Nations 246–50, 256–57;
universality 23

Vagts, Detlav 266, 267
Valladolid events 29–41; chance 37;
childlike metaphor 34; civilize, duty to
33, 36; colonization 32–33, 36–37;
constancy 33–34, 35, 36, 38; donation of

Americas 34–35, 37; foundations 30, 35; group survival 29–31; Incas 34; just war 33–34; legacy and significance 32–38; likeness 33–34, 35; nations, law of 35–37; natural law 32–33, 36; natural slavery 32; New World 29–30, 32–36; people, relations between 35–36; perfect communities 29–31, 33, 36; power 30; reciprocity 33; restitution of territory 32–33, 35; sacrifice 30; self-governing capacity of Amerindians 32, 37; *Twelve Doubts* 32–33; violence 32; virtuality 32
van Boven, Theo 263
Vattel, Emerich de 36, 44, 254
Vergès, Jacques 138, 140–41
victor's justice 145
Vienna Convention on the Law of Treaties 77
violence *see* use of force; war
Viseur-Sellers, Patricia 152
Vitoria, Francisco de 26, 29, 32, 35–38, 43–44, 47–52, 63, 254

Waldock, Humphrey 251
Waldron, Jeremy 264
war; Algerian War 97, 138–39; Cold War 92, 108–10, 118, 122, 126–28, 249; First World War 71–72; Geneva Conventions 81, 83–84, 87; Hague Regulations 81, 84; International Criminal Tribunal for Rwanda, war nexus and 165; Iraq 246–58; just war 33–34, 250, 255; laws of war 84, 85; *levée en masse* 84, 85; perfect communities 29; prisoner of war status under Geneva Conventions 83–84; regulation of violence in war 81; Second World War 83, 145–60; Tokyo Military Tribunal 145, 147, 149, 151–54, 156–60; Tokyo Women's Tribunal and fiction 145–60; total war 83
Washington Consensus 217
Weber, Max 195
Welling, James 266
Wendel, Bradley 268
Westlake, J 254
Westphalian Peace *see* Peace of Westphalia 1648
Wheaton, H 254
white slavery 155
Williamson, J 217

Winterson, Jeanette 148
Wolff, Christian von 254
women *see* Tokyo Women's Tribunal
World Bank 216–17
world government formation 202–3
World Trade Organization (WTO) 191–204; *30 Frames a Second: the WTO in Seattle* 230; anti-market 195; *Battle in Seattle* film 230–32; citizenship 224; civil society 225; civilized-uncivilized dichotomy 209; colonialism 213; comparative advantage 191–93; conditional aid 214–15; corporate capitalism 191–98, 201–2; developing countries 193, 199–200, 207–19; development 207–19; dirigiste dogma 212–13; Dunkel Draft 200; Dutch East India Company 191, 193; economics 210–11, 215–17; English East India Company 191, 193; establishment 191; European Union 200; event, aspects of the 225–27; 'Event Horizon' 224–25; foreign direct investment 192–93, 197–98; Free Association 226–27; GATT 108, 110, 193, 198–204, 210–11, 217–18; globalization 196, 201–2; government controls 215–17; Hollywood 230–32; homogenization of markets 196–97; industrialization 210–11; institutional arrangements, failing 214–15; intellectual property treaties 203–4; International Monetary Fund 216–17; joint stock companies 193–94; Latin America, economic crises in 216–17; League of Nations 208, 209; liberalization 199–201, 207, 211; mobilization 229–31; modernization theories 210–11; multinationals 193–98; nation states, interdependence of multinationals with 194–98; neo-classicalism 214; neo-liberalism 207–8, 211–12, 214, 218; outward-oriented polices 215–17; Permanent Mandates Commission 209, 214; political event, protests as a 227–30; political representations 211–12; post-switch phases 203; post-war period, development mission of 208–11; protectionism 193; protests 221–32; rational choice 207, 212–14; recession 214; ruptures in time 226; science of development 211–13, 215, 217; Seattle

protests 221–32; state socialism in 1989, collapse of 108, 110; state sovereignty 197; technical assistance 214–15; Tokyo Round 199; TRIPS 203, 204; United States 198–201, 203; Uruguay Round 191, 198–201, 203–4; video cameras 228; Washington Consensus 217; World Bank 216–17; world government formation 202–3; YouTube 228, 230

Wright, Quincy 256–57

YouTube 228, 230

Žižek, Slavoj 137, 174, 175
Zubaydeh, Abu 272